THE SOCIOLOGY OF THE THIRD WORLD
Disparity and development

THE SOCIOLOGY OF THE THIRD WORLD

Disparity and development

Second edition

J. E. GOLDTHORPE
Honorary Lecturer in Sociology, University of Leeds

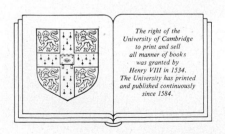

*The right of the
University of Cambridge
to print and sell
all manner of books
was granted by
Henry VIII in 1534.
The University has printed
and published continuously
since 1584.*

CAMBRIDGE UNIVERSITY PRESS

Cambridge
London   New York   New Rochelle
Melbourne   Sydney

Published by the Press Syndicate of the University of Cambridge
The Pitt Building, Trumpington Street, Cambridge, CB2 1RP
32 East 57th Street, New York, NY 10022, USA
10 Stamford Road, Oakleigh, Melbourne 3166, Australia

First published 1975
Reprinted 1977, 1978, 1979
Second edition 1984
Reprinted 1985

Printed in Great Britain by the
University Press, Cambridge

Library of Congress catalogue card number: 83-13506

British Library Cataloguing in Publication Data

Goldthorpe, J. E.
The sociology of the Third World. – 2nd ed.
1. Social history – Comparative studies
2. Underdeveloped areas – Social conditions
I. Title
909′.0972′2087   HN16
ISBN 0 521 25303 9 hard covers
ISBN 0 521 27293 9 paperback
(First edition ISBN 0 521 20521 2 hard covers
            ISBN 0 521 09924 2 paperback)

Acknowledgements

Acknowledgement is made to Princeton University Press for permission
to reproduce on page 37 the figure from Kingsley Davis, *The Population
of India and Pakistan*.

Thanks are due to President Nyerere for permission to quote from his
'Socialism and Rural Development', in *Essays on Socialism*, published
by Oxford University Press, for which he holds the copyright.

Contents

Preface and acknowledgements

My first encounter with the Third World (though the phrase had not then been coined) was during my war service as a naval radar officer in 1942–45 in such places as Mombasa, Durban, Colombo, and Trincomalee. Experiencing at first hand the economic disparities and cultural diversities of peoples with widely different preoccupations and ways of life finally decided me to try to carry over the scientific attitude with which I had been imbued as a student of the natural sciences into the study of human society. After the war, then, I did not go back to Cambridge but went instead to the London School of Economics and Political Science to graduate afresh in economics and sociology (including social anthropology). As it had been what I saw in East Africa that had first and most strongly awakened my interest, in 1951 I eagerly accepted a post as lecturer at Makerere, the nascent University College of East Africa, in Kampala, Uganda, which gave me the opportunity to learn more while at the same time taking part in a great project for the advancement of the then subject peoples of a colonial empire. There, besides pioneering the teaching of sociology as a degree subject, I made my first attempts at the analytical description of Third World societies, in general in my *Outlines of East African Society*, more specifically in *An African Elite*, a study of Makerere College students and former students, 1922–1960.

So it was with a somewhat narrowly East African focus that I came to Leeds in 1962, yet with a growing awareness that despite their profound diversities traditional societies throughout the world were subject to common forces making for change. Leeds proved to be a good place to seek a wider vision, with a strong and continuing interest in the Third World at all levels and in many departments throughout the University, and always a lively development seminar.

The idea of writing this book originated about the end of 1967, and the first edition was written during a 'semi-sabbatical' session in 1971–72.

It has been completely revised and very largely re-written just ten years later. Much has happened to make this necessary in a rapidly changing world. Up-dating statistics and other factual information has been the least part of the task. Much more taxing has been the need to condense existing material to make room for new. Many new facts have called for new interpretations; while it has also been necessary to take cognizance of new ways of looking at facts, including those already known, which around 1970 had not gathered the momentum or gained the credence they later acquired.

I have learned by experience to write much more in the past tense. Especially to one with a scientific background, propositions and statements about continuing tendencies are naturally expressed in the present. But strictly speaking we have knowledge only of past events; and if that is true in astronomy about receding galaxies, it has immediate practical importance for a social scientist writing in 1982, for whom the latest available economic and demographic statistics are for 1980 while many recent research reports are of studies carried out in the 1970s. I hope, though, that a sense of immediacy has not been lost as the problems and processes of the recent past continue to affect our world at the present time.

Though most of the chapters that follow cover much the same ground as those in the first edition, I have changed their order somewhat. I am still not sure what the right order would be, and there are two underlying problems. Sociology, being about complex inter-relations, does not lend itself to serial exposition, and in principle one could start anywhere, work one's way by any path round the whole dynamic system, and return to the starting point. So perhaps there is no right or best order, and I can only invite readers to find their own way through the book in any order they choose, while signposting the connecting paths with plenty of cross-references. Even more fundamentally, according to my conception of science, facts come before theories; we devise theories in order to try to explain or account for the facts we observe. In the early chapters, therefore, I have tried to set out to the best of my knowledge and belief what are the basic facts to be explained, before proceeding in chapter 6 to review what social scientists of various persuasions have made of them. As many of the key facts are economic, however, and many of the social scientists concerned are development economists, it seems natural to do so soon after economic conditions have been described rather than hold the theory chapter till the end as perhaps strict logic would indicate. I am aware, moreover, of the strength of the contrary view, that the categories we use in observing, describing, and ordering the facts are themselves derived from and infused with theory, so that theory is logically prior to facts. In deference to that view (though I do not share it), I have set out in chapter 1 an introductory outline of the main schools of thought that were active in development studies during the 1970s, even though I go over the same ground again in more detail in chapter 6.

In all that follows I warmly acknowledge my debt to those who taught me, including my old tutor C. P. Snow, who said a lot of what I have to say in his 1959 Rede lecture on the two cultures. I was grateful to the late

Professor Harry Hanson for encouraging me to write the first edition. It was inspiring to have Lord Boyle at Leeds as Vice-Chancellor from 1970 to 1981. Previously a member of the Pearson commission, actively and astutely interested in the social sciences, he honoured me with his foreword to the first edition; I wish I could show him this, and I mourn his passing.

I am grateful to the many colleagues and friends who have read all or part of this book and its predecessor and given me their guidance. Brenda Taylor has laboured patiently, to and fro between old text and new draft, to produce a perfect typescript. And I acknowledge with thanks the kindly help and guidance of the staff of Cambridge University Press at all stages from the first discussions of the idea of the book to the publication of this revised edition.

November 1982

J. E. G.

1   Introduction and argument

Disparity and development

The transformation of human life through the application of science did not begin everywhere and at the same time; and the uneven onset of that transformation has created a situation without precedent in history. Rich and poor there have been since the dawn of civilization, but until recently most people in every country lived at or near subsistence level, and it was only a small minority in any who were able to command enough resources to live an ampler life. What is completely new about the present world situation is that the real incomes of almost the whole populations of some countries have been raised far above subsistence, while those of others remain at or near that level. A central theme of this book accordingly is disparity. The prime disparity is that between rich and poor countries. Related to it is the disparity between rich and poor people, especially in poor countries, whose wealthy families can emulate the affluence of the well-to-do in rich countries, while the great majority still live at or near subsistence. Such disparities are indeed a commonplace of contemporary discussion, expressed in phrases such as 'a divided world' and 'the ever-widening gap'.

But ours is not a divided world. On the contrary, the world is one. The disparity in the living standards and ways of life in different societies and countries has arisen in a world in which all are increasingly involved with one another. The second major theme accordingly is that of involvement or inter-relation – a theme which in some of the older literature, especially of social anthropology, was characterized as 'culture contact'.

Anthropologists of an older generation used to write monographs about societies which, if not strictly 'untouched', had been affected by outside influences to only a limited extent. In that golden age, social anthropologists could analyse a society as a unique form of human association with its own distinctive structure and culture to be explained mainly in its own terms. Now that is clearly no longer possible. The world has broken in. International politics and the world economic system have intruded into those 'untouched societies' in the form of institutions such as mines, factories, political parties, armies, and schools, that now have to be

1

considered as integral parts of the whole which it is the business of the social scientist to study and comprehend. Yet the pre-existing diversity of cultures, and their continuing significance, has certainly not vanished overnight, as we are reminded every day when we open the newspaper and read of the militant resistance of an ethnic minority to absorption into an Asian state, or of deadly tribal rivalries in an African country. Such societies are awkward to study, for while the heritage and perspectives of social anthropology are necessary they are not sufficient, and while there is certainly material in them for the consideration of the more specialized social sciences such as economics and political science these can lead to partial and misleading conclusions unless they are informed by a constant awareness of the whole whose parts they are studying – an awareness made possible perhaps by the synoptic vision of the sociologist.

Units of analysis

For many purposes, the unit we have to consider is the *country*, that is, a defined geographical area with a human population and a *government*. Often, indeed, we have little choice in the matter, since it is the governments of countries that collect and issue statistics. Thus when we compare birth- and death-rates, GNP per capita, or school enrolments, the statistics we find in the appropriate sources are for units such as India, Kenya, and Brazil.

Governments collect and issue statistics because they wield legitimate power. They use that power also to issue currency, collect taxes, regulate banking, impose tariffs, borrow at home and abroad, and in countless other ways that affect the economic life carried on within their boundaries. So each country comes to have its own *economy*: a natural unit for analysis, even though no country's economy is isolated from the rest of the world and each is to a greater or less extent affected by what happens in the world economy as a whole.

Similarly, a government's policies about the national language, schooling, and the mass media of communication all affect its people's career prospects and cultural life, while its laws about marriage, inheritance, the care and custody of children, and such matters affect their family life. In certain respects, then, each country may come to have its own *society*. But the boundaries of country and society do not in general coincide. Many countries, especially in the Third World, are in a sense highly artificial, arbitrary creations whose boundaries might as well have been drawn along other lines on the map, and include societies with widely diverse languages and cultures, for example within Nigeria the Yoruba, Ibo, Hausa, and others. At the same time, some societies extend across the boundaries of more than one country, for example the Samia, parted by an arbitrary boundary between Uganda and Kenya, or the overseas Chinese whose society extends into Hong Kong, Malaysia, Singapore, Thailand, Indonesia, and other countries.

Industrialization and development

Industrial countries make lavish use of energy. Ever since the steam engine was invented, heat engines burning fossil fuels have put more power at the elbow of the inhabitants of the now affluent countries than was previously available to them from their own muscles, those of other animals, and a limited use of wind and water power. Today the most striking and fundamental difference between rich and poor countries lies in the vastly greater resources of energy commanded by the former.

If energy represents the critical difference in terms of physics, then in terms of economics the concomitant difference is capital. Heat engines and the machines they drive represent capital investment on a vastly greater scale than the simple tools of a non-industrial economy. Their use increases the productivity of labour; indeed, the very nature of work is transformed as it comes to be done by machines directed and controlled by human operators rather than directly performed by their own muscles. So wages are potentially high, and only a modicum of trade-union organization is needed to ensure that actual wages correspond closely to the productivity of labour. Industrialization accordingly involves a change from labour-intensive to capital-intensive methods, and this entails a process of capital formation, initially by forced saving and 'going short' out of low levels of income, later by saving and investing out of high incomes to use power-driven machines to make more machines. In the process there is a shift of the labour force out of 'primary' production (agriculture and other 'extractive' occupations like fishing and mining) into 'secondary' or manufacturing industry. This is followed in the later stages by a further shift, as manufacturing becomes more capital-intensive, out of manufacturing industry and into inescapably labour-intensive services, 'tertiary' and 'quaternary', as diverse as retailing, education, social welfare services, and entertainment. In this process the material standard of living, as represented by 'real' incomes (discounting changes in the value of money), rises roughly in proportion to the amount of energy consumed, and as dramatically.

Such has been the experience of those countries whose economies have undergone the process of change which we have come to know as industrial development, industrialization, or the industrial revolution. Some industrialization has taken place in virtually every country in the world, so it is not strictly correct to speak of 'non-industrial countries'. However, the process started at different dates, and has proceeded at different rates, in different countries. By common consent Britain was the

3

first industrial country, followed by other western European countries, then Russia and Japan. The United States was a late starter, still a mainly agrarian nation of farm and small town as late as 1900, but its industrial development was then very rapid and it quickly overtook the rest. So much is the familiar substance of economic history. The countries with which this book is concerned are those in which, for whatever reason, industrialization started late and has not proceeded very far. Even though in some of them – especially the biggest, India and China – there is now a substantial industrial sector, it is small in proportion to the immense whole, the majority of their people still live by a subsistence peasant agriculture, and their average incomes are still low accordingly. They are the late industrializing, the as yet little-industrialized countries.

Countries of this kind were first called 'underdeveloped' in a famous report to the United Nations in 1951.[1] The word had not then acquired all its present associations, and, as the report said, 'an adequate synonym would be "poor countries"' – the term often adopted in this book. Later, when 'underdeveloped' came to be thought of as derogatory, they were called 'developing' – an instance of what Myrdal called diplomacy by terminology,[2] for it is clear that not all of them are. If economic development is to be measured by the growth of GNP per head, in some countries that is a negligible or even a negative quantity. Moreover, the term 'development' and its derivatives need to be handled with caution, for, as Gellner has said, 'This language [i.e. that of economic growth] is misleading in as far as it suggests that what is at stake is something quantitative, a rate or speed or quantity of accumulation of goods. Ultimately, what is at stake is something qualitative – a transition between two fundamentally different forms of life.'[3] Furthermore, economists themselves find development an elusive concept, and they tend to refer it to conditions or processes which lie in the realms of psychology or sociology rather than economics. It is 'in the mind',[4] they say; it involves 'the upward movement of the whole social system';[5] it consists of 'the transformation of a tradition- or authority-bound society into a modern, innovating, experimenting, progressing one'.[6] To use such a term in defining our subject is to risk taking for granted what is actually problematic, a danger which is enhanced by the imprecision of the concept itself.

Classical perspectives

The disparity between the industrial nations, at that time confined to western Europe, and the rest of humanity was already a fact about the world in which sociology emerged as a recognized discipline early in the nineteenth century. In the work of the classical sociologists we find that modern industrial society was recognized as a phenomenon *sui generis* and constituted a distinctive type of society. Most of them wrote of 'social development' in the context of grand theories of social change, addressed to the question of how a society of one type is transformed, or transforms itself, into one of another, and in terms of the equally grand concepts of evolution and progress.

Thus Comte regarded it as one of the aims of sociology 'to discover through what fixed series of successive transformations the human race, starting from a state not superior to that of the societies of the great apes, gradually led to the point at which civilized Europe finds itself today' – that was in 1822. Social development was a product of intellectual development, which albeit somewhat unevenly had proceeded in three stages, culminating in positive (or as we would now say scientific) thought associated with industrial, peaceful social organization.[7] Somewhat similarly, Herbert Spencer classified societies by the complexity of their organization, and into 'industrial' and 'militant' types. He did not mean by 'industrial' quite what we understand by the term today, and classed some simple and technologically primitive societies as industrial because they concentrated on peaceful production rather than war. Nevertheless he made it clear, by implication if not explicitly, that he regarded industrial societies as superior and more advanced from the evolutionary point of view, for he wrote of 'reversions' and 'partial reversions to the militant type of structure' in advanced contemporary societies including his own. Anything involving coercion or compulsion was 'militant', while 'industrial' societies were based on the voluntary co-operation of free individuals.[8]

Following Spencer, Maine concluded from his study of ancient law that 'the movement of the progressive societies has hitherto been a movement from Status to Contract';[9] and together with the British economists from Adam Smith onwards they laid the foundations for Durkheim's analysis of the division of labour, with its distinction between mechanical and organic solidarity. Mechanical solidarity characterized a society in which there was little division of labour and people were like-minded because they performed similar tasks, and the structure of such a society consisted of homologous segments like clans. Durkheim probably erred in under-estimating the extent of individual differences in such societies, and overestimating the predominance of penal customary law in them. Organic solidarity was that of the complex society with a high degree of division of labour. Here the social structure consisted of interdependent associations, like industrial enterprises exchanging goods and services with one another. Occupational and other groups would tend to develop their own different sub-cultures, and such a society could no longer rely on common values as a source of solidarity. Durkheim differed from the British school in recognizing that self-interest mediated through free contract does not assure solidarity, since interest makes me today your friend, tomorrow your

5

enemy. He accordingly rejected Spencer's extreme individualism, and looked rather to the rise of new sources of solidarity like professional ethics to maintain long-term non-contractual relations among individuals and groups; while ritual was another way in which groups engendered and maintained their solidarity and cohesion.[10]

Although Marx and Engels differed sharply from the liberal tradition of Comte, Spencer, and the British economists; based their approach on historical materialism; and saw class conflict as a main explanation of social change, they too like their contemporaries put their ideas into a grand perspective of the stages of development of human societies. Originally property took the form of tribal ownership and the social order was an extension of the family. Then the slavery that had always been latent in the family became the dominant institution of society, so that citizens and slaves were the two classes of the city-states of ancient Greece and Rome. The third stage of development was feudal, with peasant serfs instead of slaves as the subject class of producers. And it was obvious enough that what they characterized as the bourgeois capitalist society of their own time had emerged from feudal society when the labourer ceased to be a slave, serf, or bondsman and became a free seller of labour power. To bring about that state of affairs, the industrial capitalists had to displace the feudal lords; and Marx wrote that 'The hand-mill gives you society with the feudal lord; the steam-mill, society with the industrial capitalist.'

When Marx became the correspondent of the *New York Daily Tribune* on Indian affairs, and became accordingly more aware of the civilizations of India and China, he saw Oriental society, based on the Asiatic mode of production, as a kind of alternative or by-pass to the Occidental stages of the city-states and feudalism. It was typified by centrally controlled canalization and other public works, its urban trading class was weakly developed, and it was too centralized to be feudal, while in its social order the unifying function of the tribe was usurped by the despot and his ideological reflex the deity. Marx accordingly wrote in a summary way of the 'Asiatic, ancient, feudal, and modern bourgeois modes of production' as 'progressive epochs in the economic formation of society'.[11]

Among his many contributions to sociological theory, Max Weber, like Marx, grappled with the question of the rise of capitalism, but he rejected Marx's historical materialism and the economic determinism which it entailed. While capitalism could be seen as a set of institutional arrangements including rational book-keeping, formally free labour, the separation of the household from the workplace, the separation of corporate business property from personal property (by means of limited liability), and the concept of citizenship, such a view saw only the bare bones. The whole structure had to be brought to life, and what inspired it and gave it direction Weber called the spirit of capitalism. This he identified with the Protestant ethic, whose rise he traced in the seventeenth century in the Calvinist sects and the Puritans in western Europe and America. The sense of a calling to be in the world but not of it, to lead a godly, righteous and sober life without withdrawing into a monastery, and to resist all the temptations of the world, provided the motivation for the distinctively Puritan virtues of thrift, honesty, sobriety, diligence in business and sheer hard work. With such virtues it was indeed hard not to succeed, yet if it were wrong to expend resources in personal consumption and frivolous display, what else to do with the profits but re-invest them in the business? The 'elective affinity' between the Protestant ethic and the spirit of capitalism indicated that, so far from religion being a mere superstructure, affording ideological justification for the harsh necessities of the material economic base, the converse might be the case, and religion as an independent factor could play a part in initiating social and economic change.[12]

Tönnies contrasted the 'natural, organic' relations of the family, village, and small town (*Gemeinschaft*) with the 'artificial, isolated' condition of urban industrial society (*Gesellschaft*) in which the original and natural relations among human beings are excluded and all strive for their own advantage in a spirit of competition. Western Europe had passed from a union of *Gemeinschaft* whose prototype was the family, through an association of *Gemeinschaft* with corporations and fellowships of the arts and crafts and 'relations between master and servant, or better between master and disciple', to an association of *Gesellschaft* with the rise of the joint stock company and limited liability. A fourth stage was possibly represented by movements like consumers' co-operation and British guild socialism, a revival of *Gemeinschaft* in forms adapted to the prevailing *Gesellschaft* which might become the focus for 'the resuscitation of family life and other forms of *Gemeinschaft*'. No doubt his nostalgic analysis idealizes the harmony and integration of small-scale rural communities and overrates their advantage; but the notion of *Gesellschaft*, like Durkheim's organic solidarity, expresses the complex interdependence of modern industrial society while deploring its consequent impersonality.[13]

In his work on social development, Hobhouse tried to avoid value-judgements, sought to elaborate 'criteria of advance of a non-ethical character', and identified them as growth in scale, efficiency, mutuality, and freedom. His concept of 'efficiency' resembled Spencer's differentiation of the social structure, with co-ordination of the activities of different parts. Advance in one respect might not necessarily be accompanied by advance in others; thus a growth in the scale of social organization had often been achieved by means of repression and constraint, so that for instance the Greek city-states were smaller in scale than 'some of the great Empires of the middle culture', but enjoyed more freedom. Nevertheless, on the whole the four aspects of social development were so inter-related that there had been advance in all of them together in the history of humanity. Hobhouse's criteria of freedom and mutuality may well have expressed his position as a liberal social philosopher and not been quite as 'non-ethical' as he intended. His criteria of scale and efficiency, however, clearly converge on Durkheim's view of the division of labour.[14]

In this short introductory chapter I have done no more than to allude to the work of some of the classical sociologists – perhaps enough, though, to establish that the broad theme with which this book is concerned has been a major preoccupation of sociology since its first beginnings.

The work of Talcott Parsons, the leading figure of US sociology in the 1950s and 1960s, was in large part a synthesis and elaboration of the nineteenth-century European classics, together with some other elements of western social thought, including especially Malinowskian functionalism in social anthropology.[15]

In his early work, Parsons clarified and elaborated Tönnies' distinction between *Gemeinschaft* and *Gesellschaft* into five major 'dilemmas of orientation' which he called the pattern variables:

1 Affectivity versus affective neutrality.
2 Self-orientation versus collectivity orientation.
3 Universalism versus particularism.
4 Ascription versus achievement.
5 Specificity versus diffuseness.[16]

Though he stated that 'a pattern variable is a dichotomy, one side of which must be chosen by an actor', it would appear more useful to think of the pattern variables as scales.

The processes of social change accompanying industrialization can be thought of as shifts in the prevailing choices that are made in four of these pattern variables: from affectivity to affective neutrality; from particularism to universalism; from ascription to achievement; and from diffuseness to specificity.

Affective neutrality is shown when an actor postpones or renounces immediate gratification. Clearly this is related to decisions to save and invest rather than expend resources in current consumption. It has much to do with the process of capital formation, and there are overtones of Weber's Protestant ethic. Affective neutrality also characterizes social relations in industrial societies, which tend to be contractual, impersonal, and calculating; the continuing need for affective gratification in these societies is largely met by family life, the one island of security left where a high level of diffuse affectivity prevails.

Industrialization tends to erode particularistic exclusiveness, like the practices that in some societies restrict land-holding or the pursuit of particular occupations to exclusive racial or caste groups, or exclude women from education or the professions. Such particularisms are in-efficient as they result in an under-utilization of human potential and natural resources. It is no accident that the most highly industrialized societies, including those with communist regimes, are those in which universalistic patterns prevail and careers are open to talents.

In the same way, achievement rather than ascription tends to be the basis for recruitment in a fully industrialized society. When people in less industrialized societies recruit workers or admit pupils on the basis of kinship we call it nepotism and regard it as incompatible with the ways of modern society.

And the finer division of labour and the greater complexity of organization in an industrial society are clearly related to the shift from diffuseness to specificity, from social relations wide in scope and all-embracing to relations in which, as Parsons put it, the actor confines his concern with another to a specific sphere and does not permit other concerns to enter.

In a later work, Parsons combined evolutionary and comparative perspectives in analysing changes in the structure of societies 'ranging all the way from extremely small-scale primitive societies to the new supernational societies of the United States and the Soviet Union'. In that evolution, the 'enhancement of adaptive capacity' entails differentiation, including for instance the separation of workplaces (workshops, factories, offices) from households. This does not mean that 'the older "residual" unit will have "lost function"...The household is no longer an important economic producer, but it may well perform its other functions better.' Differentiation poses new problems of integration, for example that of creating new roles in which authority is not derived from kinship. 'Adaptive upgrading thus requires that specialized functional capacities be freed from ascription.' And there is a problem which, as he puts it, is the opposite of differentiation and specification; it is that of establishing a new pattern of values appropriate to the new type of society. Here Parsons' thought echoes Durkheim's preoccupation with the problem of solidarity in a society in which all do not think alike. The establishment of new values may encounter severe resistance from groups adhering to older values which are no longer appropriate, a resistance which may be called 'fundamentalism'.[17] I return to this point in chapter 10.

It may be helpful at this point to tabulate the terms in which some sociologists of the classical tradition (including Parsons) have characterized the basic processes of change.

Spencer	from simple	to complex
	from military	to industrial
Maine	from status	to contract

Durkheim	from homologous segments	to interdependent associations
	from mechanical solidarity	to organic solidarity
Tönnies	from *Gemeinschaft* (natural, organic community)	to *Gesellschaft* (artificial, isolated association)
Hobhouse	growth in scale, efficiency (complexity, differentiation), mutuality, and freedom	
Parsons (1951)	from affectivity	to affective neutrality
	from particularism	to universalism
	from ascription	to achievement
	from diffuseness	to specificity
Parsons (1966)	adaptive upgrading, differentiation of sub-systems	

I now turn to a preliminary outline of the main schools of thought in development studies of the 1960s and 1970s, to which I give more detailed attention in chapter 6.

Modernization

With its background in the European classics, powerfully integrated and re-articulated in the twentieth century by Talcott Parsons, much mainstream thought in the social sciences has been in a broad sense evolutionary, even though that approach was decisively rejected by anthropologists of the Malinowski generation. Concentrating attention on the country, with its government and its economy, as the prime unit of analysis, led naturally to the view that if some countries were rich and others poor, that must be because the former were advanced and the latter backward; that the former had passed through the stages of development associated with industrialization ahead of the latter. The problem of the development of the poor countries, and the raising of the living standards of their inhabitants, was seen as the problem of how they could catch up – by their own efforts, or with outside help, or both. If they had not done so, or if they responded sluggishly to the efforts of their own government and outside development agencies, there must be obstacles to development. Identifying those obstacles, and helping to remove them, was seen as a contribution which social scientists might usefully make to the process. Thus in Latin America, an inequitable distribution of land was seen as an

10

obstacle to development. Peasants without land rights had little incentive to improve their methods and their holding, while the very rich landlords showed little inclination to invest in industrial development. The whole system was seen as feudal, a view based with some justification on the history of a continent which fell under the domination of Spain and Portugal at a time when the feudal system prevailed there as it did all over Europe. The social structures of Latin American countries, with their landowning military elites, were seen as archaic survivals from a pre-modern era, inappropriate for the needs of the twentieth century. Similarly, in India the caste system with its notion of hereditary occupations – or more exactly a 'lack of unrestricted choice of occupation' – was seen as one obstacle to development. Another was the complex of avoidance and observances of orthodox Hinduism, exemplified by the ban on cow-slaughter, which seriously restricts selective breeding for meat and milk and the rise of a modern animal husbandry that might provide much-needed protein for the Indian masses. And in many places an obstacle to development was found in religions which diverted resources into an unproductive monasticism, or encouraged a fatalistic resignation to the divine will, unlike the Protestant ethic that had played its part in the economic development of Europe and North America; and social scientists looked for latter-day functional equivalents of the Protestant ethic, sometimes with success.

In this style of thought, industrialization was identified with development, and both with modernization. The last was a key word especially among scholars and social scientists working in this field of study in the United States. 'Traditional' and 'modern' were contrasted antonyms, while 'modernization' was the passage or transition from one to the other. It was both political and personal. The modernization of a society and its institutions occurred when people were liberated from archaic restrictions and became free to move – particularly from country to town – to engage in trade, and to enter wage employment; while the modernization of individuals occurred as they became mentally free, through education, literacy, and exposure to the mass media of communication, to imagine things otherwise than as they are, and make informed choices. That indeed was the nub; United States scholars wrote of modernity in terms recalling those in which Thomas Jefferson had spoken of freedom, as 'the possibility of choice and the exercise of choice'. The crowning achievement of the modern society was the informed participation of its citizens in public life through a democratic electoral political system affording them genuine choices of leaders and policies.

Not all social scientists in the mainstream tradition, however, identified themselves wholeheartedly with the modernization school. Many social anthropologists, accustomed as they were to suspending their own value-judgements and those of the cultures from which they came, and to

11

discipline themselves to work within the cultural traditions they were studying, were unable to accept the prior judgement of the institutions of other cultures that was implied by the phrase 'obstacles to development'. Thus the Indian caste system found an eloquent defender in Louis Dumont.[18] Any implication of irrationality in the conduct of people of other cultures was alien to the whole tradition of social anthropology, which from the time of Malinowski had always alerted its practitioners to elucidate the rationality of seemingly bizarre practices and customs among the people they were studying. Social anthropologists have consistently appeared as the defending champions of those whom they studied, their beliefs and attitudes as well as their material interests.

Among the development economists, too, the so-called 'neo-institutional' school, mostly of Europeans, differed from their United States colleagues. Where the latter no doubt were thinking primarily about Latin American countries which had been independent for a century or more, Europeans were more likely to be interested in countries of Asia and Africa which had lately emerged from colonial rule, and laid greater stress accordingly on their ex-colonial character than on the allegedly 'feudal' nature of their institutions – an allegation that would not always have been easy to sustain. Seers and Streeten stressed the inapplicability of western economic analysis to the prevailing conditions in many Third World countries, with their different institutions and attitudes. Myrdal, too, consistently emphasized the influence of attitudes, institutions, and policies on the course of economic development. Questioning the view that development in one part of an economy necessarily spreads to other sectors, and noting the tendency for it to occur in enclaves with limited spread effects, he went further in pointing to 'backwash effects' by which development in one sector might draw in resources from others and impoverish them in the process. Redistributive policies might do much to counter backwash effects within a country, and level up economic development in different parts of its economy. Internationally they were more intractable.

Underdevelopment and dependence

Explanations of the poverty of poor countries in terms of their alleged backwardness did not go down well in those countries themselves. The very word seemed disparaging and gave offence, in the same way as the word 'primitive' came to be resented by people of the societies and cultures to which it had been applied, and was dropped accordingly from the language of social anthropology. And when the lack of economic development in poor countries was attributed to a lack of Protestant-ethic-type personal qualities such as thrift, industry, and enterprise, those explanations too seemed 'person-blamed', a case of blaming the victim. For Third World

12

countries were widely regarded as the victims of the past wrongs of colonial rule and the present inequities of the international economic system, not least among the social scientists and other intellectuals graduating from their burgeoning universities and entering the world of scholarship and the service of international organizations.

The intellectual movement associated with the terms underdevelopment and dependence (or 'dependency') began in the 1950s among Latin American economists reacting against the apparent failure of policies based on mainstream development economics to stimulate growth and begin to raise the living standards of the mass of the people. Later, in the 1960s, it became more widely known in the English-speaking world, largely through the writings of A. G. Frank. Gaining many converts, it became part of a general counterblast against mainstream social science.

In that counterblast, Parsons' view that development entails shifts in the pattern variables from ascription to achievement, from particularism to universalism, and the rest, was explicitly rebutted by reference to the particularism and ascription that prevailed in the highly efficient, and also strongly paternalistic, industrial organizations which had brought about the development of Japan. Analysis in terms of stages of development was attacked as concentrating on endogenous factors within each country and neglecting exogenous factors in the world system. It was particularly strongly denied that Latin American societies had ever been feudal; on the contrary, it was asserted that they had been capitalist from the time of the Spanish and Portuguese conquests. The notion of a pre-modern 'traditional' society was attacked as 'denying a history' to the underdeveloped countries, as it seemed to imply that they had persisted unchanged since time immemorial before the impact of industrialism. Equally strongly rejected was the idea of a 'dual economy', with a 'traditional' sector where people earned a living from the land by subsistence agriculture with 'Biblical' methods, and a 'modern' urban industrial sector where money transactions prevailed. The very notion of a traditional society and culture was thus dismissed, and pre-existing differences of language and ethnic identity were played down. On the contrary, it was asserted, there is only one world economy, and consequently one world system of social relations, and it is capitalist, penetrating every nook and cranny from the great industrial and financial centres outwards through national capitals, provincial towns, and small trading centres to the last remote rural hinterland. And if control extended from centre to periphery, profits were accumulated and surplus value appropriated from periphery to centre. The verb 'to underdevelop' was given a transitive meaning; poor countries were poor, not because they were *un*developed or backward, but because they had been and still were being actively *under*developed by rich countries. Political independence, indeed, was something of an illusion in a world in which the main

13

relationships continued to be capitalist and imperialist. It served only to hide the real dependence of the poor countries on the rich, the penetration of their economies by western influences through the multi-national corporations, and the extent to which their ruling elites owed their power to support from western countries, especially the United States.

With its underlying economic determinism, the language and the concepts of this school of thought are recognizably largely Marxist: capitalism, imperialism, the appropriation and expropriation of surplus value in the process of the accumulation of capital, and so on. For this reason, it has often been called 'neo-Marxist'. However, the extent to which it is 'really' Marxist is debatable, and depends in turn upon highly debatable questions about which version of Marxist socialism is to be regarded as authentic. In some of the writings of the school, there are criticisms of Marx as being, like his bourgeois counterparts, a western European evolutionist whose vision of the importance and revolutionary potential of the industrial proletariat is not directly applicable to the Third World today. And there are diverse strands and controversies within the school itself.

During the 1970s, it sometimes seemed as if there were just two mutually incompatible ways of looking at the processes of social and economic change in the Third World: that of orthodox mainstream social science, or as its opponents called it 'bourgeois development theory'; and the alternative view stressing dependence and the active underdevelopment of the poor by the rich countries. It would be wrong to call it a debate, for there was little or no dialogue; the two schools of thought talked past each other.[19] Now that appears too simple. To a large extent the 'neo-institutional' school of European development theorists can, as we have seen, be exonerated from the neo-Marxists' strictures. They are aware that backwash effects can impoverish the periphery while development proceeds at the centre; they attach much importance to the colonial history of the present-day Third World countries; and they give much weight to the international economic system. They can accordingly be seen as something of a 'third force', while the debate – or lack of it – between those two incompatible theories begins to look more like an American quarrel, an attack by Latin Americans upon the ideas current in the United States. In the same way, the contention that there was no traditional economy or society had some force in Latin American countries in some of which the original inhabitants were exterminated altogether, and whose latter-day institutions were in virtually all respects the creatures of outside intervention. It appeared far less convincing – indeed, it became quite incredible – when applied to countries of Asia and Africa where traditional societies and cultures remain manifestly alive and well.

14

The Third World

The term 'Third World' seems to have originated among liberal and radical French writers during the 1950s, when many looked for a 'third way' or 'third force' in the politics of their own country more congenial than either a conservative nationalism on the one hand or a rigidly dogmatic communism on the other. On a wider scale, too, a 'third force' seemed even more urgently to be needed in a world dominated and threatened by the cold war between the rich, powerful industrial nations of 'West' and 'East'. Their hopes were heightened by diplomatic moves, led by the governments of Egypt, India, and Yugoslavia, and by a conference at Bandung in Indonesia in 1955 of twenty-nine African and Asian states, many of which had recently gained their independence from colonial rule. The phrase they then coined, 'le tiers monde', interestingly embodies not the modern word 'troisième' but the archaic 'tiers', rich in historical associations with 'le tiers état', the third estate of the realm, the common people who rose in 1789 and overthrew the privileged first and second estates of the Ancien Régime, the nobility and clergy respectively.[20] At that time, then, 'the third world' came to mean those countries which, however diverse they might be in other ways, had three things in common: they were poor, they were ex-colonies, and in the cold war between 'West' and 'East' they were non-aligned. Perhaps accordingly they could be thought of as the commonalty of the earth, who might if they united possess the same potential as the Third Estate showed in the French Revolution to transform the existing order.

The term itself, and more important the view of the world it signifies, were introduced to the English-speaking public in the 1960s largely by Peter Worsley in his book of that title, published in 1964,[21] and Irving Louis Horowitz' *Three Worlds of Development* in 1966.[22] They have since become familiar commonplaces. But though the expression 'Third World' has accordingly been retained in the title of this book, it is all the more necessary to indicate profoundly important changes that have since deprived it of any very precise meaning.[23] The world has become more complicated, too much so to be accommodated in a simple division into three. The third world has disintegrated.

Partly this has been because some of the so-called developing countries have actually developed, and their rapid economic growth has closed the gap between them and the industrial nations, while others have stayed poor. Thus the development of South Korea, Taiwan, and Singapore has been nothing short of spectacular; Brazil by 1980 was producing a million motor vehicles a year and exporting large quantities of such manufactured goods as vehicles, scientific instruments, and aircraft; while Nigeria has become the second most prosperous as well as the biggest country of black

15

Africa. Meanwhile, though, India remains poor and its economic growth
rather slow; and among the poorest countries of all, including Bangladesh,
Nepal, Bhutan, and a number of African states, growth has been negligible
or even negative. So disparities among Third World countries have
increased and are increasing.

Even more spectacular has been the rise to power and riches of
the countries now designated 'high-income oil exporters'. As recently as the
1950s Libya, for instance, was a typical Third World country. From the
dawn of history it had always been part of some empire or other: Roman,
Byzantine, Ottoman, Italian; and when after a short period of British
military government it finally gained independence it was a land of poor
peasants and nomadic herdsmen some of whom – the original troglodytes
– literally lived in holes in the ground. Almost all its meagre export earnings
were spent on imported energy. No one knew at that time of the oil deposits
that lay beneath its desert surface, and none could have foreseen the wealth
and influence it enjoys today.[24] And if that group of countries are in a class
of their own because of their small populations and large oil revenues, some
other countries with bigger populations have also done well out of oil,
including Indonesia, Nigeria, Iran, and Venezuela. But while oil exporters
benefit from high prices, oil importers suffer, notably India and Brazil. Such
conflicts of interest hardly make for unity among the Third World as a
whole.

Of no less moment for the whole world situation has been the emergence
of China from a seclusion that lasted from the capture of Beijing (Peking)
in 1949 to the changes in leadership that occurred in the middle and late
1970s. One immediate consequence of the new outward-looking policies,
of some significance for social science, has been that we now have
considerable statistical information about the biggest country in the world,
which ten years ago was a blank on the map. China's participation in
international organizations, especially the World Bank, with which that
very welcome development is associated, has of course a much greater
general importance as marking the distance that now separates China from
the Soviet Union. At one time in the 1970s it looked as though the simple
model of three 'worlds' might give way to a four-way model, divided
vertically into rich and poor, horizontally into 'capitalist' and communist.
In such a model, China would have taken pride of place in the quadrant
of the poor communist countries along with Vietnam, Cuba, Mozambique,
and Angola. It soon became clear, however, that that was not the way the
Chinese leaders saw the world. On the contrary, from 1974 onwards they
adopted a tripartite model, but a different one, seeing themselves –
naturally – at the head of the Third World of poor countries, with a historic
mission to rally the powers of the second rank (such as the EEC countries
and Japan) against the hegemonic tendencies of the first world, the two

16

nuclear-armed super-powers. At first it was, in headline or slogan terms, 'USSR and USA arraigned in same dock'. Later, however, 'hegemonism' became a kind of code-word referring more exclusively to 'Soviet Social-Imperialism'.

Yet another respect, then, in which the vision of a 'tiers monde' has not been fully realized is that of its 'non-alignment'. In the days of the Bandung conference in 1955, Egypt and India had recently gained their independence from British imperial domination, while Yugoslavia had succeeded in wrenching itself free from the Soviet empire in eastern Europe. All three were eager to assert a genuine independence and avoid being used as mere pawns in the game of great power rivalries. Yet Egypt itself did not long remain non-aligned, becoming first a Soviet outpost, then changing sides and becoming an ally of the United States. It would be quite specious to call Cuba non-aligned at any time since the Castro revolution in 1959; with Cuba as proxy, Soviet influence was extended to Africa, and, with Vietnam as proxy, to other countries of south-east Asia; while more recently, in December 1979, Afghanistan was absorbed into the Soviet zone by overt invasion. On the other hand, the United States had no more dependable ally than Iran as long as the Shah was on the throne, South Korea and Taiwan practically owed their separate existence to United States protection, and North American influence is obviously strong in South and central America. And from 1978 onwards, Chinese foreign policy was devoted to building up a world front including even the United States to resist 'hegemonism'. There were hostilities between China and Vietnam; and despite the appalling excesses of the Khmer Rouge in Kampuchea, the Chinese opposed the alternative regime of Heng Samrin since it was backed by Vietnam, and hence by the Soviet Union. We may conclude that few countries indeed can be regarded as non-aligned in the world of the 1980s.

Perhaps, indeed, there was always something wrong with the old tripartite model. Simple though it might appear, it tried to do too much. A taxonomy of countries, based on some criterion measure such as GNP per capita, is one thing; a grouping of states into power blocs in terms of their alignments and alliances, their rivalries and hostilities, is another. The first is appropriate for the purpose of social science, especially economics, while the second is matter for the study of current world affairs and the more serious sort of journalism. Both change rapidly, and whatever is written about them needs frequent revision, but perhaps the second is even more transitory than the first.

Any system of categories, then, seems likely to be to some extent arbitrary. For the first edition of this book I devised my own, compiling and analysing the statistics with colleagues' assistance literally by pencil-and-paper methods. Since 1978 such a task has become unnecessary, as with their vastly greater resources the World Bank have regularly published all the relevant data in their annual World Development Report; and relying as I now do on their figures (with due caution, for all statistics are liable to error) I adopt in the main their categories, though with some rearrangement and changes of nomenclature. In particular, though the World Bank list countries in ascending order by GNP per capita, I have reversed that order so as to preserve the sequence of 'the West', 'the East' or Soviet bloc, and the Third World. The countries in each category are listed at the end of this chapter, while the appropriate statistics are given in subsequent chapters according to topic.

At the head of the list so arranged stand the industrial market economies including the United States and Canada, most of the EEC, Japan, Scandinavia, Australia, and New Zealand. Multi-party electoral systems prevail in all these 'western' countries, which their enemies call capitalist and their friends call free, whose inhabitants enjoy a combination of favourable health conditions, low mortality, and material affluence with liberties of expression and association unparalleled among human societies past and present. Next come the Soviet Union and the other non-market industrial economies of eastern Europe (though Romania is classed as middle-income). Then the high-income oil exporters already mentioned, whose small populations and large oil revenues give them per capita incomes anomalously high for their level of general social and economic development. The World Bank class remaining countries in two main groups of middle- and low-income economies respectively. However, China and India are each so large and in some respects so self-contained as to be in a class, almost a world, of its own, and I follow the World Bank's practice of distinguishing them from other low-income economies. Low- and middle-income economies together are referred to by the World Bank as 'developing countries', and though sceptical of that term I sometimes use it, in context, more or less interchangeably with 'Third World' and 'poor countries' in the chapters that follow.

APPENDIX

Industrial market economies: Switzerland, West Germany, Sweden, Denmark, Norway, Belgium, France, Netherlands, United States, Austria, Canada, Japan, Australia, Finland, United Kingdom, New Zealand, Italy, Spain, Irish Republic.

Non-market industrial economies: East Germany, Czechoslovakia, Soviet Union, Hungary, Bulgaria, Poland.

High-income oil exporters: United Arab Emirates, Kuwait, Saudi Arabia, Libya.

Middle-income economies: Israel, Singapore, Greece, Trinidad and Tobago, Hong Kong, Venezuela, Iraq, Iran, Uruguay, Yugoslavia, Argentina, Portugal, Romania,

South Africa, Chile, Mexico, Brazil, Algeria, Panama, Costa Rica, Malaysia, South Korea, Cuba, Turkey, Lebanon, Jordan, Syria, North Korea, Tunisia, Paraguay, Ecuador, Colombia, Dominican Republic, Ivory Coast, Guatemala, Jamaica, Nigeria, Peru, Albania, Mongolia, Morocco, Congo, Papua New Guinea, Nicaragua, Philippines, Thailand, Cameroon, El Salvador, Zimbabwe, Egypt, Bolivia, Zambia, Honduras, Liberia, Angola, Senegal, Mauritania, Yemen, Indonesia, South Yemen, Lesotho, Kenya, Ghana.

Low-income economies: Togo, Sudan, Madagascar, Niger, Benin, Uganda, Pakistan, Central African Republic, Guinea, **China**, Tanzania, Sierra Leone, Sri Lanka, Haiti, **India**, Mozambique, Malawi, Zaire, Upper Volta, Rwanda, Burundi, Mali, Vietnam, Afghanistan, Burma, Somalia, Nepal, Ethiopia, Bangladesh, Chad, Bhutan, Laos, Cambodia (Kampuchea).

Source and notes: World Bank, *World Development Report 1982*, based on GNP per capita in 1980; excludes Taiwan, also some 34 countries and territories with populations of less than one million. Names of countries follow current British usage, mostly as in *The Times Atlas*, sixth edition (1980).

2 Technology, society, and population

The natural history of the human population of the earth from the emergence of *Homo sapiens* to the present day (fig. 1)

There have been two great technological revolutions in human history: the neolithic revolution and the industrial revolution.* Each was accompanied by a population explosion.[1]

Ten or twelve thousand years ago, *Homo sapiens* was a relatively rare species living in small bands by hunting and food-gathering. Some human groups do so to this day, or did so till recently, including the Australian aborigines; a few small groups in Africa, such as those popularly called 'Bushmen', and the Hadza of Tanzania; the Andaman islanders; and some Amazon forest peoples.[2] From studies which have been done of the population density of people living in this way, it may be surmised that there can have been no more than 10 million humans on earth before the development of agriculture, and the actual population was perhaps 1 to 5 million.

Between about 9000 and 5500 BC, there occurred the first great technological revolution in human history. It involved a complex of inventions rather than one single crucial discovery. The domestication of a number of plant species, especially the grain seeds, greatly increased the carrying capacity of the land, or at least of land in some parts of the earth, and also made possible the storage of food, and both necessitated and permitted the growth of a settled population. This in turn stimulated the building of houses, an advance on the temporary shelters of food-gathering wanderers. The domestication of a number of animal species had equally complex and fundamental effects on human social organization; these included sheep, goats, pigs, poultry, cattle, and horses. By adding the muscle power of other animals to that of humans, they made possible the rise of techniques such as ploughing; they added a dependable food supply

---

* 'Human' here refers to *Homo sapiens*. If we count other species of the genus *Homo*, all now extinct, and extend our time-scale to the last million years, we could distinguish an even earlier technological revolution corresponding to the making of the first stone hand-axes and similar tools, accompanied by population growth from perhaps around 100,000 or 150,000 individuals to perhaps 1 million: the palaeolithic revolution.

20

The natural history of the human population

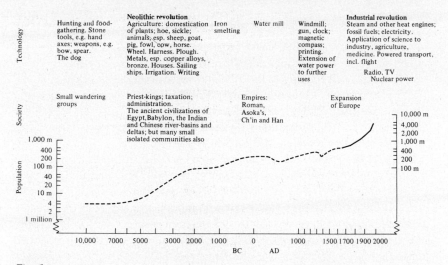

Fig. 1

Note to Fig. 1. Both time and population are plotted on logarithmic scales. Time is plotted on a logarithmic scale of years before AD 3000. This enables the long slow trends of the remote past to be somewhat 'foreshortened' while the rapid increase of the last 300 years can be seen without undue distortion. In the same way, plotting population on a logarithmic scale enables the diagram to show changes in the relative increase rate. The neolithic population explosion from 5 million to 100 million is thus kept in the same perspective as the industrial population explosion from 500 million to (so far) some 4,500 million.

of meat and milk, together with other animal products such as leather; and they afforded the means of transport and trade between the new fixed settlements of human beings. Along with agriculture, therefore, went the rise of the first towns, and correspondingly that of specialized crafts and manufactures in exchange for the food that was now available in a storable form. Other technological achievements of this period included the rise and elaboration of metallurgy and the making of tools and weapons of bronze and iron; the wheel, with its vast potential for both trade and war; and the wooden sailing ship, which added a limited use of another source of energy to human and animal muscle. And these technological developments were accompanied by remarkable economic, political, and intellectual developments, including the rise of money and systems of accounting; the rise of political authorities – mostly, it would seem, of the 'oriental despotism' type – wider than the kinship or neighbourhood principle; the invention of writing; mathematics, and its application to astronomical observation, surveying, and accounting; and the reckoning of time.

Although the neolithic revolution seems from our standpoint like a leisurely affair compared with the industrial revolution of the present time and recent history, it was nevertheless a dramatically rapid change

21

compared with the slow processes of evolution by natural selection, which had prevailed before the rise of culture. And like our own technological revolution it was accompanied by a population explosion. By the time of which we have worthwhile estimates, the largest human communities of people subject to a common political authority numbered scores of millions. The Han empire of China, Asoka's empire in India, and Roman rule around the Mediterranean basin comprised populations of around 50–100 million each, and the world's population at the beginning of the Christian era has been estimated at between 200 and 300 million.

Not that there was at any time a single neolithic culture or society. On the contrary, although the technologies of transport and war made possible the sort of empires we have just mentioned, they did not sustain a system of communications and social interaction which ever approached the scale of the whole earth. Even the empires remained comparatively isolated from one another, while in areas which they did not conquer there continued to be smaller human groups, developing in relative isolation both distinctive cultures – different languages, technologies, kinship systems, systems of political authority, etc. – and also distinctive physical characteristics through the process known as genetic drift. During the neolithic period, therefore, humankind came to be divided in two ways – by culture and by race.

After that great burst of innovative energy there followed seven thousand years of relative technological stagnation. This stagnation was not quite unrelieved, and we can distinguish two periods within it when significant advances occurred. One accompanied the development of iron smelting, apparently in about 1400 BC, and its spread, together with some inventions of minor importance such as the crane and the pulley at an early stage of Graeco-Roman civilization. The other occurred during a period around AD 1000–1300, with the invention of the windmill (possibly independently in Persia in the seventh century and in Europe about 1100), the gun, the mechanical clock, the magnetic compass and other aids to navigation, printing, and the further development of some older inventions including improved harness, making possible a wider use of animal power, and the application of water power to wider uses. The first great expansion of European influence across the world, indeed, began centuries before the industrial revolution and was based on the technology of guns and sails. Though the evidence is fragmentary, it seems not impossible that these periods of minor technological advance were also periods of population growth. In between such periods, and even to some extent during them, however, population grew very slowly, if at all, and from time to time experienced sharp setbacks from famine, pestilence, or war. From the 200–300 million which most authorities regard as a reasonable estimate for the world's population at the time of Christ, it possibly fell to not much more than half that number around the seventh century AD, rose again until about the thirteenth century, and was then severely reduced by the pandemic of bubonic plague later named the Black Death.[3]

From 1650 onwards, the increasingly reliable estimates we have indicate a continuous and ever more rapid growth. If world population scarcely doubled in the first 1,650 years of the Christian era from 200–300 million to 545 million, it nearly doubled again by the decade 1810–20 when it passed the 1,000 million mark. It then doubled in a century, reaching 2,000 million about 1920. And it has since more than doubled again in sixty years, to almost 4,500 million in 1981.[4]

Population in transition from pre-industrial to industrial conditions (fig. 2)

A useful schematic analysis of stages in the transition from pre-industrial to industrial conditions was that of the demographer and eugenist C. P. Blacker.[5] According to this analysis, pre-industrial populations were characterized by a fluctuating and precarious balance between high fertility and high mortality, which he called the 'high stationary' stage. With the rise in the standard of living and the spread of modern scientific medicine, especially in the field of public health, populations pass into the 'early expanding' stage. In this second stage, the death-rate falls, but fertility remains high, and population increases at an accelerating rate. After a longer or shorter time, however, many countries have experienced a fall in the birth-rate consequent upon the adoption of a small-family system. There has accordingly been a turning point, marking the beginning of the third stage which Blacker called the 'late expanding' stage, when although population continues to increase the rate of increase slows up. When births and deaths are again in balance, but now at low levels, we

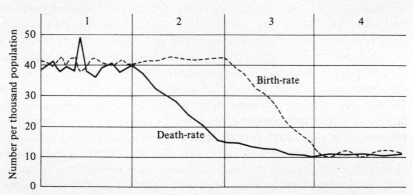

Fig. 2. The population stages (After C. P. Blacker, *Eugenics, Galton and After.*)

23

have the fourth or 'low stationary' stage; while the possibility exists that the birth-rate may go below the death-rate, so that we have a theoretical fifth or 'declining' stage.

At the end of this chapter I give case-studies of three individual countries, namely India, England and Wales, and Japan, with the object of showing the different ways in which population trends have occurred and may be related to economic and other changes. Roughly speaking, using these three societies as examples, England and Wales may be said to have entered stage 2 in 1750; stage 3 began in 1877, a date which can be 'pin-pointed' by the Bradlaugh–Besant trial; while by about 1935 or 1940 stage 3 had come to an end, though whether the trends after 1940 deserve the term 'low stationary' is more doubtful. Japan entered stage 2 some time after 1868, and stage 3 came in with the dramatic drop in the birth-rate of 1947–57. India fairly clearly entered stage 2 after the great influenza catastrophe of 1919; whether stage 3 has been reached yet is doubtful.

However, useful as Blacker's analysis is, it will become clear that it does not exactly fit the population history of any of the three countries; still less, it must be emphasized, is it an inevitable sequence to be followed by all. When we come to translate 'high' and 'low' into actual figures, things become more difficult again. Although birth- and death-rates in western Europe before the industrial revolution were much higher than they are now, it seems that they were never as high as they were in the recent past in other parts of the world.

Thus whereas in India before 1920 (fig. 4, p. 37) birth- and death-rates generally fluctuated between 40 and 50 per thousand, in England and Wales (fig. 5, p. 39) the death-rate appears to have reached only 36 at its peak in 1740, while the high birth-rates in the eighteenth and nineteenth centuries too were at levels of around 36 to 37. Studies of the demographic history of other European countries including Ireland and Norway suggest that, as in England, fertility was limited by the late marriage of women and possibly also by 'preventive' checks to achieve birth spacing, so that families were not large, especially among the poor.[6] Many authorities now regard the demographic and family patterns of western Europe, indeed, as having facilitated the early industrial revolution there, and I return to this theme in chapter 8.

Moreover in the countries which first experienced the rise of modern science, especially medical science, and of industry and agricultural improvement, the fall in mortality was slow and gradual as new discoveries were made and new developments spread through the population. In countries which experienced the impact of modern conditions at a later date, when the relevant knowledge and techniques were already fully developed in Europe, the changes which took place over a century or more

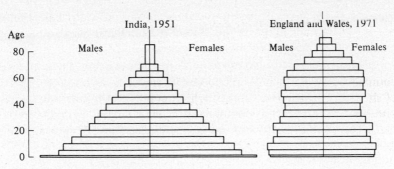

Fig. 3. Age and sex distributions

in Europe were telescoped into a small number of decades, and the fall in mortality has been swifter accordingly. This has important consequences for world population trends at the present time, for reasons to do with the age and sex distributions of different populations.

With high birth- and death-rates, many children are born, but as each age-group pass through life their numbers are much reduced, and few survive into old age. Such conditions still prevailed in India in 1951, and fig. 3 brings out the contrast between the resulting age and sex distribution and that of a population with low birth- and death-rates, England and Wales in 1971.

Since 1945, death-rates have tumbled in low- and middle-income countries generally, so that whereas a high death-rate used to be thought of as one of 40 or more, now anything over 20 is relatively high. By 1980, indeed (according to the World Bank's estimates), the 140 million people living in countries with death-rates of 20 or more were far outnumbered by those in low- and middle-income countries with death-rates of under 10.

There is no mystery about how this has been achieved; it is the result of public health and preventive medicine, an instance of the international diffusion of technology. Some diseases have been virtually eliminated, such as small-pox, whose strains are still cultivated in laboratories only in case another outbreak should ever occur. Others have been controlled, and of these probably the most important in its consequences for population trends is malaria. In one particularly striking case, the death-rate in Sri Lanka (Ceylon) was halved, falling from 22 to 11 per thousand, in eight years between 1945 and 1953, almost entirely as a result of the eradication of malaria there.[7]

The rapid current increase of population is accentuated by the very rapidity of the fall in death-rates, reflecting a rapid improvement in mortality conditions in which, however, the population of many poor countries still exhibit the 'youthful' age-structure with which they emerged

25

from the earlier stage. These improved conditions naturally have their first and most dramatic effect on the mortality of children and young adults; combating the diseases of old age is a slower process, and it is the young who benefit more from measures such as the control of malaria and the improvement of midwifery. The main improvement in mortality conditions, accordingly, is felt just in those age-groups which are most numerous; in arithmetical terms, the most reduced mortality rates are multiplied by the biggest age-groups in the reckoning of overall mortality and the summing which produces the death-rate for the population as a whole, the so-called 'crude' death-rate.

As a simple calculation will show, a stable population in which every baby born lives to the age of exactly 100 years will have a death-rate of 10 per thousand. Needless to say, no country has ever approached such favourable mortality conditions as that, and countries like Britain and Sweden, with highly developed public health services backed by adequate resources have a hard time getting their death-rates below 12 per thousand in populations which include a due proportion of old people. But in many poor countries today, where the age-structure of the population is a 'youthful' one as a result of past high mortality and present increase, a comparatively modest improvement in mortality conditions enables the crude death-rate to be brought well below 10. It was thought well-nigh incredible when in 1966 the crude death-rate in Japan was reduced to less than 7 per thousand despite mortality conditions which, age for age, were still not quite as favourable as those in western European countries with death-rates of 11 or 12. By 1980 Japan's performance had been matched by a number of middle-income countries including Singapore, Trinidad and Tobago, Hong Kong, Panama, Costa Rica, Cuba, and Jamaica; while among low-income countries the crude death-rate was little higher at 7 in Sri Lanka and 8 in China, in both of which, too, infant mortality rates were far lower than might have been expected from their GNP per capita. Such low crude death-rates could indeed be regarded as 'artificially' low, and they are likely to rise again in decades to come as the age-structure of the population matures – that is, as the big age-groups now young in those populations survive into old age and fill out the numbers of older people. Meanwhile, though, they constitute one important factor in the current rapid population growth in the world as a whole, commonly called the population explosion.

The other main factor is fertility – a much more problematic subject, as will appear below.

World population c. 1980: the Third World and the population explosion

As will be seen from table 2.1, there is a wide contrast between the industrial countries (western and communist) on the one hand and most of the Third World on the other. In the former, birth- and death-rates are comparatively low and the rate of natural increase of the population is modest. Infant mortality rates too are low, and the expectation of life is long. In the latter, birth-rates are much higher; and though death-rates too are somewhat higher than in the industrial countries, and yet in a sense (as explained above) deceptively low, giving a misleadingly favourable impression of mortality conditions, they are low enough to make for rapid population growth. China is an exception; its death-rate fell sharply between 1957 and 1980, when its infant mortality rate of 56 was the second lowest among the low-income countries; and its birth-rate too has fallen sharply in response to the one-child policy, of which more below. China apart, then, clearly it is in the Third World that the population explosion is taking place.

Awareness of that fact is now widespread, and has highlighted this as one of the great issues of our time. Although, as has been seen, there is little room for doubt about the decline in mortality and how it has been achieved with such dramatic suddenness, fertility is a much more controversial subject.

In the past, pro-natalist attitudes and policies have often prevailed among both governments and religious leaders. Some governments have been interested in population questions for reasons of military might – 'cannon-fodder' – or, more widely, national aggrandizement, or to arrest a threatened decline in their nation's power and influence in the world. Congruent with such attitudes have been the traditional injunctions of many of the world's religions: 'Be fruitful, and multiply, and replenish the earth, and subdue it.'

Such views, however, became less and less tenable after the second world war, in a world of rapidly falling mortality rates and population increase: indeed, they seemed against all reason. At the first United Nations world population conference in 1954 the prevailing atmosphere was one of Malthusian concern about population growth in relation to limited resources. Only two organized groups stood out, namely the Roman Catholic church, and the Soviet Union and its eastern European satellites. The latter were possibly most concerned to replace, and meanwhile to conceal, their appalling wartime losses, and took a strictly Marxist line equating over-population with unemployment, a disease of capitalism avoided by socialist planning. The former were adamant in their rejection of 'artificial' methods of birth control, and implacable in their hostility to abortion in

27

Table 2.1 *World population trends, 1960–1980*

	World 1960	World 1980	Industrial market economies 1960	Industrial market economies 1980	Non-market industrial economies 1960	Non-market industrial economies 1980	High-income oil exporters 1960	High-income oil exporters 1980	Middle-income economies 1960	Middle-income economies 1980	Low-income economies: China 1960	China 1980	India 1960	India 1980	Others 1960	Others 1980
Population in millions		4,414		714		353		14		1,139		977		673		511
Crude birth-rate per thousand	36	28	20	15	23	18	49	42	43	35	40[a]	21	44	36	49	45
Crude death-rate per thousand	18	11	10	9	8	11	21	12	17	11	14[a]	8	22	14	25	18
Natural increase per cent		1.7		0.6		0.7		3.0		2.4		1.3		2.2		2.7
Infant mortality per thousand live births	...	97	30	11	36	25	173	99	125	80	...	56	165	123	164	130
Life expectancy at birth, years	...	61	70	74	68	71	45	57	51	60	...	64	43	52	40	48

Notes:
[a] Figures are for 1957, not 1960.
... Not available.

Sources: World data 1960 from U.N. *Demographic Yearbook, 1961*; for 1980 from Population Reference Bureau. Rest of table from World Bank, *World Development Report 1982*; excludes Taiwan (18m.) and countries with populations of less than one million.

28

all circumstances. Such indeed is still the case, for despite continuing debate within the church successive popes have continued to reiterate traditional Catholic doctrines on these matters.[8] Other religious bodies, however, have been less inflexible. Thus among Christian churches the Anglicans at their Lambeth conference in 1958 formally recognized the propriety of implementing responsible decisions about family size by methods not involving a hindrance to married love; while Islamic, Buddhist, and Hindu religious authorities have not in general raised serious doctrinal difficulties about family limitation programmes.

In 1969 the Pearson commission identified the 'staggering growth of population' as a major cause of the discrepancy between rich and poor countries. It sharply increased the need for public expenditure on education, health, housing, and water supply. 'There is a strong inverse correlation between child health and family size. Rapid growth of the child population also delays educational improvement.' The burden of dependence was increased, to the detriment of resources that could be devoted to raising living standards. More aid was needed. Inequality was increased by developments such as the raising of land values and rents, and severe urban problems arose.

At the same time they wrote of 'a remarkable awakening to the acute problems posed by this population explosion', and reported that 'ambitious policies to spread family planning have been introduced in countries representing over 70 per cent of the population of the developing world'. Many parents wanted large families for good and valid economic reasons, not because they were ignorant or improvident; and in such cases access to family planning information and facilities would not make much difference. Nevertheless, 'many of the children born today are unwanted'. The incidence of illegal abortions, and of maternal deaths from them, was high enough to be a serious problem in Latin America and elsewhere, and indicated 'a silent demand for family planning'.[9]

They drew attention, too, to the 'major breakthrough in family planning techniques' that had recently occurred. As they implied, family limitation is much more a matter of motive than of means, and people who seriously want to avoid having children will generally find a way. However, it may be suggested that the new techniques, especially oral contraceptives ('the pill') and intra-uterine devices (IUDs, 'the coil', 'the loop'), have a significance beyond that of merely widening the range of methods available. They were developed with the Third World in mind, even though they have come into widespread use also in affluent industrial countries; and they represent methods by which women can control their own fertility, with important implications for the status of women and the relations between the sexes.

In these circumstances, the governments of many Third World countries have adopted policies explicitly aimed at slowing down the rate of population growth. The lead was taken by India, as detailed in the case-study below. Countries whose governments have followed that lead include most notably China, which has moved far from the pro-natalist position originally taken up in 1949, and since 1979 has been urging later marriage, longer spacing, and fewer children – ideally the one-child family – in order to curb population growth.[10] Other Third World governments with population policies include those of Indonesia, Bangladesh, Thailand, the Philippines, Mexico, and Turkey; while in yet others, including Brazil and Nigeria, governments permit and even quietly support family planning on grounds of health and human rights without commitment to a population policy as such. At the same time, support for family planning programmes has been forthcoming from the United Nations and its agencies including the World Bank.

In recent times, then, there has been little support for pro-natalist attitudes and policies, and widespread acceptance of the need to check runaway population growth if there is to be any hope of raising living standards in poor countries. Given that acceptance of a broadly Malthusian position, though, there has been much controversy about what governments should do and how they should do it.

At the starting point of recent and current debates is the 'fertility control' argument that if the rate of economic growth is (say) 5 per cent annually while population increases at (say) 3 per cent, then most of the effort, initiative, and investment that go into economic development are being eaten up by the extra mouths. From this viewpoint, fertility control is seen as a necessary condition of any genuine improvement in living standards, and governments are justified in devoting considerable resources to reducing the birth-rate. Thus Lord Blackett in 1969 calculated that it would pay the government of a typical poor country to spend up to $150 to prevent one birth from taking place,[11] while other authorities have estimated that 'the addition to income per head in a poor country caused by spending £100 on birth prevention is, at very least, fifteen times the addition to income from the best alternative use of £100'.[12]

The 'fertility control' approach, then, proceeds from the top downwards; it implies an active effort on the part of a government to persuade its people to have fewer children. Imbued with such ideas, a government will, perhaps, typically inaugurate a programme and entrust it to a new or existing government department under a responsible minister. An organization will be set up which will recruit staff. Targets will be allotted for the performance of field officers in persuading men to undergo vasectomies or women to be fitted with IUDs. Positive sanctions or incentives will be held out for the fulfilment or over-fulfilment of targets, while negative sanctions such as promotion withheld will be applied to those who fall short. Such pressures on the organization's field staff may be transmitted downwards to the people in the way of bribes on the one hand, threats or coercion on the other. And if that begins to read like an unpleasant caricature, it is in fact not wildly different from what happened in India in 1976, as will be seen in the case-study below.

In reaction against that, with its unpalatable ethical and political implications, some have rejected the proposition that checking fertility is a necessary precondition of economic development, and tended to assert the contrary. They argue that until people are better off, share greater knowledge and resources of literacy and understanding, can look forward realistically to security in old age without a large family to support them, and above all can expect most of their children to survive, they will have no reason to limit the number of their offspring. Large families, indeed, are a perfectly rational reaction to conditions of poverty and high mortality, and efforts by governments to promote family limitation will be ineffective, even counter-productive, until a certain threshold of economic development has been reached. Family limitation is seen from this point of view as a result, not a cause: a by-product of economic development. It arises 'spontaneously', it proceeds from below upwards, and it is to be both explained and engendered by socio-economic factors, particularly a rise in incomes; industrialization, and the growth of towns; literacy; and perhaps most important of all, the reduction of infant mortality. Hence the slogan 'The best contraceptive is development', taken up with enthusiasm at the United Nations world population conference at Bucharest in 1974, when to the dismay of many professional demographers and other social scientists the population issue was debated in frankly political terms.[13]

That position, however, has been controverted in its turn by those who consider that the reaction against the 'fertility control' approach went too far. It is a mistake to regard socio-economic development and family limitation as if they were mutually exclusive alternatives between which a choice has to be made. Governments can pursue both, and each can help the other. It is not necessary to wait till a certain threshold of development has been reached, for family limitation programmes can have some effect at any level of socio-economic development. Nor, in such programmes, need there be pressure 'from the top downwards' to arouse adverse reaction. The key phrase should rather be 'family planning', and this implies encouraging couples to make responsible decisions about parenthood, and ensuring that they have the information and the means necessary to do so. It is partly a matter of the availability alike of both the knowledge and the appliances; partly education in the widest sense, the encouragement of rational discussion in a free and open atmosphere of this as indeed of all issues; and partly of measures enabling women to decide important matters on terms of equality with men. It has been well said that

31

great social changes begin when the previously unthinkable becomes thinkable. The change of mind is what counts, and there is much that governments can do to create a climate of opinion in which that can occur.

This in turn is linked with another issue, about means rather than ends, between the 'clinical' and the 'commercial' approaches. Many of the Third World governments which have adopted family planning programmes have done so through their ministries of health, which have either set up special clinics for the purpose, staffed by doctors and nurses, or charged existing clinics with this extra task. It is argued that this is not only a great waste of the time and energy of such highly trained professional people, which should rather be devoted to relieving suffering and combating disease; it is also a mistake to put about the idea that family planning requires all the solemnity of a visit to the clinic, held perhaps infrequently and at some distance from home. According to this view, governments should concentrate more on making contraceptives available, possibly at subsidized prices, through everyday trade networks like the village store and the itinerant trader, rather as they are in western countries. On the other hand, it can be argued that the only really safe, reliable contraceptive suitable for purely commercial distribution is the sheath, which puts fertility unequivocally under male control. All the methods applicable by women require at least some professional help or supervision, whether it is a prescription for 'the pill', implantation of an IUD, or fitting a diaphragm, if they are to be either safe or reliable; while the same is even more obviously true of the surgical sterilization of either women or men. But perhaps this like other issues in the debate is best viewed in terms of 'both and' rather than 'either or'.

Europe's fertility decline reassessed

Considerations of this kind have led to a renewed interest in the history of fertility decline in Europe. Thus in the case of England, those who argue that 'development is the best contraceptive' and that socio-economic factors explain fertility decline can point to the long time-lag of a century or more of population growth, between 1760 when the industrial revolution is conventionally regarded as having taken off, and first intimations of falling fertility after 1877, before rising standards of living led to family limitation. On the other hand, at that time infant mortality was still high, even among the middle classes, who could not realistically have expected that all their children would survive, as the theory would require, before adopting the small-family system.[14]

And if England is one case, France is quite another, where – as Carr-Saunders pointed out long ago – the birth-rate followed the death-rate downwards from the early nineteenth century, with no time-lag and no dramatic down-turn like that signalled by the Bradlaugh–Besant trial in England. Confirmation that the French are indeed a special case, with a good claim to be regarded in this respect as the first modern nation, has come from studies which have traced family limitation among the French-speaking *haute bourgeoisie* of Geneva as early as the seventeenth century, before the industrial revolution, and long before it was adopted elsewhere in Europe.

In analysing the historical evidence for Europe, according to some recent writers, it is important to distinguish between 'natural fertility' and 'family limitation'. 'Natural fertility' patterns may differ in different communities as a result of differences especially in marriage ages, diet, and breast-feeding practices, even though people in those communities may be imposing no checks upon married fertility. Such differences were indeed to be found among the relatively isolated communities of pre-industrial Europe, where, as noted above, high fertility did not generally prevail, largely because of high ages of marriage among women. 'Family limitation', though, is quite different. It occurs when people, especially women, decide to have so many children and then stop. Characteristically they tend to do so in their early adult lives; so that family limitation in this sense, or 'stopping behaviour' as it might be termed, is evidenced by a much more marked concentration of births to women aged 20–24, and a faster fall of marital fertility with age.

Ingenious statistical measures have been devised to investigate the onset of family limitation in this sense in different European communities. Apart from France, where married fertility began to decline appreciably as early as 1800, in most European countries the down-turn occurred no earlier than 1880 and no later than 1920. When the data are analysed in more detail by provinces (or the corresponding administrative units) the concentration of the dates in the decades around 1900 is even more apparent. According to van de Walle and Knodel, 'Europe's fertility decline began under remarkably diverse socio-economic and demographic conditions.' Thus England was largely industrialized (with only 15 per cent of employed men in agriculture) and urbanized (rural population down to 28 per cent) when fertility started falling; whereas Hungary was an overwhelmingly agrarian economy when fertility began to decline there, as it did about the same time. So too was France when its much earlier transition began around 1800, and Bulgaria at the onset of its decline over a century later. 'Literacy was also at very different levels when fertility began to fall – low in France, Hungary, and Bulgaria, for example, and high in England and Wales.' Socio-economic explanations therefore appear inadequate, and the rapid spread of family limitation around 1900 in Europe is to be seen rather as an instance of the diffusion of ideas whose explanation may more appropriately be sought in the cultural realm.[15]

33

World fertility trends c. 1980

By the late 1970s it was becoming clear that the long- and anxiously-awaited turning-point had been reached, and that world fertility had begun to fall. Thus Bogue and Tsui in 1978 estimated that between 1968 and 1975 world total fertility had fallen from 4.6 to 4.1 births per woman on average.[16] Fertility decline had occurred in most countries, and over 80 per cent of the world's population lived in countries where an appreciable decline had occurred during that period. The governments of nine of the eleven most populous Third World countries, comprising more than half the world's population, had adopted family-limitation policies. Focussing attention on these eleven countries, Bogue and Tsui estimated that in two of them, China and Indonesia, fertility had declined by over 20 per cent. In Vietnam, Thailand, and Mexico it had fallen by more than 10 per cent, while more modest but still appreciable declines of 10 per cent or less had occurred in India, Bangladesh, Pakistan, the Philippines, and Brazil. Only in Nigeria had there been no decline in fertility, and African countries generally, indeed, seemed to be less affected by the general trend than those in Asia and Latin America. Bogue and Tsui found that five socio-economic factors were related to fertility decline. That decline was greater among the better-off LDCs (less-developed countries) than among the poorest countries, and greater in those in which more people lived in towns. It was much greater in countries with lower infant mortality rates and longer expectations of life. And it was greater in countries with fewer workers in agriculture and higher literacy rates. They also found, however, that government family planning programmes had had a direct and independent effect upon fertility almost as great as all five socio-economic factors put together. Their findings gave some support, then, to both the 'socio-economic' and the 'family planning' arguments. While both socio-economic factors and government programmes, each acting alone, could have some effect, they should be seen less as opposed alternatives than as complementary and mutually reinforcing influences.

Clear evidence of fertility decline in many Third World countries has come most recently from the findings of the World Fertility Survey.[17] Appropriately enough for so momentous a subject, this has been called 'the biggest social survey ever conducted'. Initiated in 1972, it has been organized by the International Statistical Institute with funds from the United Nations and individual donor countries, and it consists of surveys, carried out by national statistical offices, in 42 'developing' and 20 'developed' countries comprising some 39 per cent of the world's population. In these surveys, samples numbering 3,000–11,000 women have been asked, almost invariably by women interviewers, when (and if) they were married, how many children they had had, when born, and if and when

34

any of their children had died; about their schooling, childhood residence, and employment; how many children they wanted to have, whether they knew about contraception and if so by what methods, and whether they were currently exercising birth control or had ever done so. The field work was carried out in most participating countries between 1975 and 1980; and by March 1982, results were available for 29 developing countries and 16 developed countries.

In all but two of the developing countries (Nepal and Senegal), most women were aware of at least one efficient modern method of conception control as well as of measures traditional in the local cultures; in most of these 29 countries, 90 per cent or more were so aware. The methods they knew about tended to be those applicable by women, particularly 'the pill' and IUDs, rather than male methods such as the condom and male sterilization or vasectomy.

The extent of contraceptive use, however, differed widely. In some countries it was very widespread; for example, in Costa Rica 77 per cent of younger women liable to become pregnant were currently using contraception at the time of the survey, as high a proportion as in the United States. In others it was much less so, especially Kenya, where only 29 per cent of women had ever tried to control their fertility, only 11 per cent had ever used a modern method, and only 6 per cent were currently using a modern method.

There was unequivocal evidence of a fall in fertility in most of the Asian, Latin American, and Caribbean countries reporting. Although women in those countries characteristically had a total fertility of four to six children, more than twice as many as women in industrial countries, and twice as many as needed to replace the population, their total fertility had fallen in most cases by at least one child per woman. Only in Bangladesh and Nepal was there no clear evidence of fertility decline.

In Syria and Jordan likewise there was no clear-cut evidence of a fall in fertility; and in none of the four African countries reporting was there any indication whatever of fertility decline. In Kenya, indeed, it seemed likely that already high fertility rates had risen still higher in the fifteen years before the WFS survey. With a total fertility rate of nearly eight children, the mean desired family size was more than seven, and few women stated that they had had enough and wanted no more. While Kenya was probably the country with the highest fertility and the fastest-increasing population in the world,[18] the WFS findings seem consistent with the impression already mentioned that family limitation has made less headway in Africa than in other parts of the Third World.

In developing countries generally, fertility was closely related to infant mortality, an important subject about which I say more in chapter 4. Countries with relatively lower fertility were found to have lower infant

makes economic development more difficult of achievement. The time factor is so pressing, and the population growth so formidable, that we have to get out of the vicious circle through a direct assault upon this problem as a national commitment.[3]

The effect of that 'direct assault' was political disaster. By April 1976 there were widespread complaints that junior officials had shown an excess of zeal in carrying out the sterilization programme and gone far beyond government policy in order to meet their monthly targets. Some groups felt they had been unfairly picked on, such as teachers in Uttar Pradesh who were told to be sterilized or lose a month's pay. Even though the extent of the abuses may have been exaggerated, rumours of coercion and harassment were rife. There were riots and a major political storm; and the ensuing general election in 1977, held after a postponement in an atmosphere of crisis, resulted in the fall of Mrs Indira Gandhi's government. After such turbulent controversies, both the Janata Party who succeeded to power in 1977 and Mrs Gandhi when she was re-elected in 1980 adopted a more cautious approach, but the family planning policy was continued with a generally rising trend in sterilization and other con-traceptive measures.[4] By the end of the 1970s, though India's birth-rate had fallen somewhat, current estimates still put it as high as 33–36.

Case-study 2: England and Wales (fig. 5)

Our knowledge of the pre-industrial population history of this country is sketchy, and before the census of 1801 and civil registration of births and deaths in 1837 there are only parish registers, not all of which were ever complete, and many of which have been lost. Parish register material, however, has enabled estimates to be made of national birth- and death-rates from about 1700 onwards,[1] while the detailed analysis of one register – that of Colyton in Devon[2] – affords strong presumptive evidence of family-limitation practices during the hard times from about 1650 to 1780. Men married late, around 26–7; they married women older than themselves, often nearing 30 and more than half-way through their childbearing period; and births were widely spaced, though we can only guess at how this was done.

Nationally the death-rate, which was probably rising during the early eighteenth century, fell after about 1750. There has been much controversy about whether the birth-rate rose or merely remained high,[3] but the balance of evidence now suggests that it rose in response to new opportunities in rising industries, with earlier marriages and the abandon-ment of old family-limitation practices. Large families were accordingly a response to industrialization, rather than a traditional pattern.

The fall in the death-rate, however, was arrested by the 'health of towns

38

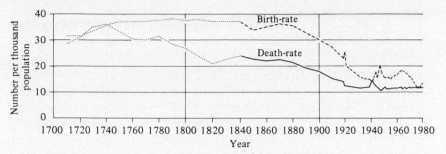

Fig. 5. Birth- and death-rates, England and Wales. Earlier data averaged and smoothed. Data for 1979 and 1980 are for UK.
(Sources: 1710–1932, A. M. Carr-Saunders, *World Population* (1936). Subsequent data from Registrar-General, *Statistical Reviews*; UN *Demographic Yearbook, Historical Supplement*, 1979, and *Monthly Bulletin of Statistics*.)

problem' in the early Victorian era, and it hesitated around 21 to 24 from about 1820 to 1880 until the sanitary reforms which were the achievement of that unsung hero of English history Edwin Chadwick.[4] That long hesitation was a special feature of the experience of this country, part no doubt of the penalty of being the first industrial country, and not repeated elsewhere.

The circumstances in which the birth-rate began to fall in the late 1870s are now fairly well understood.[5] Following Malthus' work, published in 1798, there had been some advocacy of family limitation, especially by the early radical Francis Place, but it had fallen on deaf ears.[6] By 1870, however, the rising middle class were experiencing a number of checks to their standard of living – falling prices which disproportionately reduced profits and investment,[7] and an absolute shortage of domestic servants – along with other changes that made children a source of new expense, such as the introduction of examinations for the civil service, Army, Navy, and other professions, the concurrent rise of the so-called Public Schools (actually private and very expensive), and some minor changes like the custom of taking holidays by the sea. At the time when the middle classes were motivated to limit their families, the trial of Charles Bradlaugh and Annie Besant in 1876–7 on charges of obscenity arising from a book on birth control, and the wide publicity it received in the press, gave them a knowledge of the means. The use of contraceptives, beginning among the well-to-do, spread down the social scale and by the 1950s was widespread throughout the population.[8] The death-rate meanwhile had levelled at around 12 per thousand. Since the second world war there have been two 'baby booms'. The first culminated in 1947 when the birth-rate was 20.5 per thousand, the second in 1964 when it was 18.6. In between it fell to 15 in 1955, and in the late 1970s it fell below 12 per thousand, about

39

the same as the death-rate. Population growth has accordingly been slow and irregular at rates between one per cent and, recently, zero.

Blacker's four stages, then, may be seen as having occurred in this country as follows: the first before 1750; the second from 1750 to 1877; the third from 1877 to 1940; and the fourth since the second world war. The other main feature of the experience of this country lies in the extreme slowness of the changes, which took over two centuries here in contrast to the way they have been telescoped in some later-developing countries into scarcely more than two or three decades.

Case-study 3: Japan (fig. 6)

For over two hundred years, from the gradual expulsion of foreigners in 1615–28 to the incursion of Commodore Perry in 1852, Japan was completely secluded from the rest of the world by the deliberate policy of the ruling Tokugawa shogunate. Censuses were taken at frequent intervals during this period, and though these enumerated only the commoners and excluded the nobles, samurai, and rich merchants they show a variation of no more than 10 per cent. The checks which kept population so remarkably stable included natural disasters like volcanic eruptions, but also deliberate measures – infanticide among peasants, and abortion among the nobility and gentry – to preserve a limited inheritance on land which was visibly limited.

After 1852, and especially after the Meiji Restoration of 1868, the new ruling class decided that rapid industrial development was essential if the country was not to be conquered and subjected to the colonial rule of one or other of the European powers. The immediate effect on population was an increase from its Tokugawa level of 35 million in 1873 to 55 million in 1918. It is not known exactly how this occurred; certainly the death-rate fell, but its fall may not have been immediate, while the birth-rate may well have risen with the abandonment of traditional family-limitation practices in response to the rise of new opportunities and the migration to the new industrial towns.

Modern vital statistics were instituted in 1920, from which date we have a clearer picture of trends. Fig. 6 shows that the fall in the death-rate from 25 in 1920 to 11 in 1950, comparable to that which took 130 years in England and Wales (*c.* 1810 to 1940), was achieved in Japan in 30. Meanwhile, the birth-rate remained high at first, though with a suggestive slight drop in the late thirties. Population growth was fairly rapid accordingly at around 15 per thousand or 1.5 per cent, from 55 million in 1918 to 73 million in 1940.

At this time it began to be recognized that population growth was a problem, and a government commission in 1927–30 recommended that

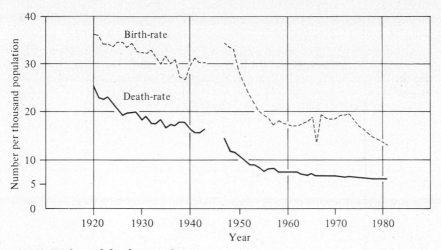

Fig. 6. Birth- and death-rates, Japan
(Sources: 1920–1955, Irene B. Taeuber, *The Population of Japan* (1958). Subsequent data from UN *Demographic Yearbook, Historical Supplement*, 1979, and *Monthly Bulletin of Statistics*.)

planned parenthood should be encouraged and there should be a reasonable diffusion of birth control. The government rejected this report; in the then climate of opinion, the obvious answers to population growth lay rather in agricultural improvement at home and imperial expansion abroad. However, some influential people continued to believe in the desirability of birth control, and the government did not interfere with the sale of contraceptives and the spread of information.

But the decisive events took place in 1948 with the passing, amid great political confusion, of the Eugenic Protection Law, which came into force in 1949 and in effect legalized abortion. The effect was dramatic. By the early 1950s well over a million abortions were performed annually in Japan, something like one to every two live births; and the birth-rate fell with unparalleled rapidity from 34 in 1947 to 17 in 1957.[1]

The great wave of abortions at that time has been followed by a quieter spread of the knowledge and use of contraceptive methods, and as in other industrial countries the birth-rate has fluctuated at levels well below 20 per thousand. Meanwhile, the death-rate has fallen to the extremely low level of 6–7, for reasons analysed above; so that population growth has continued at around 1 per cent – a rate of increase, however, that does not appear to be beyond the capacity of a country whose industrial growth rate has reached 10 per cent in recent years. Moreover, as already indicated, the death-rate must rise in decades to come as the older age-groups fill out, and unless Japanese attitudes to family size change once more it is likely that the population will stabilize over about the next thirty years.

41

SUGGESTIONS FOR FURTHER READING

Carlo M. Cipolla, *The Economic History of World Population*, revised edition, Harmondsworth: Penguin, 1978.

Georges Tapinos and Phyllis T. Piotrow, *Six Billion People*, New York: McGraw Hill, 1978.

Population Bulletin, Washington, D.C.: Population Reference Bureau.

3 The colonial episode and the race question

Most of today's poor countries underwent at some time the experience of colonial rule. There were many variations of that experience, and it ended in some places before it had begun in others. Thus after the conquests that began around 1500 in the age of Columbus, the former Spanish colonies in South America became independent republics in the wars of 1810–26, while Portugal peacefully ceded Brazil's independence in 1822. British supremacy in India, established in fact by about 1805, was formally declared in 1858, and came to an end in 1947, while a number of other south Asian countries also became independent about that time. In much of Africa the colonial experience was even later and even shorter; partition among the European powers took place after 1880 and colonial administration was not effectively established in many areas until after 1900, and there was a rush to independence around the so-called 'year of Africa', 1960. Meanwhile, although the European states did not completely subjugate China, they asserted their power there during the nineteenth century when their nationals enjoyed extra-territorial rights and immunity from Chinese law, and territorial concessions created enclaves of foreign rule on Chinese soil. The Japanese, having narrowly escaped a similar fate, took the initiative by annexing Taiwan (Formosa) in 1895, and after defeating the imperial Russian forces went on to occupy Korea and Manchuria in 1905. Less successfully they attempted to extend their empire to Mongolia and China in the 1920s and 1930s; more briefly still they overran all of south-east Asia and the western Pacific in the early 1940s, before their defeat in the second world war brought their overseas expansion abruptly to an end in 1945.

Leaving aside the empires of ancient and medieval times – Roman, Ch'in, Asoka's, Byzantine, Ottoman, Mongol – I concentrate in what follows on the overseas expansion of Europe, though it may be that some aspects of the colonial experience can be more widely generalized. For example, the position of Koreans in Japan in the aftermath of empire seems not unlike that of people from the Caribbean and the Indian sub-continent in latter-day Britain.

Over large areas of the globe, the expansion of Europe resulted in people of 'white' appearance and European descent dominating 'native' or 'coloured' populations. The sheer fact of conquest gave rise to myths about

43

superior and inferior races which were readily believed by the white conquerors. In some countries, political independence from the original colonial power was attained by 'white' communities who continued to dominate populations of non-European descent. In that way a colonial situation became internalized in such places as South Africa and the southern states of the USA, while the independence of Brazil and some other South American countries may be seen in a similar light. Elsewhere, too, attitudes of racial superiority have persisted although the circumstances that made them plausible have long since passed away. Equally persistent have been the bitterness and resentment of the formerly subject peoples once regarded as backward or primitive. Even though the age of empire has come to an end, an awareness of the colonial past and demands for 'decolonization' continue to be important in the modern world.

The meaning of the word colony has changed. Originally 'a settlement in a new country', in its dictionary sense the term was applied, for example, to British settler communities in countries such as Canada, Australia, and New Zealand. After the first world war those colonies gained greater autonomy and for a time were officially styled Dominions; while Colonies were countries such as Nigeria, Jamaica, and Kenya, where small numbers of Europeans dominated large non-European populations, and which could literally have been called dominions. The latter usage of the word colony has persisted in common speech too, and I have adopted it here.

A thumbnail sketch of colonial history, c. 1500 to 1960

1 Sixteenth to early nineteenth centuries

The age of European expansion falls into two major periods. The first was that of 'guns and sails', when in only a few decades after 1500 Europeans gained an absolute predominance over the oceans that enabled them to conquer the Americas, wholly occupy many islands round the world, and establish small enclaves on the coasts of the African and Asian continents. For nearly three centuries, however, their dominion did not extend far inland. No serious attempts were made to extend territorial conquest inside Asia, while Africa, with its lethal diseases, long resisted Europeans and as late as 1876 only 10 per cent of the continent was under white occupation. The Americas were different, sparsely populated by technologically primitive peoples who readily succumbed to European infectious diseases; even there, however, until the eighteenth century the areas under effective European control, as distinct from nominal sovereignty, were mostly close to the sea.[1]

The search for gold was a prime object of many European overseas ventures, while some settlements were established also to trade in tropical products such as spices and handicrafts such as silk, and others like St Helena to act as supply and repair depots for the sailing ships that carried on the trade. South African history, indeed, began unpretentiously with a Dutch settlement at the Cape to establish 'a cabbage patch on the way to India'.[2] Settlements in temperate zones, such as the original 13 colonies in New England, lived off the land by means of family farming. In some tropical colonies, large-scale plantation agriculture became the main economic base.

Some places where Europeans established themselves were uninhabited before (for example, Mauritius, the Falkland Islands); in others, the native population became extinct, or was extinguished (for example, the Caribbean islands, Patagonia, Tierra del Fuego, Tasmania). In some such places the present-day population is wholly of European descent, the society is a transplanted version of a European society, and the colonial situation in the later sense of the word does not exist; Tasmania and the Falkland Islands are cases in point. Elsewhere, Europeans brought in labourers from an African or Asiatic mainland. In Mauritius, for example, French settlers brought in indentured labourers from India, while later immigrations added 'Creoles' (of mixed descent including African ancestry) as clerks and skilled workers, and Chinese shopkeepers, to make up the latter-day plural society.[3] Similarly, Indian labourers were brought under indenture agreements to the plantations of Guiana and the West Indies. But by far the biggest population movements of this period resulted from the trade in African slaves.

That trade began in the mid-sixteenth century with the shipment to Brazil of slaves from the Portuguese West African possessions of Guinea, São Tomé, and Angola. People of other European nationalities soon joined in, including French and British, while the first twenty black slaves in North America were sold from a Dutch warship to Virginia settlers in 1619. It expanded in the mid-seventeenth century when the Portuguese administration in Brazil, under Jesuit missionary pressure, stopped the enslavement of native Indians there; while the growth of French and British plantations in the West Indies provided a market for British slave traders. Those plantations were important too as the main source of supply to the southern United States of plantation workers born into slavery and already 'broken in'. The trade reached its peak in the late eighteenth century, when slaves were taken from Mozambique as well as from the west coast of Africa; by 1790 there were 700,000 black slaves in the United States, and there was a vast influx into South America also at that time.

Slavery was a traditional institution in many African societies, and those involved in the trade included African chiefs who made war on their neighbours, captured slaves, and sold them for guns to make further wars.

On the east coast of Africa, Arabs too were involved both as captors and traders. Europeans traded in slaves rather than captured them, and in the case of British merchants a further complication was Lord Justice Mansfield's judgement in 1771 which effectively meant that slaves could not be brought to England or they would at once become free. The shipowners of Liverpool, Bristol, and London accordingly worked the 'black triangle' – out with trade goods (cloth etc.) to West Africa, across with slaves to the West Indies, and home with plantation goods.[4]

By the end of the eighteenth century, slavery had become a major issue in British politics. The anti-slavery movement whose parliamentary spokesman was William Wilberforce drew support from the humanitarian convictions of men such as Samuel Johnson, Horace Walpole, and above all Thomas Clarkson. It was also supported by the political opponents of the upstart West Indian plantation magnates whose monopolies had been discredited by the rising school of liberal economists. Free trade, private enterprise, individual liberty and the abolition of slavery cohered in a new set of social, political, and economic principles, and the anti-slavery movement achieved its two prime objects with the prohibition of the slave trade in 1807 and the liberation of all slaves in the British empire in 1833.[5]

Following Britain's lead, the United States outlawed the foreign slave trade in 1808, though slavery remained a domestic institution until after the civil war in the 1860s. Elsewhere too the British government took the initiative in suppressing slavery, subject as it was to the converging pressures of humanitarian reformers on the one hand, and, on the other, British plantation owners who, having been forced to give up slave labour themselves, did not see why their competitors should still have that advantage. Thus it was in a treaty with Britain that Brazil agreed in 1831 to outlaw the slave trade, though it was not effectively stopped for another 20 years, and not until 1881 that slavery was abolished in Brazil itself. Meanwhile the Royal Navy maintained anti-slave patrols around the coasts of Africa from 1807 to 1869, intercepting consignments of slaves and putting them ashore at settlements like Freetown in Sierra Leone.[6] A British consul was posted to Zanzibar in 1841, partly to look after the interests of Britain's Indian subjects there, and partly to help curb the Arab slave traders. And British public opinion hero-worshipped David Livingstone not least for his lifelong dedication to suppressing the slave trade, while the conclusion some drew from his life and death was that it would never be stopped until much of Africa was brought under British rule.[7]

This first period of European expansion, then, ended in the early nineteenth century with the independence of the white-dominated societies of the Americas, and the suppression of the slave trade.

2 *Mid-nineteenth century to 1960*

During this period, substantial areas of the major continents, away from the sea, were brought under European control. Lands in the temperate zones of North America, Australia, New Zealand, and southern Africa were opened up to white settler farmers, while the Russian empire extended eastwards across northern Asia. These developments were made possible by technological innovations, particularly the railway, the steamship both at sea and in inland waters, and later the internal combustion engine; and some crucial medical discoveries, especially quinine, which enabled Europeans to survive despite the diseases of Africa and Asia.

Thus, for example, the extension of British rule in India was a lengthy process and it was not until 1860 that most of the country was either under direct administration or indirect rule through the princes. Burma was annexed in two bites in 1852 and 1886. A British trading base was established at Singapore in 1819, but it was several decades before Malaya came under effective administration. Meanwhile in the mid-nineteenth century the French and Dutch too were consolidating their 'spheres' in Indo-China and Indonesia respectively.[8] As for Africa, even the basic geography was still unknown and being explored in the 1860s and 1870s, the 'scramble for Africa' took place after 1870, the spheres of influence of the major European powers were not settled till the late 1880s, and actual administration in some of the remoter areas was not a reality till after the first world war.[9]

Between the two world wars, as already noted, some parts of the European empires were already becoming more independent in fact, and there were the beginnings of resistance to European rule especially in India. The Cripps mission of 1943 made Indian independence certain as soon as the war was over; once India was independent there was no holding the rest of the Asian empires, while 'freedom' movements in African colonies could hardly be denied their independence in their turn; and so, by what seemed like an irresistible logic of events, soon after 1960 (and with certain exceptions of which more below) colonial rule was a thing of the past. It remains to emphasize how short was this second period of European expansion and colonial rule. In some places it all happened in a single lifetime; thus Harry Thuku, honoured at the independence ceremonies in Kenya in 1963, remembered the days before the white man came.[10]

The nature of colonial society

The salient feature of colonial society was foreign control. In European colonies this was particularly true of economic life, Christian missions, and government.

47

Economic institutions

Not all colonies were acquired in the direct prospect or hope of economic gain. On the contrary, many in Europe saw them as 'millstones round our necks'; for example, a reluctant Liberal cabinet in Britain was with difficulty persuaded to annex Uganda, partly to forestall German control of the source of the Nile, and partly by a church campaign to protect the missions and their converts there.[11] But clearly it was important to make a colony pay its way, and all colonial regimes were concerned to promote economic activity that could serve as a tax base.

In a few places this could be done by encouraging indigenous enterprise, as for example in Uganda where cotton and later coffee as export cash crops were introduced by the combined efforts of the British administration, the Anglican mission, and the local African chiefs. Such cases were exceptional, however, and reliance on native sources of supply was more usually regarded as unsatisfactory; the goods were not always available in sufficient quantity, and the quality was variable, so there was always a tendency for foreign enterprises to secure sources of supply such as mines or plantations under their own control. Thus wild rubber tapped from forest trees gave place to the standardized product of rubber plantations.

In some places, the soil and climate and the sparseness of the native population made for family farming by white settlers rather than plantation agriculture; thus the United States were long divided between the north, where the family farm predominated, and the plantation economy of the south. Similarly, farming prevailed in Australia and New Zealand, where the native populations were small and greatly outnumbered at an early stage by the settlers. There a colonial situation arose to a limited extent, as large stock farms in Australia rely on the services of stockmen of aboriginal or mixed descent, while in New Zealand there were wars over land rights between Maoris and Pakehas (whites) in the nineteenth century and some tension persists today. More pertinent perhaps to the Third World is the settlement by farmers of European descent that occurred in countries such as South Africa, Zimbabwe, Algeria, and Kenya. Though their technical and economic achievements were in many cases very great, such white minority communities posed intractable political problems with their ruggedly possessive attitudes towards the land and the country they occupied.[12] Under colonial rule they were often at loggerheads with the administrative officials sent out to govern them, whom they characteristically regarded as fatally 'soft on the natives'. It was partly over this issue, indeed, that American colonists rebelled against British, Spanish, and Portuguese rule in the eighteenth and early nineteenth centuries. Similarly, though British governors in Australia enjoined settlers to 'live in amity and kindness with' the aborigines, they had the greatest difficulty in restraining them from punitive expeditions that degenerated into cruel and indiscriminate shooting.[13] White settler communities tended to identify themselves strongly with the mother country and loudly protest their loyalty; hence 'Algérie française!' and the long-continued insistence of the Rhodesian settlers on their British identity. When the home government has seemed determined to betray their own kith and kin by handing the country over to the majority of its people, however, there has been an abrupt swing into disillusionment and a determination to maintain a 'civilized' state of affairs in a unilateral declaration of independence with white minority rule.

Where the predominant form of agricultural enterprise was the plantation, however, different situations were created. European managers came and went on leave and retirement, and did not put down roots like settler farmers. As Myrdal pointed out, plantations represented extensions in tropical colonies of companies incorporated in the metropolitan countries. Their alien control and management led to dividends and a large part of salaries being remitted abroad or used to purchase foreign goods rather than to stimulate demand on the local market. Not only did the higher salaries go to alien managers, but also skilled workers, foremen, and even some unskilled workers were brought in from other countries. In south Asia the gulf between the European upper caste and the masses of unskilled workers was widened by the employment of middlemen, many of whom were 'Oriental aliens', and by the system of managing agencies. Though managers might sometimes be uneasy about the way these intermediaries were treating the workers, they were too dependent on them to be able to do much about it.

In Myrdal's judgement, plantations as a form of industrialized agriculture played an indispensable part in economic development, raising average income levels (though not everyone shared in the increase) and stimulating investment in the infra-structure of buildings, roads, ports, and railways. Even though these, like the associated commercial and financial institutions, were geared to the foreign-dominated export sector, they could become part of the local economy and be used for wider purposes. And on the whole the independent governments of south Asia left them alone. Threats to nationalize them, as in Sri Lanka, or actual nationalization, as in Indonesia, were on the whole disastrous; the threats scared off new capital, while the actuality led to inefficiency and corruption.[14]

Large international corporations still control plantations in many poor countries, where they exemplify the 'big firm, small country' syndrome to which I refer in chapter 4. Though from an economic point of view they represent a somewhat inassimilable legacy of the colonial period, socially and politically they have posed fewer problems than farming by European settlers. Even more than the latter, however, plantations and mines alike

49

depended on a plentiful supply of cheap labour. In the early period of
colonial history this was largely provided by slaves. After the abolition of
slavery, recourse was had to other methods of recruitment.

In many societies there were traditional obligations to work for public
purposes for a few days or weeks a year. Thus in many Asian societies
people were required to turn out when needed to repair and maintain
irrigation canals, dams, and embankments. In some African societies
people had to mend the chief's fence and till his fields, yielding food for
councillors and litigants at his court, and a famine reserve. Sometimes these
customary obligations could be usefully modernized, like *bulungi bwansi*
(literally 'good works underfoot') in the kingdom of Buganda, by which
people were required to maintain minor roads and village tracks. In effect
it was a tax payable in labour rather than money. Under colonial rule,
however, there were instances where forced labour was raised, not for
public purposes, but for private employers, and not for a few days or weeks
but for long periods.[15] Thus according to Myrdal the indigenous systems
of forced labour which colonial regimes inherited in south Asian countries
were adapted to induce large-scale movements of labour. Such practices
could be challenged and made the subject of campaigns in the home
country. For example, in the early days of British rule in Kenya similar
activities on the part of the administration there were publicized and
discredited by missionaries led by J. H. Oldham, and the government was
forced in 1921 to abandon the formal compulsion of Africans to work on
the settlers' farms.[16] Moreover, forced labour of this kind was officially
proscribed by international agreement in 1926.

Another method of labour recruitment, with some elements of 'voluntariness' about it, was by means of contracts or indentures. These often
involved men in working in places far distant from their homes and with
restrictions, sometimes severe, on their freedom of movement. As Myrdal
put it, 'Foreign labourers, isolated in unfamiliar surroundings, were more
docile, more easily organized for effective work, and more permanently
attached.' In south Asia he gave as examples the Indian and Chinese
labourers respectively in the rubber plantations and tin mines of Malaya,
Indian workers in Burma and Sri Lanka, and the Chinese brought into Java
both as coolies on the tobacco plantations and as intermediaries between
the government and the indigenous population.

Yet another form of pressure upon men to enter employment was that
of imposing money taxes in circumstances when there was little option but
to earn the money by working for settlers, mines, or plantations, at
whatever wages were offered – and clearly such circumstances put native
workers at a disadvantage and made for low wages. To cite Myrdal again,
it was private employers who consistently complained of labour shortage
and urged colonial governments to do something about it. The difficulties

of attracting local people into wage employment were indeed serious, but 'the matter was never considered on any assumption other than an extremely low level of wages'. Governments themselves do not seem to have had the same problem: 'some very large undertakings, such as the construction of railways and public works in India after 1860, seldom suffered seriously from labour shortage, though wages rose conspicuously as the demand for labour increased'.[17]

It will have become clear how strongly the economic institutions established under colonial rule were oriented to the export of primary products for a world market. The point is made most vividly by a map which shows how the railways built in African colonies linked the mines, the plantations, and the white-settled farming areas to the sea; they did not link one African country to another.[18] Though an infra-structure was certainly built up, it may not have been the precise infra-structure that the present independent governments would have preferred. As will be seen in chapter 4, many poor small countries remain very dependent on primary exports, and this perhaps has been the most persistent economic consequence of their colonial past.

Missions

Christian missions were integrally involved in European overseas expansion in ways that went far beyond the preaching of the gospel. They founded branches of the churches that had sent them, which were long dominated by European clergy until these were replaced by men locally born and ordained. They concerned themselves with healing bodies as well as with saving souls, so that in association with mission stations there grew up dispensaries and hospitals, soon followed by schools for training nurses and other medical personnel. Schools were needed too for the general spread of literacy, well-nigh indispensable as that was for membership of the church, while higher and more specialized education was required for the training of native clergy and catechists. Schools needed books and other equipment, so that the missions' activities extended into commerce and industry as they initiated and controlled printing works, bookshops, and workshops where materials such as school furniture were manufactured. Furthermore, in some areas it came to be felt that people's material standard of living had to be raised if they were to be able to care as Christians should for their children and other dependants in a house with minimum sanitary and hygienic arrangements, such as soap and mosquito nets. Some missions accordingly developed an 'industrial' side, training men as skilled craftsmen, and introducing cash crops to enable people to earn money for bibles, clothes, and school fees. For example, in Uganda the Church Missionary Society's industrial missionary, Mr Borup, in partnership with government officials was largely responsible for introducing cotton as a cash crop. Moreover, it was the CMS who set up the organization for collecting, processing, and exporting the crop with capital raised in Britain largely from wealthy Christian philanthropists who for many years got very little in the way of dividends.[19]

In Africa a large mission station was like a whole town, with its hospital, schools, seminary, workshops, bookstore, and houses of foreign missionaries and native adherents, all centred on a large church or cathedral. Some like medieval European cities even had walls round them, for some missions were established before colonial government and the whole station might have to be defended against attack. That necessity has arisen again in more recent times in a country such as Uganda, as mentioned below in chapter 12.

Mission stations thus afforded a refuge for those who needed protection. For example, freed slaves found safety in stations like that at Freretown near Mombasa, while during the female circumcision crisis of the 1920s (see below) the Protestant missions similarly extended protection to girls who refused clitoridectomy, and were themselves attacked in consequence. Such circumstances further heightened their character as settled communities with an economic base, different from the surrounding areas and acting as change agents in relation to the life of those areas.

Throughout colonial history, the missions championed the rights of the natives against exploitation by European enterprises or unjust treatment by government officials. For example, Jesuits in Brazil resisted the enslavement of the native Indians, establishing stations at strategic river confluences to stop slave raiders penetrating up-stream, to intercept convoys coming down-river, and to settle the freed captives on land where they could live and be evangelized.[20] Similarly, I have already mentioned the missions' successful campaign against forced labour in Kenya.

Missionaries, however, did not always make themselves popular with the native people of colonial territories. Despite their concern for the latter's welfare, they were necessarily deeply committed to changing many aspects of the indigenous cultures. The local deities were condemned as false gods, to be abjured by the convert along with customs and practices which from a Christian point of view were immoral. Some of those practices may now seem to us comparatively harmless, and missionaries were not always able to distinguish between the essential core of Christian teaching and western European cultural preconceptions; it was only half in jest that some were said to have brought Christianity, chemistry, and cricket in a single package. Forms of dress and dancing, for example, which by today's standards seem inoffensive enough were stigmatized as indecent by Victorian missionaries. Not all the traditional practices they condemned were so innocent, however. In Kenya there was a storm over clitoridectomy, traditional among the Kikuyu in initiating young women. The missionaries objected not only to the dangerously unhygienic way that was done, for the same objection to male circumcision could be met by having it carried out by trained staff in a hospital or dispensary, as was in fact done in Christianized versions of similar rites elsewhere in Africa. 'Female circumcision' was different, as it had lasting harmful results. Missionaries accordingly urged their converts not to allow their daughters to undergo initiation, and (as already mentioned) sheltered those who refused it. From a Kikuyu point of view, however, that seemed a totally unwarranted interference in an integral part of their traditional life. In the conflict that ensued, government officers who not long before had been under missionary pressure to stop forced labour now found themselves leading forces of police to protect the lives and property of their missionary critics who, as it appeared, had made themselves quite gratuitously unpopular by their tactless handling of the matter.[21]

And there was resentment of the long-continued occupancy of positions of authority in the churches by Europeans. Different churches had different approaches to this problem. Roman Catholic missions soon established schools from which a few young men with the necessary intelligence and vocation might pass into seminary training and eventually be ordained. It was a slow process, and many dropped out, though those who did were a source of educated manpower as teachers and in the government service. Once ordained, there were no distinctions between local and expatriate priests; their celibacy helped, as they lived without wives and children in the same clergy houses, and when there were enough local priests a whole diocese eventually passed from missionary hands into those of a local secular clergy. Some Protestant missions, too, took higher education and the training of clergy seriously. Among Anglicans, however, there was a distinction between the mission, financed from donations in England, and the 'Native Anglican Church' (as it was often called) which was locally supported. Frugal though the living standards of Anglican missionaries were, native Anglican clergymen and their families were even poorer materially, and this caused a certain amount of feeling within the church. At the same time, some other Protestant denominations tended to be slower to ordain local men, thus giving an appearance of trying to keep control of church affairs in white hands.[22]

Resentment of foreign domination extended accordingly to Christian missions and missionaries, dedicated though they were to the good of the people among whom they worked. It had much to do with movements to set up independent churches, as detailed in chapter 10.

Government

The government of colonies was characteristically regarded as administration rather than politics. Power in a colony was wielded by officials of the metropolitan country who were responsible to the home government rather than to any local body. Local legislatures were, it is true, set up to distinguish when the Governor or Viceroy was giving an order from when he was making a law. Typically they consisted of a majority of senior government officials and a minority, usually appointed rather than elected, of 'unofficials', influential local whites whom the government wished to placate and conciliate by involving them in the process of law-making. In some British colonies white settlers complained that such arrangements amounted to taxation without representation and denied them their basic democratic rights. That argument was used to sustain a claim for making government responsive, if not altogether responsible, to a very undemocratic electorate, namely the local white minority. Under strong settler pressure, that claim was conceded in some settler-dominated colonies such as Kenya and Southern Rhodesia (now Zimbabwe). Elsewhere, generally speaking, it was only in the later stages of colonial rule that non-whites were nominated to membership of legislative councils, and only on the eve of independence that they were elected by popular vote. Meanwhile, administering a colony was viewed as an art comparable to administering a government department at home – making sensible rules and seeing that they were obeyed, collecting revenues and using them efficiently for approved purposes to the satisfaction of a government auditor, and generally attending to the business of government in an orderly manner.

Traditional societies differed widely in the extent to which their institutions could form the basis of modern administration under colonial rule. Thus at one extreme Indian civilization included indigenous scripts and literatures; money, banking, and credit institutions; and a tradition of political organization extending back to the empire of Asoka. At the other, the social and political organization of some East African tribes was not recognized as 'government' at all by the early European explorers, there was no indigenous writing, and a rudimentary currency had only recently been introduced by Arab slave traders. Modern administration clearly had to start from the beginning in such places, and there are records of the well-nigh comic confusion that occurred when taxes in kind were introduced before money was familiar and widespread. African political systems themselves, however, differed widely, and in places such as the emirates of northern Nigeria and the interlacustrine Bantu kingdoms of Uganda there were despotic monarchies with appointed chiefs and organized courts recognizable as 'government' by Victorian Englishmen. A policy of indirect rule was appropriate in such areas and (whether or not under that name) was adopted by the British also in others including the sultanate of Zanzibar and the kingdom of Tonga, and above all the princely states in India, and likewise by the Dutch in Indonesia. Indirect rule had great advantages. People were governed in the way to which they had been accustomed. The legitimacy of traditional authorities was recognized and confirmed, backed in the last resort by the metropolitan power. Control was exercised over what those authorities did with their powers, and they could be required to use them to introduce health measures, schools, cash crops, and the like for the general benefit and advancement of the people; the introduction of cotton in Uganda, noted above, was a case in point. At the same time the lower levels of administration were staffed cheaply with local subordinate officials rather than expensively with expatriates; thus it used to be said in jest in colonial Africa that the only member of the administration not entitled to go on leave to Britain was the chief. For such a person, though, there were difficult dilemmas. The more modern his style and the measures he introduced, the more discontent and opposition he was likely to arouse. But if he failed to make the changes required of him, or represented too vigorously the views of his people, he was subject to pressure from above by officials who in the last resort could dismiss him and send him into exile.[23]

In colonies where there was a native population, some account had generally to be taken of the indigenous system of law. On the one hand, the colonial administration existed precisely in order to ensure that Europeans' lives and property came under the same kind of protection as they might at home, and that contracts to which they were party could be relied on, if necessary, for enforcement in the setting of a congenial legal system. On the other hand, however, where the local people had their own institutions for dealing with offences and settling civil disputes, there might be little need to interfere, and much to be said for leaving well alone. So native law and custom might be recognized, though generally only so far as it did not conflict with 'natural justice' or some such concept, meaning the fundamental preconceptions of the colonial power's law. It applied only to minor criminal cases in which the accused was a native, and civil cases in which both parties were native. Generally, too, there was a right of appeal to the colonial power's courts. Furthermore, in the plural societies that grew up under colonial rule (see below), immigrant communities other than those of the colonial power might have their own customary laws, especially about marriage and inheritance, and these were not always well accommodated into the laws of the colony.

The effect was generally to sharpen distinctions between different communities or categories of people, and to give legal sanction to them. Where two systems of law existed enforced by two sets of courts, the question of who was subject to which had to be legally defined. For example, in East Africa under British rule the prime distinction was that between 'Africans' or 'natives' on the one hand, and 'non-natives' on the other. An African or native was defined as 'a person who is a member of, or one of whose parents is or was a member of an indigenous African tribe or community'. Persons whose legal status was so defined were subject to the jurisdiction of officially appointed or recognized chiefs, and had to obey their lawful orders in matters like health control, soil conservation, and the brewing of local beer. Non-natives were not subject to the jurisdiction of African chiefs, but they did pay more tax. Within that category, distinctions between Europeans and Asians were made as a matter of administration rather than law.[24] Elsewhere in Africa, in French and Belgian colonies a distinction was drawn between '*indigènes*', who were subject to customary law, and others, who were subject to metropolitan law. The latter were of course primarily the Europeans, but they included also those Africans whose superior education and occupation put them into the category variously known as *assimilé*, *immatriculé*, or *évolué*.[25] Thus where the British adopted a set of categories based on birth and amounting to a race distinction, the French and Belgian administrations enabled a small elite to move out of the category of 'natives' and gain the same rights and responsibilities as Europeans.

All colonial governments, then, exercised law-and-order functions, collected taxes, and set up the framework of modern administration, though in doing so they often drew invidious distinctions between categories of people, particularly Europeans and natives. In partnership with Christian missions, and to an extent that differed in different places, they introduced modern social services such as health and education. Most also laid the foundations for economic development by public investment in the infra-structure of harbours, railways, roads, and public buildings; indeed, that aspect of the colonial legacy is visible today even in such minor details as police uniforms and the rule of the road.

Another legacy of empire in most former colonies is that of a language of wider communication. Although Japanese does not seem to have taken deep root in Taiwan, Korea, or other parts of the former Japanese empire, at the other extreme Spanish was firmly implanted in most of Latin America during centuries of colonial rule and is now the universal language of the region, while Portuguese is the language of wider communication not only in Brazil but also in Mozambique, Angola, and the other former Portuguese colonies of Africa. In Africa and Asia, whatever the variety of the local vernaculars, at least some people in a colony learned to speak and write English or French, or some other language with a wider currency in the world. Thus an elite were left with the key to a wider world of knowledge, culture, and political and commercial opportunities. As a result, the educated elites of former British colonies enjoy close and easy communications with the whole of the English-speaking world, including the United States, while those of former Belgian and French colonies gravitate more naturally to the French-speaking world. Most of Africa is accordingly divided at present between Anglophone and Francophone countries, whose leaders communicate more readily among themselves and with outsiders than they do with each other – a cultural equivalent of those railways that run straight to the sea and not to neighbouring African countries. I return to the question of language in chapter 9.

Under colonial rule, nearly everywhere a start was made on education, or more strictly schooling. (It can of course be maintained that no society lacks a system of education, for all prepare and socialize children somehow for their adult roles; not all, however, traditionally did so through specialized institutions like the school.) Colonial governments generally ensured from the first that there were schools for Europeans' children, while schools for the natives were mostly pioneered by missions and later maintained and extended in partnership between the two. Widely different policies were pursued in different colonies. In some there was an emphasis on primary schooling; for example, in the former Belgian Congo (Zaire) it was assumed that while some Africans needed to be trained in basic industrial skills as craftsmen, railway workers, and the like, higher posts would be filled by Europeans for the foreseeable future. When in the 1950s that assumption was clearly open to question, the rapid establishment of higher education, including three universities, had all the appearances of a death-bed conversion, and the institutions concerned had had very little effect on the situation when independence eventually broke upon the country. In some other colonies, in contrast, governments early assumed a responsibility for native education including higher education; among British African colonies, Uganda and the Gold Coast were notable in this respect. In yet others such as Kenya, the rise of African education took place in a difficult atmosphere of opposition from white settlers, though it went ahead there rapidly nonetheless.[26]

Colonial governments therefore faced the issue still central to educational policy in poor countries, that of the balance between primary schooling for the greatest number on the one hand and higher education for a fortunate few on the other. Under colonial rule, emphasizing primary schooling could look suspiciously like holding back native advancement. It was associated with settler pressure in colonies such as Kenya and Rhodesia, and campaigned against by missionaries and nationalist political leaders; while colonial governments less subject to settler pressure, like Uganda, did more to encourage the emergence of an indigenous elite. Ironically, the latter policy has more recently been stigmatized as elitist for engendering disparities of income and privilege, while the former has been endorsed as egalitarian, cost-effective, and more conducive to economic development. I discuss the issue further in chapter 9.

Western medicine too was introduced into colonies by Europeans, for whom indeed it was a necessary condition of their very survival. In modern times an expedition, to the Himalayas for example, will include a medical member to treat the others if they are sick or injured and advise on hygiene, diet, and the like. He or she may also practise to the extent that time and resources permit among the expedition's porters, and try to relieve sickness and suffering in the valleys through which the expedition passes; but they are not his or her primary responsibility. It was in rather similar expeditionary circumstances that colonial government medical officers worked in the early days; their first responsibility was the health and survival of the European officials, then that of others: European 'unofficials', natives employed by the colonial government as policemen, clerks, and the like, and lastly the native population at large. Where public health was concerned, the first requirement was to create townships, cantonments, and government stations as islands of health control – pure water, sanitation, refuse disposal, malaria eradication – where Europeans could live and work efficiently. Arrangements for treating the sick followed a similar pattern, with government hospitals for Europeans separate from those for the native population. At the same time, western medicine was also introduced by the missions, for whom, as already noted, healing bodies and saving souls were inseparable. As with schooling, therefore, medical services and hospitals had dual origins in government and missionary initiatives.

The European community

Although as seen by the native or subject people the white conquerors may have seemed a united force, there were diversities and conflicts of interest among different groups of Europeans. Settlers clashed with government officials over land questions and the conditions of native labour, while missionaries championed native rights against both. All tried to out-manoeuvre one another, not only in the colony itself, but also in the metropolitan country, where missionaries could enlist support from their parent churches while commercial interests too could bring pressure to bear in the home capitals. Generally speaking, however, the native population knew little of these conflicts, as many Europeans much of the time assented in effect to a conspiracy of silence out of a sense that, however deep the disagreements, white prestige and even perhaps their very survival depended on maintaining a united front.

Moreover, in British colonies the appearance of white solidarity was accentuated by one special and peculiar institution known as the Club.

Writing of Uganda in the 1950s, Sofer and Ross described how in a small European community this was the focus of European activities, providing the only recreational facilities for many miles. Membership was open to both sexes, and members met there after work for drinks, conversation, and games, as well as for organized activities such as amateur dramatics. In the smallest stations, non-membership involved isolating oneself almost completely from the European community. In the larger centres other facilities were available, but it was considered the 'right' thing to be a club member. The club's exclusiveness was heightened by the fact that not even all Europeans were regarded as suitable for membership, as those whose work bordered on the manual or whose English was not good were assigned to the 'non-clubbable' category.[27] The club was accordingly the meeting place for those who exercised authority at the local level – the District Commissioner and his senior assistants, specialist officers of the government service (medical, education, agriculture, veterinary, police, works, etc.), the bank manager, senior managers of the oil companies, and the like. Here, in a setting and an atmosphere that reinforced their sense of national and racial identity, the top people and their families mingled informally in circumstances giving every plausibility to the suspicion that they could from time to time settle important affairs behind closed doors – closed, as we have seen, even to some Europeans, and certainly closed to all natives.

Populations of mixed descent

In many colonial societies, sex relations between people of different 'race' – which meant primarily between Europeans and others – were subject to an ambiguous disapproval. Ambiguous, because it might well be a sign of manly prowess for a white man to have a black mistress, while sex relations the other way about between a black man and a white woman were much more heavily penalized as symbolizing the black man getting above his place. Such attitudes extended the usual dual morality of sex relations into the race-relations situation. A man must gain experience, but equally he must protect his sister's honour; so there are two sorts of women, the virtuous who are good for marriage, and the other sort, who are socially inferior. In a race-conscious society white men clearly tend to class black women in the latter category.[28]

Colonial societies differed widely, however, in the extent to which such unions might be regarded as legal marriages whose children were legitimate. That affected both the number of people of mixed descent and their status, with important consequences for the latter-day social structures of former colonies. Two contrasting examples will illustrate the point.

In Brazil, despite some evidence of prejudice and discrimination in the past, hard-and-fast colour bars were avoided and racial categories kept flexible and open. From the earliest times of Portuguese settlement, intermarriage and the founding of legitimate families of *mamelucos* were encouraged both by church and state, since they increased the Catholic population and added to the number of loyal subjects of the Crown.[29] Those attitudes set patterns that long persisted, according to studies carried out in the 1940s and 1950s mostly by North American scholars. Thus Wagley quoted a study by Hutchinson of a rural community among whom only a small minority including the local planter-aristocracy could trace a purely European descent. A second class of bureaucrats, professionals, and technicians included the rest of the pure whites and some of mixed ancestry. There was a third stratum of fishermen, craftsmen, and wage workers, and a fourth of casual workers without a regular income. These two lower groups included a few *brancos de terra* (of ancestry mainly white but known to be mixed) with mulattoes and a majority classed as Negroes.[30]

Paler skins and European appearance predominated at the higher levels of income, power, and prestige. There was, however, a widespread acceptance of 'whitening' or 'purifying the blood' through mixed marriages, resulting in a complex, fluid class structure in which race was only one factor and wealth, occupation, and schooling also counted. Brazilians said that 'a rich Negro is a white man and a poor white is a Negro', and had a rich vocabulary of racial terms – *branco, branco de terra, indio, negro, mulatto, mameluco, preto, cabra, cabo verde, caboclo, escudo, pardo, sarara* – reflecting a fluid situation characterized by ambiguity and vagueness. The flexibility of racial categories was exemplified by Roger Bastide's report that 'In regions with a high percentage of Africans, the census officials tend to class Negroes as mulattoes and light-skinned mulattoes as whites. In regions where the European element predominates, mulattoes tend to be classed as Negroes.'

Both prejudice and discrimination were to be found, and Bastide quotes a Brazilian gentleman's response to a social survey carried out by René Ribeiro:

You know that, as a Catholic intellectual...I have not, cannot, and must not have any racial prejudices...My evidence, however, will not be that of the intellectual ...brought up in the doctrine of the Church but of the man, the grandson of a *senhor de engenho* who is full of prejudices...I have never reacted violently when a coloured man has sat down in the same omnibus, at the same table or in the same cinema as myself. What irritates me is...the mulatto's wanting to take the place of a white man, dressing like a white man, wanting to marry a white woman, owning a car...Inferior race. Good for work. They have a soul and must be baptized. They must seek salvation and go to Heaven. But be equal with the white man, no...I think that it is the Catholic intellectual who is right, but it is the man who actually lives and feels.

As for discrimination, Bastide put it epigrammatically: 'A Negro is not refused a post because he is a Negro – he is told that unfortunately it has just been filled; he is not refused promotion – he fails to pass the medical examination.' The interracial etiquette of avoiding reference to people's colour was at variance with the actualities of prejudice and discrimination. Nonetheless, both the practical difficulties of rigidly classifying so mixed a population, and the official view of Brazil as a colour-blind society, had prevented social colour bars or overt legal discrimination from arising.[31]

From similar origins South African society evolved along completely different lines. The early Dutch settlers at the Cape brought in slaves from Madagascar, Mozambique, and the East Indies, and assimilated the indigenous Hottentot population into serfdom. Unions between the settlers and the women of these slave communities were sometimes recognized as marriages, especially if the woman had been baptized; as time went on, however, they came to be regarded as concubinages, and the woman's children however begotten were slaves, until the abolition of slavery in all British dominions in 1834. Later in South African history the attitudes of white people towards unions with non-whites became more and more unfavourable. Entrenched as an integral part of South African white culture, those attitudes were embodied in laws denying the status of marriage to any union between a white and a non-white person (Prohibition of Mixed Marriages Act, 1949), and making sex relations between such persons an offence (Immorality Act, 1927, amended 1950 and 1957). Since mixed unions have become so difficult, it seems likely that most of the so-called Coloured population of South Africa are the descendants of the early unions referred to above. Most speak Afrikaans as their home language, and keep up their original culture, especially the Malays who remain Muslims though otherwise their culture is Afrikaans and western. To a large extent, then, the Coloured people may be regarded as a self-contained and mainly endogamous group. In contrast to the complex and fluid system of racial categories in Brazil, therefore, in South Africa there are just four: White, Coloured, Bantu, and Asian. The process of 'whitening' as it is known in Brazil has its equivalent in 'passing' in South Africa; but the Population Registration Act of 1950 had the express aim of eliminating it, and an administrative framework has been set up in which each person's race is a legally defined status, from which it is very difficult to get reclassified.[32]

Plural societies[33]

Finally, in many places colonial expansion created a society of the sort that has been called 'plural' in which people thought of themselves, and were thought of by others, as belonging to different 'communities' associated with different occupations and social statuses, marked off by racial appearance, and distinguished by cultural features such as language and religion.

In a colonial society there were always at least two such communities, white and natives; usually, however, there were more. The slave trade took populations of African descent to the Americas, and migrations of free or indentured labour took many more people to distant parts including East Indians to the Caribbean, Chinese and Indians to many parts of south Asia, and Indians to South Africa. Slave and labour migrations are only part of the story; others besides Europeans migrated on their own initiative in search of trade, such as the Indians who took part in the opening up of East Africa, and the Chinese in Malaya and Mauritius. Migrant communities of this sort became closely associated with particular occupations or other economic interests such as retailing. In many countries, indeed, a person's identity as a member of one or other of these communities might be more important than citizenship of the new state. The governments of newly independent countries have accordingly had an uphill struggle to engender a common culture and sense of identity as part of the task of nation-building.

Though it is necessary to refer only briefly here to this aspect of the colonial heritage, it is one that has been of the utmost importance in shaping the present-day social structures of many poor countries.

The question of exploitation

It is often alleged that the present-day rich countries owe their affluence to their past and continuing exploitation of the poor. In so far as it concerns the colonial past, the question calls for some consideration here.

Exploitation may be said to occur when a transaction or relationship between two persons or groups makes one better off at the expense of the other. Unlike bargains freely made that benefit both parties, such arrangements are clearly unlikely to be entered into willingly if the disadvantaged party understands the consequences. Generally they involve coercion, or ignorance and gullibility, or both.

It will have become clear from the foregoing that there was much exploitation in colonial history, particularly in the early period. Slaves were victims of the grossest exploitation of all, forced as they were to work for no more than the barest subsistence to enable them to live and breed more slaves. Forced labour too was exploitation. Other labour recruitment practices like the contracts and indentures mentioned above had a semblance of voluntariness about them, yet it may reasonably be surmised that workers' ignorance and gullibility were often exploited when they ventured into the unknown on long-term contracts to far distant places where their freedom of movement was restricted. Such practices were by no means universal, however, and by the end of the colonial period employment in foreign enterprises often paid far better than alternative occupations, particularly traditional subsistence agriculture; a state of affairs that has continued, as seen in the next chapter.

Exploitation could also be said to occur when people were deprived of access to land or other resources on which they relied for their subsistence, and left with little choice but to work on plantations, mines, or settlers' farms. However, plantations and farms often made more productive use of land than formerly, and were a source of employment and incomes. Thus in south Asia, according to Myrdal, 'Of the four main types of agriculture, plantations yield by far the highest returns per unit of land, followed by wet paddy, sedentary dry farming, and shifting cultivation'; moreover, the plantations were 'labour-hungry', though many managements shopped around for the cheapest labour and the employment did not always benefit the local people.[34] Widely different land policies were adopted by different colonial governments in pursuit of the 'dual mandate' doctrine that required them to balance the rights and interests of the native peoples on the one hand and the most effective use of natural resources on the other.[35] For example, in British East Africa there was the greatest possible contrast between Uganda and Tanganyika, where paternalistic administrations laid prime emphasis on protecting native land rights and made very little land available for plantations and settlers' farms, and Kenya, where wide areas in the so-called Highlands were set aside exclusively for white settlement.[36] Moreover, improved health conditions under colonial rule resulted in population growth, but in Kenya extra land for African subsistence agriculture was not available as it had been pre-empted by its alienation to white settlers. The land issue became bitterly contentious and had much to do with the guerrilla campaign in the 1950s known to Europeans as 'Mau Mau'. Similarly, in Ceylon (Sri Lanka), according to Myrdal, 'the planters laid their hands on uncultivated land in the hilly districts around the villages in the very period when an extension of the land under food crops was becoming urgent as population was increasing'.[37]

Some colonial governments, especially in the early days, forbade or discouraged native competition with European interests, either locally or in the home countries. A much-cited example is that of Indian cotton textiles, undercut in the early nineteenth century by British machine-made goods which entered India duty free, while Indian manufacturers could not retaliate as the export of textile machinery to India was at first prohibited, then subject to a duty which was in turn repealed in 1860.[38] Similarly, restrictions were imposed on coffee-growing by Africans in Kenya from the early days of British rule till about 1950. The Kenya settlers even tried to get similar restrictions imposed in Tanganyika, but the administration there resisted their pressure and encouraged native coffee-growing on Kilimanjaro and elsewhere. Later, the Kenya administration reversed its policy and encouraged Africans to grow coffee there too.[39]

The colonial exploitation thesis prompts two wider questions: are those Third World countries that missed the colonial experience now better off than ex-colonies? and what difference did having colonies make to the prosperity of the now-rich industrial countries?

Although few Third World countries escaped colonial rule altogether, three that did maintain an independence, however precarious, during most of the colonial period are Afghanistan, Thailand, and Ethiopia (though the last-named was under Italian colonial rule from 1936 to 1945). Comparing each with its ex-colonial neighbours by their GNP per capita, the case of Thailand supports the colonial exploitation thesis; in 1980 it was a prosperous middle-income country comparable with the Philippines and far better off than either Burma, Cambodia, Laos, or Vietnam. However, the other two are contrary instances. Afghanistan on the eve of the Soviet occupation in December 1979 had a lower GNP per capita than India, and far lower than Pakistan; while Ethiopia in 1980 was another very poor country with an average income about the same as that of Somalia and only about one-third that of Kenya and Sudan. Furthermore, some of the most prosperous and rapidly developing countries of the Third World have been those in which European colonial rule made its longest and deepest impression, particularly Latin American and Caribbean countries. In the light of the evidence, then, it does not seem easy to sustain an argument systematically relating the present-day poverty of nations to past colonial exploitation.

To be sure, profits were made from colonies. As Myrdal pointed out, they accrued to a few, including shareholders in the metropolitan countries and Europeans settled in the colonies; while the costs of empire, in so far as they were not borne by the colonies themselves, fell upon the whole nation, including the working class whose sons died in colonial wars. After the second world war, national liberation movements in the colonies increased the costs of policing them, and it became increasingly difficult to justify those costs to the home electorates. In Britain's case, according to Myrdal, after the first period of crude exploitation the colonies were probably never very profitable. It was free trade with, and investment in, the areas of European settlement in temperate zones, rather than colonialism in Africa and Asia, that built up Britain's prosperity in the late nineteenth century. So 'the British were cool and rational rather than generous and idealistic in giving up their South Asian colonies...The French and Dutch acted differently because they did not see their own interests.'[40]

It seems quite clear, indeed, that industrial countries have prospered more without colonies than with them. Thus of the five industrial countries with the highest GNP per capita in 1980, four – Switzerland, Sweden,

Denmark, and Norway – had no colonies, while Germany was deprived of them after the first world war. Japan's spectacular rise as an industrial nation took place with redoubled vigour after they too had been deprived of their overseas possessions in 1945. As for the United States, despite phrases like 'American imperialism' they never had much of an empire, and for long were indeed the leading anti-imperialist power, whose representatives frequently chided countries like Britain and France for the sin of having empires.[41] Thus it was under United States pressure that the British government sent the Cripps mission to India in 1943, so ensuring India's independence as soon as the war was won. And when countries such as Britain and France divested themselves of their colonies they too may have benefited in their turn. Freed of their imperial commitments ('east of Suez', in the symbolic phrase) after 1960, and relying on nuclear weapons for defence against a direct attack upon themselves, like other western states they were able to reduce their armed forces and military expenditure to unprecedentedly low levels and devote correspondingly more of their resources to their public health and welfare services.[42]

In Britain's case, mention may also be made of the Colonial Development and Welfare scheme. Initiated in 1929 and extended in 1940 and 1945 despite the war, this took effect mainly in the 1950s when substantial grants were made from the British treasury to colonial territories for purposes such as rural development and the establishment of university colleges, and was a forerunner of what we now call aid.[43]

We may therefore conclude that though exploitation did occur at some times and in some places, in general colonial rule became less exploitative as it went on, and was a source of benefits as well as costs. Despite some exploitation, the economic returns from colonial empires were disappointing, and those industrial countries that had them were better off when for one reason or another they gave them up.

In the foregoing I have mainly considered economic exploitation. The term may be extended, however, to cases where there is an appearance of exploitation even though none, strictly speaking, is taking place, which may be called 'quasi-exploitation'. Domestic service, for example, is not necessarily exploitative if people are not forced to be servants and if their remuneration in cash and kind is as good as in other occupations open to them, even though the result is that rich people appear to be making themselves comfortable at the expense of poor. As seen in later chapters, domestic service reflects wide disparities of income, and is still widespread in poor countries. During the age of colonial expansion, western European societies were highly inegalitarian, and well-to-do people employed servants. In the colonies they employed black servants, so adding a racial distinction to an economic disparity. Later, when income disparities diminished in the metropolitan countries and domestic service declined there, in the colonies

65

white people could still employ black servants. Thus, writing of Uganda in the 1950s, Sofer and Ross singled this out as a main reason why European immigrants decided to stay, or to return.[44]

And if material, economic exploitation is classed as 'instrumental', following de Vos we may further distinguish 'expressive' exploitation when, as he put it, 'socially dominant members of a society make indirect use of others for a psychological advantage'. This occurs in caste societies when socially exploited pariahs as part of their occupation perform tasks regarded as innately polluting. The dominant group depend on these out-castes, want them to continue, and cannot practise violence against them, so separate themselves off as 'sacred' from the 'unclean' out-castes who accordingly become necessary for the maintenance of a secure definition of their superior social status.[45] Some personalities may thrive in a society in which they have someone to despise and patronize, even though they may be doing nothing but good to the despised and patronized; and this may have applied in colonial societies to the more paternalistic kind of missionary, administrator, teacher, or technical officer.

The view from below

I have emphasized throughout that colonial regimes were widely diverse. Some were economically exploitative and politically repressive, alienated much land to white settlers, used forced labour for mines, plantations, or settlers' farms, and neglected native education, health, and economic development. Others by contrast were mild and beneficent, imbued with a 'development and welfare' mentality, alienated little land, encouraged native education and welcomed the emergence of an indigenous elite. Thus among African colonies we may contrast Kenya and Algeria on the one hand with Uganda, Tanganyika, and Senegal on the other. All, however, were characterized by invidious distinctions. To adapt Jean-Paul Sartre's epigram, not so very long ago the earth had 2,000 million inhabitants: 500 million people, and 1,500 million natives.[46] Colonial society embodied white superiority in every aspect of modern life: their technological mastery, their control of economic, political, and religious organizations, legal distinctions between Europeans and others, and even the arrangements for health care which seemed to show that some people's lives were considered more valuable than others. In such circumstances, benevolent paternalism seemed to diminish human dignity scarcely less than outright exploitation.

For example, Maguire recounted how in Sukumaland in central Tanganyika a development scheme which, it can hardly be doubted, would if implemented have materially raised people's living standards, came to grief through being imposed from above. Plans were at an advanced stage before local people were informed, let alone consulted, and the scheme was linked with ambitious but unpopular proposals for representative local government on multi-racial lines. Widespread non-co-operation with government orders for livestock improvement and the like drew from the administration the fatal response that 'sometimes people have to be coerced for their own good', and mass demonstrations degenerated into riots that were brutally repressed.[47]

Whether harsh or mild, exploitative or beneficent, then, colonial regimes were almost always resented by those upon whom they were imposed, and especially the more intelligent, educated, and urbanized people among them. What was resented was first and foremost foreign rule, then the exploitation, real or imagined, associated with it. Thirdly there was a reaction against some Europeans' disdain of indigenous cultures, and fourthly a resentment of colour bars and the personal humiliations that went with them. Those sentiments found expression in a literature of protest which has had a continuing influence in shaping intellectual and political movements in the Third World, as men who later became political leaders set out their manifestos, often in autobiographical form.[48]

This literature ranged in style from the dignified, urbane and moderate tone of Jawaharlal Nehru[49] to the wildly intemperate polemics of Frantz Fanon.[50] It embodied two responses to the white-dominated world. One was to assert that 'men of colour' were fully equal to whites, and could perform similar tasks and rise to similar challenges. The other was more backward-looking. An early example was the preface to Jomo Kenyatta's *Facing Mount Kenya*, an ethnological text imbued with a political message: 'To Moigoi and Wamboi and all the dispossessed youth of Africa: for perpetuation of communion with ancestral spirits through the fight for African Freedom, and in the firm faith that the dead, the living, and the unborn will unite to rebuild the destroyed shrines.'[51] It was poignantly expressed in Aimé Césaire's poem:

> Exult for those who have never invented anything...
> who have never explored anything
> who have never conquered anything
> but who yield themselves, captivated by the essence of things
> ignorant of appearances...
> truly the elder sons of the world...
> spark of the World's sacred fire.[52]

It was hard to reconcile the two responses, for the more competent the formerly subject peoples showed themselves at coping with the modern world, the more it was by acquiring and exercising scientific knowledge and administrative skills not particularly characteristic of the indigenous cultures of 'those who had never invented anything'. That posed deep dilemmas for cultural and literary movements like that of *négritude* or 'the

African personality', about which Wole Soyinka remarked that 'A tiger does not go around proclaiming its tigritude – it just pounces.'[53]

Decolonization

The call for decolonization, loudly voiced in recent times, linked two demands. One was that the expansion of Europe should be reversed by its contraction, and required the former colonial powers to relinquish their overseas possessions. The other was for the end of foreign rule, or in other words the self-determination of peoples. Nearly everywhere the two coincided, the former colonies' inhabitants were glad to see the backs of the white conquerors, and the liberation (or abandonment) of colonies was almost completed by the early 1960s.

Nearly, but not quite. In the aftermath of empire, and particularly of the British empire, a few places remained where the two demands did not coincide. The last colonial dependencies are diverse, and particular circumstances applying to each make it hard to generalize. Some are islands of strategic and scientific importance with few if any permanently settled inhabitants, such as Ascension, South Georgia, and the South Sandwich Islands, while the French likewise retain such possessions as Kerguelen and the Crozet Islands. In others, however, colonial rule has continued at least in part because the inhabitants clearly do not want it otherwise, and see it as preferable to any likely alternative. Thus the inhabitants of Gibraltar have consistently shown that they do not want to live under Spanish rule, while the Falkland Islanders likewise made it abundantly clear that they did not wish to be handed over to Argentina. And by far the biggest population still under colonial rule are the five million inhabitants of Hong Kong, to whom similar considerations apply, and whose future was under discussion when these words were written in October 1982.

SUGGESTIONS FOR FURTHER READING

Philip Mason, *Patterns of Dominance*, Oxford: Oxford University Press, 1970
Carlo M. Cipolla, *European Culture and Overseas Expansion*, Harmondsworth: Penguin, 1970

4   Economic conditions

Income

The most obvious way of starting to investigate the differences between rich and poor countries, or individuals, is to compare their incomes. As I explain below, there are certain pitfalls in this approach to the differences between rich and poor countries, but up to a point it is a good and useful one.

There are three possible measures of a country's collective income, and of these the one most commonly used is the gross national product or GNP. The *gross domestic product* or GDP is the value of all goods and services produced in the country, usually valued 'at factor cost', that is, adjusting for indirect taxes and subsidies. *Gross national product* is the gross domestic product at factor cost, plus any balance of income received from abroad. *National income* is gross national product net of depreciation. It represents the resources available for current use after setting aside sufficient to maintain the nation's stock of capital equipment, and is the best measure accordingly; however, it is more difficult to calculate, since it is hard to arrive at estimates, or even a satisfactory definition, of depreciation; and it is not available for as many countries as is GNP.[1]

Most countries have statistical departments which calculate and publish an annual estimate of the GNP in the national currency. This can be converted into a standard currency (by convention US dollars) at an appropriate rate (usually the official rate of exchange). The average for the population, or GNP per capita, enables us to see at a first rough approximation what the average income is in each country and how it compares with others. These estimates, along with other data, are nowadays compiled annually by the World Bank from data supplied by national statistical offices together with other sources, and I summarize the most recently available figures in table 4.1.

They show, first, how wide a difference there is between the western industrial countries at the top of the scale and the poorest countries at the other. Secondly, they show that differences in money income do correspond to differences in real resources and living standards. Even though figures showing a more than forty-fold difference in GNP per capita between the

69

Economic conditions

Table 4.1

	Type of economy (No. of countries)	Industrial market economies (19)	Non-market industrial economies (6)
GNP per capita (range)	1980	$16,440 – $4,880	$7,180 – $3,900
GNP per capita (average)	1980	$10,320	$4,640
Average annual growth rate, %	1960–1980	3.6	4.2
% of GDP generated in agriculture	1980	4	15
% of GDP saved	1980	22	25
% of GDP invested	1980	23	24
Energy consumption per capita[a]	1960	4,257	2,913
(Kg of coal equivalent)	1979	7,293	5,822
% of labour force in agriculture	1960	18	41
	1980	6	16
% of population living in towns[b]	1960	68	49
	1980	78	62
No. of people per doctor	1977	620	340
No. of people per nurse[d]	1977	250	200
% of population with access to safe water	1975	…	…
Diet: calories per day,	1977	3,377	3,489
as % of requirement[e]	1977	131	137

Notes:

[a] Includes coal, oil, gas, hydro-electric and nuclear energy; excludes firewood and traditional fuels.

[b] Towns as defined in each country.

[c] Unofficial estimates by Population Reference Bureau suggest a much higher figure of 26.

richest and the poorest countries represent something of a statistical mirage, for reasons explained below, they correspond closely to differences in real resources, particularly energy; in the availability of health services, in diets, and hence (see table 2.1) in infant mortality rates and general mortality as measured by the death-rate.

Thirdly, they show that it is now misleading to pose the problem of Third World development in terms of a gap between rich industrial and poor non-industrial countries. In fact there is no gap; the GNP per capita measure is a continuous variable, rising in an unbroken scale from the poorest countries Cambodia, Laos, Bangladesh, and Chad to West Germany and Switzerland at the top, as it were, of the industrial league.

Furthermore, account must be taken of trends over time. Economic development has taken place in many countries, and in some the rate of

70

High-income oil exporters (4)	Middle-income economies (63)	Low-income economies		
		China	India	Others (31)
$26,850	$4,500			$410
−$8,640	−$420			−$80 and below
$12,630	$1,400	$290	$240	$230
6.3	3.8	...	1.4	1.0
1	15	31	37	45
62	25	30	20	7
24	27	31	23	15
1,015	418	560	111	62
2,609	965	734	194	87
63	61	...	74	81
46	44	71	69	73
30	33	...	18	11
66	45	13[c]	22	19
1,380	5,840	1,100	3,630	19,460
3,010	2,510	480	5,700	13,200
88	50	...	33	29
...	2,561	2,441	2,021	2,113
...	107	103	89	94

[d] Includes nursing auxiliaries.

[e] As % of requirement for normal health and activity, taking into account climate, age and sex distribution, and average body weight in each country.

... Not available.

Source: World Bank, *World Development Report, 1982.*

growth has been rapid, while in others it has been nil or negative, so that positions in the league table are constantly changing. Particularly rapid economic growth, indeed, has occurred in some countries that would formerly have been classed as underdeveloped, notably Brazil, Korea both North and South, Taiwan, Singapore, Hong Kong, and probably in some respects China. Looking at the figures for whole groups of countries, too, it is not surprising to find that growth rates in the middle-income countries have far exceeded those in India and other low-income countries; presumably that is how the former have raised themselves, so to speak, into the second division of the world league.

The limitations of the GNP measure

Published figures of GNP per head are useful only as a first approximation. If taken too literally they can be misleading; besides obvious sources of inaccuracy and error, they are subject to reservations on a number of grounds. On the whole there are reasons to think that they exaggerate the real differences of living standards between rich and poor countries – wide though these are, they are not as wide as the figures, taken literally, would lead us to think.

First, it must always be remembered that they are average figures. They conceal the differences in income levels between rich and poor people within countries; and as indicated later in this chapter, these differences are particularly wide within many poor countries.

Secondly, official statistics persistently underestimate the value of goods produced and services rendered without money transactions in what is variously termed the non-cash, traditional, or subsistence sector (of which more below), which still accounts for a substantial part of the gross domestic product of many poor countries.

Thirdly, there is the rate-of-exchange problem. In compiling the statistics, figures computed initially in each country's national currency have then to be converted to a common standard, conventionally the US dollar. Official exchange rates, however, are unsatisfactory for this purpose. They change suddenly when a national currency is devalued overnight, and they can be artificially manipulated by governments. Particularly in the case of some poor countries, they reflect supply and demand conditions for a few key export commodities in uncertain world markets. And there are fundamental reasons why they systematically underestimate the purchasing power of poor countries' currencies and their real incomes. International trade tends to equalize the prices of traded goods throughout the world. Wages in different countries are strongly affected, if not quite determined, by differences in the productivity of labour in producing those goods. In industrial countries, productive methods are capital-intensive, so labour productivity and wages are high. High wages in manufacturing industry set standards of comparison for incomes in other sectors of the economy, especially services, which are highly priced accordingly. In poor countries, methods of production are labour-intensive, the productivity of labour is low, and wages and other incomes are low, so services are cheap, much cheaper than the corresponding services in rich countries. What is needed is a set of exchange rates based on purchasing power parities, as they are called, or in other words a method for comparing incomes according to the real resources needed in different countries to purchase precisely specified goods and services. Such a comparison encounters formidable statistical difficulties. It is the subject of an International Comparison

Project, launched by the United Nations in 1969, which by 1982 had calculated a purchasing-power-parity exchange rate for 34 countries. According to these calculations, the official exchange rates for some low-income countries' currencies, including India, Pakistan, and Sri Lanka, were undervaluing them by some three- to three-and-a-half-fold, and those of some middle-income countries by two- to two-and-a-half-fold. Average incomes in those countries should accordingly be multiplied by factors of that order of magnitude to give an idea of their real value in terms of the goods and services they can buy.[2] When an adjustment of that kind is made, it may be concluded that, rather than a forty-fold difference, average real incomes in western industrial countries are something like 10 to 12 times those in low-income countries, and 3 times those in middle-income countries.

And while GNP per capita as currently calculated may not be a very good measurement scale, there seems no reason to doubt its usefulness as an ordinal scale. In other words, when we range countries in order according to their GNP per capita we are doing almost if not quite the same thing as to range them in order from better off to worse off.

Real indicators

Besides comparing incomes, we need to compare living standards in ways that do not depend on the money measure. Some of the indicators that can be used for this purpose represent real goods and services, particularly food and energy. Others, such as infant mortality and the expectation of life, directly reflect the conditions of life; yet others, such as the numbers of people for each doctor or nurse, represent the availability of social services. Comprehensive, world-wide data on some of these indicators have been included in tables 2.1 and 4.1. In the discussion that follows, these average figures are amplified by reference to individual countries. Aggregated as they are, they conceal the differences among countries at similar income levels; for example, the strikingly low infant mortality rates in Panama, Costa Rica, and Cuba among middle-income countries, and in Sri Lanka and China among low-income countries. And if there are disparities among countries, so there are within them. For example, how many of the 26,810 people for every doctor in Uganda ever see one? – presumably in such a country modern scientific medical care is largely the privilege of an urban elite.

Diet

In recent years comprehensive data on the most basic measure of diets, the average number of calories per day, have been published annually by

73

the World Bank, and I summarize them in table 4.1. Older figures formerly compiled by United Nations agencies included the percentage of calorie intake derived from animal sources, and the number of grams of protein per day, for some countries.

In most industrial countries, western and communist alike, the average diet yields well over 3,000 calories a day and exceeds basic needs by more than 30 per cent. The proportion derived from animal sources ranged from as much as a half in New Zealand and Canada down to 18 per cent in Italy and 15 per cent in Japan, while protein intakes ranged from over 100 grams a day in New Zealand to 75 in Japan.

At the other end of the scale, in India and other low-income countries the average diet of little more than 2,000 calories a day is not enough to maintain health and normal activity, even taking into account age and sex distributions, average body weights, and the warm climates of many of these tropical and sub-tropical countries. By that test the average diet in India in 1977 was 11 per cent short of basic needs. Even greater deficiencies were reported from a number of African countries including Ethiopia, and also Nigeria where agriculture had languished despite oil revenues. In such countries, the older studies indicated low protein intakes, commonly of around 50 grams a day, while as little as 3–5 per cent of the diet was of animal origin.

Between the richest countries and the poorest, the average diet in China was reported to be at least adequate, while the same could be said for middle-income countries taken as a whole. Within that large group, however, there were wide differences in diet corresponding quite closely to income levels. Deficient diets were reported from a number of the less well-off middle-income countries, including Nigeria (as already mentioned), Ghana, Bolivia, and both Yemen and South Yemen. On the other hand, notably well-fed middle-income countries – Romania, Yugoslavia, Argentina, Singapore – were among the better-off in terms of GNP per capita in that group.

Generalizing very broadly, then, we may say that the inhabitants of rich countries eat about half as much food again as those of the poorest countries, including nearly twice as much protein. But a high GNP is not a necessary condition of an adequate diet, and in suitable conditions people in quite poor countries can nevertheless eat reasonably well.

Many factors affect what people eat, among them being their tastes and preferences, the methods of agriculture and stock-keeping, and the resources of land and labour available for producing food. Traditional diets in many poor countries consist of a basic carbohydrate source eaten in enormous quantity once a day, after cooking, usually by boiling in the form of a paste or porridge. The basic source may be rice, as in much of Asia; wheat in the temperate zone and cooler tropics; sorghum or millet in the drier tropics; a starchy root crop such as cassava or yams; or the plantain or banana. Other foods may be taken in small quantities as a relish or sauce, but the overall effect is often monotonous. Eaten in sufficient quantity, such a diet may yield enough calories to sustain life, and may also be rich in fibre, yet also lack other dietary constituents – protein, vitamins, minerals – necessary for full health and energy as distinct from mere survival.

Broadly speaking it is the rice- and wheat-eaters who fare best, for these food grains are reasonably good sources of vegetable protein, while the same could be said of those African peoples who traditionally cultivated the grains known collectively as the millets. In recent times, however, millets have tended to be displaced by the high-yielding exotic maize, whose protein profile lacks certain essential amino-acids. Maize should accordingly be supplemented with good animal protein such as meat and milk; but the same population pressures and local land shortages which have been associated with the change to maize have also resulted in more land being used to grow the basic carbohydrate crop and less being available for grazing – an instance of a problem which is found in many poor countries. Not all climates and vegetations are suitable for cattle, while in addition to shortages of resources there are also cases where local food taboos, or even mere tastes and preferences strongly ingrained in local cultures, work against an adequate protein intake. For example, religious prohibitions on the eating of meat seriously affect the diets of people in many countries of south Asia; while an FAO report on Siam (Thailand) stated that 'Milk, unfortunately, is not relished, and even children get little of it.'[3] Diets based on the potato are vulnerable to disaster, as the experience of the Irish in 1848 showed; yet, according to Connell, even the potato was able to provide an adequate basis for the diet if eaten in sufficient quantity, and if supplemented by high-grade protein from milk.[4] Probably the worst traditional diets of all were based on the plantain, like those of the region around Lake Victoria especially in Uganda, which became notorious for their gross deficiency in protein. The resulting disease or condition, named kwashiorkor in the Ga language, was identified in the 1930s as a clinical syndrome almost simultaneously in West and East Africa, where it was found that children who at weaning were put straight onto the almost protein-free local diet showed a well-marked set of symptoms, including a lack of the black pigment melanin which led to their skin colour being pale reddish-brown rather than black, and the hair pale and loose rather than black and tightly curled. Kwashiorkor has since been recognized as a very widespread deficiency in many tropical and sub-tropical areas, and since children need protein for growth where adults need it only for replacement, it is in the nutrition of children that the starkest contrasts appear between the diets of rich and poor countries.[5] Deficient diets in childhood undoubtedly contribute much to high rates of infant and child mortality in poor countries. By adversely affecting growth, they must also contribute indirectly to diseases and deficiencies later in life.

Lest the comparison seem too one-sided, though, it should be added that some diseases are more prevalent in industrial countries, and many of them are associated with over-refined and over-processed foodstuffs, especially sugar and white flour. Lacking in dietary fibre, these foods are blamed for conditions including dental caries, some forms of diabetes and of heart disease, constipation, appendicitis, and possibly cancer of the lower bowel.[6] Whatever their other deficiencies, Third World diets of the kind I have described above were traditionally rich in coarse vegetable fibre, though they may have been adversely affected by commercially processed and marketed foods in recent times. Similar misgivings have been expressed about the impact of proprietary baby foods supplanting former breast-feeding practices, with adverse consequences for both hygiene and nutrition, particularly upon the infants of women with more schooling and those living in towns. Reports based on the World Fertility Survey indicate that, despite advertising blandishments, the great majority of mothers in Third World countries still breast-feed their babies; but they do not do so for as long, and average breast-feeding periods have dropped by two to three months in a generation.[7]

On balance, then, while some improvement is no doubt called for in the diets of industrial countries, raising levels of nutrition in poor countries is without doubt a far more important and challenging task for humanity. Not only is it a worthwhile end in itself, but it is also one with instrumental value in increasing people's working capacity and efficiency. That was why Myrdal insisted that it was wrong to regard expenditure on food in poor countries merely as consumption; rather it should be thought of as investment.[8] Improved nutrition, releasing human energies, is associated with general economic development both as cause and as effect. For it seems clear that many people in poor countries are underfed not only because of supply constraints, but also because of a straightforward lack of purchasing power,[9] and I return to this important point in chapter 5.

Housing and sanitation

In industrial countries, most people live in houses built of brick, stone, or concrete, with slate or tile roofs, floors of wood or cement and usually with a covering for comfort and ease of cleaning, with electricity and an inside water supply to kitchen, bathroom, and flush toilet. When censuses or housing surveys reveal that some people live in houses that lack these amenities, the reaction is one of shame and outrage, a matter for campaigns by charitable organizations and political pressure groups. By

76

contrast, according to censuses, in Tunisia in 1975 people lived three to a room in most houses, only one in four of which had piped water, one in three electricity, and less than one in two had any kind of toilet. Somewhat similar conditions were reported from the Dominican Republic in 1970, though only one in five houses there were occupied at a density of three to a room, and one in seven had a flush toilet. In the Philippines in 1970, people lived three to a room in two houses out of five, and though a majority had piped water and some kind of toilet, fewer than one in four had a WC or electricity.[10] In low- and middle-income countries generally, it is usual to find many people living in houses built of dried mud, with grass-thatch roof (though superseded increasingly by corrugated metal) and earth floors. Water may be carried from a well, spring, or pond for distances to be measured in kilometres, and on this subject at least we have comprehensive statistics (see table 4.1) for 1975; in middle-income countries only half the population had reasonable access to safe water, defined as treated surface water or such untreated but uncontaminated water as that from boreholes, springs, and sanitary wells; while in India and other low-income countries it was fewer than one in three.

By these tests, housing and sanitary standards are generally much lower in rural areas than in towns. To some extent this does not matter; in particular, earth sanitation may be adequately hygienic in a sparsely populated rural area, while serious troubles arise (as they did in nineteenth-century Europe) when the traditional building methods and sanitary habits are attempted in the slum areas of the rapidly growing towns. I take up this point again in chapter 7.

Infant mortality

The infant mortality rate has long and rightly been regarded as the final test of a society's state of material civilization. In most low-income countries, though progress had been made, rates in 1980 of between 100 and 200 infant deaths for every 1,000 live births resembled those of Europe in the nineteenth century. As seen in table 2.1, the long-term improvement in conditions in western industrial countries continued between 1960 and 1980 with a fall in their collective infant mortality rate from 30 to 11, and to single figures in some countries. By this test things had not gone quite so well in communist industrial countries, and in 1980–81 there were reports that the remarkable improvements achieved in the Soviet Union during the first 40 years after 1917 had been partly undone by the neglect of the national health service in favour of increased military spending.[11]

In the Third World, although on the whole the lower-income countries have the higher infant mortality rates, there are considerable variations among different countries. Two things, it seems, are needed to achieve a

Economic conditions

low infant mortality rate: resources, and the political will to devote them to public health and welfare services. Thus among western industrial countries it is no accident that the one that has consistently taken the lead in this field is Sweden, with its long tradition of social democratic government. Elsewhere too we find that the countries which, in relation to their resources, report strikingly low infant mortality rates are those whose governments, whether communist, liberal, or social democratic, have pursued appropriate health and welfare policies. Among middle-income countries, with an average of 80, these notably include Jamaica (16), Cuba (21), Panama (22), and Costa Rica (24); among low-income countries, with an average of 94, Sri Lanka (44) and China (56).

Energy

By far the best single indicator of real economic resources is that of energy consumed. The scientific units involved are internationally standard, independent of money, and free of rate-of-exchange problems. Comprehensive statistics are available for energy derived from coal, oil, gas, hydro-electric and nuclear energy, though for lack of reliable data they do not include firewood and other traditional fuels which contribute substantially to meeting people's energy needs in the poorer countries.

As table 4.1 shows, there is a fairly close relation between energy consumed and GNP per capita. Certainly the poorest countries have very little energy at their disposal. If at the other extreme the correspondence between energy and income in western industrial countries is not quite as close in the 1980s as it was in the past, that may be partly because the steep rises in the price of oil in the 1970s forced these countries to adopt energy-conserving measures, even though as yet to a very limited extent. And just as the middle-income countries as a whole have been developing fastest in GNP terms, so has their consumption of energy been increasing fastest. In some, indeed, it has been spectacular; between 1960 and 1979 it increased eleven-fold in Singapore, seven-fold in South Korea, and two-and-a-half-fold from a much higher initial base in North Korea. There, indeed, like the old north of England industrialists' 'Where there's muck there's money', President Kim Il Sung has been heard to boast that 'the smoke from our chimneys darkens the skies'.

Economic development

Income: what it comes from and where it goes

Finally, table 4.1 brings out important differences among groups of countries in the sources of their incomes and the allocation of income between investment and current consumption. Even though these comparisons involve a money measure, they are confirmed by the distribution of the labour force among different sectors of the economy.

Thus it is a most striking fact that although the western industrial countries as a group are virtually self-sufficient in food production, they manage to be so with (in 1980) only 6 per cent of their combined labour force in agriculture and only 4 per cent of their income generated in that sector. Many more people work on the land in low- and middle-income countries, and proportionately more of their income arises from agriculture. However, these proportions have fallen as the industrialization of these countries has proceeded, and more people have been employed and more income generated in industry and in services. Table 4.1 shows how the share of agriculture fell between 1960 and 1980.

How much of a country's income is saved and invested is of central importance for its economic development. It used to be thought that whereas industrial countries could save up to 20 per cent of their gross domestic product and invest it in productive equipment yielding increased income, poorer countries could save only a smaller proportion of their much smaller incomes, so their economies could grow only slowly, if at all, and rich and poor countries would be divided by an ever-widening gap. In more recent times that has proved not to be the case. While western industrial economies save and invest around 22–23 per cent of their gross domestic product, middle-income countries save and invest even more, and their economic growth rates are faster. Among low-income countries, too, domestic saving in India at 20 per cent of GDP nearly suffices for investment at 23 per cent, while China is even more remarkably self-reliant, saving and investing no less than 30–31 per cent of its GDP. Only in the other low-income countries, then, is domestic saving seriously deficient, and between 1960 and 1980, according to the World Bank's estimates, it actually fell from 9 to 7 per cent of their combined GDP. Clearly such considerations have an important bearing on aid, to which I turn in chapter 13.

Patterns of development[12]

When we range out present-day countries in order according to their GNP per capita, then, we find quite consistently the following tendencies. In countries with higher incomes, fewer people work on the land, and the income generated in agriculture forms a smaller part of the whole domestic product. More people work in industry and in services, and more income is generated in those sectors of the economy. Accordingly, more people live in towns. They use much more energy from inanimate sources such as the fossil fuels and hydro-electric power. They have more to eat, and apart from a lack of fibre their food is of better quality. They are healthier and live

79

longer. Mortality conditions are more favourable, though public health measures in poor countries have brought about great improvements there too; death-rates are lower despite there being more old people in the population; above all, infant mortality rates are far lower. Birth-rates are much lower, and so rates of natural increase are lower, approaching zero in the most affluent countries. There is much greater provision for the care of the sick. And as will be seen in chapter 9, more children go to school and more go on to secondary and higher education.

A most important observation follows: these were exactly the trends which occurred over time in the history of the present-day industrial countries. The increased use of coal and later oil; investment in new machinery; migration from country to town, with the movement of labour at first from the land to the mines and factories, then at later stages the levelling-off of the labour force in industry as it became more and more capital-intensive, with self-regulating machines producing more goods with fewer people, and a further move accordingly into services; the improvement of public health and education; the fall in the death-rate, especially the infant mortality rate; the fall in the birth-rate – these are the commonplaces of the economic and social history of the industrial revolution.

It is this whole complex combination of inter-related trends which may be regarded as constituting economic development, of which a rising GNP per capita is the single and not very adequate criterion measure. If economic development means anything at all, this is it. Further, this observation makes the notion of stages of development well-nigh inescapable, despite the critical attacks that have been directed against it. And it lends some initial strength to the recapitulation thesis, that the present-day low-income economies are likely to experience similar trends and go through similar stages to those undergone by the now-rich industrial economies in the past, even though that thesis needs some qualification, as will appear below. And indeed it can be seen that it is happening. Comparing the figures for 1980 with those for 1960 in tables 2.1 and 4.1 confirms that during the last two decades these were the trends in the low-income countries, and still more markedly in the faster-developing middle-income countries.

The economic characteristics of poor countries

The dual economy

As a first rough approximation, the economy of any country may usefully be regarded as composed of two sectors, variously termed the 'cash', 'monetary', or 'modern' sector, and the 'non-monetary', 'household', 'traditional' or 'subsistence' sector. In the first, goods are produced and services rendered for money, cash transactions prevail, and money values are placed on everything. In the second, goods are produced and services rendered without money payment (though money may be used in gifts), and things are valued in more personal terms of reciprocity, family ties, honour, or neighbourliness. Pretty universally, it may be guessed, men are more involved in the first sector, and women in the second. This may affect such matters as the languages they speak; for example, in Uganda many men and few women speak Swahili, the lingua franca in trade and employment (see chapter 9).

Because the second sector is non-monetary, it largely escapes statistical notice. To some extent, indeed, it represents a hidden economy, though it is not to be confused with the so-called black economy of illicit cash transactions and tax evasion. The goods produced and services rendered in the second sector either do not figure in the official national income accounts at all, or are underestimated, often grossly so.

In all countries much production is carried on by unpaid family labour in the non-monetary household sector, for example preparing and cooking food. In Third World countries people's needs are met in this sector to a much greater extent than is the case in industrial countries, and traditionally were so even more. Peasant families produce all or almost all their own food without money changing hands, while groups of men go hunting and fishing together and divide the catch among their families, and traditionally in Africa a house was built in a day by kinsfolk and neighbours in a social gathering for which the first task was to brew the beer.

Economic development is, among other things, a process in which goods and services formerly produced or rendered in the non-monetary sector are made the subject of money values and transactions. House-building is a case in point, though we should not overlook the 'do-it-yourself' maintenance and decorating of houses in the non-monetary sector of industrial economies. In general, the more developed the economy the larger is the modern cash sector in relation to the subsistence traditional or non-cash household sector. The latter, however, continues to operate, and its importance continues to be overlooked and underestimated, especially in relation to the unpaid work of housewives in the home; it would be a mistake to regard it as vestigial.

In low-income countries the extent to which the non-monetary sector is overlooked and underestimated is even greater, and with it the economic activity of women. There is indeed much irony about the way in which the phrase 'economically active' has come to mean involved in paid work in the cash economy, for the original derivation of the word economy itself was from the Greek for household management. And to imply that women who are not in paid employment are not working is both inaccurate and insulting, for in most countries they do most of the housework and look after the old and the very young, while in many Third World countries they do much of the cultivating too.

In Third World countries, then, many needs are met (however inadequately) in the traditional subsistence sector without the intervention of money. By contrast, the modern cash economy is represented by such institutions as mines, factories, banks, and commercial offices, pervaded by a thoroughly businesslike outlook and the fullest use of money, credit, and international exchange. At least one commodity or product in each of the poor countries is thoroughly modern in this way – copper in Zambia, the tourist trade in Kenya, or in India such sectors as the iron and steel complex at Jamshedpur, the commercial centre of Calcutta, or the Bombay stock exchange. Often such sectors appear as enclaves or islands of economic and technological modernity in contrast to the life that surrounds them.

Leading sectors, spread and backwash

The very prosperity of such sectors or enclaves tends to heighten the disparity between them and the rest of the economy and society. To some extent such 'growth poles' generate economic growth in nearby sectors. For example, industrial or mining development in one part of an African country may stimulate food-growing as a cash crop in nearby rural areas, and some of the earnings of workers in mine or factory may generate increased incomes among peasant farmers. Further afield, however, the migration of men to the mines may result in depressed conditions in the rural tribal areas as those left behind – women, old people, children, the sick and handicapped – struggle to maintain themselves and their dependants by traditional methods on the land. As with men, so with capital; even one with quite a modest capital to invest, such as a small shopkeeper, may rate his prospects better in the thriving industrial area than in the impoverished countryside. Such effects cumulate and reinforce one another. So, in the language of development economics, while a 'leading sector' is generating 'spread effects' in neighbouring sectors, those more distant may be experiencing 'backwash' or 'polarization'. A leading sector may be an industry, such as cotton or railways. Or it may be thought of in geographical terms as a town and its hinterland, while the areas experiencing backwash are more distant rural areas. Or the leading sector may be a minority – a class, a racial group, or one of the communities in a plural society like the Asians in East Africa or the Chinese in Malaya. Economic development by its very nature seems prone to engender regional, class, and communal disparities. These have serious political and other repercussions, and I revert to this important point in subsequent chapters.

The precariousness of the cash sector

The modern cash sector of the economy of many poor countries, however, has hitherto tended to be narrowly and precariously based on the export of a small number of primary commodities. Thus the Brandt commission reported in 1980 that in recent years some countries had obtained almost all their export earnings from one commodity, apart from oil; they included Zambia (94 per cent from copper), Mauritius and Cuba (90 and 84 per cent respectively from sugar), and Gambia (85 per cent from ground-nuts and ground-nut oil). 'Between 1970 and 1972 over half the non-oil developing countries obtained more than 50 per cent of their export earnings from one or two crops or minerals.'[13] Moreover, not only is the foreign trade of some such countries dependent on a few exports, but the whole economy is also dependent on foreign trade. Thus in 1980 merchandise exports amounted to 20 per cent or more of the gross domestic products of Zaire (mostly copper), Sri Lanka (tea and rubber), Guinea (bauxite and alumina), El Salvador (coffee), and Nicaragua (coffee and cotton), while in the case of Zambia the export/GDP ratio was no less than 45 per cent. Bolivia's exports, mostly of tin, amounted to 17 per cent of its GDP, and Bangladesh was scarcely less dependent on jute.

Dependence of this kind does not prevail everywhere in the Third World, and has been diminishing. China and Brazil derived less than 10 per cent of their GDP from exports in 1980, and India less than 5 per cent. No longer are India's mainstays tea, cotton, and jute; in the late 1970s Indian exports were remarkably diversified, with no one commodity contributing as much as 7 per cent to total export earnings, tea less than 6 per cent, and cotton less than 5 per cent, while jute had dropped off the list altogether. By 1980 Brazil's export earnings from machinery and vehicles exceeded those from coffee. And even Costa Rica, with an export/GDP ratio of 20 per cent in 1980, derived 40 per cent of its export earnings from manufactured goods and other products, compared with 25 per cent from coffee and 20 per cent from bananas.[14]

Nevertheless, the primary products on which many Third World countries depend have in recent decades been exported into highly competitive and unstable world markets. On the whole the terms of trade in commodities other than fuels turned against low- and middle-income economies between 1960 and 1980, though they were very much in favour of oil-exporting countries such as Indonesia, Nigeria and Venezuela. But long-term trends were quite outweighed and overshadowed by short-term fluctuations in the prices of primary products far wider than those of industrial products.

In the case of agricultural commodities like tea, coffee, cocoa, and rubber, the vagaries of the weather lead to variations in the supply, while the period of years between planting and marketing may lead to excessive swings in price. Producers who respond to high prices by planting may thereby bring about a glut in which prices tumble – an effect known to students of economics as the 'cobweb theorem'. Moreover, some agricultural products produced by poor countries can be stored, so that buyers in rich countries with stocks in hand may be able to afford to wait until prices have gone really low before buying again. In the world market for products of this nature, much dealing is in fact done in futures, which tends to bring about an oversensitive market, liable to precisely the fluctuations against which the consumers (who largely are the big manufacturing concerns in the rich countries) are trying to protect themselves.

Countries exporting such products as cotton, jute, and rubber have further had to contend with competition from synthetic fibres and other industrial products. Metals too have had to face competition. Copper from countries such as Zambia and Zaire can be replaced for some purposes by aluminium, produced mainly in industrial countries with ample supplies of electrical energy; and like sugar and rubber it is subject to wide fluctuations in price. For example, in April 1974 the price of copper peaked at $3,034 a ton; by the end of the year it was $1,290, reducing Zambia's GDP by 15 per cent and the imports it could afford to buy by 45 per cent.[15]

Such misfortunes can have wider political consequences. For example, the fall in the price of cocoa in 1970–71 led the government of Ghana, burdened as it was by debts inherited from President Nkrumah's regime, to devalue the currency by 48 per cent. This caused an immediate sharp rise in the prices of imported goods (as indeed it was intended to do), causing unrest which led the army to withdraw their support from Dr Busia's government and restore military rule in January 1972.[16]

Involvement in the cash sector of the economy is clearly a risky business, then, and subsistence production in the non-monetary sector may well continue to have its attractions if only as an insurance against failure in the other. Buying land offers such an insurance. In conditions of general disorganization like those in Uganda from the mid-1970s onwards, with the collapse of legitimate political authority and great personal insecurity of life and property, it seems clear that many people survived by retreating into the subsistence economy, growing their own food when it was too dangerous for lorries to bring it in to the town markets, and bartering with neighbours when money prices reached absurd heights.

'Big firm, small country'

Another aspect of the modern international economy which makes it precarious and uncontrollable from the point of view of poor countries, and especially of their governments, is what may be termed the 'big firm, small country' syndrome. Much of the modern-sector activity in poor countries tends to be in the hands of large firms – the so-called 'multi-national corporations' – whose economic resources tower above those of all but the biggest and richest states in the world. If even the more powerful states sometimes have a hard time bringing some of these corporations' activities into line with their domestic economic policies, it may well be appreciated how little influence a small state in a poor country can exert over the activities of the giants.

This was well brought out in Beckford's study of plantation agriculture in the Caribbean. Like Myrdal he characterized plantations as extensions in poor countries of the activities of firms based in rich countries. Besides their metropolitan ownership and control, these firms exhibited a high degree of vertical integration; their plantations were only part of the whole, and it was the profitability of the whole that mattered more than the efficient use of resources in the plantation itself. Particularly where a firm produced some of the raw material (such as fruit or sugar cane) in its own plantations, and bought and processed some from local independent suppliers, lower prices might mean lower profits for the plantation but higher profits overall.

Secondly, such firms spread their agricultural operations out among a number of countries so as to minimize the risk of losses alike from natural hazards of weather and plant diseases and from political risks and labour troubles. This, said Beckford, 'leads to perverse supply responses for individual countries. For although the firm may increase overall acreage and output in response to an increase in the relative price of its output, it may, in the process, contract acreage and output in a particular country.' The response to price changes might be rational from the point of view of the multi-national firm, yet fail to take advantage of the situation from the point of view of the agricultural sector of each country. Clearly, for a firm to reduce production at a time of rising prices constitutes exasperatingly capricious behaviour from the point of view of the government of the country concerned.

Thirdly, a large firm might control much or most of the exports of a particular commodity from an individual state. For example, according to Beckford, in 1966 the United Fruit Company controlled 100 per cent of export banana acreage in Guatemala, 70 per cent in Costa Rica and Panama, and 56 per cent in Honduras, in addition to which it purchased and handled for export slightly more fruit than it produced in its own plantations. In such cases, the land area covered by the plantation enterprise might be so great as to make it virtually the only source of employment in substantial parts of the country concerned. Rising productivity due to technical improvement might enable relatively high wages to be paid, especially if the workers were able to organize themselves in a trade union, though at the cost of increased unemployment – an important point, about which more below; but the country's economic and political dependence on the firm was clearly both great and precarious.[17]

Very similar considerations apply to mining; while in manufacturing industry, two further factors contribute to the same effect, namely technology and tariffs. In manufacturing, indeed, the recapitulation thesis has to be considerably qualified, for unlike the present industrial countries at earlier stages of their development, today's poor countries live in a world in which there are already rich industrial countries, with whose highly developed technology they are hard put to it to compete. In the past it was enough for one country or even one firm to develop the new technology at all; when Boulton and Watt were making steam engines they, and Britain, had few competitors. Now, to take hypothetical examples, it is not much use a firm in (say) Hong Kong being able to make plastics, or a firm in (say) Chile being able to make automobiles, unless they can do it cheaper or better than ICI or Ford. It is true that tariff protection may sometimes enable infant industries to make a start in poor countries, and this is indeed one of the classic arguments in its favour. But many kinds of industrial development in the modern world involve such large indivisibilities as to require large markets to secure the requisite economies of scale. Accordingly, for example, it is only in a handful of Third World countries – most notably Brazil, and on a more modest scale India – that vehicle manufacturing has been fully developed, though several more assemble vehicles from imported components. In such developments, small countries, most of whose inhabitants are poor, and whose internal markets are very small, are at a disadvantage. The rich industrial countries have consistently protected their manufacturers with tariffs which discriminate against the manufactured exports of Third World countries.[18] And major industrial developments involve competing in world markets with giant industrial corporations which not only possess the technological 'know-how' that put them in the lead in the first place, and which is protected by patent laws, but also ensure, by massive expenditure on research and development, that their technological lead is maintained. A single big international company may spend more on research and development alone than many a small country's whole GNP, and more than the aid allocation of a major industrial state.

Rather than striking out on their own in such circumstances, businessmen in poor small countries may well see their best hope of success in entering into a relation of some kind with one or other of the giants, manufacturing components under licence, for example, or assembling and marketing the big firm's products in the small country. So they become in effect little more than subsidiary companies of the multi-national corporations, and there is a 'big firm, small country' syndrome in manufacturing as in plantation agriculture and mining.

On being a latecomer

It may be useful at this point to summarize the advantages and disadvantages of being a latecomer on the scene of economic development.

On the one hand, late-industrializing countries can take advantage of the experience gained, often slowly and at great cost, in the countries where the industrial revolution began. By adopting solutions already devised, their later development can be telescoped, sometimes dramatically so. In no field is this more evident than in that of public health and preventive medicine, where, as has been pointed out in chapter 2, improvements in mortality which took a century or more to achieve in western European countries have been accomplished in later-industrializing countries such as Japan in two or three decades. In manufacturing, too, despite the handicaps noted above, some latecomers have profitably copied the models and methods devised in the countries of the first industrial revolution. It seems strange to recall the time in the 1930s when Japanese goods were sneered at as 'cheap imitations' and western workers demanded protective tariffs against competition from the products of 'sweated labour', now that Japanese technology is no longer imitative but at the forefront, and Japanese workers are no longer low-paid compared with their western counterparts. More recently it has been from some of the newly-industrializing countries such as Taiwan and Korea (both North and South) that the mass markets of the world have been flooded with goods such as tennis shoes and transistor radios, and so close to the originals have the imitations of some standard goods been, even down to the labels, that there have been murmurs of complaint in western countries about trade marks and patent rights. Another example of imitative development has been that of village industrialization in the Punjab, where local craftsmen began by making spare parts for western products such as sewing machines, diesel engines, pumps, and farm machinery, and went on to produce all the components and assemble them.[19]

And if the technology can be borrowed in a metaphorical sense, so can the capital literally be. As we have seen, taken as a whole, Third World countries have recently been financing high rates of investment mostly from their own resources, and a serious deficiency of domestic savings is a problem mainly confined to the smaller low-income countries. However, it can be argued that much of their recent development, especially that of the faster-growing middle-income countries, was initiated in the past by external capital inflows both public and private, or in other words that they would not now be developing as they are if they had not been able to borrow. Further, it is clear enough that external loans especially to the poorest countries still enable developments to be initiated for which local savings would be insufficient.

On the other hand, the technology available to be 'borrowed' from countries now at an advanced stage of economic development is characteristically capital-intensive, making available highly paid employment for a few, and quite inappropriate to the circumstances of low-income countries; I return to this important point below. And as for borrowing in the literal sense, many Third World countries have become burdened with debts which have reached astronomic proportions, so that much of their future development is already heavily mortgaged, especially their future earnings of precious foreign exchange. Meanwhile their need to borrow is increased by balance-of-payments deficits, most acutely in oil-importing countries. Repayments and interest charges due on old debts require yet more new borrowing, and so the problem is compounded.

Furthermore, as noted above, whereas the early-industrializing countries exported their manufactured goods in a world in which they found ready markets and few competitors, later-industrializing countries find export markets closed against them both by tariff barriers and by the commanding positions of already established industrial enterprises. It is for reasons of this kind that the recapitulation thesis needs to be somewhat qualified, and it has to be recognized that later-industrializing countries cannot pass through exactly the same stages of development in a world that has changed. Some would go further and say that it has changed to their disadvantage. The early-industrializing countries, it is said, in their role as imperial powers, set up a world division of labour in which they themselves concentrated on manufactured exports to exchange for raw materials produced in their dependencies. Now those countries have abandoned their empires and sought self-sufficiency in protected markets, relying on their own resources and depending less on the rest of the world; and their former colonies have been left in the lurch, deprived of markets for the export of goods for whose production they have natural advantages.

Thus to take one particularly important class of goods, the industrial market economies taken as a whole meet most of their needs for food by trading among themselves. People in an industrial country such as Britain eat wheat from Canada, bacon and dairy produce from Denmark and the Irish Republic, lamb from New Zealand; they do not live on rice bought at low prices from starving peasants in Asia. Only a few foodstuffs produced in poor countries are consumed in rich; they include sugar, fats, and oils. Sugar is produced at least cost from sugar cane grown in tropical countries. But cane sugar produced in the West Indies and Mauritius has been ousted from the markets of western Europe by beet sugar produced at greater cost within the European Economic Community with its protectionist common agricultural policy. Moreover, with its surplus disposals the EEC has in recent years become almost the world's biggest exporter of sugar, second only to Cuba.[20] On the other hand, perhaps it might be argued that land in West Indian countries that used to grow sugar for Europe can now be used to grow food for home consumption, and that the former domination of these countries' economies by plantation interests (like those analysed by Beckford) can now be reduced.

Labour, employment and earnings

Some factors at work in Third World economies make for low wages, others for high. The apparent paradox is soon resolved when it is recognized that both high and low wages are to be found in the same economy. Indeed, wide disparities or differentials in earnings are a leading characteristic of Third World economies.

The lowest levels of earnings, including wages, in poor countries are very low indeed by comparison with wage rates in industrial economies, and this has to be seen in relation to the low opportunity cost of labour where many or most people live on the land. When people – mostly men – leave the land and enter employment, all they forgo are the meagre returns on subsistence agriculture, even supposing the traditional way of life on the land to have been left undisturbed by modern changes. In such a case, wages need only be 'subsistence-plus', perhaps half as much again as the returns to subsistence agriculture, for people to be willing to accept them. In fact in poor countries earnings in some occupations are found to be at that kind of level, especially agricultural wages in commercialized farming in rural areas, and earnings from occupations such as hawking and domestic service in towns.

Quite generally, though, the traditional way of life on the land has not been left undisturbed. Technical improvements in agriculture have raised the productivity of labour on the land, so that enough food for all can be grown by fewer people, and the results have been higher incomes for farmers, rural unemployment, and migration to towns. The same basic economic forces which operated in England in the age of the inclosures and the industrial revolution can be seen in the more recent history of the Green Revolution (about which I say more in the next chapter), in agricultural improvements in Latin America, and elsewhere in the Third World. In response to the falling demand for labour resulting from these changes, agricultural wages, already low, have fallen even lower. For

89

example, according to data amassed by Azizur Rahman Khan, in 1949 agricultural labourers in Bangladesh could earn 2.36 taka a day, in 1975 only 1.28 (at constant 1963 prices). In a village in Uttar Pradesh, a ploughman's daily wage could buy 6.58 kilos of wheat in 1954–5, but only 3.12 kilos in 1967–8. And real agricultural wages in the Philippines dropped from 3.84 pesos a day in 1957 to 1.48 a day in 1974 (at constant 1965 prices).[21]

So people seek work of other kinds, as they did in the classical industrial revolution of the eighteenth and nineteenth centuries in Europe. But the dominant technology in the urban-industrial sector too is now highly developed and capital-intensive, providing work for a few highly paid workers, in contrast to the masses of unskilled labourers who in former times dug the canals, laid the railways, and hewed coal by hand. In the urban-industrial sector of the present-day developing countries accordingly, some wages tend to be well above the 'subsistence-plus' level which would in theory characterize an economy in which there was development with unlimited supplies of labour.[22] Indeed, it was with only slight and pardonable exaggeration that Meier coined the phrase 'development without employment'.[23] It was vividly illustrated by Lord Campbell:

I first became connected with the sugar industry in 1934 in what was then British Guiana. Then, there were over fifty factories producing 160,000 tons of sugar a year and employing something like 60,000 people. Now, there are less than ten factories producing nearly 400,000 tons of sugar a year and employing only 30,000 people. Of course, sugar-workers are now paid much higher wages, and the mechanical bulldozer may do the work of gangs of five hundred men – what happens to the four hundred and ninety-nine men who aren't driving the bulldozer?[24]

According to Meier, in the 'less developed countries' taken as a whole, between 1948 and 1961 employment in industry grew by only 3.5 per cent annually while the urban population increased at a rate of 4.6 per cent and industrial output by 7.5 per cent annually. These trends did much to explain the extremely high rates of open unemployment in urban areas in poor countries, commonly as high as 15–25 per cent, quite apart from any questions of 'disguised unemployment' or 'underemployment' of people still living in rural areas. Men clearly move into towns in the hope of being among the favoured few who get work and earn wages which are sometimes as much as twice or three times the income of a whole family in the traditional subsistence sector.

In these circumstances, Sir Arthur Lewis warned of the consequences of 'premature decasualization':

Modern personnel theory is against casual labour. Men on the permanent staff feed better, work more effectively, have a higher morale, and cause less trouble. Unions also object to casual labour, because it is more difficult to organize. Decasualization does not increase the average level of unemployment, but it makes unemployment less supportable. If 100 men each work 3 days a week they can all live. When 60 work 5 days a week and 40 become continuously unemployed, one faces a major social problem. High wages stimulate decasualization, since the employer seeks to get best value from those he employs; and also because high wages make him put in machines, which require him to train a staff and keep it.[25]

In a capital-intensive industry with a few relatively skilled workers, wages play a comparatively small part in total costs and management have little reason to resist wage claims when they are pressed by a well-organized trade union. The governments of poor countries, too, may favour the payment of high wages especially by big foreign enterprises; high wages may be viewed as a kind of 'tax', limiting repatriated profits and making more of the benefits available locally. Similar considerations may apply to generous fringe benefits. Local pressures both by governments and unions for such benefits may in turn predispose enterprises to invest in capital-intensive methods, importing the necessary machinery.

To an increasing extent, selection for the few highly paid jobs in the modern sector has been by means of formal educational qualifications gained through the school system. This puts a premium on schooling and certification, with important consequences alike for disparities of income, discussed later in this chapter, and for schooling itself, to which I turn in chapter 9.

For the rest, however, unemployment is too simple a term. Outside the ranks of the favoured few in modern-sector jobs – the aristocracy of labour, as some writers have called them[26] – people are not on the whole found to be sitting helplessly about doing nothing. On the contrary, many struggle for a livelihood in ill-rewarded labour-intensive activities in what I called the 'indigenous private sector', now more generally termed 'informal'. The need to recognize this sector introduces a qualification into the dual sector model with which I began, useful though that is as a first approximation. As detailed in chapter 7, the informal sector includes the myriad tiny businesses and self-employed individuals who in poor countries carry on small-scale manufacture by handicraft methods, minor repairs, food processing, and the like, along with the activities of small shopkeepers, street hawkers, water sellers, and casual labourers. Domestic service, too, which has all but disappeared in industrial societies, is still a widespread institution in the Third World in response to much wider disparities of income which make it possible for substantial numbers of people to employ others for no more than a twentieth or a thirtieth of their own incomes.

Through these informal sector activities, purchasing power is diffused more widely from the favoured few in modern-sector jobs to the poor. Another way in which this happens is through kinship networks, as well-paid town workers remit part of their earnings to their families in rural areas.

Much attention was paid to remittances of this kind in earlier studies of labour migration, particularly in Africa, where modern-sector employment represented for many men an episode, though it might last anything from two to twenty years, rather than an irreversible commitment. They have implications both for town life and for the family and kinship to which I turn in later chapters. In those studies, the emphasis was on migration from rural communities to modern-sector employment in plantations, mines, factories, and towns. For the most part it was internal migration within a country or territory, or could be so regarded at a time when, for example, Uganda and Kenya were not sovereign republics but adjoining territories under British rule between which people moved freely. Some migratory movements had their international implications, though, such as those from Rwanda and Burundi under Belgian mandate into Uganda under British rule, and the migration of men to work in the mines of South Africa from countries such as those now named Lesotho, Malawi, Mozambique, and Zimbabwe.[27] In more recent times the international aspects of labour migration and workers' remittances have come to the fore as it has been recognized that several Third World countries can now be regarded as major exporters of labour. Thus in 1978, according to the World Bank, workers' remittances added 18 per cent to India's earnings from merchandise exports and 21 per cent to those of Bangladesh, 33 per cent to those of Mali and 60 per cent to those of Upper Volta; they nearly equalled the merchandise export earnings of Egypt and Pakistan; and they were almost the only source of foreign exchange for Yemen and South Yemen.[28]

Corruption

No country is free from corruption; it has political as well as economic aspects, and I have more to say about it in chapter 12. And in the nature of things it is obviously impossible to cite statistics. Nevertheless, the impression is well-nigh inescapable that corruption is far more widespread and pervasive, even blatantly so, in the poorer non-communist countries than it is in either the West or the communist world.

Its economic consequences were well analysed by M. J. Sharpston, who distinguished between 'efficient' corruption which occurs when scarce resources command an illicit price which corresponds to their scarcity value, and 'inefficient' when the price is lower. From an economic point of view, efficient corruption has the same effect as a complete absence of corruption in rationing scarce resources for which a government licence or permit is required, though it tends to put the proceeds of the sale of those licences or permits into private hands rather than the public exchequer. It may happen, though, that corruption is inefficient because people, including officials, are 'naturally obliging and more inclined to give you the stamp you need on your document than not'.

Generally speaking, high rates of customs duty, and complex and stringent controls on economic life, combined with 'inefficient' corruption, make for the widespread evasion of laws and regulations. Thus smuggling will be commonly practised if rates of duty are high but customs officers do not ask for large bribes; if the rate of duty is lower, it may be as cheap, or almost as cheap, to pay it. Corruption may 'oil the wheels', for example in securing the prompt import of a vital spare part without which much production is being lost. In some circumstances, too, it may stimulate investment by affording a means for the accumulation of capital; for example, corrupt politicians may invest their ill-gotten gains in bus companies or similar enterprises with a local development potential – though they may also invest them in Switzerland or Wall Street.

On the other hand, corruption may well lead to 'the diversion of resources – particularly that really scarce resource, practical and intelligent manpower – into "fixing" rather than producing'. Secondly, corruption tends to lower the standard of the services provided by all parts of the public sector. If officials are overworked but corruptible, so that a small bribe will lead to prompt attention to important papers while others wait, then the temptation will be to introduce delays in order to attract bribes for circumventing them, and the level of the bribe needed will tend to rise. Though this may be a way of rationing scarce resources like officials' time, it is not one that affords them an incentive for the prompt and efficient despatch of business; rather, it introduces delays and inefficiency and hence costs to the economy generally. At higher levels of decision-making, planning and policy may be affected in a manner that does not make for the greatest good of the greatest number, for example when 'a few local industrialists may obtain effective control of government policy in so far as it affects their industries', and tariffs, government contracts, tax laws, and the like may be manipulated accordingly. And these effects may be compounded when it is not local industrialists who are primarily concerned, but large foreign firms. 'In an extreme case,...foreign interests with large investments in a developing country may virtually buy up the government and run the country as an unconsolidated subsidiary'[29] – an extreme case indeed of the big firm, small country syndrome.

On balance, we may surmise that corruption probably tends to enhance inequality. The effects will not be all one way, and corruption may also have some redistributive effects, especially by spreading the benefits of office among the wider kinsfolk of the official. In some statements by educated men in East Africa which I collected in the course of a study of

93

the educated elite there, it was suggested that the demands of kinsfolk for a return on the 'investment' which they considered they had put into his education might be one of the factors leading a government official to accept bribes if they were offered, and the same would apply to other educated men such as teachers.[30] Turning to an example from modern African fiction, one of Chinua Achebe's characters was blamed by his uncles for not demanding big enough bribes.[31] However, the redistributive effects of this nature probably only partly offset the tendency for persons in positions of power and influence, who are in most cases already well rewarded in overt and legitimate incomes from salaries and the like, to command a covert, illegitimate extra price for their services. To quote Sharpston again, 'effective tax rates will be lower, especially on high incomes, and...with a corrupt government money can breed money in a very direct way; government contracts, grants, concessions, exemptions and subsidies go to those who can pay for them'.

Disparity and development

Disparities within poor countries

Many writers have stressed the wide disparities of income and wealth among persons and family households in poor countries. Thus Brazil has been likened to 'a Sweden superimposed upon an Indonesia', while Indian authors have coined such phrases as 'the island republic' and 'Middle India' for the well-to-do minority, some 2 or 3 per cent of the population of that vast country, with their middle-class attitudes and way of life.[32] Wide disparities must constantly be borne in mind when interpreting the data presented earlier in this chapter; averages per head, low as they are, may yet mislead if the great majority receive much less than the average.

Much has become known about this important subject in recent years, especially from research initiated by Hollis Chenery and his colleagues and carried out with the World Bank's resources. Their statistics on income distributions, mostly in the 1970s, need to be treated with caution and are not available for all countries, but are certainly illuminating.

To parody George Orwell, all income distributions are unequal, but some are more unequal than others. The simplest measures of inequality indicate the share of all household incomes received by different groups of households: the top 10 or 20 per cent, the lowest 20 or 40 per cent. From the different possible measures I single out the percentage of all household income received by the top 10 per cent of households.

By this test, western industrial societies are not only healthy, prosperous, and free, but also quite egalitarian. In the 1970s the least unequal income distributions were those of the Scandinavian countries and the Netherlands,

94

along with Yugoslavia, where the top 10 per cent of households received around 21–23 per cent of all household income. The United Kingdom was not far behind at 23.8 and the United States at 26.6 per cent. In other industrial market economies the share of the top 10 per cent was somewhat more: Japan 27.2, Italy 28.1, and West Germany 28.8, but only in France was it as high as 30 per cent.

Comparable data for communist industrial countries are not available, but studies by western scholars of wage- and salary-structures and farm incomes in the Soviet Union and eastern Europe indicate that income distributions there are about as unequal as they are in the West.[33]

In contrast, in few Third World countries was the top 10 per cent's share less than 30 per cent: Sri Lanka 28.2, Bangladesh 27.4, South Korea 27.5, and most notably of all perhaps Taiwan 24.7. In most of the middle-income countries for which data are available, the figures ranged between 34 and 45 per cent. They included Chile, Argentina, and Venezuela where the top 10 per cent's share was around 35 per cent; Costa Rica, Malaysia, Mexico, and Turkey where it was around 40 per cent; and Peru, Panama, and Kenya, where it was 43–46 per cent; while the highest figure of all was that for Brazil, just over 50 per cent. Among low-income countries, apart from Sri Lanka and Bangladesh, the most important by far was India, where the top 10 per cent's share was 33.6 per cent of all household income.[34]

Such disparities have to be seen in relation to a number of factors. In many countries there were wide differences of wealth, power, and prestige before modern industrial development began. In a pre-industrial economy, by far the most important asset is land; and land was distributed very unequally indeed in most countries, so that there were wide differences between the privileged minority of landowning families and the rest of the population. Nowhere was this more true than in Europe in the eighteenth and nineteenth centuries, on the eve of the industrial revolution; more recently, somewhat comparable conditions have prevailed in many Asian countries, and most of all in Latin America, where the distribution of land ownership is strikingly unequal compared with other regions. Characteristically, too, the landed gentry are or were the military class; they exercised political power through patronage and through their control of the organs of government (in eighteenth-century England the House of Lords); and they were also the educated class, able, since they could afford a privileged education for their sons, to dominate the professions and the administration of government. In some countries such landowning aristocracies have been overthrown, and in others their dominance has been undermined as industrial capital has overtaken land as the leading economic asset in an industrial economy. In yet others, however, economic development has been such as to consolidate or even enhance their privileged position.

95

Pre-existing disparities apart, economic development itself often appears as a process in which some people become better off while others at best stay as they were, if they are not actually made worse off. Reference has already been made to growth poles and leading sectors, spread and backwash effects. Especially in the early stages of development, these are ways in which disparities widen as an industry, a region, a religious denomination or an ethnic minority does well while others are left behind.

We have also seen how involvement in the modern sector brings high if precarious rewards. At the top of the occupational scale, indeed, a few people in poor countries are often found to be remunerated as highly as their counterparts in affluent industrial countries. This can hardly be avoided when they work for the same firms, the big multi-national corporations, or when like medical practitioners, university professors, or senior government officials they can 'brain-drain' (supposing they are free to do so) to comparable posts in the West or in international organizations. Applying world standards of comparison to the top salaries of top people, however, clearly stretches out the scale of income disparities in poor countries enormously compared with poor peasants and low-paid urban workers. At less exalted levels, too, differentials are wide. Thus, writing of the 1960s, Jolly reported that in Uganda a typical primary teacher earned between six and thirteen times the average national income, a secondary teacher between twenty-five and forty times, and a university teacher up to one hundred and twenty-five times. African contrasts were rather extreme, but even in India the corresponding figures ran from two-and-a-half to four-and-a-half times the average national income for primary and secondary teachers and from nine-and-a-half to fifteen times for university teachers, significantly higher than the proportions in rich countries where the primary or secondary teacher rarely earned more than three times average income and often less than twice. Turning to wages and the difference between town and country, Jolly stated that 'increases in money wages of 7 to 10 per cent per year have not been uncommon over periods when prices have risen by only 2 or 3 per cent and when agricultural prices (which largely determine rural incomes) have fallen or remained constant.' In such circumstances, 'Far from defending the right of the underdog to a reasonable share of the national income, the [trade] unions are a pressure group for the already privileged, against the interests of both the unemployed and those in the rural areas.'[35]

Such considerations bring out the number of different axes or dimensions along which income disparities in developing countries may be arrayed. They are related to pre-existing inequalities in the distribution of land, the greatest asset in pre-industrial societies. They often arise in the process of economic development itself as some prosper while others are left behind. There are urban–rural differentials. Among people working in towns, wage earners in capital-intensive modern industries, in many cases controlled by multi-national corporations, may constitute a relatively well paid aristocracy of labour, especially if they are organized in trade unions. Wide occupational differentials also arise partly because the most eminent and highly qualified can sell their skills in a world market, while in part they are related to education (or more exactly schooling) and formal certification. For, as will be seen in chapter 9, educational diplomas and professional qualifications are economic assets yielding their possessors high returns, and the opportunities to gain them are not equally open to all.

Redistribution with growth

If, following Chenery, we range out countries in order by their GNP per capita, we find a general tendency for inequality to be somewhat less at the ends of the scale and somewhat more in the middle.[36] According to one interpretation, this is what we should expect. In the poorest countries of all there is so little to go round that if it were more unequally distributed many would perish. At the other end of the scale, the ample resources of the industrial countries has enabled them to distribute these widely among their people through egalitarian policies and welfare state measures. In between, however, inequality must get worse before it gets better; economic development engenders inequality, which cannot be remedied until there is more to go round; the first thing to do is to increase the size of the cake, after which it will be time to think about cutting it into more nearly equal slices.

That, however, is not the most striking thing to emerge, nor is it Chenery's conclusion. Rather, it is the extreme diversity among the middle-income countries in this respect, which appears in the form of a widely dispersed distribution on the graph relating income to inequality. In these countries there is ample scope for different circumstances, most of all different government policies, to affect the outcome. In some, economic development has indeed involved some people getting much richer while others have been little or no better off, and the relative deprivation of the poor has increased; but in others the reverse has happened, and lower-income groups and households have shared more than proportionately in the gains from rapid economic development. In Chenery's phrase, there can be redistribution with growth.[37]

To explain such wide diversities we need to consider in detail different countries' historical circumstances and the policies of their governments.

Brazil

Brazil in the 1960s and 1970s combined rapid industrialization with the most unequal income distribution of any country for which the data are available. The military government who seized power in 1964 determined to place their country within one generation in the category of the developed nations. Meanwhile the size of the cake had to be increased before it could be cut more equitably. Meanwhile, too, they would tolerate no resistance. Any kind of opposition or criticism was identified as subversion by 'the enemy within'. Associations such as peasant unions and most political parties, through which people could represent their economic and political demands, were repressed, while trade unions were firmly controlled, and the methods adopted to enforce that repression made Brazil the subject of an international campaign against alleged violations of human rights. According to Peter Knight, there were also economic consequences. 'The style of Brazilian economic growth (not only how much was produced, but what was produced for whom) was strongly influenced by the fact that the poor and a large part of the working class had neither effective political voice nor economic power.'[38]

The chosen policy was to encourage private enterprise. The lessons of the 'dependency' school of Latin American economists (see chapter 6) were heeded to some extent; while capital might be borrowed from abroad, it must be on terms that did not entail loss of control to outside agencies, or 'denationalization' in the Brazilian sense of the word. In that development, the leading sector was a capital-intensive heavy industry producing durable consumer goods such as refrigerators for the 'Sweden' of affluent town-dwellers and not doing much for the 'Indonesia' of the rural poor. Most of all it was concentrated on motor vehicles, of which Brazil was producing well over a million a year by 1980, and the related infra-structure of roads, service stations, and the like – perhaps unwisely so in view of Brazil's dependence on imported petroleum, though (as detailed in chapter 5) Brazil also pioneered the large-scale production of vegetable alcohol as a motor fuel.

Economic growth was spectacular. Between 1960 and 1979, per capita GNP rose at an average rate of nearly 5 per cent a year, while during the peak years of the 'economic miracle', 1968–73, it grew at an average annual rate of over 8 per cent. Furthermore, according to Knight, the available evidence suggested that to some extent growth did benefit the poor. 'Most Brazilians shared some of the real economic growth. But the gains of the rich were enormously larger than those of the poor in absolute terms. And in relative terms the rich grew richer faster than the poor grew less poor.' That gave rise to much unease among diverse Brazilian elites, including those of businessmen, intellectuals, and the hierarchy of the church, and there was a growing conviction that 'the social question' of the extreme disparity between rich and poor must be addressed. Despite the regime's suspicion of independent social and political movements, the Roman Catholic church supported trade unions and participated in

98

grassroots groups called Basic Christian Communities, and the Pope called for social justice during his visit in July 1980.

It became increasingly difficult for the government to reconcile liberal private-enterprise economic policies with political repression, giving people freedom with one hand and denying it to them with the other.[39] In 1974 and again in 1978 the permitted opposition party, the Brazilian Democratic Movement, won resounding victories in congressional elections conducted in an atmosphere that turned them into plebiscites against the government; and although the latter did not fall, it responded with policies of political liberalization. There was an amnesty for political prisoners, the freedom of the press was restored, and a somewhat greater freedom of discussion was permitted on television, though race apparently continued to be a sensitive topic.[40] Unions engaged in collective bargaining and strikes occurred, while new political parties were allowed to organize. And much greater attention was paid to basic public welfare services, though not to land reform. It seems clear, however, that the distribution of income and wealth in the early 1980s was still extremely unequal, and the structure of effective demand unlikely to shift resources much from the production of private motor vehicles, colour television, and the like into schools and health services, water and sewerage, housing, food, clothing, bicycles and buses. Meanwhile Brazil's infant mortality rate of 77 in 1980, though no more than average for middle-income countries generally, was markedly higher than those of other Latin American countries with comparable GNP per capita such as Chile, Panama, and Costa Rica (not to mention Cuba). At that rate, of the three and a half million babies born annually in Brazil, some 275,000 could be expected to die within a year. If Brazil had Chile's infant mortality rate of 43, that number would be reduced to 153,000; if the rate were as low as 22–24, as in Panama and Costa Rica, it would be no more than 80–85,000. Such is the cost in human terms of unmet social needs in inegalitarian economic development.

Cuba

If Brazil has represented in Chenery's terms the leading case of growth without redistribution, Cuba in the 1960s appeared as that of redistribution without growth; however, growth followed in the 1970s.

After the revolution in 1959 there was a drastic redistribution of assets. According to Dudley Seers' account, tenants took possession alike of rural smallholdings and town houses, and much property was simply abandoned as many people fled to the United States. Nationalization, starting with foreign-owned companies and land, spread to productive assets of all kinds. United States asset-holders were not compensated at all; local owners were paid annuities on terms that involved a degree of expropriation for

99

them too. At the same time, public expenditure and investment concentrated upon the needs of the poor, especially in the health and education services, and upon rural areas, where big inroads were made into unemployment and urban–rural differentials were reduced. Income was redistributed as wages were increased while salaries were cut, so that occupational differentials fell to a ratio of no more than about three to one. Extra earnings from piece rates, bonuses, and overtime were abolished or discouraged. Charges were abolished for medical care and schooling, which became free public services, while basic foods were rationed at low prices, and public transport fares were kept low.[41]

In the early years a revolutionary zeal and an aversion to a market economy extended to a policy, if not directed expressly at abolishing money altogether, at least of playing down its importance. It seems clear that this led to inefficiency and mismanagement as financial accounting was abandoned alike for individual enterprises and for the economy as a whole. According to Seers, 'Managers of factories and farms ceased to keep accounts, or even to know their costs of production.' No attempt was made to offset price reductions, price controls, and free services by reducing the quantity of money in circulation, and there was no currency reform apart from the confiscation of large notes soon after the revolution. Excessive money demand for goods and services soon led to shortages, queues, and a black market. According to Seers' estimates, national income probably rose about in line with population growth from 1961 to 1968, but then declined between 1968 and 1971. By the latter date, dire poverty and unemployment had been eliminated, but progress in the production of food and of exports was slow, and so was rehousing. Great efforts were made to extend schooling and adult literacy, and the medical services, but there were difficulties. According to Brundenius, about one-third of all doctors left the country soon after the revolution; and to make up the number quickly, the Ministry of Education and the universities lowered the requirements for qualification. Health conditions deteriorated, and the infant mortality rate rose to a peak of 46.7 in 1969.[42]

The problems of the 1960s stimulated a great debate about how to remedy inefficient management and planning without reverting to the materialist incentives of a market economy. A policy of rapid industrialization was decided upon, even though it involved a well-nigh total dependence in the medium term on exports of one primary commodity, sugar, to pay for imported investment goods. A link was restored between wages and productivity. And in order to absorb excessive purchasing power in the economy, the prices of some public services including electricity and water rates were raised, the abolition of house rents was postponed, and there were substantial increases in the prices of durable consumer goods, cigarettes, and rum – a set of measures some called 'socialist inflation', though their aim was counter-inflationary, and the state continued to provide for basic needs at low cost.

Between 1970 and 1974 the world price of sugar rose eight-fold, and Cuba quickly earned large amounts of western currencies. When it slumped again many industrial projects had to be abandoned, but the Soviet Union came to the rescue, buying Cuban sugar at well above the world price. Consequently, although the 1960s had been a decade of nil and in bad years even negative growth, there was a veritable growth spurt after 1970 with average annual growth rates paralleling Brazil's at over 8 per cent, and though the pace slackened to around 4 per cent after 1976 growth was still consistent. By 1980 the infant mortality rate was 21 – almost the lowest in the Third World, lower than in the Soviet Union, and comparable with those of western European countries only 20 years before.

India

More briefly, India may be characterized as the case of little redistribution with slow growth. Land reform, impressive on paper, was not fully implemented. According to P. K. Bardhan, the laws included deliberate loopholes and exemptions, and their enforcement was vitiated by corrupt administration and a slow and costly judicial process. In many cases the benefits of government schemes intended for the poor have been diverted by the well-to-do and locally well-connected. Thus the subsidized credit made available through village co-operatives has been appropriated by big farmers and village moneylenders, while the distribution of canal water from irrigation works has been influenced in their own favour by powerful local figures. Infra-structure development such as roads and land improvement has been utilized mostly by the well-to-do, while schooling benefits the rich more than the poor, and in the urban-industrial sector the better-off gain most from public transport and communications and low-cost housing.[43] As has been seen, the distribution of income has remained rather unequal, while between 1960 and 1980 the average annual growth rate was 1.4 per cent, and India's infant mortality rate at 123 in 1980 was similar to that in other low-income countries.

Sri Lanka

Some redistribution and some growth have taken place in Sri Lanka, along with expensive but effective social welfare and public health programmes.

According to Jayawardena, rural landholding was never very unequally distributed. Small tenant cultivators were protected by a law of 1958, and although the land reform of 1972 did not go as far as some international

agencies had urged, notably the International Labour Office, it was nevertheless quite important and quite effective. Farmers did well out of import substitution policies which, though primarily aimed at reducing a balance-of-payments deficit, included price maintenance and credit facilities that enabled them to take full advantage of Green Revolution technical improvements.[44]

During the 1970s the government embarked on ambitious schemes for subsidizing and rationing basic foods. To distribute rice to the special ration shops entailed setting up an effective system of government procurement, with some benefit to farmers. At the height of the scheme about 50 per cent of all rice consumed was being distributed through the ration shops, and about 20 per cent of all caloric consumption and 14 per cent of all income was from the rations. It was costing from 15 to 24 per cent of the budget, and no doubt benefiting many who did not need it as well as most who did; but it resulted in there being very little malnutrition, and the infant mortality rate fell to 44, the lowest in any low-income country.

After 1979 there was something of a retreat to a means-tested coupon scheme, and the cost to public funds fell to around 11–14 per cent of the budget. Farmers benefited once more from a shift to full-cost producer pricing. After 1981 there was evidence of some deterioration in nutrition as inflation eroded the value of the coupons. Nevertheless, even this less ambitious scheme still covered the poorer half of the population both urban and rural, while 30 per cent of all rice consumed was distributed through the ration shops.[45] Accordingly, while economic growth proceeded at a modest average annual rate of 2.4 per cent between 1960 and 1980, it seems clear that there has been considerable redistribution and much improvement in the conditions of the poor. And this has been achieved in the only low-income country apart from India with a multi-party electoral political system.

South Korea

However, the most striking cases of redistribution with growth have been South Korea and Taiwan. In both countries these developments occurred after a period of severe dislocation following the end of Japanese colonial rule in 1945.

In Korea that was again followed by a devastating war from 1950 to 1953 and the partition of the country, leaving more than a million dead and millions homeless. The country was laid waste, its society disrupted, and with much property destroyed many social distinctions were obliterated. In such a situation drastic measures were necessary, and under strong pressure from the United States the opportunity was taken for a thorough-going land reform. According to Irma Adelman, Korea had been a land of rack-rented peasants paying 50–90 per cent of the value of their crop to absentee landlords; it quickly became a country of very small owner-operated farms, few of which reached the statutory limit of one hectare of paddy. As in Sri Lanka, these smallholders did well out of import substitution policies. At the same time, there was little inequality of wealth in industry either; most of it had been owned by the Japanese, and the few private South Korean fortunes were soon eroded by the loss to the North of the major coal deposits, heavy industry, and electricity generating capacity.[46]

Between 1953 and 1963 the government pursued a policy of import substitution industrialization. This achieved some success, but by 1958 the limits of import substitution were being approached, and the developments it indicated were highly capital-intensive. Though literacy rose from 30 to 80 per cent, graduate unemployment also soared to 50 per cent, there was unrest among students, and the economy was plagued by inflation and corruption.

In 1964, rather than pressing on with import substitution, the government decided on a different strategy, characterized in economists' jargon as that of export expansion in labour-intensive consumer non-durables. That strategy was chosen primarily to promote economic growth; its consequences for distribution, though not unwelcome, were not foreseen. Through its control of the banks, the government forced the private sector to comply with its plans for rapid labour- and skill-intensive growth with a heavy emphasis on incentives. Interest rates went sky-high to 30 per cent, representing real rates of 20 per cent after allowing for inflation at around 10 per cent; and although such extremely high rates did not make existing industry any less capital-intensive, they strongly disposed employers to look for labour-intensive ways of doing things without costly capital investment, while they also stimulated savings and made greater domestic resources available for investment in new developments. At the same time the currency was devalued by 50 per cent to promote exports and diminish imports, and inflation was successfully countered. The results were phenomenally rapid increases in both exports and GNP. Between 1964 and 1970, employment in the urban-industrial sector rose by 1.6 million, while unemployment fell from 7.7 to 4.5 per cent, and nearly half the increase in employment was in production for export. The real incomes of the poorest 20 per cent of the population doubled, agricultural wages also doubled, and real wages rose by 85 per cent during the same period, a rise in which trade union activity played no part. It would be wrong to call this a period of redistribution with growth; as has been seen, the great levelling of South Korean society took place before 1964. What is significant is that between 1964 and 1970 the poor fully shared in the general prosperity, the real incomes of the bottom 40 per cent of the

103

Economic conditions

population increasing at the same average rate of 9 per cent annually as the GNP per capita of the country as a whole.[47]

Taiwan

The island of Taiwan has had many vicissitudes. Originally a province of the Chinese empire, and known to the outside world by its Portuguese name of Formosa, it was under Japanese colonial rule from 1895 to 1945. In 1949 the Kuomintang government of China retreated there when Beijing (Peking) fell to the communist forces, and the island became known for a time as the Republic of China. More recently its formal international status has become somewhat obscure and contentious; but for purposes of economic analysis it can be regarded as a country with its own economy about which statistical data are available.

According to Gustav Ranis, the Japanese left behind a strong agricultural infra-structure, and as in Sri Lanka and South Korea farmers did well out of import substitution policies in the 1950s. At that time too there was an influx of people with skills and capital from the mainland. Foreign earnings were invested in capital goods, and the general policy was aimed at self-reliance. After 1960, that gave way to one of export-oriented growth. Import quotas were replaced by tariffs. Inflation was checked and the currency devalued, while as in South Korea interest rates were raised and there was land reform. The growth rate, already 'respectable' at 7 per cent, rose further to 10 per cent. The productivity of labour on the land increased while people left the land for jobs in an expanding labour-intensive urban-industrial sector. As a result an unusually low differential prevailed between agricultural and industrial incomes, with the latter only about 15 per cent above the former. As Ranis put it, the upward pull on wages of such forces as multi-national corporations and trade union pressures was apparently much weaker in Taiwan than in other less-developed countries. The rapid shift from agriculture to industry did not make the overall distribution of income more unequal, therefore. Both agriculture and industry were very labour-intensive; moreover, the ownership of both land and industrial assets was widely distributed from the first. Wages lagged behind productivity, but rewards to ownership and enterprise were widely dispersed, so that income distribution was not much affected; and there was ample social mobility. And United States aid helped, especially when the crucial decisions were being made around 1960 to move away from a protective import substitution industrialization policy to a liberalization of imports and an export-promoting industrial development.[48]

Such was the extent of redistribution with growth that between 1953 and 1961, when the economy as a whole was growing at 7 per cent annually, the incomes of the poorest 40 per cent grew at 12 per cent.[49]

104

As already noted, in 1971 the share of the top 10 per cent was not much more than in Yugoslavia or the most egalitarian western European countries; and the infant mortality rate in the late 1970s was 25.

SUGGESTIONS FOR FURTHER READING

World Bank, *World Development Reports* (annual)

Everett E. Hagen, *The Economics of Development*, Homewood, Ill.: Richard D. Irwin, 1975

Margaret Hardiman and James Midgley, *The Social Dimensions of Development*, Chichester and New York: Wiley, 1982

Hollis Chenery et al., *Redistribution with Growth*, Oxford: Oxford University Press, 1974

5 Environmental constraints

But is it possible? It is a much controverted issue whether the economic development of poor countries, and particularly their industrialization, can be carried to a level approaching that of rich countries without the world as a whole running into environmental constraints.

Thus Paul and Anne Ehrlich wrote in 1970 that most of the under-developed countries would never, 'under any conceivable circumstances, be "developed" in the sense in which the United States is today. They could quite accurately be called the "never-to-be-developed countries"'. The earth was overpopulated already, as the limits of food production by conventional means had very nearly been reached. Indeed, 'world agri-cuture today is an ecological disaster area'. It was already leading to loss of soil fertility and erosion, and was vulnerable to even minor natural disturbances. As for other resources, the annual production of such materials as iron, copper, and lead would have to be increased six- to eight-fold if the world's population used them at United States rates. However, to bring the present world population up to United States standards of equipment – railways, automobiles, electric wiring, structural steel, etc. – would require the extraction and smelting of far greater quantities at far higher rates, ranging from 75 times as much for iron to 250 times as much for tin. Even if that were possible, the energy consumed might endanger the heat balance of the earth, with possibly disastrous effects on climate. The partial industrialization of the earth had already caused intolerable pollution of air and water; 'our environment cannot stand "world industrialization"'. Accordingly Ehrlich and Harriman did not hesitate to describe the industrial nations as 'over-developed' and call for their 'de-development'. The underdeveloped countries should at the same time be 'semi-developed', that is, their standard of living should be improved, but not to the extent of raising their GNP per head to contemporary United States levels.[1]

Such views were not unanimously endorsed by other scientists, and some were strongly controverted. They were criticized by John Maddox as exaggerated and alarmist, lacking in historical perspective and innocent of economic understanding. Maddox also pointed to the danger that statements by citizens of affluent industrial countries that others could never hope to enjoy a similar affluence, though made in all good faith by scientists of integrity primarily in criticism of trends in their own society, were likely to be misunderstood and misrepresented. They risked alienating people in countries 'not yet rich enough to aspire to the kind of freedom from pollution on which the more prosperous nations have set their sights'. Suspicion that conservationist arguments might be a means to thwart the industrialization of poor countries seems to have contributed to the difficulty in finding a common platform for the international conference on the human environment at Stockholm in 1972.[2]

In the same vein, in 1972 the first report by Donella and Dennis Meadows and others to the Club of Rome (an unofficial group inspired by the Italian industrialist Aurelio Peccei), using computer models, foresaw that resource exhaustion and pollution would set limits to growth.[3] An earlier computer model 'World 2' by Jay Forrester had indicated down-turn and collapse soon after AD 2000 when increasing resource costs would inhibit growth and lowering standards cause population to decline. With more real-life data the Meadows' model 'World 3' indicated a sharp rise in pollution precipitating catastrophe, and drastic assumptions or remedies had to be fed in to ensure stable population and living standards without undue resource depletion.

There were many criticisms of these models, both detailed and general. Thus Boyle traced the crisis in World 3 to a transcription error multiplying pollution by ten. When that was corrected, re-runs indicated far less disastrous consequences, and the model was more amenable to policy changes such as the discouragement of capital-intensive agriculture before soil deterioration became serious.[4] Similarly, scientists at Sussex University pointed to misplaced aggregation and over-simplification in the model; for example, industrial output was related to only one factor of production, capital, with a constant capital–output ratio of three. No allowance was made for adaptations such as investment in pollution-reducing technology, which in the real world would lead to a higher capital–output ratio, less pollution, and slower growth. It was a fundamental criticism of all such models and predictions that they disregarded human ingenuity and adaptability, which was evident in the real world in response to price changes which in turn signalled changes in the relative scarcity of resources.[5]

Such criticisms did not go unheeded. Apocalyptic visions of overshoot and collapse gave place in later contributions to more complex and realistic discussions which, however, did not lose sight of the main issue. Thus the second report to the Club of Rome dis-aggregated global data into ten regions and projected different possible trends in such variables as the price of oil.[6] A later report by Dennis Gabor and others constituted an explicit reply to the criticism that the Meadows did not consider how far techno-

107

logical development might solve problems of resource scarcity and prevent, or at least delay, mankind's approach to the material limits. It looked in much finer detail at the resources available for the production of energy, food, and materials, and I quote from it below.[7]

At the same time, economists have recognized the importance of these issues. For example, Everett Hagen stated unequivocally in the 1968 edition of his standard work on the economics of development that 'there is no technical or economic reason why growth should not continue indefinitely'. In the 1975 edition, however, he added a new chapter on the questions of minerals supply, energy, and pollution, including a discussion of the Meadows' model and its critics, and substantially re-cast another to deal with the issue of the world food supply as a possible limit to growth.[8]

It is common ground in this debate that, at the very least, population growth makes the raising of standards of living more difficult, and checking human fertility is an important condition for such improvement. Controversies surround four inter-related issues, which may be summarily called those of pollution, food, non-renewable resources, and energy.

Pollution

People in the industrial nations have vastly increased their output both of agricultural and industrial products over the last two hundred years, but only, it is suggested, by the use of methods which have already caused unacceptable levels of pollution of the air and water. Were these methods to be extended and become general in the poor countries too, the self-righting mechanisms of the natural world and its various cycles might be seriously or even irreversibly impaired. For example, the extensive burning of fossil fuels in the typical processes of the industrial economy – heat engines, metal smelting, etc. – has given rise to anxiety both on account of the carbon dioxide which is released into the atmosphere and the heat which is generated. The burning of fossil fuels certainly increases the heat energy in the earth's atmosphere, over and above the amount currently received and absorbed from the sun, and this suggested that there might be a change in the heat balance with possibly long-term effects upon climate. Changes in average temperatures since the start of the industrial revolution, however, have been small and erratic, and do not suggest any serious interference with the earth's energy balance. Moreover, the amounts of energy released by the combustion of fossil fuels are minute compared with those received from the sun – something of the order of 1 to 20,000. However, local effects may be more serious, and there are anxieties about such questions as the heating of rivers from the discharge of cooling-water from factories and power stations. As to carbon dioxide, the fear is that this also might lead to a world-wide rise in temperature since this gas has

108

a strong tendency to absorb radiation at the wavelengths at which it is mostly emitted from the earth. More carbon dioxide in the atmosphere would mean that more of this radiation was trapped, and give rise to what has been called a 'greenhouse effect'. However, though it is said that the carbon dioxide level in the atmosphere has definitely increased, as has been stated there is no clear evidence of any particular trend in temperature. Some authorities have speculated that the 'greenhouse effect' may be being offset by the increased screening of the earth by dust and smoke, partly from industry, partly from the increased extent of agricultural burning in the tropics, and partly also from volcanic eruption. In any event, the higher levels of carbon dioxide may not persist for long. For one thing, the oceans, which contain sixty times as much carbon dioxide as the atmosphere does, will begin to absorb the excess as the mixing of the intermediate and deeper levels of water proceeds. For another, the increased atmospheric content of carbon dioxide will stimulate a more rapid growth of plants – a phenomenon that has been utilized in greenhouses.[9]

Such considerations emphasize the extent to which the human use of combustion in industrial and other processes depends on the activities of green plants to restore the oxygen–carbon dioxide balance. Oxygen, in fact, only occurs in the atmosphere at all because living organisms keep putting it there; it is a highly reactive element and unless continually renewed would soon combine with other elements and be lost to the atmosphere. The dependence of an industrial society on the organic oxygen cycle is highlighted by a calculation which suggests that in the land area of the forty-eight coterminous states of the USA, the amount of oxygen produced by photosynthesis in plant life amounts to only 60 per cent of the amount used in the combustion of fossil fuels. The balance is made up by a net 'import' of oxygen by atmospheric circulation from outside the boundaries of the USA, mostly it is thought from the marine diatoms in the Pacific (and it is now estimated that about 70 per cent of the earth's annual supply of oxygen comes from the oceans). While the availability of oxygen for industrial combustion may not be an immediate limitation to the industrial development of other countries – indeed, the world seems more likely to run out of fossil fuels before it runs out of atmospheric oxygen to burn them – it does point to the dependence on a cycle which could be impaired by the pollution of the oceans. If what has happened to Lake Erie and some other bodies of enclosed water were to happen to the Pacific Ocean – if, for example, DDT pollution were to increase, or if large quantities of defoliants were to be released into the oceans – then, it is suggested, we would start running out of oxygen.[10]

However, some other authorities have dismissed such fears as exaggerated. The scale of human industrial activity and its pollution of the atmosphere remain puny compared with natural hazards. Indeed, the

109

Ehrlichs conceded as much when they referred to the effects of major volcanic eruptions like those of Sumbawa in 1815 and Krakatoa in 1883 which resulted in the pollution of the atmosphere by vast quantities of ash with climatic effects which were felt all over the world. In 1816 there was 'no summer at all' in the northern United States, and in Britain the lowest summer temperatures ever recorded were in that year and in others following similar eruptions.[11] In contrast, the climatic effects of human industry are so small as to be hardly detectable with available measurements.

A class of substances about which there is controversy is that of the nitrogenous fertilizers. The fixation of atmospheric nitrogen is an essential part of the life-cycle, and it occurs naturally, to some extent in lightning flashes, to a much greater extent through the nitrogen-fixing bacteria in the root nodules of leguminous plants including peas, beans, clover, and soya beans. In addition, nitrogenous fertilizers are produced industrially by means of the Haber-Bosch process in which ammonia is synthesized by combining atmospheric nitrogen with hydrogen, mainly from natural gas, at high temperatures and pressures. The increased yields of food crops made possible by industrial fertilizers are so great that it has been estimated that 30 per cent of the world's population now depend on them for their food supply, and it is not surprising that some authorities have regarded their increased production and use in Third World countries as a hopeful development. Thus in 1971 the FAO reported with satisfaction the prospects for increased production of fertilizers in Africa,[12] and Lipton had 'no doubt that enormous expansion of fertilizer use would pay many of the farmers of the Third World'.[13] Above all, the Green Revolution (which I discuss below) involves the lavish use of fertilizers and pesticides.

In some industrial countries, however, where farmers have used these substances on a large scale, they have drained into lakes and rivers and there stimulated plant growth, notably that of certain algae. That unwonted and excessive growth has been followed by the rapid decay of plant material, which had used up the oxygen dissolved in the water, so the fish have died. Another environmental hazard has been the pollution of drinking water, with the long-term accumulation of nitrates in ground water.[14] For reasons of this kind, ecologists have expressed serious reservations about synthetic fertilizers, at just the time when hopes for agricultural improvement in poor countries have been pinned on their use.

At the same time, other objections have been voiced. According to Postgate, the Haber process is highly capital- and energy-intensive and depends on the availability of natural gas. The use of synthetic fertilizers, especially in poor countries, entails production and distribution costs and tends to increase dependence on industrial countries' manufacturing capacity. The biological process in which nitrogenase (the naturally

110

occurring bacterial enzyme) fixes atmospheric nitrogen is about three times as efficient as the Haber process, uses only solar energy, and is of course completely non-polluting. From a Third World point of view there seem strong reasons for reversing the current trend and reverting to biological nitrogen-fixing, by methods that could no doubt be improved with further research. Besides those already mentioned, other useful plants associated with nitrogen-fixing micro-organisms include lupins, used in some places as cattle fodder. Paspalum, a grass much recommended in the tropics to combat soil erosion, also makes a limited but definite contribution to nitrogen fixation; while one of the most efficient plants of all for this purpose is azolla, a water fern grown in south-east Asia on flooded rice fields between crops.[15]

Equally controversial has been the use of chlorinated hydrocarbons like DDT as insecticides. Following the publication of Rachel Carson's *Silent Spring* in 1962, these substances came under suspicion on the ground that, unlike organic insecticides such as pyrethrum, they were relatively stable and persistent, and tended to be accumulated up the food chain from crops treated with DDT through herbivores till they reached toxic proportions in higher predators such as the birds of prey. Likewise they could be accumulated in the human body, with unknown but possibly harmful effects. Environmentalists accordingly campaigned for their use to be put down by law.

That campaign ran counter to the policies of the FAO and the World Health Organization, which regarded DDT as still essential both for malaria control and as an agricultural pesticide. It was acknowledged that chlorinated hydrocarbons had been misused, wild life had been harmed, and high levels of residues had been found both in humans and other animals. But alternatives were costlier and less effective, and an experimental decision to outlaw DDT in Sri Lanka had resulted in a renewed outbreak of malaria there. In the circumstances, the continued use of DDT had to be approved, though it should be kept to the absolute minimum, and used in conjunction with other methods in integrated systems of pest control.[16]

In the ensuing controversy, distinguished scientists who defended DDT included Thomas Jukes, professor of medical physics at Berkeley. As a result of its use, 960 million people who had been subject to endemic malaria were free of it, and another 288 million lived in areas where it was being vigorously attacked. That aspect of the matter had not been publicized, he suggested, because most ecologists were healthy, well-to-do whites.[17] Even more outspoken was Dr Norman Borlaug, one of the authors of the Green Revolution. He considered that its continued success depended on farmers being allowed to go on using agricultural chemicals. 'If agriculture is denied their use because of unwise legislation that is now being promoted

111

by a powerful group of hysterical lobbyists who are provoking fear by predicting doom for the world through chemical poisoning, then the world will be doomed not by chemical poisoning but from starvation...No chemical has done as much as DDT to improve the health, economic and social benefits of the people of the developing nations.'[18] A more cautious view was that of A. H. Bunting, professor of agricultural botany at Reading. He thought that fears of the 'death of the oceans' had been greatly exaggerated, and that urban and industrial effluents were far more important than agricultural chemicals in their likely effects on biological processes in the sea. Nevertheless, 'insecticides should be used with greater care and precision'; and he added that 'The current successes with ultra-low volume spraying may permit welcome economies in dosage.'[19]

More recent researches and controversies have drawn attention to the danger that, perversely and paradoxically, the over-use of DDT as an agricultural pesticide may have contributed to a resurgence of malaria by creating conditions favourable to the emergence of insecticide-resistant strains of the *Anopheles* mosquito. The authors of one such study even estimated that each kilogram of DDT results in 105 more cases of malaria. That calculation was greeted with considerable scepticism by other scientists working in the field of tropical medicine and malaria control. In the ensuing controversy, however, it was conceded that the over-heavy use of residual insecticides such as DDT had led to the development of resistant strains, and there was a further reiteration of the wisdom of the policies of the FAO and WHO in favour of integrated pest control and management. One authority wrote that 'Sri Lanka has very wisely banned the use of DDT and malathion in agriculture and reserved them for the anti-malaria campaign, but still has a hard struggle to contain and reverse its resurgent malaria problem.'[20]

It may be further argued that, precisely because the dangers of pollution have been so intensively publicized in recent years, it is highly likely that appropriate remedial action will be taken. It may take time before new forms of pollution are recognized, and harm may be done meanwhile. The abatement of pollution always involves costs, which may fall on the individual industrial enterprise, farmer, or householder, or may be borne by the taxpaying public through a subsidy from public funds. But anti-pollution laws in industrial countries have had their successes. In this movement the 1956 Clean Air Act in Britain may be regarded as a pioneering instance which has succeeded in very greatly reducing air pollution by smoke. In Britain, too, considerable progress has been made in reducing the pollution of rivers, and fish including salmon have returned to the London reaches of the Thames after a century's absence. At the time of writing, the use of tetra-ethyl lead as an automobile fuel additive has come under strong suspicion, and as a result of a current campaign it seems

112

likely that it will be much reduced if not abandoned altogether. The problem is no doubt part legislative, part technical in the design of automobile engines to run smoothly and economically with lead-free fuel. A combination of public laws with the adoption of appropriate technology to abate pollution as and when its harmful effects are recognized seems more likely than not to be a continuing trend, and the pollution of the environment may well cease to be regarded as an inevitable concomitant of industrial development and scientific agriculture.

Food

Since the Reverend Thomas Malthus published his *Essay on Population* in 1797, there have been recurrent fears that world population was about to outstrip food supply. Such Malthusian fears were strongly voiced in the early 1950s, and again in the early and mid-1970s. Again and again the spectre hovers, then recedes. By 1980 the problem was not that of a world food shortage. Over the previous 20 years, world food production, particularly that of the food grains, had increased faster than population. The same was true of the developing countries taken as a whole. World grain prices rose sharply in the crisis years of 1972–74, but then fell again, and their general trend from 1966 to 1980 was markedly downwards. Some serious problems emerged, however. Production and consumption of food per capita fell in some poor countries, especially in Africa. And according to the World Bank,

While there is no evidence that outright starvation has become more pervasive, nonetheless the number of malnourished people has probably increased and the position of particular groups and certain areas may have deteriorated seriously. Most of the undernourished live in the countryside...In both low- and middle-income countries, the poorest urban and rural groups are chronically undernourished. The worst affected are those living in rural areas where agricultural production fluctuates widely. Children and pregnant or nursing mothers bear the brunt when food is short. Seasonal variations (less food in the months immediately preceding harvests) and crop failures (because of weather and pests) are the main supply-related causes of actual starvation. In many low-income countries, these conditions are an ever-present threat to life. Yet the most common cause of undernutrition is a demand, not a supply, factor – a straightforward lack of purchasing power.[21]

Changes in the world food situation since the 1930s, and especially between 1970 and 1980, are brought out in the figures for the international trade in cereals in table 5.1. In 1934–38 western Europe imported food from all other regions. Since then, and especially since 1970, the pursuit of self-sufficiency through the common agricultural policy of the EEC has reduced though not eliminated western Europe's grain imports. Meanwhile, most other regions became importers from the United States, Canada, Australia, and New Zealand, though as late as 1970 the Soviet Union was

113

just about self-sufficient. Events during the 1970s profoundly changed the whole situation, and highlighted the apparent ability of the North American prairie farmer to feed the world, with a little help from his Australian and New Zealand counterparts. A momentous decision – arguably one of the most important in recent history – was made by the Soviet Union in 1972, when rather than slaughter livestock to meet the shortage of grain caused by a bad harvest they resolved to import grain, mainly from the United States, in unprecedented quantities.[22] Grain prices doubled or trebled between 1972 and 1974 accordingly, and their rise coincided with equally drastic rises in the price of oil as a result of concerted action by OPEC countries. That double shock had serious enough consequences in the industrial market economies; in some Third World countries the effects were even more serious. In 1973–74 there was a poor monsoon in south Asia and an exceptional drought resulting in famine in the Sahel and the Horn of Africa. According to the World Bank, 'Bangladesh suffered severe shortages and malnutrition in 1973–75, when its own food production was poor, the international market was tight, and it had to find extra foreign exchange to pay for more expensive oil.' But food aid dropped in response to the general shortage, at just the time when some of the poorest countries needed it most.

Serious though the crisis of 1972–74 was, however, it did not prove to be the harbinger of general disaster, and it did not affect all countries, nor even all poor countries, to the same extent. India in particular came through remarkably well, thanks largely to the Green Revolution. The generally rising trend of food-grain production there was barely halted in 1972–74, and that crisis was met almost entirely by drawing on stocks. Later in the 1970s stocks were built up to higher levels than ever before, and proved enough to meet a severe drought in 1979 which set back production by 17 per cent with nothing like the hardship inflicted by comparable droughts in the past, such as that in 1966. Though once the chief recipient of United States food aid, India virtually ended food-grain imports in the 1970s. Substantial amounts of foreign exchange were thereby saved, helping to pay for more expensive oil without curbing other imports.[23]

Although human beings do not live on grains alone, there is another reason for regarding them as central to a discussion of the world food situation. In poor countries, most of the grain produced is eaten by people. In rich countries, much of it is fed to livestock and converted, very inefficiently, into products such as meat and milk. Thus according to Gabor *et al*, in Canada just over 10 per cent is consumed directly; in India, by contrast, direct consumption amounts to 83 per cent.[24] Furthermore, the more privileged classes in poor countries emulate their counterparts in affluent countries by increasing their demands for animal protein. This is

Table 5.1   *World grain trade: net imports and exports, by regions, in millions of metric tons*

	1934–38		1970		1980	
	Imports	Exports	Imports	Exports	Imports	Exports
North America (USA and Canada)		5		56		131
Latin America		9		4	10	
Western Europe	24		30		16	
USSR and Eastern Europe		5	0	0	46	
Africa		1	5		15	
Asia		2	37		63	
Australia and New Zealand		3		12		19

Source: Lester R. Brown, 'World food resources and population: the narrowing margin', *Population Bulletin*, vol. 36, no. 3 (September 1981).

why, according to the World Bank, middle-income countries have stepped up their grain imports and become the world's largest market for cereal exports. 'Their growing need for imports has resulted primarily from the increasing affluence of urban dwellers...In addition, livestock production has become more important, so that over a third of total cereal consumption (and well over half of total imports) have been used to feed animals rather than going directly to people.'[25] Such considerations explain why the EEC piles up surpluses of animal products ('butter mountains') while importing grain; it imports the latter to produce the former. And they focus attention again on that momentous decision in Moscow in 1972. Clearly, it seems, it was not to save the Soviet people from imminent starvation that the Politburo decided to import grain, but to safeguard the supplies of milk and meat to which they had become accustomed. It may further be suggested that if there were ever to be a general Malthusian world food shortage, a major contribution to survival would be for the inhabitants of rich countries, and the well-to-do in all countries, to eat less meat. As noted in the last chapter, more unrefined vegetable fibre would be good for us. In part, such a change could be accomplished by reverting to patterns of the fairly recent past – less beef, more carrots? – while in part it may be happening already, almost imperceptibly, in response to market pressures, with the development of foods which look and taste like meat but are actually made with vegetable protein from soya beans or other plants.

Meanwhile, if the world food problem is to be seen less in terms of a danger of global shortage than of national and local problems, that is

115

largely because of a number of developments which have collectively been called the Green Revolution.

This began in 1943, when the Rockefeller Foundation entered into a collaborative programme for agricultural research and development with the government of Mexico. The improved strains of wheat developed at the institute then set up under Dr Norman Borlaug raised the country's food production by 7 per cent annually during the next 20 years, while population grew by 3 per cent a year, and Mexico was turned from a wheat-importing to a wheat-exporting country. During the 1950s a similar partnership between United States foundations (Rockefeller and Ford) and the government of India embarked on a similar project with similar results. In 1960 an International Rice Research Institute was set up in the Philippines. It developed a whole series of improved rice strains including the famous IR8 and a further improved successor IR24, which by 1970 had turned the Philippines from a rice-importing country to one with a surplus for export. Later in the 1960s the foundations' work in Mexico was extended to maize as well as wheat, while institutes of tropical agriculture were set up in Colombia and Nigeria.[26] The main effects of these developments were felt from the mid-1960s onwards.

Plant breeding to produce high yielding or high response varieties (HYV, HRV), however, is only one aspect of the Green Revolution. The new seeds have to be cultivated in the right way if their potential yield is to be realized. They form as it were only part of a total package, of which the other components often include irrigation, sometimes machinery, and usually the plentiful use of fertilizers and pesticides – an aspect I have touched on above.

Has the Green Revolution been a triumph or a disaster? Opinions differ sharply. Those in favour include most natural scientists, some economists, and authorities such as the World Bank; those against, other economists along with political scientists and sociologists, especially of a radical persuasion.

Some of the reasons for a favourable view are obvious: higher yields; increased production of food at rates faster than population growth; famines averted; food plentiful and cheap where it was, or was expected to become, scarce and expensive; countries that used to depend on imported food becoming self-sufficient, like India, or becoming food exporters, like Mexico and the Philippines. Furthermore, the Green Revolution has made modern scientific agricultural practices reliably profitable, and furthered the general development of roads, transport, distribution services, and the like to deliver the inputs to the farmer at the right time and the right price. And in some areas, notably the Punjab, profits from the new agriculture have provided the capital for remarkable developments in village industrialization.

Radical criticisms have something to do with the environmental misgivings noted above, but are directed much more at the effects of the Green Revolution on the rural class structure. It is the well-to-do farmers and landowners who benefit, since they can afford the new inputs of improved seeds, fertilizers, and pesticides, and in some cases irrigation and new machinery. Moreover, in their efforts to put together land holdings of an economical size to make the new methods pay, they may dispossess share-cropping tenants and subsistence peasants who used to give a hand at harvest and other peak periods, but whose services are no longer required. Thus according to Erich Jacoby, in central Luzon in the Philippines the new strains of rice made possible a more than 100 per cent increase in yield for only 50 per cent extra labour. The labour input per ton of rice was therefore one-third lower than before. Rising productivity of labour in this case made for rising unemployment, since there was no great increase in demand for rice on the home market, while the export market too was glutted with other south-east Asian countries also producing more rice. The new technology put a premium on effective management, exact calculation, market-oriented production, a reliable labour force, and modern machinery. It was incompatible with traditional forms of tenancy, share-cropping, and seasonal work, so that a lot of people lost their livelihoods, and the general result was the enhancement (or as Jacoby called it the deterioration) of social inequality.[27] It was these effects which led a political scientist from a Green Revolution country to comment sardonically on the award to Dr Borlaug of the Nobel *Peace* prize (rather than a science prize) when his discoveries had created class conflict and a potentially revolutionary situation. What is the good, radical critics ask, of plentiful cheap food when people who used to grow it themselves are now malnourished because they cannot afford to buy it?

Non-renewable resources

Apart from fossil fuels, with which I deal below, 'non-renewable resources' are materials such as metals of which only a finite stock exists in the earth, as distinct from renewable resources like those derived from agriculture. As already noted, conservationists like the Ehrlichs consider that for United States patterns of consumption to become general throughout the world, impossible demands would be made for iron, copper, and the like. Some of the early computer models of the Club of Rome likewise foresaw materials shortages as imposing limits to growth.

However, the apparently simple question of how much there is of a material turns out in practice to be difficult and complex. 'Reserves', economically recoverable with existing technology, are to be distinguished from 'resources' known to exist and possibly recoverable under more favourable technical or economic conditions. The degree of certainty of our knowledge varies, so that reserves or resources may have been measured, or their existence may be known but not how much, or it may be inferred with various degrees of probability.[28] No doubt with good reason, the estimates of mineral reserves by official bodies such as the US Geological Survey err on the side of caution; and the use of estimates of that kind as if they were definite limits in the early Club of Rome studies was one of the grounds on which they were later criticized.[29]

Moreover, although there is only a finite amount of the substances in question in the earth's crust, they are not lost by being mined and put into human use. They may be discarded, but can if necessary be recovered and re-used. That is, after all, the business of the scrap metal trade, and it is again a matter of price.

What, indeed, do we mean exactly when we say that we shall one day 'run out of' a particular resource? The process is likely to be gradual, not abrupt, as the more accessible deposits are worked out and mining enterprises incur higher costs as they work less accessible ones. As the price rises, presumably at some point recycled supplies compete with newly mined. Perhaps we shall know when we have 'run out of' minerals when city refuse tips are quarried and used as low-grade ores.

Such considerations have, it seems, led to a somewhat less pessimistic view of this aspect of world development. However, greater use of minerals entails more energy consumption, especially with a shift to lower-grade resources, and greater disturbance of the earth's crust. We may well conclude with Gabor *et al* that 'recycling, waste prevention, increased efficiency in utilization, conservative use and substitution of abundant for scarce materials are the principal means of exter-ling supplies'.

Energy

All the energy available for human use is derived ultimately, after the lapse of a longer or shorter time, from the sun. Some solar energy is used by humans instantaneously, as when we lie on a beach and gratefully absorb its warmth. Solar energy which powers atmospheric depressions, and of which we may use a tiny proportion to drive sailing ships or windmills, is used within a few hours or days. Energy from atmospheric circulation may also be used after a slightly longer time when rain falls on high ground and runs back through water mills or hydro-electric power stations. Here the time-lapse depends on the capacity of the lake or dam in which the potential energy is stored. This may range from a few days in the case of a simple water mill powered by a river or stream to a few years in the case of a large modern dam, or even as much as a century when the largest lakes are used. For example, the arrangements for controlling Lake Victoria

118

envisage 'century storage', averaging out the controlled outflow of the lake with the vagaries of the rainfall over that kind of period. Much of the energy which we use ourselves in our own muscles is derived from the sun after a time-lapse of the order of a year, assuming the growth of annual crops like the food grains; some over a small number of years, as we eat meat or fish that has been growing and feeding on plants for periods of that order. The same is true, of course, of the energy of domestic animals like the horse which are put to human use. When people burn firewood they are using solar energy after a period represented by the age of the tree when it was pruned or felled, a period normally of less than a century.

In pre-industrial technologies, the time-lapse between the arrival of solar energy at the earth and its human use is (or was) characteristically rather short. Most work was done by human and animal muscles, and the predominant fuel was wood. Thus the energy cycle involved the possibility of regeneration or recycling over a comparatively short period. Given wise husbandry and a population not so dense as to press upon resources, land used for growing food and fodder crops, or for pasture, could be used again another year. Likewise the forest cropped for firewood could regenerate within years or decades; indeed, a balance could be struck between the annual growth of a given area of forest and the off-take of timber for firewood, building, furniture, and other uses. Not of course that a balanced cycle of this kind has been universal or even particularly characteristic of pre-industrial economies. On the contrary, we know only too well that 'primitive' technologies too have ruined forests and caused soil erosion, and that the impairment of vital cycles is not something for which industrial technologies alone are responsible. The history of Britain, for instance, is the history of continuous deforestation from the Bronze Age to the present day, though it is fair to add that the inroads made into the indigenous forest in these islands by the comparatively sparse population of pre-industrial times were far outdone by the havoc wrought by a few decades of charcoal-burning for iron smelting in the early industrial period.[30]

With the rise of industrial technology, a new dimension has been added in the use of solar energy after very much longer time-lapses, to be measured in millions of years. That extra dimension is, of course, the use of fossil fuels. As has been seen in chapter 2, it was the use of these sources of energy that gave the decisive impetus to the industrial revolution in history. Moreover, it has been made clear in chapter 4 that the most striking difference between the real resources available to the people of the rich and poor countries respectively lies in the vastly larger quantities of energy available to the former.

Yet the fossil fuels are a non-renewable resource, or indeed one should rather say *the* non-renewable resource. The solar energy that is used when we burn coal and oil is derived from that which fell on the earth millions of years ago. In the case of metals I argued that they were not lost, and could be recovered. In the case of coal and oil the same is true in a sense – the carbon dioxide which results from their combustion will be absorbed by plants, a proportion of which may conceivably rot down into peat beds which will form the coal seams of the future. But this can occur only after a lapse of millions of years, and certainly not within the kind of time-span that is of any relevance to human life over the next few decades or centuries, with which we are concerned. As Cipolla has put it:

One can summarize the story of our happy generations in the following way. For millions of years wealth was stored and cumulated. Then, someone in the family discovered the hoard – and started to dissipate it. We are now living through this fabulous dissipation. Humanity today is consuming more coal in a single year than was generated in a hundred centuries or so during the process of carbonization.[31]

Coal was the first fossil fuel to be exploited on a large scale. The industrial revolution was built on coal, which long provided most of the energy used in industrial countries, and its share in world energy production did not fall below a half until the late 1950s. After 1950 it was eclipsed by oil, which by 1980 provided nearly half of the total world energy supply. However, world coal reserves far exceed those of petroleum, so that a revival of coal as a primary energy resource is a distinct possibility. India and China are already major producers, but many other Third World countries lack both coal and oil.

The current domination of the world energy scene by oil divides Third World countries sharply between oil exporters and oil importers. It has put the high-income oil exporters into a class of their own, while as has been seen in chapter 4 other oil exporters such as Nigeria and Indonesia have also done well by borrowing on the strength of their oil revenues to further their general development. In contrast, according to the World Bank, in some countries including Brazil, Turkey, and India, oil imports in 1980 absorbed over 50 per cent of export earnings,[32] while Bangladesh was in dire straits in the 1970s to pay for both oil and food.

Nevertheless, although astonishing discoveries are still made – for example, who would have thought in 1950 that by 1980 Britain and Norway would be major oil producers? – no one questions that fossil fuels are finite and non-renewable resources. If greatly increased energy use is to be possible over a long term as the people of the poorer countries improve their standard of living, it is timely to look for other sources. The current possibilities seem to be two-fold. One is a much greater use of nuclear energy; the other is to increase the proportion of solar energy currently falling on the earth which is put to human use, and the efficiency with which it is used.

No subject is more controversial than nuclear energy. This is mainly

120

because its civil and military aspects are so closely related as to be hardly separable. As a matter of science and of history alike, nuclear reactors produce weapons material as well as heat that can be used to generate electricity, and this close association has no parallel in the case of any other energy source. It is controversial also because of the terrifying hazards of the substances and processes involved. The stringent security precautions necessary to ensure that they do not get into the wrong hands are yet another cause for anxiety.

Although it is no exception to the statement that all energy is ultimately derived from the sun, it is also a very special case. A nuclear reaction represents the conversion of matter into energy, and the matter in question is derived from the sun only in the same sense as the whole earth is derived from the sun. In that sense, then, it too depends on fossil fuels. The first such 'fuel' to be used was, and is, uranium-235, a rare isotope of a rare element. Natural uranium contains it in a proportion of 0.8 per cent with 'normal' uranium-238, and it is the only naturally occurring element which without exposure to extreme conditions is capable of 'fissioning' or splitting spontaneously in such a way as to make possible a chain reaction. When one of its atoms disintegrates, it emits neutrons; when an atom is hit by a neutron, it disintegrates with the emission of neutrons. In nature this does not lead to a chain reaction, partly because the neutrons fly off too fast, partly because the element is so dispersed that there is little chance of the neutrons from the disintegration of one atom hitting another. The controlled use of this chain reaction involves either concentrating uranium-235, or slowing down the neutrons by means of a moderator such as graphite or heavy water, or both. (Heavy hydrogen or deuterium is an isotope of ordinary hydrogen; heavy water occurs naturally as one part in 6,760 of ordinary water.) An uncontrolled chain reaction occurs when a certain quantity, known as the critical mass, of uranium-235 is brought together, when it disintegrates in a flash with the release of enormous amounts of energy. That was done in one of the first nuclear weapons, the one that destroyed Hiroshima in 1945. Other nuclear weapons, including that which destroyed Nagasaki, have made use of similar uncontrolled chain reactions in other fissionable substances, particularly plutonium. This does not occur in nature in any appreciable quantity, and is produced in controlled conditions in nuclear reactors.

Modern nuclear technology is exceedingly complex and can hardly be discussed without much technical detail. Over-simplifying perhaps, the method adopted in most of the countries that have embarked on a nuclear programme uses enriched uranium with a higher proportion of uranium-235 than that occurring in nature. Enrichment is generally done by diffusing the gas uranium hexafluoride through porous metal membranes, partially separating the lighter uranium-235 from uranium-238. Enormous factories are needed to carry out the process on a sufficient scale. In an alternative method devised and applied in Canada, natural uranium is used in reactors with a moderator of pure heavy water, separated from ordinary water by a long and costly process. In both methods, then, a large initial investment is required, in the one case in the fuel which is consumed, in the other in the moderator which, apart from small losses, can be used indefinitely. That investment can be thought of equally in terms of money or of energy, and the initial investment of energy in setting up a nuclear industry must of course come from non-nuclear or 'conventional' sources.

Depending on the design of the reactor and how it is operated, the spent fuel contains a mixture of substances, many of them radioactive and some fissionable in the same way as uranium-235. Notably these include plutonium. Recovering substances of some potential use is done in reprocessing plants, which like other installations in the nuclear industry are immensely large and costly. The residues of substances for which no use is at present foreseen constitute nuclear waste, whose disposal gives rise to daunting problems.

Although the spent fuel from the reactors described above may contain fissionable products, less comes out than goes in, and these have been called 'burner' reactors accordingly. The aim in 'breeder' reactors is a conversion factor of more than one, so that more fissionable materials come out than go in, and after being extracted from spent fuel in a reprocessing plant can be used as reactor fuel in their turn. For instance, by the reaction which transforms uranium-238 into plutonium-239, use can be made of 'depleted' uranium from which some of the uranium-235 has been removed to be concentrated in enriched uranium. In this way, too, commoner materials can be used, such as thorium from granite, by means of the transformation of thorium-232 into uranium-233.[33] So the nuclear industry can 'breed' or create its own fuel, and by moving away from its dependence on one extremely rare substance broaden its resource base and ensure its continuing contribution to energy supplies.[34] However, little use has as yet been made of thorium, and the breeder reactors hitherto developed depend on producing, reprocessing, and using larger and larger quantities of plutonium. Not only is this weapons material, it is also fiendishly toxic; a few micrograms probably constitute a lethal dose, yet breeder reactors use it by the ton.

Beyond the fission reactions already in use lie the possibilities of controlled fusion reactions. Where fission reactions involve a large atom splitting into smaller ones, fusion reactions occur when small atoms fuse to make bigger ones, in both cases with the emission of energy. (Uncontrolled fusion reactions, detonated by a fission reaction, are used in the more powerful nuclear weapons.) One such reaction, simple in principle, is the fusion of two atoms of heavy hydrogen or deuterium (D–D); another,

122

perhaps more workable in practice, is the fusion of heavy hydrogen with tritium, a rare isotope of hydrogen (D–T). Such reactions are hard to achieve continuously in controlled conditions since they require temperatures comparable with those of the sun and the containment of the resulting plasma in a limited volume by extremely intense magnetic fields. They offer great attractions, especially D–D as the 'fuel' is non-radioactive and abundantly available from ordinary water. In the 1950s there were high hopes that they might offer the ultimate solution to the world's energy problem, but after thirty years of research they still seem not to be technically feasible on the requisite scale, let alone economical.[35]

The advance of nuclear technology on the one hand, and steep rises in the prices of oil and coal on the other, have made nuclear energy competitive with fossil fuels as a source of electrical power. Thus the World Bank in 1980 put nuclear light water reactors on a par with conventional coal-fired power stations, and breeder reactors at a somewhat higher cost level comparable with oil-fired generators. The nuclear option, however, is open only to very large countries. 'Its capital cost is high, and smaller countries do not have grids with the minimum capacity – some 6,000 MW – to handle the minimum reactor output efficiently. If countries also lack the skilled labour and management needed for a nuclear programme, the peculiar hazards of nuclear energy production may make it an unwise choice. And all must be as concerned as the industrial countries about the security and safety of nuclear plants.'[36]

China and India are accordingly the only Third World countries which have (at the time of writing) invested in a full-scale nuclear industry including the testing of nuclear weapons. China did so with its own resources, and in 1969 detonated a weapon underground. In 1974 India carried out an underground test of a device using plutonium from a research reactor codenamed CIRUS that had been built with Canadian help from the early 1950s onwards to use natural uranium and heavy water. The spent fuel had then been reprocessed and the plutonium extracted in a plant built in India with imported components. The Canadians were furious as they had believed that their aid would be used only for peaceful purposes. Yet the Indians had not violated any agreement. They had always refused to sign the non-proliferation treaty, which they regarded as perpetuating the great powers' nuclear supremacy from which, in their view, arose the greatest danger of a nuclear catastrophe; and though they were parties to the 1963 test-ban treaty, that does not prohibit underground tests.[37]

Such are the difficulties of nuclear non-proliferation, well exemplifying the dilemmas posed by nuclear energy for the world as a whole. If it has a contribution to make to economic development, the governments of poor countries will claim its benefits for their people, and the justice of their claims will be hard to resist. Many will flinch, however, from the appalling dangers of the wider availability of nuclear materials, especially plutonium. If because of those dangers nuclear technology is limited to a few countries, then the smaller Third World countries will be excluded and disadvantaged, and nuclear energy even in its peaceful applications will divide nations from one another as deeply and perhaps as bitterly as it has divided public opinion within some industrial countries.

And though nuclear energy may have a role in electricity generation, it seems unlikely to be able to provide for that other evidently felt need of human beings for a power source which is mobile, self-contained, and under the user's control. That need has been met in the twentieth century by the internal combustion engine, which has been readily adapted to uses like farm and garden cultivation, fishing, forestry, and small-scale manufacturing as well as personal and family transport in the ubiquitous motor vehicle. If and when petroleum is exhausted, a fuel that suggests itself is alcohol; I return to the point below.

This brings us to the other broad range of possibilities; why not make more use of the nuclear fusion reactions that go on continuously and abundantly at a safe distance in the sun? Compared with fossil fuels, the greater and more efficient use of solar energy directly or after short time-lapses has the appealing implication of relying on current income rather than squandering a capital inheritance.

After considering nuclear energy and rising oil prices, it is salutary to be reminded by the World Bank that 'for almost half the world's population energy problems take the form of a daily search for wood with which to cook food'. Firewood, crop residues, and animal dung together represent about a quarter of the energy used in developing countries as a whole; in Africa south of the Sahara, wood provides three-quarters of all the energy used.[38] As forests are used up, people burn more vegetable waste and dung, which would be better used as fertilizers, and crop yields fall, so more land is deforested and taken into cultivation. There is an urgent need to plant more trees, while research into ways of improving the efficiency with which fuel is used and designing better stoves that people can afford presents a challenge to scientists and engineers.[39]

As liquid fuel for internal combustion engines to replace petroleum gasoline (petrol), alcohol from renewable vegetable sources has already been mentioned. More strictly one should say alcohols, for the possibilities include methyl alcohol (methanol) from wood as well as ethyl alcohol (ethanol) from crops such as sugar and maize. Before 1970 the cost of these fuels was not competitive with petrol, but since the great oil price rises they have come within the petroleum range. The country which has taken these developments most seriously is Brazil, where a vigorous fuel alcohol programme was launched in 1975. Ethanol from sugar was selected as the

124

most promising alcohol, mixed with petrol to form 'gasohol', as it has been called. By 1980, 19 per cent of motor fuel in Brazil was alcohol. Some other countries in which developments of this kind are taking place include the United States, Australia, New Zealand, and South Africa. However, as with the Green Revolution, solving one problem seems to have created others. In Brazil, sugar growing for 'gasohol' competes for good land with both food production and export crops; and it has contributed to a still greater concentration of land-holding and wealth, especially as it has been financed with highly subsidized credit at the instance of a powerful lobby allied with the motor vehicle manufacturing interest.[40]

Hydro-electric power offers another way of using a renewable source of energy derived from the sun with a modest time-lag, and its cost compares favourably with all but the cheapest fossil fuels. Little of the potential water power available is being used as yet, and it is in the poorest regions of Africa, South America, and south-east Asia that the greatest unused potential is to be found. In some cases there have been political difficulties. For example, the Cabora Bassa scheme on the Zambezi was condemned by the Organization for African Unity and attacked by African nationalist guerrilla forces when Mozambique was still under Portuguese rule and it was seen as representing foreign interests and benefiting mainly whites. And it is not always easy to get agreement for schemes using rivers that flow through more than one country.

Another possible way of replacing fossil fuel sources is to use more solar heat for space heating in temperate climates where it is necessary. Experiments have been reported which seem to suggest that buildings such as houses and schools can be designed to trap the sun and keep the warmth in with modern insulating materials, while heat from electric lights and human bodies contribute to warming a dwelling that needs topping up only on the coldest and least sunny days. Solar panels to heat water have not proved economical, at least in Britain,[41] but a Canadian government agency has experimented, apparently with success, with the year-long storage of solar heat in a huge tank of water some three metres deep underneath a house.

The direct use of solar radiation to generate electricity in photo-cells has been sucessfully developed for special purposes such as spacecraft, but its cost is high and seems likely to remain so. Likewise, according to the World Bank's estimates, the unit cost of wind-generated electricity is high. But further research and development may change the picture. Since the poor countries are mostly those in the tropics and sub-tropics – between roughly latitudes 30°N and 20°S – they should be well placed for future development of the more direct use of solar energy. From a Third World point of view as well as that of the world as a whole, this seems to be the right direction in which to look.

125

SUGGESTIONS FOR FURTHER READING

Paul R. Ehrlich and Anne Ehrlich, *Population, Resources, Environment*, San Francisco: W. H. Freeman, 1970

John Maddox, *The Doomsday Syndrome*, London: Macmillan, 1972

Donella H. Meadows, Dennis L. Meadows, et al., *The Limits to Growth*, Washington, D.C.: Potomac, 1972; London: Pan, 1974

H. S. D. Cole et al., *Thinking About the Future: A Critique of The Limits to Growth*, London and Brighton: Chatto and Windus and Sussex University Press, 1973

Dennis Gabor et al., *Beyond the Age of Waste*, Oxford: Pergamon, 1978

6 The social sciences and the Third World

Before the second world war, the only social scientists to take much interest in the countries we now know as the Third World were the social anthropologists. For them, indeed, the 1920s and 1930s represented the golden age of the classic field studies, of Tikopia and Samoa, the Bemba, the Nuer, and the Azande. Evolutionism was rejected, and the prevailing approach was functional and comparative. Here were peoples with their own ways of doing things, different from 'ours' (that is, the western societies from which most of the anthropologists came), yet viable, internally consistent, and not irrational, enabling them to meet their basic needs and survive.[1] Although changes in the cultures and social structures they studied were not always entirely neglected, many anthropologists aspired to be early on the scene in their search for what Margaret Mead called 'untouched societies'[2] before these had been much affected by colonial administration, missions, schools, labour migration, and other outside influences.

From about 1950 onwards, however, all that changed. Political scientists, who had taken little interest in colonies and regarded their government as mere administration, not politics, suddenly became aware of the political scene in the newly independent states of Asia and Africa. Among economists there was a similar awakening; whereas in the 1930s the supreme economic problem had been seen as that of mass unemployment in the West, by the 1950s a similar challenge was presented to a new generation by 'the hideously great, and alas, ever widening disparity between the standards of living in the rich, developed countries and the poor, underdeveloped countries of the world'.[3]

The 1951 United Nations (Arthur Lewis) report

That interest was both signalled and stimulated by a report to the United Nations in 1951 by a group of experts headed by Professor W. A. Lewis (now Sir Arthur Lewis), 'Measures for the Economic Development of Under-Developed Countries'.[4] True to the preoccupations of economists of their generation, they devoted a good deal of attention to unemployment and underemployment, and their recommendations were 'regarded as a

127

counterpart to...measures required to achieve full employment in economically more developed countries'. 'Under-developed', the term used in the title, was interpreted as referring to countries whose per capita real incomes were low compared with the United States, Canada, Australia, and western Europe; 'an adequate synonym would be "poor countries"'. Measures to be taken included those by governments of developing nations and by international action. 'Economic progress will not occur unless the atmosphere is favourable to it. The people must desire progress, and their social, economic, legal and political institutions must be favourable to it.' Property institutions, for example, must be such as to create incentives, and legal institutions must protect the rights of tenants to the benefit derived from their improvement of the land. The public sector must perform all the tasks which in developed countries had come to be thought of as its traditional sphere, and must indeed perform them particularly well in underdeveloped countries, providing a sound infra-structure of roads and other communications, education, public health, and other public and social services. In addition, public action might be necessary in such fields as market research, geological surveys, and prospecting for minerals, the establishment of new industries, and the creation of financial institutions to mobilize savings and channel them into 'desirable private enterprise' notably in the form of capital for the small private farmer and artisan. The importance of education was stressed, and its scope was shown to be wider than the mere training of technicians. In general, because the market might misallocate resources, governments must be alert to intervene in fields beyond that traditionally allotted to the public sector. Some guarded but favourable remarks were made about the desirability of fertility control.

Measures to be taken by international action included, as a first priority, arrangements for stable terms of trade, favourable to developing countries. There was a good deal of criticism of the 'unfair' policies of some industrial countries in subsidizing the home production of commodities which could be produced more cheaply in underdeveloped countries. For example, subsidized beet sugar production in Europe deprived tropical countries of part of their market for an important export – a point often made in later criticisms of the economic policies of European countries. Some industrial nations were further accused of encouraging, and even subsidizing, exports of primary commodities produced in competition with underdeveloped countries. Secondly, the report called for the transfer of capital from rich to poor countries on a scale 'far beyond what is currently envisaged', thereby taking the lead in calling for what we now term aid.

Stages of development

In 1958 Walt Whitman Rostow gave a series of lectures at Cambridge which were published in 1960 as *The Stages of Economic Growth*, a book that remains the most explicit statement of the thesis embodied in its title.[5] Basing his analysis on his earlier studies of the development of the British economy in the nineteenth century, he identified five stages or categories within which all societies 'in their economic dimensions' lay: 'the traditional society, the preconditions for take-off, the take-off, the drive to maturity, and the age of high mass-consumption'. The preconditions included a shift out of agriculture and an enlargement of the scale of economic relations in which the orientation of commerce and thought passed from a regional to a national and a still larger international setting. In recent history this had occurred 'not endogenously but from some external intrusion by more advanced societies...[which] shocked the traditional society and began or hastened its undoing'. Family limitation was at least foreshadowed, and there was a shift from ascribed status to individual ability, a disposition to invest, and a spread of rational scientific and technological ideas.

The take-off was marked by a big rise in net investment, from 5 to over 10 per cent of net national income. Rostow identified this as occurring in Britain between 1783 and 1802, the United States 1843–60, Japan 1878–1900, and India and China since 1950. But at this stage modern technology was applied only in a few 'leading sectors' – cotton in England, railways in the United States – and the requisite personal qualities of enterprise in these sectors came in many cases from a minority who formed a leading elite in economic growth. Weber's Protestant ethic is clearly relevant here, and Rostow acknowledged his insight, but remarked that 'John Calvin should not be made to bear quite this weight'. Other enterprising minorities besides the Calvinists had included the Samurai, Parsees, Jews, Russian civil servants, and one might add Chinese and Indian minorities overseas; I return to this point in chapter 10.

In the drive to maturity, some 10–20 per cent of the national income was steadily invested, and a modern technology extended from the leading sector throughout the economy. Finally, a mature economy could use its resources in three ways: the pursuit of external power and national aggrandizement; the 'welfare state', redistribution, the social services, and leisure; or 'high mass consumption', represented above all by the private motor vehicle.

Many criticisms have been made of Rostow's thesis. Since his book is sub-titled 'A non-communist manifesto', dissents from a Marxist analysis, and refers to communism as 'a disease of the transition', it is not surprising that Marxist critics have been hostile.[6] Some of the criticisms by radical

129

writers seem wide of the mark. Thus, as mentioned above, Rostow did not concentrate wholly on endogenous factors in development, and he acknowledged the importance both of the colonial experience and of involvement in the international economy; while to say of so distinguished an economic historian that his work was 'a-historical' or 'denied a history to' the underdeveloped nations would plainly be absurd. Exception can be taken to his use of the term 'the traditional society'. As has been seen, radical underdevelopment writers deny that there is or ever was such a thing. From a quite opposite point of view, however, to lump together in such an undifferentiated category all pre-industrial, non-Western societies is to pay scant regard to the evidence of social anthropology showing the diversity of pre-existing cultures and their persistence despite the unifying forces at work in the world today. Non-Marxist economists, too, have been critical. Hagen suggested that the stages of growth were not really as clear-cut as Rostow made them out to be. The supposed upward surge in investment occurred in only a few countries, particularly England, the Soviet Union, and Japan, but elsewhere capital formation was a steadier process and Rostow's division into periods was 'entirely artificial'.[7] More fundamentally, Myrdal attacked Rostow for teleology, that is, for imputing to abstractions like 'history', 'society', or a 'nation' human attributes they cannot possibly possess, especially a capacity for purposive action. Thus growth once started seems automatic, and the importance of decisions and policies, especially on the part of governments, is down-played.[8]

Balanced versus unbalanced growth

A perennial issue in development economics is that of the relative merits of 'balanced growth' on the one hand and a concentration on a 'leading sector' on the other. As long ago as 1943, Rosenstein-Rodan imagined 20,000 underemployed Eastern European peasants leaving the land to work in one large factory making shoes. Their wages would be spent partly on food, so agricultural production would be stimulated; but not much would be spent on shoes, and the shoe factory would quickly go bankrupt. If, however, a million underemployed peasants went to work in a thousand factories producing the whole range of goods on which workers and peasants spend their earnings, all would prosper. He accordingly advocated 'the planned creation of a complementary system', or industrialization in 'one big push';[9] and in this he was supported by other development economists including Ragnar Nurkse.[10] Such ideas had their critics; thus Viner thought they neglected the possibilities of international trade, through which those 20,000 shoe workers might dispose of all their products, if they were specially good, and import their other wants.[11] Youngson acidly pointed out that it might really be quite easy to think up a whole set of uneconomic, unprofitable industrial enterprises linked in supply-and-demand relations and say that one had planned a 'complementary system'. Thus an uneconomic hydro-electric scheme might look more economic if an uneconomic cement industry were linked with it. The current from the first turbines could be used to manufacture cement for the next dam, while uneconomic factories producing textiles, beer, and soap could be linked with the scheme as consumers of electrical energy, and protected by tariffs on an 'infant industries' argument, so concealing the uneconomic nature of the whole.[12] (To one who lived in Uganda in the 1950s, it all seems remarkably true to life.) It was widely acknowledged, though, that poor countries were unduly dependent on primary export industries, which were precarious and had weak spread effects; and that diversification and industrialization were badly needed.

A leading critic of balanced growth, and advocate of the opposite policy, was Albert O. Hirschman. In his book published in 1958,[13] he argued that Rosenstein-Rodan's thousand factories would need at least a thousand managers; but underdeveloped countries just did not have managerial resources in such abundance, and if they had they would not be underdeveloped in the first place. He agreed that 'The grudge against what has become known as the "enclave" type of development is due to the ability of primary products from mines, wells, and plantations to slip out of a country without leaving much of a trace in the rest of the economy.' He distinguished, however, between export enclaves and those devoted to import industries. In the latter, beginning with the mere assembly of imported components, packaging, etc., industrialization might proceed by 'backward linkages' to the local production of components and finally basic raw materials. This strategy of import substitution industrialization, or ISI as it later became known, has been followed successfully in many countries, including for instance motor vehicle manufacture in India.

Contrary to much received opinion, Hirschman was not averse to capital-intensive methods, on the ground that they might stimulate learning and demonstrate efficiency. There might even be something to be said for 'show-piece' projects with a 'compulsion to maintain'. For example, in the transport sector a failure to maintain aircraft is likely to lead to spectacular crashes in which many lives are lost, while failure to maintain roads only leads to inconvenience and annoyance, and, in between, failure to maintain railways is more likely to lead to crashes than in the case of roads but less so than in the case of aircraft. And so we find that poor countries run their airlines well, their railways are mediocre, and their roads are usually in a parlous state of disrepair.

Hirschman accepted that unbalanced growth was likely to lead to 'polarization' and tension. For example, an industrial region ('the North') might be the scene of growth in contrast to a relatively backward area ('the

131

South'); or an innovative minority ('the Jews') may be enriched before other groups. He was optimistic, though, about 'backward linkages' and 'trickle-down effects', and thought it neither feasible nor desirable to suppress those tensions altogether. 'Under-developed countries already operate under the *grand tension* that stems from the universal desire for economic improvement oddly combined with many resistances to change. Much is to be said for breaking down this grand tension, a highly explosive mixture of hopes and fears, into a series of smaller and more manageable tensions.' Governments had the dual task of inducing growth, with all the imbalance that it brought in train, and of restoring balance. Foreign aid should 'embolden a country to set out on the path of unbalanced growth'. And economic advisers should be less concerned with establishing priorities than with 'discovering under what pressures people are operating and toward what forward steps they are already being impelled'.

Modernization

Freedom is the right to choose, the right to create for oneself the alternatives of choice. Without the possibility of choice and the exercise of choice, a man is not a man but a member, an instrument, a thing.

Thomas Jefferson

Modernization as a non-economic process originates when a culture embodies an attitude of inquiry and questioning about how men make choices...The problem of choice is central for modern man...To be modern means to see life as alternatives, preferences, and choices.

David Apter[14]

The terms industrialization, development, and modernization are much confused, and their meanings overlap. In so far as it is possible to distinguish them, industrialization is the most straightforward. Like the Industrial Revolution in the history of western countries, it refers to real changes, objectively observable and statistically measurable, particularly including the shifts from agriculture to industry and from country to town, falling mortality and rising literacy. Development, as we have seen, is a somewhat more problematic concept. Growth in GNP per capita is generally taken as the criterion measure, but many economists look deeper in search of underlying preconditions, institutional or psychological. If in industrialization the focus is technological, in development it is economic. Modernization is one way of looking at both. It refers to a school of thought, an approach to the understanding and interpretation of industrialization and development, that particularly characterized social thought in the United States in the 1950s and 1960s, though its origins can be traced much further back to the dictum of Thomas Jefferson quoted above.

Modernization is seen as the change from a 'traditional', pre-industrial state or condition, the starting-point for development, to 'modernity',

132

through an intermediate 'transitional' condition. The process affects both societies and individuals in mutually reinforcing ways. In traditional societies, most if not all people are traditionally minded. Transitional societies include some modern-minded people, and others who are transitional in their outlook and attitudes, as well as many who are still traditionally-minded. Modern-minded people propel their society into modernity; equally, the institutions of a modern society encourage and engender individual modernity in its members.

Traditional societies are viewed as static and unchanging. They are characterized by subsistence economies using 'Biblical' methods – the ox-drawn wooden plough, hand sowing and planting, head carrying, 'cottage industries' using little or no mechanical power.[15] Their social structures are various, but many can be characterized as feudal. Religious institutions are powerful and dogmatic, engendering personal attributes that include submission to authority and fatalism. In particular, fertility is uncontrolled, and there is an acceptance of 'as many children as God sends'. In such societies there is little effective choice; traditional cultivation is the only alternative to starvation, while there is equally little alternative to submission to traditional political authority.

By contrast, modern societies are viewed as dynamically changing, characterized by innovation, technological advance, and economic development. Such societies engender in their members flexible, rational minds given to 'having opinions'. Modern-minded people assert autonomy in making important decisions, notably in deciding for themselves how many children they shall have, and rationally implementing their decisions by technically effective means. They are imbued with a conviction that we can shape our world, the very antithesis of fatalism. Religious dogma and traditional political authority alike are rejected, or at least questioned. The politics of a modern society are correspondingly based on the informed participation of citizens in the political arena. There is a choice of parties and policies, government is rationally legitimated by the consent of the governed, and, in a word, there is freedom.

The transition from traditional to modern is regarded as a transformation, not a transfer; that is, it is not just a matter of transferring the capital or the technology, nor even the outward forms of social and political institutions, from one set of countries to another. When their ideas were first formulated in the 1950s, the modernization school clearly supposed that the process would be irreversible, and that once people had tasted freedom and participated in the political arena there would be no getting them out. By the 1970s it was clear that that did not always happen, and contrary evidence of 'departicipation' in some countries prompted a reassessment of the whole concept of participation and its relation to modernization; I take up the question in chapter 12.

If the stages of development thesis was most explicitly articulated by Rostow, the modernization approach was pre-eminently that of Daniel Lerner, whose book *The Passing of Traditional Society* was published in the same year that Rostow lectured in Cambridge.[16] Based on field observations in Turkey in the 1950s, it opens with the parable of the grocer and the chief in Balgat, a village not far from the capital. While the chief represented traditional authority, the grocer, who had seen American films in Ankara, had images of a wider world including a well-stocked supermarket. What distinguished him, according to Lerner, was 'empathy', a capacity to imagine things otherwise than as they are, and to project oneself in imagination into other social roles and other states of society. Thus the chief, when asked what he would do if he were president of Turkey, replied 'I am hardly able to manage a village, how shall I manage Turkey?' But the grocer had a ready answer; he would make roads so that people could travel to town and see the world, not stay in holes all their lives.

'Empathy', then, was related to mobility. Physical mobility through ease of travel led to urbanization as people moved to towns and became more involved in the modern cash economy. 'Psychic mobility' resulted from literacy and exposure to the mass media of communication. The modern style of life was 'distinctively industrial, urban, literate, and *participant*'. It involved 'having opinions', and culminated in voting 'in elections which actually decide among competing candidates'.

Extending his analysis to the statistics then available from UNESCO and other United Nations sources for some 54 countries, Lerner found that urbanization, literacy, and media exposure were indeed correlated, and he concluded:

When the underdeveloped lands of the world are tested by our model of modernity, the enormous hurdles in the path to modernization stand out more clearly. What the West accomplished gradually over three past centuries is not so easy for the East to achieve rapidly in the present century...

We come, then, to political participation. Democratic governance comes late, historically, and typically appears as a crowning achievement of the participant society. That the voting coefficient is so high indicates that these 54 countries have achieved stable growth at a high level of modernity. In these countries the urban literate tends also to be a newspaper reader, a cash customer, and a voter.

It is perhaps not unfair to remark that in such a view modernization seems to mean becoming more like the United States. While the Jeffersonian ideals may indeed represent for many a model worthy of emulation, it seems plain that we have here not just a social science theory or set of explanatory ideas helping us to understand what is happening in the world, but also a set of evaluative criteria by which to judge the policies and performance of Third World countries and their governments. Perhaps this analysis may have been addressed, among others, to modernizing elites in those countries, of whom Riggs has succinctly written that 'A transitional society, however contemporary, is one whose leaders have an image of themselves as molders of a new destiny for their people, as promoters of modernization, and therefore as initiators of industrialization.'[17] Perhaps, too, it was intended to encourage those whom Lerner calls 'moderns' and others might designate as 'innovators' or 'change agents', such as teachers, business managers, and agricultural extension officers.

The modernization school continues to have many adherents, especially in the United States,[18] and I deal in chapter 11 with studies of individual modernization especially by Alex Inkeles and David H. Smith. It has also stimulated much criticism. There was a rather confused debate about 'internal' and 'external' influences in which it was not clear what units the supposed influences were internal or external to: what is internal to a country or society may be external to an individual, but international influences are external to both. Lerner's analysis spanned the individual and societal levels, but failed to distinguish between societies and countries; and apart from American films he had little to say about the international influences changing countries, societies, and individuals. His analysis can be criticized too as lacking in historical awareness.

Such deficiencies, however, were amply made up by Reinhard Bendix, who pointed the way towards a possible rehabilitation of the modernization analysis.[19]

According to Bendix, the 'societies of the original breakthrough' into modernity were 'England' and France. It will be noted at once that he said England when he meant Britain; and though the error is commonplace enough among United States scholars, it exemplifies the confusion between country and society which Bendix shared with other writers in this field.

From Britain ('England'), the rest of the world learned that modernity involved industrialization; it was a matter of coal, iron, railways, steamships, textile mills, and the like. From France, the rest of the world learned a different lesson; modernity involved a united nation-state with a common language and a common citizenship. In the powerfully evocative words of the Marseillaise, 'Allons, enfants de la patrie...Aux armes, citoyens!'

In the decades around 1800, their 'original breakthrough' put Britain and France into the positions of world leadership, and all other countries into the position of 'backwardness' or 'follower' status in an international system of social stratification, a key concept that Bendix approvingly derived from Nettl and Robertson.[20] Just as individuals low in the social scale within a country experience relative deprivation or *atimia*, so do countries in an international system of social stratification – or, to be more exact, so do their ruling elites. Smarting under the stigma of backwardness, they strive to catch up. In Europe around 1800, that aspiration was immensely sharpened by the imminent threat of conquest as Napoleon's armies, inspired by revolutionary and patriotic zeal, overran Europe from the Peninsula to Moscow, only to be defeated largely by the industrial and naval might of Britain (allied, it must be said, with Russian numbers and the Russian winter). It seemed like a case of modernize or go under.

There accordingly followed successive waves of catching up by follower countries: in the early nineteenth century, Germany, Belgium, Scandinavia, and Italy; after about 1860, Russia and Japan; after about 1890, the United States. It may be noted, though, that although what we would now call modernization was certainly on the agenda in Russia, there was a great debate there between the 'westernizers' and the 'Slavophiles'. For the former, modernization meant westernization, though they debated among themselves the merits of three possible models represented by 'England', France, and Germany. Respectively, those represented liberal private-enterprise industrialization, radical reform, and state-directed development according to the ideas of the German economist Friederich List which would leave the existing social and political order intact. According to the Slavophiles, however, Russia should be true to her unique historical heritage. 'Catching up' was a mistake. Parliamentary democracy would make no sense there and economic development would be an embarrassment. As for the threat of conquest, the sheer size of the country and the numbers in their army should be able to take care of their defence, as they had against Napoleon. But the westernizers won, and chose the German model; and the Tsar's chief ministers, successively Witte and Stolypin, thereby became perhaps the first modernizing autocrats and, like many of their kind, made themselves thoroughly unpopular in the process.[21]

Of the later-industrializing countries, only the United States wholeheartedly followed the British private-enterprise model of development epitomized in the work of the great Scottish economist Adam Smith. In virtually all others, including France, much greater initiatives were taken and control exercised by the state. In the process of catching up, too, it was not always clear what were the essential elements in modernity and what were merely adventitious traits that happened to be characteristic of the early modernizing countries, or societies. Thus the high prestige of the French language throughout Europe, and its value in France itself as a source of national unity and pride, long antedated the 'original breakthrough' around 1800 and can be traced back to the age of Richelieu if not even earlier. Yet the model of the nation-state with a common language and a common citizenship, as has been noted, has been accepted without much question as part and parcel of modernity. It was energetically pursued in Italy after the Risorgimento and the reunification; and it has been adopted in more recent times by many Third World countries with even more diverse languages and cultures.

Accordingly, as Bendix contended, one model of modernization will not do, and we need several. He was distinctly sceptical of arguments that a 'logic of industrialization' prevailed to such an extent that the process was likely to follow the same pattern or stages of development in each country. On the contrary, he asserted, at least as good a case could be made for the converse proposition: 'Once industrialization has occurred anywhere, this fact alone alters the international environment of all other countries... Industrialization cannot occur in the same way twice.' Scientific and technological progress, painfully slow in the 'societies of the original breakthrough', could be drastically telescoped and their lead-times shortened in later-developing countries, most notably perhaps in the field of death control. Awareness of the gap between advanced and backward countries 'puts a premium on ideas and techniques which "follower" societies may use to "come up from behind"'. Educated elites were thus in positions of strategic importance; the gap between educated and uneducated widened; education was seen as having instrumental value as a source of income, prestige, and security, rather than an intrinsic or consummatory value in itself; and there was a corresponding tendency to invest too much in educating a bigger elite than a country needed or could afford.

Underdevelopment and dependence: the counterblast

During the 1960s, many writers on development and related subjects expressed a radical dissatisfaction with the prevailing ideas of the orthodox, mainstream social science tradition.[22] Among the first to debate different ways of looking at the problem of underdevelopment were certain Latin American economists, some of them associated with the United Nations Economic Commission for Latin America, or ECLA,[23] and it seems that the sequence of their thought ran somewhat as follows. It had been widely agreed during the 1950s that poor countries were unduly dependent on a few primary exports. That state of affairs could be attributed to the international division of labour that was first enforced under colonial rule, according to which the colonies were to be raw material suppliers while the metropolitan countries specialized in manufactures. Although it might have been expected that in that role they would have shared in the great surge in prosperity that followed the second world war, and made the industrial nations into affluent societies, that had not occurred. Although western consumers were paying, and able to pay, much more for coffee (for example) than they had in the past, much of the increased price was due to the greater value added in processing, packaging, and marketing the instant coffee products sold in the supermarkets, and little of it went to the original growers of coffee in countries such as Brazil. Clearly the

137

remedy was to do more of the processing and packaging in Brazil; and indeed there was general agreement about the need for the diversification of the economies of poor countries and the development of industries there. But how was that to be achieved? and, in particular, how was the capital to be raised? In order to earn the foreign exchange they needed to buy the machinery and other capital imports, the underdeveloped countries had to depend even more in the short and medium term on their primary exports, thus intensifying their problem. Moreover, world markets for their products were readily glutted, so that increased production for export only led in many cases to such a drop in price that total receipts were reduced rather than increased; quantities of Brazilian coffee, indeed, had sometimes had to be destroyed to maintain its price. Some economists recommended solving that dilemma by means of what they called 'industrialization by invitation'; rather than attempt to raise the capital for industrial development themselves, the underdeveloped countries should let the multi-national corporations do it for them, even offering them inducements through tax exemptions and the like. But that strategy too had adverse consequences. While it was not denied that something worthy of the name of development might occur in that way, the subsidiary enterprises the multi-national corporations set up in poor countries created only small enclaves of prosperity with limited spread effects. Much of the profits and some of the personal incomes generated by those enterprises was repatriated to the metropolitan countries. Thus not only were the poor countries denied a full share of the proceeds, but their dependent status was also enhanced by the fact that the important decisions were taken out of national hands and made elsewhere.[24] And the interests of the big international firms might be the occasion, or even the pretext, for diplomatic and political pressure from other governments – especially, of course, the United States – constraining the host country from pursuing its own policies and making its own decisions. Even aid was suspect from this point of view. Bilateral assistance from one donor country to another recipient country could be used by the former to exert 'leverage' on the latter; while multilateral aid was channelled through agencies, in particular the World Bank, which were seen as dominated by the rich non-communist countries and responsive to their point of view and their interests.[25]

At this point, it may be surmised, some gave up in despair. Whatever the poor countries might try to do to break out of their poverty trap and promote their own development, it seemed as though their efforts would be thwarted. The rich industrial countries, their multi-national corporations, and the international agencies they dominated, would always somehow manipulate the world economic system in their favour and to the detriment of the poor countries. There was only one remedy: opt out of the world system altogether, sever all links with the West, and pursue a Spartan policy of self-reliant development, perhaps in co-operation with friendly socialist countries. If that meant revolution, so be it. Much of the voluminous literature of the school of thought associated with the terms underdevelopment and dependence seems to be inspired by that conviction.

The early debates of this school of thought were conducted largely in Spanish, and it was not until 1967 that it became widely known in the English-speaking world through the outspoken advocacy of A. G. Frank.

Brought up in the United States, Frank studied economics at Chicago. Later he rejected the whole approach he was taught there, especially as applied to Latin America, and changed to a radically different view according to which 'Economic development and underdevelopment are the opposite faces of the same coin.' They are attributable neither to 'supposedly different economic structures or systems' nor to different stages of economic growth. On the contrary:

One and the same historical process of the expansion and development of capitalism throughout the world has simultaneously generated – and continues to generate – both economic development and structural underdevelopment...

Yes, *development of underdevelopment* – because underdevelopment, as distinct perhaps from *un*development, did not pre-date economic development; nor did it spring up of itself; nor did it spring up all of a sudden. It developed right along with economic development – and it is still doing so.

The metropolitan centres of world capitalism were linked with peripheral satellite countries; and that relationship was also found within the latter among their regions, and between their towns and industrial centres and their declining agricultural districts:

An obvious consequence of the satellite economy's external relations is the loss of some of its economic surplus to the metropolis...Analogously, the regional, local, or sectoral metropolises of the satellite country find the limitations on their development multiplied by a capitalist structure which renders them dependent on a whole chain of metropolises above them.

Therefore, short of liberation from this capitalist structure or the dissolution of the world capitalist system as a whole, the capitalist satellite countries, regions, localities, and sectors are condemned to underdevelopment.[26]

Frank's analysis, along with his polemical criticisms of mainstream development theories, was published in 1967 at a time of unrest in western universities, and merged with other streams of thought then current with which it was generally congenial. The very idea of a social science was being repudiated, and objectivity was regarded as neither possible nor desirable. Radical social thought was extolled as fusing theory and practice in revolutionary action. It was hailed as emancipatory, whereas mainstream social science was condemned as justificatory of the existing social order. Characterized as 'positivist' and 'empiricist', social science was said to represent merely the rationalization or intellectual camouflage of the status

139

quo, and was dismissed as 'bourgeois'. At that time, too, the United States government was unpopular among intellectuals and students both at home and abroad, largely in relation to the war in Vietnam. There was sympathy with revolutionary movements in Third World countries, and leaders such as Fidel Castro and Che Guevara were idolized. At such a time there was a ready hearing for a radical analysis that whole-heartedly rejected orthodox social science and pointed to revolutionary action – the kind of actions and policies, indeed, that had already been taken by the regime in Cuba.

As already noted, it was of the utmost importance for this school of thought to establish that Latin American societies had never been feudal, and that the world system established from *c.* 1500 onwards was capitalist from the outset. Not to do so would have been to accept the mainstream ideas about dual-sector economies, part traditional and part modern, and about stages of development, that had been so decisively repudiated. But there were difficulties about that position. It was a widely accepted view among Marxist and non-Marxist authorities alike that the Spanish and Portuguese conquests in the Americas had occurred when feudalism prevailed in Europe, and no societies were more feudal or 'seigniorial' than those of Spain and Portugal. It seemed obvious that the institutions implanted by the conquistadores were feudal in nature; and indeed the kind of landholding with servile peasants and a wealthy landed class that characterized many Latin American countries could without difficulty be recognized as resembling that of European feudal society.

Radical underdevelopment writers accordingly found themselves at odds not only with those whom they could dismiss as 'bourgeois', but also with much orthodox Marxist thought including that of Marx himself. Thus Frank controverted not only the 'bourgeois thesis' that Latin America began its post-discovery history with feudal institutions which survive today, but also 'the traditional Marxist theses' that:

(a) feudalism predates capitalism,
(b) feudalism coexists with capitalism,
(c) feudalism is invaded or penetrated by capitalism.

And he continued:

There is a remarkable similarity in all fundamentals between the bourgeois and the Marxist analyses – both metropolitan born. Both maintain that society consists of two substantially independent sectors. The one is more modern because it took off independently and is capitalist; the other, the agrarian sector, still holds back both its own progress and that of the modern sector because it remains feudal.[27]

More recently, Immanuel Wallerstein has devoted monumental scholarship to establishing a like thesis, that 'In the late fifteenth and early sixteenth century, there came into existence what we may call a European world-economy...based on the capitalist mode of production.' He noted an 'intra-Marxist debate' about the 'periodization' or dating of the different stages, and the association in the view of many between the rise of capitalism and the industrial revolution. His own usage of the term capitalism was very much wider, however, for he asked: 'Why different modes of organizing labor – slavery, "feudalism", wage labor, self-employment – at the same point in time within the world-economy?' And he continued: 'That is why slavery could flourish in the Roman Empire and why it is preeminently a capitalist institution, geared to the early preindustrial stages of a capitalist world-economy.'[28]

Clearly, it depends what you mean by capitalism; and it may be that so wide a usage renders the term undiscriminating.

Radical underdevelopment writers taking this view have been criticized for confusing capitalism as a system of exchange with capitalism as a mode of production.[29] For a Marxist, no doubt, wherever there is capitalism there is exploitation. But the converse is not necessarily true; where we find exploitation, as in the Spanish and Portuguese American colonies in the sixteenth and seventeenth centuries, it is not necessarily attributable to capitalism. Exploitation occurs in all societies in which men are divided into two antagonistic classes, whether as masters and slaves, as lords and serfs, or as capitalist proprietors and wage labourers. Linked with this criticism has been the accusation that the radical underdevelopment school neglect the whole subject of class.

It seems that different writers have, so to speak, taken different leaves out of the Marxist book. The radical underdevelopment school have looked at the one on which are inscribed the words surplus value, its expropriation from the original producer (worker or peasant), its appropriation by the capitalist, exploitation, and the accumulation of capital. Their critics have taken another, on which appear the words productive forces, mode of production, means of production, social relations especially class relations, classes and class conflict, base and superstructure, and class consciousness.

Among the latter, some of the intellectual exercises which the debate has stimulated seem to an outsider to be of purely scholastic interest. Thus there has been much debate about the status of pre-capitalist modes of production,[30] and attempted elucidation of what Marx really meant by the Asiatic mode of production. However, in their acknowledgement that other modes of production coexist with capitalism, and are penetrated by it, writers of the latter school seem to have moved to a position not far from that of mainstream theory with its dual-sector model. Perhaps, too, the concept of the articulation of modes of production recalls that of culture contact in the older anthropology, though no doubt with a much more materialist bias.

And there have been attempts to synthesize the new radical perspectives,

141

most notably perhaps by Samir Amin. He distinguished five modes of production, different from those of Marx: the 'primitive communal' mode, anterior to all others; the 'tribute-paying' mode; slave-owning; the 'simple petty-commodity mode'; and capitalism. His analysis of underdevelopment as 'extraversion', or dependence on primary exports, was rather like Frank's. However, in his consideration of 'the contemporary social formations of the periphery', Amin proceeded to a detailed delineation of the class structures of underdeveloped societies.[31]

It will have become apparent that ideas about underdevelopment and dependence have been influential since the late 1960s in persuading some of those engaged in development studies to change their outlook and cross over to a radically different school of thought.[32] Those ideas have stimulated much controversy among Marxists and other radicals, though how far it is necessary to distinguish between those two categories, and whose point of view is the most truly Marxist or radical, are questions not perhaps of the greatest interest to outsiders. It remains to add that some at least of the 'stagnationism' or pessimism about the possibility of development within the existing world system, on which the whole intellectual movement was predicated, appears to have been falsified by events, as at least some formerly poor Third World countries have achieved rapid economic growth while remaining involved in international trade and the world system generally.

The Neo-Institutionalists[33]

Some eminent development economists, while remaining broadly within the mainstream, dissented from some aspects of conventional social science and took up a distinctive position. They included Gunnar Myrdal, Dudley Seers, and Paul Streeten.

They were much concerned about the fundamental problem of value in social science. Myrdal maintained that social science was not as objective and value-free as its orthodox practitioners represented. Choice of research subject, concepts, and analytical approach were alike value-loaded. Rather than permit the intrusion of tacit value-premises under the guise of objectivity, scientific integrity demanded that the investigator's value-premises should be made explicit. Streeten too was concerned about 'value-seepage' in a subject such as development economics in which it was not always easy to separate prognosis from programme. However, 'It does not follow that social science is impossible, or that it must plunge at once into valuations and ideologies. On the contrary. To be useful and truthful, the social scientist, and particularly the economist, should start with the actual political attitudes of people, not with their rationalizations and pseudo-theoretical ideologies.'

Secondly, they were sceptical of theories that suggested that economic growth – or indeed economic activity in general – was in some way automatically generated or regulated. Myrdal as a Swedish social democrat saw nothing wrong with state intervention in the economy, and it was to justify that interventionist position that he broke with the classical *laissez-faire* market economics. Similarly, Rostow's metaphor of an aircraft gathering flying-speed in a 'take-off into sustained growth' seemed too mechanistic. Myrdal's analysis consistently stressed the importance of attitudes, institutions, and policies. The course of economic development was not to be understood as the outcome of blind impersonal forces, but was largely determined by conscious choices and decisions, particularly on the part of governments.

Gunnar Myrdal came to the study of 'the poverty of nations' while Fru Alva Myrdal was Swedish ambassador in India from 1957 to 1961. He had already carried out a massive survey of race relations in the United States, and then as head of the Economic Commission for Europe had become aware of the cumulative nature of regional disparities. That led him to formulate his analysis of 'backwash effects': centres of economic activity could attract resources of people and capital from retarded or depressed areas, leaving the latter trapped in a vicious circle of low expectations and with an undue burden of dependants. Within rich countries, governments could intervene to redress regional disparities, but to do so made great claims on public funds, which governments were likely to sanction only in response to the thought that even unemployed workers and depressed peasants had the vote. While Myrdal also saw 'spread effects' from the growth poles, like Hirschman's 'trickle-down', he was less optimistic that they would prevail.

Backwash effects were compounded by international boundaries. Clearly the poor in poor countries can exert no political leverage on the governments of rich countries, and not always much on their own. International trade had had strong backwash effects, undercutting traditional handicrafts like the weaving and metal-working industries of Asian countries. In the colonial past, some capital from Europe had gone into the export enclaves of countries such as India, and also into their public utilities such as railways, but much more had gone into setting up areas of European settlement in empty lands in the temperate zones. Compared with internal migration within countries, international migration was very limited in scale, being hampered by nationality laws, immigration controls, and in some cases colour bars. Differences in law, administration, *mores*, language and values made national boundaries 'much more effective barriers to the spread of expansionary momentum'.

Turning to the institutions of India and its neighbours. Myrdal conceded that colonial rule had brought many benefits including roads, ports, railways, political security, law and order, a civil service, sanitation, education, and contacts with the outer world. On the other hand it had also brought restrictions on the growth of their industries; for example, the indigenous Indian textile industry before 1860, as narrated in chapter 3. 'Enforced bilateralism', sometimes politely called 'close economic and political ties', between metropolitan countries and their colonies had restricted the markets open to the latter. Racial and cultural differences between European and native peoples had been associated with practices of segregation that had hampered the transfer of cultures, especially technical skills and a spirit of enterprise. The end of colonial rule had left some countries, notably India, with a genuine sense of national identity, but others remained artificial states with little unity or common purpose.

Myrdal conceived of the situation in each south Asian country – as in any country – as a *social system* consisting of causally inter-related *conditions* in six broad categories: output and incomes; conditions of production; levels of living; attitudes toward life and work; institutions; and policies. In south Asia the conditions in all six 'can be categorically called undesirable because a one-way change in them is deemed desirable for engendering and sustaining development'. Data on output and incomes were useful as an index of the 'level of under-development', but not as a definition. 'The movement of the whole system upwards is what all of us in fact mean by development.'

Many previous writers had analysed conditions in poor countries in terms of 'vicious circles'. Poor people do not eat enough, cannot work hard, and so are poor. The process can be reversed and turned into a 'virtuous circle': poor people are given more to eat, their health improves, they can work harder and get more to eat. While Myrdal did not dissent from that analysis, he recognized its somewhat tautological nature (poor countries are poor because they are poor) and regarded it as far too limited in scope. The 'low-level equilibrium' was to be seen rather as the stability of social systems.

The great bulk of historical, anthropological, and sociological evidence and thought suggests that social stability and equilibrium is the norm and that all societies, and under-developed societies in particular, possess institutions of a strongly stabilizing character. In view of those findings the real mystery is how they can escape from equilibrium and develop. The Western experience of scientific, technological, and economic advance may well be unique: a series of extraordinary circumstances.

The main resistance to change in the social system 'stems from attitudes and institutions. They are part of an inherited culture and are not easily or rapidly moved.'

The 'decolonization hurricane' had deservedly swept away many of the old ideas about 'backwardness', especially racialist myths. But institutions were still important, and the honest economist had to point out that many of the institutions of many underdeveloped countries were not conducive to development. Their social structures were highly inegalitarian, and Myrdal firmly believed that 'policy measures leading to greater equality could lead to more rapid growth'. Land reforms were urgently needed, and though countries embarking on them would have done themselves no harm in the eyes of United States official opinion, few had actually done so, while some had enacted land reforms on paper but had not put them into effect. Educated elites whose emergence had been encouraged under colonial rule now had a vested interest in maintaining the gap between the educated and the masses. 'In no other field is there greater inequality in these countries than in the availability of health facilities. These are mostly monopolised by the upper classes.' Ill-health, ignorance, and lack of incentives contributed to a massive under-utilization of human resources.

Prominent among the political institutions of underdeveloped countries was what Myrdal termed 'the soft state'. By this he meant 'a lack of social discipline'; deficiencies in law enforcement; disregard of the rules by public officials at all levels, and their collusion with powerful persons whose conduct it was their duty to regulate. In particular, 'tax evasion by the affluent is colossal'. Paradoxically, although in one sense the soft state was systematically lenient and let individuals do as they pleased, it was also capable of displaying much harshness towards individuals and groups, especially in military dictatorships. Corruption was an integral and important part of the soft state, and one generally neglected by economists despite its bearing on the whole structure of economic incentives and the irrationality it introduced into the situations in which individual and collective decisions and plans were made. It hampered growth and development, and was a major contributory factor to inequality.

The soft state and corruption were linked in turn with an elitist conspiracy in which landowners, moneylenders, local officials in collusion with them, industrialists, higher officials, legislators, and the educated elite acted together to hinder reforms, manipulate them in their own favour, and obstruct their implementation. Despite their lip-service in many cases to the egalitarian ideals of a classless and even a socialist society, such elites were not willing to give up the advantages they enjoyed. Pressure from below was needed. And it was the elite with whom the outside world had to deal, just as in colonial times the metropolitan powers and their officials found it expedient and even necessary to deal with their subject peoples through the latter's established traditional authorities. Today it was members of the elites in underdeveloped countries who turned up at international conferences to plead for a new world economic order. 'They certainly did not find it opportune to stress or even mention the need for a new economic order at home.'[34]

Dudley Seers, like Myrdal, regarded the developed industrial economy as a rare and special case. Such economies had existed for little more than a century, and they covered only a small part of the earth's surface and included only a minority of its inhabitants. Yet conventional economics treated the special case as if it were the norm. Textbooks and lecture courses with titles like 'Economic principles', 'Banking', and 'Public Finance', turned out on inspection to be analytical and somewhat theoretical descriptions of those aspects of the economy of the United States, Britain, or other advanced industrial countries. Worse, those textbooks were being used in the universities of non-industrial countries, translated into languages such as Spanish for the purpose, despite the manifest inappropriateness of much of their empirical content quite apart from their theoretical perspective. The case was not much better with books written for use in the Soviet Union and recommended, again in translation, in the universities of a country such as Cuba. Some Marxist analysis was highly relevant, for example, 'the "industrial reserve army" of the unemployed is after all to be seen in the streets' in many a Latin American country, while the attitudes of the landowning classes confirmed Marx's analysis, and foreign-owned plantations exemplified imperialism. But there was no attempt to adapt the analysis or content to underdeveloped countries as they are today, nor was there any scholarly analysis of the growth process.

Seers spelled out in detail the characteristic features of the special case, the developed industrial economy, and showed how special they were. He conceded that it should be studied; many economists would spend their whole working lives in economies of that kind, while others in non-industrial societies should study their characteristics if they were to understand their impact. For, as he emphasized, 'non-industrial economies cannot be understood unless studied in the context of the world economy.' Above all he argued for a comparative approach, perhaps with the slogan 'Economics is the study of economies.'[35]

Paul Streeten too criticized the limitations and biases of orthodox economics in dealing with the problems of development. 'One-factor analysis' or 'single-barrier theories of development' referred to different schools of thought, ideologies, and even changes of fashion among economists singling out first one particular factor and then another in their efforts to diagnose the root cause of underdevelopment and recommend measures to remedy it. 'If the Physiocrats stressed Land as the source of all wealth and the classical economists Labour, Capital has recently played the strategic role...Education is now the craze...or..."investment in human beings"..."Research and development" are already popular, and perhaps we shall soon study the returns from appropriate child training, which produces experimental innovating personalities, or from expenditure on child prevention.' (Both of the last-named have in fact occurred, and are mentioned elsewhere in this book.) But the removal of any one barrier had not proved to be a sufficient condition for development, while development had taken place in some countries despite the presence of unfavourable conditions, and had failed to take place in others despite their absence. 'Such considerations suggest scepticism towards any single-barrier explanation. Obstacles are numerous and interrelated.'

For example, while he suspected that a breakthrough in agriculture might be urged by some with an urban-industrial bias to squeeze surplus workers, food, and savings out of the rural sector into industry, Streeten saw the prerequisites for such a breakthrough largely in institutional terms. As well as an adequate infra-structure of roads, irrigation, etc., it was necessary to improve farmers' skills by training, and for the farmer and his family to have a minimum level and the right kind of education, health, and nutrition. It was necessary to increase the availability of incentive goods, which farm families would work harder to get, while resistance to work in the country on the part of urban youth and technicians had to be broken down. There had to be a system of land tenure which permitted the farmer to reap the benefits of his efforts. Credit had to be available at low interest, and marketing arrangements had to prevent middlemen from creaming off so much as to leave the farmer inadequate incentive to switch from export crops to domestic food production. Prices must be stabilized, and technical assistance available.

Conventional economists were prone to lump together for analytical and statistical purposes things that were really diverse, a tendency which Streeten called 'misplaced aggregation'. For example, 'if economies are divided into sectors between which there is little or no substitution... aggregation of incomes or prices is inappropriate...The income of an industrial enclave may grow, while real income per head of the indigenous population stagnates or declines. In what sense is "average income" rising?' Similarly, if for various reasons the notion of a single labour force did not make sense, then concepts of unemployment, underemployment, or disguised unemployment were likewise inappropriate. 'Any attempt to calculate "disguised unemployment" also presupposes a value judgement as to the length of the appropriate working day and working week.'

A complementary tendency to separate things that were really inter-related Streeten termed 'illegitimate isolation'. For example, it was false to separate expenditure on education on the one hand from investment in physical assets on the other. Particular kinds of education presupposed and were linked with investment in particular kinds of physical assets – agronomy with agricultural implements, engineering with industrial equipment. Likewise, much expenditure that in western countries would be classed as consumption, especially on the social services of health and education, could be regarded in poor countries as investment, since it had the direct effect of raising output and incomes. It was misleading to separate investment in agricultural improvement from expenditure on health and even from institutional reform. 'Much of the potential benefit of irrigation schemes is wasted because schistosomiasis is spread and reduces human efficiency, or because land ownership systems deprive peasants of both incentives and opportunities to make use of the water even if they wanted to raise yield.'[36]

Indigenous economics

Yet another critic of conventionally trained economists was Dr Polly Hill, who carried out a pioneer study of migrant cocoa farmers in southern Ghana and went on to a series of studies of 'grassroots' economic development in West Africa by methods combining economic analysis with the field techniques of the social anthropologist. In a plea for indigenous economics, as she named this approach to 'the basic fabric of economic life', she pointed to economists' earlier interest in the points of contact between West African and European economies – external trade, and organization of exports and imports – rather than with the production of crops or internal distribution. Such important matters as land tenure were neglected along with the ways in which native producers raised capital and managed labour, and myths grew up about West African economic behaviour, a kind of 'economic folklore', which became accepted by sheer reiteration in books and official publications.

The neglect of indigenous economics during the colonial period had not been rectified since independence; on the contrary, it had taken hold of the attitudes of modern West African governments and their economic advisers, who deplored the backwardness of the peasants and were apt to initiate large-scale mechanization projects without adequate consideration of the consequences. Furthermore, the whole ideology of economic development planners was opposed to indigenous studies. They were reluctant to introduce into their models ideas drawn from anthropological research, to look at the humdrum problems involved in the collection of the statistical data they so finely manipulated, and to reserve judgement in cases where their knowledge was inadequate.

Although the 'indigenous economist' was in some ways opposed to the 'development economist', both were concerned with the processes of change and modernization, though perhaps the former tended to regard them more from a non-governmental standpoint. Indigenous economics resembled conventional western economics in its general approach, but those who guessed on the basis of western experience were apt to go wrong even on fundamentals. The economic behaviour of West Africans was basically rational, but the structure of that rationality required studying in the field.

148

We must study the farmer, not patronize him; we must assume that he knows his business better than we do, unless there is evidence to the contrary...though...this is not to say that the farmer will be unappreciative of skilled technical advice and help.[37]

SUGGESTIONS FOR FURTHER READING

Daniel Lerner, *The Passing of Traditional Society*, New York: Free Press, 1958

Gunnar Myrdal, *Asian Drama: An Inquiry into the Poverty of Nations*, 3 vols., New York and Harmondsworth: Twentieth Century Fund/Random House/Penguin, 1968

Reinhard Bendix, *Embattled Reason*, Oxford: Oxford University Press, 1970

Paul Streeten, *The Frontiers of Development Studies*, London: Macmillan, 1972

Ian Roxborough, *Theories of Underdevelopment*, London: Macmillan, 1979

7   The rise of towns

Town life is not new; indeed, it is more than just a play on words to say
that it is as old as civilization. However, while hunting and food-gathering
people have no towns, and the neolithic culture which was the basis of
the pre-industrial civilizations supported an urban minority, the rise of
industry has been associated with a process of urban growth in which most
people in industrial countries have come to live in towns. Although in the
present-day poor countries the urban proportion is smaller, it is growing,
and indeed one of the most obvious changes that are taking place in these
countries is a world-wide movement of people from the country to towns
which are experiencing rapid, even headlong growth. But in a world in
which the dominant technology is capital-intensive, that migration is not
generally matched by a corresponding expansion in employment opportunities in modern industry. It is this which gives contemporary urbanization
in the poor countries its special character, and many of its special
problems.

Urban development in historical perspective

The first towns, such as Ur of the Chaldees and Mohenjo-Daro in India,
seem to have arisen before 4000 BC, and their life was clearly related to
aspects of neolithic technology. Agriculture made it possible to accumulate
stores of food, and this enabled some people to live by working at crafts
other than agriculture and selling the products for food. At the heart of
every town, indeed, then as now, is a food market. Stocks of food could,
in particular, be accumulated by persons or groups possessing political
power; taxes or tribute from the surrounding countryside stimulated the
development of writing and counting, and enabled the rulers to employ
bureaucrats, soldiers, and servants, as well as to pay others to build their
palaces and temples, dress them in fine clothes, and deck them with jewels
traded by caravans across the deserts from distant places. And so the
'services' which the town 'exported' to the surrounding countryside, in
exchange for food, included political services or administration, and also
religion; for it seems likely from the excavations that have been made of
ancient cities that their rulers in many cases owed their power at least in

150

part to beliefs that they were of divine origin, or priest-kings uniquely able to perform ceremonies thought vital for the fertility of the land and the survival of men. Thus among the contributions to human culture of the neolithic cities must be counted organized religion, bureaucracy, and organized military forces, the last being necessary to keep order within the city-state and repel the envious nomads prowling round its outskirts. As Keyfitz has pointed out, the relation between these early cities and the surrounding countryside was probably highly exploitative, based as it was on force, bureaucratic organization, and legitimate power. In later civilizations there was more of a balance, with the city dominating its region in an ecological and cultural rather than a political sense, the scene of an uncontrolled market exchange of goods and services which find their own price. Later still, in the most advanced civilizations, cities' taxes may actually subsidize the countryside through agricultural price-support schemes and the like. In the non-industrial societies today, however, it is more likely that the taxation of the peasant generates the capital for industrial development, for example through import duties on consumer goods. Eventually the peasants may be expected to benefit, but after how long?[1]

The greatest cities of the ancient world had populations of as many as a million, and in the most highly developed pre-industrial civilizations between 10 and 20 per cent of the population lived in towns. Rome at the height of its power around AD 150 had a million inhabitants, and of its empire's total population of 50–100 million some 10 million lived in cities. With the decline of the Roman empire these cities decayed; by the ninth century Rome's population is put at 17,000, and it is only in modern times that Rome has again reached the million mark – still depending, incidentally, on the sewers laid down in the classical period.[2] Similarly, according to Kracke, in China there were cities of well over a million in the thirteenth century AD, far bigger than any in Europe at that time, and in the prosperous eighteenth century as many as 20 per cent of China's population lived in towns.[3] Such estimates accord well with early modern censuses of pre-industrial and early industrializing societies. In 1801 nearly 10 per cent of the population of England and Wales lived in London, while just over a further 7 per cent lived in other towns of 20,000 or more.[4] In India the urban population was between 9 and 10 per cent of the total according to the British censuses from 1881 to 1921, rising thereafter to 20 per cent in 1971 and an estimated 22 per cent in 1980.[5]

Rapid increases in the size and importance of towns first affected the early industrializing societies; as Kingsley Davis put it, 'Before 1850 no society could be described as predominantly urbanized, and by 1900 only one – Great Britain – could be so regarded.'[6] The 1851 census, which for the first time showed more people living in towns than in the country, was

151

a landmark in human history, not merely that of Britain. Here the proportion of the population classed as urban went on rising till it reached a peak of just over 80 per cent in 1951; since then it has fallen slightly as people find it possible with modern transport to live in the country and work in the town. Britain, it is true, imports much of its food, exporting industrial products in exchange, and the same could be said of other highly urbanized countries such as Belgium and Hong Kong. But even in a fully industrialized country which also, broadly speaking, feeds itself from its own agricultural production, namely the United States, we also find the proportion classed as urban rising to over 70 per cent since 1970.

Comparisons between countries and the assessment of trends over time encounter statistical difficulties because different countries define towns differently according to the way they organize local government. In the past there have been attempts to standardize, but the most recent sources give figures based on national definitions of the term urban (see table 4.1). There can be no doubt that the world's urban population has risen dramatically, and much faster than the population as a whole. Thus according to data assembled by Breese, in 1800 2.4 per cent of the world's population of 906 million lived in towns of 20,000 or more, and in 1900 the proportion was 9.2 per cent of 1,608 million. By 1960 it had risen to 27.1 per cent of the world's population of nearly 3,000 million. Thus between 1900 and 1960, while the world's population as a whole had not quite doubled, the urban population had increased some five-and-a-half-fold from under 150 million to over 800 million.[7] And that trend has continued. By the early 1980s the proportion of the world's population classed as urban in each country was put at around 40 per cent.[8] Moreover, most of the increase has been in Third World cities. According to the World Bank, average annual growth rates of the urban populations of low-income countries other than India and China were around 5 per cent in the 1960s and 1970s, and 4 per cent in middle-income countries, compared with under 2 per cent in the industrial market economies. Such growth in the poorest countries' cities was surpassed only in those of the high-income oil exporters.[9]

The character of urban growth

In the historical development of the present-day industrial societies, towns that had traditionally been based on handicrafts and trade grew rapidly as they became the centres of the new large-scale industries based on mechanical energy, while some new towns were created in what were previously rural areas. There was a great influx of workers, displaced in many cases from their peasant holdings by agricultural improvement, and living in poor and squalid conditions since neither the capital nor the knowledge was available at that time to house them in decent and sanitary conditions.

In many respects this process is now being paralleled in the poorer countries. Here too some industrial centres, large and small, have arisen out of nothing (for example, Nairobi), while there has been a rapid growth of some existing towns accompanied by a change in their character (for example, Mombasa) and the rise of some industrial conurbations (for example, the Copperbelt and the Witwatersrand). Migration from country to town brings into dense urban settlements large numbers of people who are not used to the conditions of town life. The rapidity of the influx, and the lack of resources, have meant that building to modern standards has not kept pace with the growth of the urban population, and the provision of essential services like water, drainage, and electricity supply lags behind.

In the urban areas of the poor countries, therefore, living conditions are often extremely squalid, and large numbers of people live in 'shanty towns' in shelters which they have made for themselves out of makeshift materials. The official agencies of administration and law and order in such urban areas are often ineffective, partly because of inadequate resources and partly because in many cases they are mistrusted by the people. In such areas there is a good deal of crime and 'vice' – prostitution, illegal manufacture and sale of liquor, extortion rackets, confidence trickery, and the like. People accordingly tend to rely for help and protection on networks of social obligation which they formed in the country areas. Kinship is used as a source of benefits – help in finding a job, accommodation, money, and credit – while people of similar ethnic origin and language tend to stick together and make common cause against others, and create networks of nepotism and patronage, so that some trades may come to be regarded as the preserve of particular ethnic groups, who introduce one another to employers and their agents, and use various devices to exclude others, or get rid of them if they intrude into their preserve. Geographical areas of the city, too, may come to be associated with particular ethnic groups, who take up residence near others speaking the same language, practising the same religion, and using common facilities like shops which sell their particular types of food. Once created, such areas may acquire a life and character of their own. If closed in upon themselves by the hostility of others, they may become 'ghettos' – the name originally applied to the Jewish quarter of European cities in the Middle Ages, and now extended to, for example, the black quarters of American cities. If, however, the structure of opportunity is relatively open, people may migrate out of the ghetto into better-class residential districts as they become more prosperous, and there may be an urban succession like those in which, for example, the Jews moved out and some other group of poor immigrants moved in. The nature of the migration from country to town differs, though, between different towns. Sometimes it is a once-for-all movement in which the new townsmen stay and take up permanent residence. In other cases there may be a circular migration, with some people moving out of the town and back to the country as others replace them. Chicago in the nineteenth century is the classic example of the first; once people had made the long and expensive sea journey from Europe they stayed in America, though Poles (for example) might move out of the Polish quarter and into the prosperous outer suburbs as they made money and became more Americanized. The towns of Africa have in the past afforded examples of the second case, with a good deal of circulation between town and country and a rather small number who settled in town and became permanently urbanized.

In this highly general description we might as well be referring to nineteenth-century Liverpool or Chicago as to the twentieth-century cities in Asia, Africa, or South America. There are, however, some important differences. When the first of the new industrial urban areas grew up in the nineteenth century, their rise was unprecedented; never before had there been anything like them, and there was no previous experience to draw on. I have already referred, in particular, to the 'health of towns' problem in Victorian England, and the way in which modern systems of drainage and water supply had to be thought out from the beginning. As Kingsley Davis put it: 'During the 19th century the urbanizing nations were learning how to keep crowded populations in cities from dying like flies. Now the lesson has been learned, and it is being applied to cities even in countries just emerging from tribalism. In fact, a disproportionate share of public health funds goes into cities.'[10] Disproportionate, one would add, from the point of view of the people in the rural areas in the poorer countries – scarcely so in relation to the sanitary needs of the cities.

Health expenditure, though vital, represents only one of the ways in which the industrial cities and conurbations of the West serve as models of urban life, to emulate which becomes a point of pride for the cities of the newly developing countries. Grandiose municipal and government buildings, stately avenues, skyscraper blocks, sports arenas, and theatres become legitimate objects of municipal aspirations; Manaos has to have its opera house, with performances by Caruso and Melba. The aspirations, like the economies, of the poor countries tend to be oriented to a world market dominated by the West, and these aspirations take concrete architectural form in the buildings and planning of their cities.

It was remarked in chapter 4 that a feature of the economic life of the present-day poor countries is what has been called 'development without employment', and this is nowhere more vividly to be seen than in the new cities of the Third World. The capital-intensive nature of modern industrial development, which has already been noted, means that industry can grow and produce more goods without employing many more workers, and in

154

fact it is the usual experience in these cities for their industrial employment to grow much less fast than their population. This gives rise to situations which, as a first approximation, are often described as unemployment, though the term is too simple and the situation too different for this word to be readily transferred from a western industrial context. More precisely, the economy of new cities can often be regarded as made up of three major sectors.

First, large-scale modern capital-intensive industry. This sector is generally dominated by foreign-owned firms whose management, if not actually conducted by foreigners, is carried out along lines similar to those of large western companies, which are often indeed the parent corporations. Wages in these firms tend to be good, at least by local standards, while working conditions are generally exemplary, and the workers benefit from welfare provisions such as clinics for their families. This is not from pure benevolence on the part of managers; such firms have an interest in a stable, healthy, contented labour force of people aware how much better off they are in the firm's employ. Moreover, there is an element of 'best behaviour' on the part of a firm vulnerable to criticism both locally, because of its position as a guest enterprise, and in its home country. Such a firm will therefore meticulously observe both the local labour laws and good employment practices as they are understood in rich industrial countries, even though its managers may know perfectly well that local firms are not so scrupulous. Characteristic of the latter, according to Lloyd, are firms owned by members of ethnic minorities, or pariah entrepreneurs, as well as ones that have grown from the initiative of an indigenous trader or artisan. In such firms, wages tend to be lower and working conditions markedly inferior. The labour laws are flouted or circumvented, while casual employment prevails, especially in the building industry, which employs many unskilled migrant workers.[11]

Secondly, the state sector. This is not particularly capital-intensive, and it employs considerable numbers of workers at wages near the local market rate as sweepers, cleaners, messengers, road workers, construction workers in public health and housing schemes, and so forth. The state as guardian of the public purse has an interest in keeping the minimum wage of these unskilled workers low. State bureaucracies and those of public corporations, however, embrace many grades from the lowest to the highest, where senior officials in most countries are to be found enjoying a style of life comparable alike with their counterparts world-wide and their compatriots in the private sector. Unless severely constrained by public policy (as, exceptionally, in Tanzania), such bureaucratic hierarchies are a source of income differentials and contribute to the contrasts between rich and poor that characterize life in Third World cities.

Thirdly, a large and highly labour-intensive indigenous private sector.

155

which probably hundreds of thousands of people died of disease, exhaustion, and hunger, if not deliberately executed.[21]

SUGGESTIONS FOR FURTHER READING

Gerald Breese, *Urbanization in Newly Developing Countries*, Englewood Cliffs, N.J.: Prentice-Hall, 1966

Gerald Breese (ed.), *The City in Newly Developing Countries: Readings on Urbanism and Urbanization*, Englewood Cliffs, N.J.: Prentice-Hall, 1969

Peter Lloyd, *Slums of Hope? Shanty Towns of the Third World*, Harmondsworth: Penguin, 1979

8 The family and kinship in a changing world

In no aspect of culture are the diversities of human societies more striking than in the institutions of the family, marriage, and kinship. There are many possible arrangements for meeting the basic human needs of mating, reproduction, the care and upbringing of children, and the care of the aged. Patrilineal, matrilineal, bilateral, and double descent systems; different arrangements for the transfer of possessions and rights from the older to the younger at marriage and at death; the different extent to which kinsfolk are organized in descent groups such as lineages and clans, and the extent to which these groups (where they exist) hold property and make decisions corporately; the varieties of marriage – polygyny, polyandry, or monogamy; the different ways in which a marriage leads sooner or later to the formation of a household, its size and composition, and the position and rights of men and women in it; whether a marriage can be dissolved, and if so on what terms; the many different elements are combined in different societies in a vast variety of permutations, making the comparative study of kinship a happy hunting ground for social anthropologists and constituting a great part of the subject-matter of their science.

If the diversity of kinship is the first lesson of social anthropology, the second is its importance. Every society has a kinship system organized around the universal processes of mating and reproduction. Not every society has highly organized and relatively autonomous institutions such as the state, industrial enterprises, the army, schools, churches, sporting and recreational associations, trade unions, and political parties. As a consequence, many activities which we in a complex society would class as political, or economic, or educational, or religious, etc., are in other societies subsumed under and carried out in the performance of kinship roles. Thus for example the discussion of law and order in Evans-Pritchard's classical study of the Nuer proceeds at once into an analysis of the lineage system.[1] It is not intended to imply that people's behaviour is determined or narrowly prescribed by their kinship roles.[2] Most individuals occupy more than one kinship role, so that a woman is at one and the same time a daughter, a wife, a sister, a mother, an aunt, a sister-in-law, and so on; and the requirements of one role may be hard to reconcile with those of another, so that there may be dilemmas and choices. And there are often conflicts; clans and lineages may fight over land, or engage in deadly intrigue in vying with each other for a king's favour. Faced with choices and conflicts, individuals may *use* their kinship roles (in the sense that the latter do not dominate or determine their actions); we could, however, equally well say that in small-scale societies it is their *kinship* they use to gain their ends, since in the absence of other well-articulated institutions it is all they have.

The processes of social change of the kind with which this book is concerned involve societies in becoming more complex. Additional institutions – office, school, factory, mine – are grafted onto the previously existing social structure in which kinship loomed large. People are faced with problems as they learn to bring their new roles into relation with the roles they already occupy in the kinship system. Sometimes the requirements of the two can be fulfilled without dilemmas and conflicts arising. For example, in Ogionwo's study of Nigerian peasant farmers (detailed in chapter 11), some men found that they could fulfil their obligations to provide their dependants with resources by growing cash crops according to the new methods urged by government agricultural extension officers. For such a man, being a good farmer helped him to be a good father. From one point of view, he was an innovator, a progressive farmer; from another, his actions were highly traditional, representing the thoroughly old-fashioned idea of duty to his family. This example, incidentally, does much to invalidate the view of the modernization school that traditional and modern are at opposite poles.

As a second example of a relation between traditional kinship and the modern economy we may take van Velsen's study of the Tonga of Malawi in the 1950s, when between 60 and 75 per cent of the adult males were absent, mostly working in the mines in Rhodesia (now Zimbabwe) and South Africa. They did not take their wives and children with them for reasons which, as he put it, 'are corroborated by the literature on urban conditions for Africans'. For the same reasons, most men wanted to return home when they retired. Although on the face of it such a system of labour migration might appear grossly disruptive of traditional kinship and village life, van Velsen thought otherwise and regarded it as a positive factor in the continuity of tribal life. Men could rely on their kinsfolk to look after their wives and children, while they remitted home much of their miners' pay for the benefit of their families and kin. They helped kinsmen to find work by providing them with contacts, introductions to employment, and papers (genuine or forged) to facilitate their entry to South Africa. Meanwhile they relied upon their own claims to status and land in the village being kept for them, and took part in the politics of village feuding to that end. 'It is within this framework that Tonga hold gardens, marry, have children, occupy political office, seek for the protection of their rights – in brief, expect security in life.'[3]

In societies of this kind, then, although the institutions of the modern world may have begun to take root it may not be possible for all to avail themselves of their services. In central Africa in the 1950s men could not look to state old age pensions to maintain them in old age. Nor was commercial life assurance a practicable alternative. Although there were banks, they did not have branches in remote country districts, and it would have been distinctly unusual to say the least for African mine workers to handle their money through a bank account. And when it came to the management of village affairs, representative local government institutions of a modern sort did not exist. So people's needs to borrow, save, and mobilize capital, to assert and maintain their rights to land, and in general to secure their future, were met through the kinship network. To reiterate: in such societies people use kinship to gain their ends because that is all they have.

Consequently, in changing societies there are new demands on the kinship system – which is only a more abstract way of saying that people make new demands on their kinsfolk, and respond to family claims in new ways and with new resources.

This poses questions for empirical research. What are the new demands which people make on each other, the new needs they seek to satisfy, and the ends they seek to gain through the kinship network? How adequately does the existing kinship system enable people to meet those needs or gain those ends? What new resources have people at their disposal in the fulfilment of old or new expectations in their kinship roles? And how far do these changes promote change in the kinship system itself? The last is the biggest and in some ways the most difficult question. We tend to assume that, for the time being at any rate, and in the early stages of industrialization, other institutions grow while the kinship system continues to operate along existing patterns. Family and kinship generally seem to change rather slowly, showing indeed a massive continuity compared with more rapid changes in other institutions. Yet changes do occur, and it is important to recognize them.

Some notable studies along these lines were carried out by social anthropologists in the colonial period, especially Audrey Richards' account of Bemba marriage in the economic conditions then prevailing in Zambia.[4] In more recent times there has been a dearth of such studies. Much of our systematic knowledge about the family during industrialization comes from research into the history of the family in western societies, while we also know quite a lot about what happened in Japan. One comprehensive study of the process in a wider perspective is that of W. J. Goode.

165

The family and industrialization in western societies

By western societies in this context I mean those of north-western Europe together with those of similar origins in North America, Australia, New Zealand, and elsewhere. Kinship in these societies has special features, unusual in a world comparison. They include bilateral kinship, reflected in a symmetrical kinship terminology; thus the English language does not distinguish between father's and mother's kin, and for instance both father's sister and mother's sister are called aunt. There are no corporate, or potentially corporate, kin-groups such as clans or lineages. The set of persons whom an individual recognizes as 'related' to him- or herself, properly called the kindred, is not a group and cannot act as one. Marriage is monogamous, and probably was so even before the pagan tribes of north-western Europe were converted to Christianity. A monogamous marriage sets up a new household, that is, marriage is neolocal. The nuclear family household of a married couple and their dependent children, though not isolated, is regarded as a more or less independent economic unit, responsible for its own budgeting and catering, while the responsibility of the nuclear family also for such matters as the way the children are brought up is recognized alike by outside agencies and by other kin. Related households do not normally pool their resources or regard the resources of other households as being at their disposal by right. Nevertheless, though the nuclear family household may be autonomous, it is certainly not isolated. Ties of affection between parents and their offspring, and between siblings (brothers and sisters), formed in childhood, last for life. Young and middle-aged married people retain close links with their parents even though they do not normally share a dwelling with them, and some studies have indicated that relations are particularly close between married women and their mothers.[5] Though not co-resident, the three-generation family is strong. Relations between grandparents and grandchildren are generally close and affectionate. When resources need to be mobilized to meet illness, infirmity, and other misfortunes, or marriage or the birth of children, financial and other help is generally forthcoming even though it is neither claimed nor granted as a matter of right. Thus Colin Bell showed the extent of the support, both financial and in help in emergencies, which middle-class families received from their wider kin, especially the spouses' parents,[6] and Townsend showed that the great majority of old people are looked after by their middle-aged children.[7] As for the wider kindred, though effective kinship generally seems to extend no further than first cousins, nevertheless Firth found that households in London typically recognized between 100 and 200 people as kin, and could name up to 150 of them.[8] Finally, though the last Roman Catholic bastions have yet to fall, in most western countries there is provision for the

166

dissolution of marriage as a safeguard against the breakdown of relations in an area of life in which people tend to have many emotional and financial eggs in one basket.

But though other kin are not lost sight of, and relations with them are important, nevertheless the emphasis is on the autonomous nuclear family household as the residential group in intimate daily interaction. As suggested in chapter 2, pre-industrial family patterns in western societies were those of small households, late marriage, and few children.

Sociologists of a past generation used to believe that such patterns arose in response to the rise of industry, before which there was an extended family system in which numbers of related kinsfolk lived and worked together and mutual aid prevailed. Such views are now regarded as quite mistaken, though they still linger. Much recent research shows that few households in pre-industrial north-western Europe and colonial North America were of a compound or extended type, including for instance the married children and grandchildren of the household head, or the widowed parent of the husband or wife. On the contrary, it has been shown that though little change took place in the average size of the household in these societies, if anything it tended to increase, not decrease, in response to the rise of industry, for reasons considered below.[9] 'Extended family' is an unsatisfactory term. In the sense of a co-resident household, it may be said that there never was an extended family in these societies (whatever may have been the case in southern and eastern Europe). In another sense, however, that of the kindred as a mutual aid network, it could equally be said that the extended family is as much in evidence today as ever it was.

Some other features of the pre-industrial western family are related to the tradition of service. In these societies, people seem never to have employed their own kinsfolk as servants – in contrast, as has been noted, to the practice in some contemporary urban societies in the Third World. The well-to-do gentry and aristocracy in the country, masters and merchants in towns, employed people of a lower social class as living-in servants, so that while their households were numerous (giving rise to mistaken beliefs among later sociologists about extended family households), the households of the poor were correspondingly depleted as some of their members, especially adolescents and young adults, left home to go into service. That included many other kinds of work besides domestic service; agricultural workers on the home farm of a landed estate, apprentices and journeymen in a town master's establishment, were alike regarded as servants along with the groom, the cook, and the housemaid. Further, many western countries such as England and Holland had a maritime tradition, in which for centuries some men ventured in sailing ships on long voyages, lasting sometimes for years. Soldiers too served in distant parts. Nor did people work only for one master; rather, they moved at intervals of a year or more

167

at the annual hiring fair. Some, especially men, may have spent their whole lives in service, while others left it after a while – women to get married (rather late in life, it will be recalled), some men to take up land vacated by the death of a father, others to set up as masters on their own account after serving their time as apprentices and journeymen.[10] Nor was service confined to the lower classes. In the middle ages, the sons of the gentry became pages and knights in the service of lords other than their own fathers, while later in English history a genteel young lady might become a governess or companion in another household.

The tradition of service in pre-industrial western societies, then, meant that there was nothing new about young men and women leaving home, fending for themselves, seeking their fortune (the Dick Whittington syndrome), establishing themselves before marrying, and assuming responsibility for the support of their own households when married.

As noted in chapter 2, one effect of the rise of industry in England may well have been to make earlier marriages possible; women had more children, and the birth-rate rose. We may now see another reason why the average size of households increased: the rise of industry made it possible for teenage children to work while still living at home, instead of going out into resident service, and to stay at home until they married.

This is shown particularly clearly in a study by Michael Anderson of family life in the Lancashire cotton town of Preston in the nineteenth century.[11] To judge from contemporary pronouncements in books and in evidence before Parliamentary committees, the conclusion might well be drawn that family life was disintegrating and in danger of imminent collapse under the stresses of industrialization. A particular occasion for alarm was the threat by young people to leave home and move out into lodgings, or share houses with friends – 'that they may be more at liberty to follow their own inclinations', as one witness put it; and to quote another, 'the result of this precocious independence is, of course, the utter relaxation of all bonds of domestic control'. An examination of the census returns, however, showed that the proportion of young persons living at home with their parents was considerably higher in industrial Preston than it was in agricultural villages in Lancashire. The fact seemed to be that young men and women in Preston indeed stayed at home as long as it suited them – they could live more cheaply at home while working in the cotton mills, in contrast to the living-in type of service which was traditional in pre-industrial society, and still the norm in the nearby rural areas. Another way in which people made use of their family relations to meet the new needs of industrial life was the practice of having a grandmother living in as a resident baby-minder while mother went out to work – female labour, of course, being specially important in the textile industry generally. This certainly suited the grandmothers, and it also saved mothers the expense of putting their small children into the care of child-minders who did it for a living.

Anderson demonstrates that in 'critical life situations' generally, there was an almost complete absence of viable alternatives to the kinship system as a source of help. This was true not only of Preston families, but also of migrants, who were seen as making positive efforts to build up and maintain a kinship net in town – despite, again, the widely held view that migration disrupts kinship bonds.

It seems clear, then, that industrialization did not create the modern western family. On the contrary, the kinship and household institutions characteristic of north-western European societies long antedated the industrial revolution. They included the autonomy of the nuclear family household, congenial as that was to individual thrift and self-help, the accumulation of capital, and decisions to devote resources to the education of children. As noted in chapter 2, there is strong evidence of pre-industrial family limitation in these societies, abandoned temporarily though it may have been in the early stages of the industrial revolution. The tradition of service in others' households, especially among the poor, contributed to the late marriage of women and hence to small families and households and rather low birth-rates in these societies. And it was clearly related to their adaptation to the new opportunities for employment in industry and the migration from country to town; while migrants were sustained by the mutual aid network of the kindred, and the nuclear family household afforded a base for young industrial workers.

But is the association between the particular kinship system that prevailed in north-western European societies and their industrialization merely fortuitous? We might well be inclined to suspect so, were it not for the case of Japan. There we find a society remote from them, isolated indeed during the all-important period, and totally dissimilar in language, religion, and many other important respects, yet whose kinship and family institutions prove to be strikingly similar to theirs, and to be related in similar ways to the rise of industry. This points to the conclusion that a kinship system of this kind, so far from being the result of industrialization, may well be one of its causes, or at least a major facilitating factor.

The family and industrialization in Japan

Some of the background factors affecting the family and society in Japan have been outlined in chapter 2. In the traditional kinship system as described by Chie Nakane, the basic unit was the *ie* or *iye*, a household headed by a man who exercised exclusive control of the household property.[12] He was succeeded, usually in his lifetime, by one man, normally his son. Succession and inheritance were not divided, and there was no joint family or corporate lineage among whom property might be divided or who might exercise joint control. If the household head had no son, then a son-in-law might be designated as successor (a process confusingly called 'adoption' in some of the older literature in the English language); in rare cases an unrelated person such as a servant might be so designated. The object was to maintain the *ie* as a going concern capable of providing its members with a living, including its retired members, the former household head and his wife. The consequent discrimination between the successor and other sons led naturally to jealousy and rivalry, and Nakane quotes a Japanese proverb that 'a sibling is the beginning of a stranger'. Non-successor sons had to fend for themselves and set up new households. They might expect some family help in doing so, but among the peasant classes there was very little help that could be given, while among the wealthier classes the share of non-successor sons in the family property was traditionally minimal. The 1947 Civil Code attempted to remedy what had come to be seen from a modern point of view as an injustice by giving all children, even daughters, equal rights to inherit. Both Nakane and Fujiko Isono report, however, that only urban families with modern ideas avail themselves of the new provisions, while in the country the family land is still in fact transmitted undivided, and non-successor sons in effect waive their rights in order to avoid the fragmentation of holdings which would clearly be uneconomic and disadvantageous to all concerned. In modern times, many non-successor sons have been able to move to towns and get jobs in industry, while others who have stayed in rural areas have found non-agricultural work. According to Isono, although around 1960 there were six million families on the land, only a quarter of them were living exclusively by agriculture, and for the majority their non-agricultural earnings exceeded their agricultural income.[13]

Traditionally a household set up by a non-successor son was a branch, *bunke*, of the original stem household or *honke*. A set of households so linked was called a *dozoku* (and there was confusion here too as this term was mistranslated as 'lineage'). The links between stem and branch households were partly those of natural sentiment and partly ritual, with family reunions to celebrate the ancestor cult. Only aristocrats, however, maintained long genealogies, and for most commoner families there were only two ancestral ceremonies, one for the founder of the stem household, one for that of the branch.

Japanese kinship terminology is perfectly bilateral, and in this it is like those of western societies and most unusual among non-western cultures. Indeed, it is rare to find a non-European language in which English terms such as aunt and cousin have exact equivalents. The only difference in this respect is that in Japanese there are four terms for siblings, distinguishing elder from younger brothers and sisters, where in English there are only two. Moreover, the word *shinrui* means exactly what sociologists term the cognatic kindred, the circle of recognized kinsfolk whom we in vernacular English call our 'relatives'. And as in the West, there are no clans or lineages in Japan. Although, as mentioned, western anthropologists at first thought the *dozoku* was a lineage, that was clearly a mistake. It is not exogamous, and both parallel-cousin and cross-cousin marriages may take place within it; while unrelated servants' households too may be included in it.

Japanese marriage is monogamous, legally so since 1898, in practice traditionally so before that. The essential rule seems to have been that just as a household could have only one male head, so it could have only one mistress. Extra-marital sex relations were not unknown, and prostitution was traditional; but though a man might have a mistress, and might father children outside a marriage, even if he brought her into his household (and a dutiful wife was supposed to accept that with fortitude) her status would be that of a servant, not a co-wife. The status of the mistress of the household was unassailable, and traditionally she would exercise a petty tyranny over her daughter-in-law, the wife of the successor son. On the retirement of the household head, however, in a simple ceremony of handing over a wooden spoon, that tyranny was brought to an end and the daughter-in-law became the unchallenged mistress of the household in her turn. The strength of traditional feelings on this area of family life may be judged from the controversy over the provisions of the 1898 Meiji Civil Code, which, in attempting to modernize the law of marriage and the family, prohibited marriages, *inter alia*, of men under thirty and women under twenty-five without their parents' consent. This was bitterly opposed by traditionalists, on the ground that marriage without the parents' consent ought not to be legal at *any* age!

Some changes in Japanese family and kinship have taken place, and continue to take place in the conditions of modern life. Vogel in his study of the urban professional middle class – the 'salary-men' – reported a weakening of the *ie* ideal, though this caused apprehension among old people who wondered who would look after them in their old age, a point also emphasized by Isono. Traditions of arranged marriage were still strong, though opposed by many young people who were seeking the same sort of freedom of choice and search for 'love' as their counterparts in western industrial countries. Isono reports that the understanding parents of a young couple who fall in love might try to disguise a love-match as an arranged marriage, in order to placate older and more traditionally minded relatives. Vogel, however, found that not all young people were really wholehearted in their attachment to 'love' and freedom of choice. While that might suit some, there were others – 'the over-protected, the bashful, the cautious, those with high standards, those with a proud family history,

171

and the "left-overs"' – who might be quite willing to acquiesce in arrangements or suggestions made by their parents. There was, however, a difference; where the old institution was unequivocally one of arranged marriage, the new practices consisted rather of arranged introductions for a formal first meeting or 'interview', after which the young couple find out for themselves whether they will be suitable marriage partners. Isono puts it quite clearly: 'The favourable attitude to the "interview" is not a remnant of traditional mentality, but *a rational utilization of a traditional practice*' (italics mine).

Modern-minded Japanese families were not inclined to take the ancestor cult very seriously, and there was little that a man had as head of an *ie* that he did not have as a husband and a father. Vogel states accordingly that 'the nuclear family has replaced the *ie* as the basic social unit in Mamachi' (a 'salary-man' residential area).[14]

Although Japanese family and kinship differed in important respects from those of western Europe, there were also striking similarities. Descent was bilateral and marriage in practice monogamous. Although traditionally many Japanese households were of an extended three-generation composition, with the former head and his wife living on in retirement, they were nevertheless small, autonomous, and self-reliant. There was neither a joint family nor a clan or lineage structure. Non-successor sons were expected to move out and fend for themselves, with little or no material help from the stem family. Even though there were some differences in detail, in essentials the Japanese family like its western counterpart proved readily adaptable to the new circumstances, and must be counted as a facilitating factor in the rise of industry. Changes that have occurred, especially among the well-to-do, modern-minded, urban population have tended to make the Japanese family even more like that of the West, and there is evidence too of the ways in which people have made use of traditional institutions to meet their needs in modern conditions.

W. J. Goode's two theses: 'fit' and 'convergence'

The foregoing summary thus tends to support the first of the two major theses advanced by W. J. Goode, namely that there is a 'fit' or congruence between the conjugal family and the modern industrial economy.[15] Goode used the term conjugal as a shorthand expression for the whole complex of characteristics of the western family much as I have outlined them – an emphasis on the nuclear family household as the normal residential unit, bringing up children and managing its own affairs in relative financial independence; monogamy, relatively free choice of marriage partner, egalitarianism in relations between spouses, some provision for divorce in case of marital breakdown, though with checks and safeguards for the interests of dependent children; bilateral descent, an absence of clan or lineage structures and of joint family systems giving other kin (the 'elders' as he called them) the right to interfere in the choice of marriage partner or the affairs of the nuclear family household.

Goode's second thesis was that as other societies become industrialized their family patterns may consequently be expected to converge on the conjugal type. That put him in the company of writers such as Clark Kerr who maintained that there is a logic of industrialization impelling all industrial societies towards similar institutions – a point of view broadly in line with that of the modernization school.[16]

Goode investigated those hypotheses in a monumentally comprehensive review of the available evidence from most of the major continents and culture areas of the world: the West, Arabic Islam, Africa south of the Sahara, India, China, and Japan. His coverage was not quite world-wide, and he noted with regret the paucity of studies of eastern Europe and of Latin America, while the Islamic world outside the Arab states was also omitted. In considering India, China, and Japan he dealt with the material from one large state, while his other areas consisted of a number of states, as in Europe, Arabic Islam, and Africa. From each area he amassed a wide variety of evidence, including laws (together with the reports of government commissions on family law and related topics), official statistics (of much of which he was properly sceptical), social surveys, and the field reports of social anthropologists. This evidence he analysed under similar broad headings, adapted as necessary. They included practices relating to the choice of mate, plural marriage (polygyny or polyandry), marriages with relatives, age at marriage, the birth-rate and fertility along with related factors such as infanticide, abortion, and contraception; the extended family, household, clan, and kin network beyond the nuclear family; divorce and the remarriage of widows and divorced persons; the position of women in the wider society, women's work and rights, the equality of sexes; and relations internal to the family, especially those between spouses. Sometimes it proved difficult to separate material under these heads. For instance, the marriage or betrothal of children obviously came under 'age at marriage', but it also affected choice of mate, and had a bearing on the power of parents and other elders in a wider kin network to exercise that choice on behalf of dependent minors.

From that study of the literature, Goode concluded that where changes in the family were taking place at all there was indeed a convergence. In many countries laws had been enforced prohibiting such traditional practices as infant marriage and betrothal, and bringing legal minimum ages into line with internationally accepted standards. Arranged marriages had declined and there had been a general trend towards individual choice of marriage partner. Very large 'extended family' households were more of a myth than a reality in most civilizations, yet modern changes had tended towards nuclear family households as the norm. Relations with wider kin were of continuing importance, no less in the West than elsewhere, but the power and indeed the inclination of kinsfolk to interfere in the running of, or share the benefits of, the nuclear family household had been reduced. Where divorce had been easy and divorce rates high, it had become more difficult, in some cases with the interposition of a judicial process, and rates had fallen; where it had been hard, shameful, or even quite impossible, it had been legally instituted and tended to lose some of its former stigma. It was in this respect that convergence had been most striking, with a movement in contrary directions from the two extremes towards the middle position of most western countries where divorce is possible but not easy, with checks and safeguards for the children.

However, change had been neither uniform nor rapid. Thus in India, though infant marriage had been abolished, it was not yet generally accepted that young adults had the right to meet, engage in courtship, and decide whom and when to marry. Arranged marriages were still normal and girls were strictly chaperoned. Caste endogamy was generally observed, most people supported the joint family at least in principle, and though divorce had been legalized it remained hard and shameful. Contrary to Hindu traditions most people favoured the remarriage of widows, but women did not yet mingle freely with men in most walks of life. Similarly in Africa little or no change had taken place in such institutions as polygyny, clan and lineage structures, traditional courtship, or divorce.

The qualifying phrase 'where changes were taking place at all' was an important one, therefore, and in a good many areas of family life no change was to be discerned. But the strongest point in favour of Goode's thesis was that according to his evidence there were no contrary changes. Nowhere, for example, had there been a tendency for parents to exercise *more* control over their children's marriages, for the wider kin network to be *strengthened*, for *more* men to take plural wives, or for hard and shameful divorce to become even harder and more shameful.

As has been seen, there are reasons for agreeing with Goode that the particular forms of the family that prevailed in the West and in Japan were such as to facilitate industrialization in those countries.

If that is the case, then change in the family may be expected to be more radical in societies with other kinship systems. While there may well be a convergence, and the kinship systems of those countries may come to resemble those of the early-industrializing nations, nevertheless the discontinuities are likely to be sharper. For a time at least, the transitional forms of the family (in the Third World) may differ substantially from those of industrial societies, in relation to the widely different traditions that were their starting-points for change.

Conclusion: continuity and change

Paradoxically, it seems, a realistic consideration of the family has to emphasize both continuity and change.

On the one hand, family relations are lifelong relations, partly as a matter of sentiment and partly on account of property. Emotional relations among near kin may be of love or hate, or most often perhaps a mixture of both, but seldom indifference. Widely if not universally in all cultures, people have legitimate expectations that their offspring will care for them in their old age. Family relations also involve a long-term interest in property, especially land, houses, and household effects – the assets and resources that provide for lifetime needs and for those of succeeding generations. Such considerations alone seem likely to make the pace of change in family relations a slow one compared with the rapid changes that take place during a lifetime in the world outside the family. That perhaps is the residue of truth in the otherwise much disputed view of the family as an island of stability in a changing world.

Thus, as already noted, Ogionwo found that what he termed familism was unrelated to progressiveness among Nigerian farmers. Similarly, in his studies in Africa and the Caribbean Doob found that people changing from old to new ways in other aspects of life retained traditional attitudes to the family. I refer to their work in more detail in chapter 11.

On the other hand, family and kinship institutions have proved resilient in their adaptation to change. Kinship networks have sustained people in new vicissitudes and (in Anderson's term) new critical life situations. Industrialization has not disrupted kinship but rather strengthened it. Thus Yonina Talmon-Garbier found in her study of immigrants from Islamic countries to Israel that 'the initial reaction to social change is neither attenuation and decline nor mere persistence but an upsurge of kinship solidarity and heightened commitment... The stability and security of kin bonds generate flexibility and receptiveness to change while instability and insecurity generate defensiveness and rigidity.'[17]

Among the changes that seem likely to affect family relations in the Third World, none is more important than the world-wide tendency towards greater participation by women in activities outside the domestic domain. Too much should not be made of the fact that in India and Sri Lanka as well as in Israel, Britain, and Iceland women have risen to the highest political office. Such outstanding individual cases are not incompatible with what has been called 'tokenism' and 'the statutory woman' at the middle

175

and lower levels in politics, business, and administration, though no doubt they illuminate the way in which the emancipation of women has been seen as an important aspect of general modernity. More important perhaps is the general extent of women's economic activity outside the household. It was noted in chapter 4 that, in so far as it is useful to distinguish between a traditional or subsistence sector and a modern cash sector in the economy of a Third World country, hitherto women have been more involved in the former and men more in the latter. That may be the case to a diminishing extent as new opportunities open for women's employment and their activity in the cash sector generally. And even if much of that employment is in the stereotypical female occupations, such as primary teachers, nurses, and secretaries, it entails the schooling of girls, and so runs counter to the tendency to favour boys, as seen in chapter 9. It involves women in taking responsibility and making decisions, and so runs counter to traditional attitudes requiring their subservience to men and acquiescence in the latter's decisions. And it makes many women at least partially and potentially independent of a man's economic support, which cannot but have profound consequences for relations between the sexes and family relations generally.

Inkeles and Smith, in their study detailed in chapter 11, found that modern-minded individuals were imbued with a conviction that we can make our world by means of rational decisions effectively implemented. This general attitude applies with particular force to fertility decisions, especially on the part of women, with vital implications for population trends. Thus it is in this light that we can see the significance of the findings of the World Fertility Survey, referred to in chapter 2, that it was about the methods of fertility limitation applicable by women that women in Third World countries were most aware. Is it entirely speculative to suggest that the down-turn in world fertility began when women decided to take matters into their own hands?

SUGGESTION FOR FURTHER READING

W. J. Goode, *World Revolution and Family Patterns*, Glencoe, Ill.: Free Press, 1963; paperback edition with a new preface, 1970

9   Cultural diversity, language, education, and the mass media

Cultural diversity

In the neolithic world of limited communications, human communities in relative isolation developed different cultures. The term culture in this context refers to a whole way of life: a complex whole including language, material culture or technology, social institutions, and religious, moral, and aesthetic values. A culture is a combination of these elements in a total pattern recognizably different from other cultures, even those with which there are elements in common. Thus neighbouring societies might get their living in similar ways yet speak different languages and have different forms of political organization. There may be problems of delineation, as cultures shade over into one another; for instance, it may be a moot point whether two tongues are different languages or dialects of the same language. So we cannot say with precision how many different human cultures there are, or were, before the forces that in our time have made for the breaking down of isolation. But that should not lead us to minimize the extent and depth of cultural diversity, to which the whole science of social anthropology bears witness.

Cultural diversity, though a common characteristic of many Third World countries, is not equally well marked in all. Some areas have long been exposed to the overlordship of a dominant people, whose culture has more or less heavily overlaid the indigenous folk-cultures, or even (as noted in chapter 3) extinguished them altogether. That is most clearly so in Latin America, though even there the persistence of pre-conquest cultures should not be overlooked, for instance among the Amazon forest peoples, while in Bolivia more people speak Amerindian languages than Spanish as their mother-tongue, and there are four and a half million Quechua-speakers in Peru.[1] A common language, religion, and related institutions such as kinship are equally evident in the Arab-Muslim region. Cultural diversity is rather more marked in Asia despite the unifying factor of religions – Islam in Pakistan and Indonesia, Buddhism in Burma and the adjoining lands. In India, a recognition of cultural diversity and tolerance of different ways of life and worship have always characterized the Hindu attitude to life, and non-Hindu communities found an accepted place in society through the caste system. It is in Africa that cultural diversity is most marked, presumably because of the short time since, under colonial rule, government was established over wider areas than the tribe and barriers to communication were overcome.

As an illustration, Uganda is a comparatively small country whose population was some four million when British rule was established around 1900, and about thirteen million in 1980. That population includes some twenty-five to thirty groups, each with a language, culture, and identity recognized as distinctive by themselves and others.[2] (Under colonial rule such groups were called tribes; I discuss the word below.)

The indigenous languages of Uganda have been classified in four main groups as Bantu, (Central) Sudanic, Western Nilotic, and Eastern Nilotic (formerly termed Nilo-Hamitic). Within each group the individual languages resemble one another, though the degree of mutual comprehension varies. Thus the Bantu languages are about as alike or as different as English, German, Danish, and Dutch. Nilotic, Sudanic, and Bantu languages, however, differ much more fundamentally in grammar, vocabulary, and tone.

Though kinship systems in Uganda are not as diverse as elsewhere in Africa, there are important differences between peoples with a fixed number of clans (especially in the Bantu-speaking south) and those with flexible and fissiparous lineage systems (especially in the Nilotic-speaking areas). These were related to differences of political organization. In the south there were the highly centralized kingdoms of the interlacustrine Bantu – BuGanda, BuNyoro, Ankole – with strongly authoritarian and inegalitarian attitudes about political relations and human relations generally. One of the titles of the Kabaka or king of BuGanda was Sabataka or chief of the clan-heads, and the latter held traditional fiefs including county chieftainships, military commands, and courtly offices. Elsewhere political authority was weak or absent, and political relations were conducted at the level of feuds among lineages. Unlike Kenya, few of the peoples of what is now Uganda practised circumcision or organized young men into warrior age-sets, though some did including the BaGisu. Politically the area was a kaleidoscope of small kingdoms or chiefdoms expanding, conquering their neighbours, reducing them to tributary status, and establishing small empires that fell apart again after a generation or two.

European intervention and colonial rule had the effect of simplifying the pattern and fixing it in a more definite form. The British arrived on the scene late in the nineteenth century when one little empire, that of Bunyoro-Kitara, was in decline. The province of Toro had lately asserted its independence, and the neighbouring kingdom of Buganda was aggressively expanding. The British based themselves on Buganda and extended their rule to adjoining areas in alliance with its remarkable missionary-

178

schooled elite, and the very name of the protectorate, Uganda, is the Swahili version of the name of the kingdom.[3] Their central position, their alliance with the British, and their head start in schooling and economic development put the Ganda in a position of privilege if not hegemony over other tribes in the Uganda Protectorate. As elsewhere in Africa, the boundaries of that protectorate were settled by statesmen in the chancelleries of Europe drawing lines on a map – lines that parted like from like as often as they united unlikes under a common overrule. There is scarcely a point at which the boundaries of Uganda do not divide people who had a common language and culture, and in some cases a traditional political unity.

Uganda can thus be seen as a highly artificial and arbitrary creation. For about sixty years it was subject to British rule, with the establishment of a common official language – the completely alien English – along with common systems of taxation, justice, schooling, traffic regulations, and the like, while shortly before independence the forms of representative government were set up. When it became independent in 1962, however, it was a country with no common indigenous language or culture, nor any deeply felt traditional loyalty or sense of national identity on the part of its people. Those sentiments belonged rather to the primordial groups such as the interlacustrine Bantu kingdoms; and attachments to and rivalries among those groups dominated Uganda's stormy and tragic post-independence history, to which I return in chapter 12.

In these respects Uganda is by no means unusual among modern African states. It is rather the countries with a single indigenous language and a common political tradition – Lesotho, Swaziland, Somalia, and Madagascar – that are the exceptions. Elsewhere a similar diversity prevails. In neighbouring Tanzania, for example, there are not twenty-five to thirty but well over a hundred recognizably different cultural groups; while rivalries between such groups in other countries too, notably Nigeria, have led to devastating civil wars.

What word shall we use?

Not long ago it was the common practice for a social anthropologist to use the term 'tribe' for the human group, with its distinctive culture, that was the object of his or her study. That usage was, as it were, unselfconscious; neither pejorative nor patronizing, but neutrally descriptive. To be sure, there were imprecisions. As La Fontaine put it, 'There are thus two types of meaning for "tribe": one which refers to cultural homogeneity, usually symbolized by a single language, and another which denotes a group organized as a political unit.'[4] Evans-Pritchard, adopting the latter usage, stated that 'within a tribe there is law', and used the term 'congeries of tribes' for the wider cultural community of which the politically fragmented

179

Nuer tribes were segments.[5] Other social anthropologists have preferred a definition like Gulliver's 'any group of people which is distinguished, by its members and by others, on the basis of cultural–regional criteria'.[6]

Colonial administrations too used the word tribe, and it was among the questions people were asked on occasions such as seeking employment or entering a school or college. For purposes of that kind it had a commonsense justification; if a person's tribe was known, then one also knew such essential things as his or her mother-tongue and home area. From the point of view of social science, one of the most important such occasions was the census. Demographic data were useful as a background to more detailed studies by social anthropologists; indeed, one of the first things the reader of a monograph about a people wants to know is how many of them there are. They were important too to geographers and economists; for example, internal migration patterns within an African country could hardly be studied without reference to census data on tribes.[7] Such data had a bearing on the planning of school systems, for example in deciding on the allocation of resources to the production of text-books in the different vernacular languages; while by comparing the tribal composition of students at a university college (as I did at Makerere) with the population of the tribes from which they came, it was possible to lay bare the patterns of regional and ethnic disparities in the incidence of higher education.[8]

In modern times, a person's tribe became an important aspect of his or her ascribed status, and this led to inter-tribal rivalries and conflicts. In many cases some tribes came to dominate particular occupations; this arose partly from stereotyping by employers who believed, for example, that some tribes were physically strong, others quick-witted, etc.; and partly from attempts on the part of workers of a particular tribe to project a favourable image and so create a partial monopoly of the trade for themselves.

Factional rivalries over such things as employment, housing, and education accordingly led to a heightening of tribal consciousness at a time when traditional tribal identity was being transferred into new, non-traditional situations. Thus Parkin traced the rivalries between the immigrant Luo and the local Ganda tenants in a municipal housing estate in Kampala in the 1960s,[9] while Grillo showed how the Luo and the Luyia-Samia factions grappled for control of the Railway African Union in Uganda at the same period.[10]

Finally, after independence, tribal rivalries have broken out in many new states over the biggest prize of all – the control of the state with all its power and resources.

It is not hard to understand why modern governments in poor countries, especially in Africa, should have come to regard factionalism and particularism of this kind as a negative force to be opposed, a danger to be

checked. Tribalism got a very bad name as a result of events like the
Nigerian civil war. Katanga separatism in Zaire, and Buganda separatism
in Uganda. It is not surprising therefore that modern African leaders have
played down tribal differences in the name of nation-building, however
artificial and arbitrary the nations to which the new sentiments of loyalty
are to be attached. Thus the government of Tanzania departed from the
practice of its colonial predecessors and omitted any question on tribe from
the 1967 census, a decision which, however understandable politically,
was much to be regretted from the point of view of social science. As we
have seen in chapter 6, a nation-state with a common language and
common citizenship has come to be regarded as the badge of modernity,
while tribalism is associated with the stigma of backwardness and repudiated
by the modernizing elites. And so, as Audrey Richards well put it, some
African political leaders wished to forget the different tribal polities by
which Africa is inhabited, and wrote as though the colonial powers had
invented tribal differences, though such a view seemed clearly disingenuous
and involved turning a blind eye to the immense diversity of African
cultures.[11]

Perhaps partly in deference to the feelings of African political leaders
and intellectuals, some social scientists too have tried to avoid the word
tribe, even though it merely entailed using an equivalent term such as
ethnic group, cultural group, people, or (in the context of language)
mother-tongue group. That seems a clear case of what Myrdal called
'diplomacy by terminology'. Some have gone further; thus Vincent wrote
'Surely the "tribe" may best be viewed as a colonial administrative unit
given legitimacy, and indeed in some cases reality, by colonial
recognition?'[12] while in the same vein Apthorpe stated that 'the colonial
regimes administratively *created* tribes as we think of them today'.[13]
Another consideration that may lead some writers not only to reject the
word tribe but also dismiss the whole subject may be a view that such
institutions as language, kinship, religion, laws, and morals are merely
superstructural epiphenomena unworthy of serious attention from the
point of view of economic determinism and a materialist conception of
history and of society. Thus, as noted in chapter 6, some radical underdevelopment writers have repudiated the very notion of a traditional
economy and society, and seen only the capitalist world system. But the
reality is still there; it does not become something else when we decide to
call it by another name, nor does it go away if we decide not to take it
seriously.

Language

In most industrial societies most people speak the same language, which is also the official language of the state. Most, not all, for complete uniformity does not everywhere prevail; for example, among the people of the United Kingdom are those whose mother-tongues are Welsh and Gaelic, Arabic, Gujarati, and Polish, yet English is overwhelmingly the majority language. Some countries, such as Sweden and Japan, are called linguistic states because their language is peculiar to them and not much spoken elsewhere. In other cases, the national language of one state is widely spoken and officially recognized in other countries too, as French is in Belgium, Canada, and Switzerland; German in Austria and Switzerland; Spanish throughout Latin America except Brazil; and English in the United States and other countries. Among industrial countries, multi-lingual states are the exception rather than the rule; and though the difference may be one of degree rather than of kind, the contrast with the Third World is clear and wide.

In many Third World countries, the diversity of languages is much greater, and the local indigenous languages have only limited currency and do not serve as languages of wider communication. In order to cope with employment, education, dealings with officials, and everyday communication in shop and street, their people are forced to be linguists, learning at least one other language besides their mother-tongue, and often more. Some indeed become remarkably adept at language-switching according to the social situation; thus hotel workers in Kenya have been heard to switch from one to another of four or five languages including their mother-tongue such as Kamba, the lingua franca Swahili, English, and German, spoken by many tourists.[14]

On the whole it is men who have hitherto been under the greater necessity to learn languages other than their mother-tongue, since (as noted in chapter 4) they have been more involved in the wider social milieux of employment, trade, and migration to towns, while women (on the whole, with some exceptions as in West Africa) have been more engaged in those of the household, family, and neighbourhood, where the vernacular prevails. For example, a survey in Uganda in 1968 found that 52 per cent of men but only 18 per cent of women could converse in Swahili; 28 per cent of men, 13 per cent of women in English.[15] Local languages accordingly continue to be mother-tongues, learned by children of both sexes. Later in life, different languages may be needed for different purposes. Manual workers may need to know an oral lingua franca for work, traders for business, and town dwellers for communication with neighbours; while those who aspire through schooling to better-paid jobs in management and administration need to learn a language of wider communication as well. Since some people need to know the formal, literary language of wider communication, and it is not always possible to know in advance who they will be, such elite languages may have to be taught in schools to many who will have little or no use for them in later life.

Thus in Tanzania, although more than a hundred different vernacular languages have been recognized, nearly all of them are Bantu. That has facilitated the rise of Swahili as the lingua franca spoken and understood by virtually all men, though probably to a lesser extent by women. Swahili is basically Bantu in its grammar and structure, with a vocabulary enriched with Arabic, Portuguese, and English words adapted to the needs of modern life; this includes a fully developed system of number, lacked by most Bantu languages. It has been written in Roman script since the nineteenth century, and can also be written in Arabic script, in which there is a somewhat limited older literature. It was much encouraged too under both German and British colonial rule.[16] Its advantages as a national language, however, were offset by its limitations as a language of wider communication. Though spoken quite widely in neighbouring Kenya and Uganda, parts of Zaire, and the coasts of Somalia and Mozambique, it does not give access to a wider world of science, technology, literature, trade, or diplomacy. That continues to be the role of English, the legacy of the colonial period, which retains an important place in the secondary school curriculum. Educated young Tanzanians therefore have to learn three languages – their vernacular mother-tongue, Swahili, and English – unless they live at the coast or in Zanzibar, where Swahili is the mother-tongue.

In Uganda no lingua franca gained so strong a foothold under colonial rule. Many men in fact learned Swahili in trade and employment, but its use was deprecated and opposed by the people of Buganda, who under British overrule enjoyed a privileged position of hegemony. It was a houseboy's language, they said, spoken by white bwanas to their servants in Kenya, and it was not the mother-tongue of any indigenous group in the protectorate of Uganda. It was, however, the language of the army, since under colonial government Ugandan units formed part of a regiment, the King's African Rifles, which drew units also from Kenya, Tanganyika, and Nyasaland (as they were then named), and in which Swahili was the obvious lingua franca. At the same time, fears of Ganda hegemony on the part of the other tribes of the protectorate led to resistance to any suggestion that Luganda (the Ganda language) should become the general lingua franca there, and so after independence the only choice for an official language was the completely alien English. One advantage of this situation was nevertheless that in the education system it was possible to go straight from the vernacular to English, without the intervening step of Swahili. Ganda disdain for Swahili later caught up with them in an

183

unpleasant and unexpected way. As related by Mazrui, after the downfall of the Kabaka of Buganda and the suppression of the Ganda kingdom, 'a linguistic test [began] to be used as a way of determining the degree of humiliation to which a captured person was to be subjected'; soldiers tended to beat up any black man who could not answer them fluently in Swahili, and whom they thought likely accordingly to be a subject of the departed Kabaka – including on one occasion a Jamaican colleague of Mazrui.[17]

The decision to adopt a local language as the official language of a new state, therefore, while it may be a natural choice and one which can focus national consciousness, can also have politically divisive effects if the language is that of a group whose dominance is feared and resented, and it may also lead to a partial abandonment of a language of wider communication. These are points of more general application, as will appear below.

And language problems have arisen even in states based on a single language and culture. When the Somali Republic became independent in 1960, there were no fewer than three languages of wider communication: Arabic, the language of Islam, and English and Italian, the legacies of colonial rule in the north and in the south respectively. There was no generally accepted script for Somali itself. It had long been written in Arabic script, but not very satisfactorily. About 1920 an entirely new script had been devised, named Osmaniya after its originator, which was championed by Somali nationalists, and did not readily give way to the claims of a Roman orthography. The language question itself was a vexed one and it was many years before an orthography could be agreed. Meanwhile written communication within the country was in English, Italian, and to a lesser extent Arabic; while rivalries between English- and Italian-speaking elites, each with their distinctive heritage of ideas about how the country should be governed, made for factionalism within the new state. Only their common cultural nationalism can, it seems, account for the success that was achieved despite these difficulties in binding north and south together in one Somali nation.[18]

Most traditional African cultures did not include writing, a generalization to which cases like Swahili and Somali in Arabic script afford only partial exceptions. Most African languages were committed to writing from the late nineteenth century onwards, mainly by Christian missionaries, and in the Roman script. Like other phonetic alphabets such as Greek, this assumes a sequence from the idea through the sound to the written symbol. Although Roman is not perfectly suited to every language, it can be adapted to most, and it has very great advantages. Literacy in one language can readily be transferred to another, so that though many Africans have to learn more than one language, they do not have to learn more than one script. For example, Kikuyu, Swahili, and English are all written in Roman. Furthermore, the comparatively limited number of symbols required – basically the 26 letters of the alphabet – make it highly convenient and economical for international use in printing and type-writing. On the other hand, since it associates shapes with sounds completely arbitrarily, it is not an easy script to learn, and many children have difficulty with it, as evidenced by controversies in western countries over methods of teaching and initial teaching alphabets. And though once learned it can be applied to other languages, it does not help people to communicate with those who speak other tongues.

By contrast, as its name implies, in the ideographic script of China the written symbol represents the idea, not the sound. The sequence from the idea to the symbol is in principle independent of that from the idea to the sound. Thus at the most elementary level at which young children learn to write, the symbols for 'man', 'woman', 'house', etc., consist of styl-ized pictures (rather like the non-lingual ideograms for basic needs to be seen in public places in western countries too nowadays). This makes an ideographic script delightfully easy to learn in the early stages, literally child's play, indeed. Its other great advantage is that people who speak different languages can nevertheless communicate with ease in writing. In China, a land of several different languages, the common ideographic script is thus regarded as indispensable for national unity. On the other hand it has serious disadvantages. The simplicity and obviousness of the ideographs for commonplace objects are replaced by extreme complexity and difficulty when it comes to more advanced concepts, which require allusions (often to similar-sounding words) and other conventions de-manding an enormous expenditure of time and effort to learn. Thus in contrast to Roman's 26 letters, ordinary literate Chinese may know perhaps 3,000 symbols, newspapers use 6,000–7,000, and the most literate people know as many as 30,000–50,000. In traditional China that meant that the education of the elite was in the narrowest sense literary, a matter of learning thousands of symbols and their meanings and knowing how to use them in context. In modern times, too, the difficulties for printing and typing can readily be appreciated.

Among the spoken Chinese languages the one that used to be called Mandarin, named the national language under the Kuomintang republic, and latterly re-named Putonghua or everyday speech, has become more and more widely understood in twentieth-century China. Writing it in Roman script, however, runs into the difficulty that words may have different meaning according to whether they are pronounced with a rising, falling, or level tone, which is not readily represented in Roman. Various orthographies were devised in the nineteenth and twentieth centuries, and the system of conventions known as Pinyin was officially adopted in 1958

185

for transcribing Chinese personal names and place names into Roman in foreign language publications. Meanwhile there has been a policy of simplifying the traditional symbols for printing and writing in China itself.

India like China has a rich and ancient heritage of literary culture, but each of the major Indian languages has its own script, and there are also ritual scripts such as Gurmukh in which Punjabi is written for the purposes of the Sikh religion. Each of these scripts, and the language and culture associated with it, was regarded as a precious heritage, and the post-independence history of India was marked by violent disputes as the country was reorganized into linguistic states. Under British rule English had taken firm root as the official language, and hence the language of opportunity for the intellectual and bureaucratic elite, so that many families at the highest social level adopted it as their mother-tongue. Ironically it was they who were the 'Anglicists' in the nineteenth-century controversies over educational development, while the British officials tended to be 'Orientalists' and included men with a deep respect for Indian culture who exerted themselves to save Sanskrit from oblivion.

The government of independent India faced difficult problems over language. While the English-speaking elite were a considerable national asset for the communication of scientific and cultural ideas with the rest of the world, as well as for diplomatic and business contacts, they were correspondingly cut off from the great majority of their fellow-countrymen, and the use of English as the official language emphasized a distance between government and people that was quite inappropriate after the departure of the British. The decision in 1963 to adopt Hindi in the Devanagari script as the official language could be said to bring government nearer to the people – but only some people. It was a contentious decision by which people in non-Hindi-speaking areas felt disadvantaged, not least because their children now had to learn an extra language at school compared with those whose mother-tongue was the new official language. Well-meaning proposals to equalize the handicap by making Hindi-speaking children learn some other Indian language seemed unrealistic and ineffective.[19] Feelings ran high and riots broke out over this issue in 1965, particularly in Madras, and the government was forced to modify its policy.

In India, too, people have to be not bi-lingual but tri-lingual, and (to coin a term) tri-scriptal as well, as they learn first the language of their state with its traditional script, then Hindi in Devanagari, then English in Roman. More time spent on language leaves less time for substantive subjects such as mathematics, science, and history, and there are said also to be indirect effects in an emphasis on memory work and rote learning which spread to the way other subjects are taught as well as the little time left to teach them, and led Myrdal to exclaim that 'people are not merely being insufficiently educated; they are being mis-educated on a huge scale'.[20]

Although India may be regarded as something of an extreme case, 'bi-scriptalism' is also called for in Arabic countries in so far as the Roman script is needed for English or French as languages of wider communication. And similar problems arise in some other south Asian countries. In Sri Lanka, for instance, there are three languages – Sinhalese and Tamil, each with its own script, and English with Roman script. In Pakistan the language spoken by the biggest number of people is Punjabi, with a script different from that used for the official language Urdu. Both regional and national languages have to be taught in Burma and Thailand. Another example of linguistic complexity is the Philippines, where there are several Malayo-Polynesian vernacular languages of which the one spoken by the biggest number is Cebuano. Another, however, was chosen as the national language since it was the vernacular language of the region of Manila, had greater prestige, and was spoken more widely as a second language; this was Tagalog, renamed Pilipino as a matter of national pride. Spanish has been used in the islands for many centuries, and continues to be taught in schools; while English has also been taught in the primary schools since the beginning of the American administration as the premier language of wider communication. At least, however, all these languages, including the vernaculars, are written in Roman script.[21]

Enough has been said, perhaps, to show the importance of language and linguistic diversity in Third World countries. That importance is particularly marked in education, politics, and the mass media of communication, to which I turn below.

Science, culture, and development

Science is a social institution whose manifest function is discovery. Scientists aim to make statements about the world that shall be true irrespective of who makes them. Scientific propositions (hypotheses, theories) are open to be tested by any competent observer against observations of the real world, and knowledge consists at any time of tested and not-yet-falsified theories. Science is accordingly the most truly international of all institutions, and the knowledge with which scientists are concerned is trans-cultural, transcending the national and ethnic cultures in which they were severally brought up. Yet there is a paradox here, for knowledge is an essential constituent of every culture. Without reliable knowledge of the world, peasant cultivators, herdsmen, and fishermen could not survive, any more than an industrial society can survive without a scientific technology. While all cultures embody some science, though, they differ widely in the extent to which they have (so

187

to speak) domesticated science, and the extent and complexity of the not-yet-falsified knowledge which they embody. Science is everywhere at loggerheads with false belief, and western societies are no exception; there seems no warrant whatever for viewing ours as in any sense a specially scientific culture. Yet it was in western countries that modern science was nurtured, and overwhelmingly in industrial countries that it is now pursued. Whether measured in terms of the resources devoted to it, the numbers of scientists engaged in it, or their published contributions to knowledge, something like 95 to 98 per cent of scientific activity is carried on in industrial countries.[22]

Science is an intensely competitive and selective activity, and though in principle it is open to all, in practice, because of their systematic advantages, most scientists turn out to be white rather than black, men rather than women, and of upper- or middle-class social origins.[23] The centres of excellence where research of world renown is carried on are overwhelmingly located in industrial countries, where they afford apt examples of growth poles giving rise to backwash effects in 'brain-drains' and the paucity of scientific work in poor countries. At the level of applied science, too, it is often said that topics chosen for research tend to be related to the problems of industrial rather than agrarian societies, of temperate rather than tropical climates and crops, and towards capital- rather than labour-intensive technology.

Education

Some indication of the extent of schooling and of literacy in Third World countries may be gained from United Nations statistics. Tables 9.3 and 9.4 show how unequivocally each is a part of the modern sector, affecting males more than females, town more than country. Tables 9.1 and 9.2 show how rapidly each has spread in poor countries since 1960. Third World countries in general, indeed, have devoted immense effort and resources to this aspect of their development. In most countries formal education is the biggest single item of public expenditure, and its share in the budgets of Third World countries typically rose from 10–15 per cent in the 1960s to 20–25 per cent in the 1970s. Public expenditure on their school systems has risen something like twice as fast as GNP in developing countries as a whole, while in many this has been the only sector of the economy in which planned targets have regularly been achieved and even exceeded. Much of this effort, too, has gone into secondary and higher education, which have absorbed disproportionate shares of budgets, while population growth and rising numbers of children of school age have led some governments quietly to postpone or abandon their goal of universal primary schooling. Nevertheless, much progress has been achieved, as the figures show.

Table 9.1 *Primary school enrolments and adult literacy, 1960–1979*[1]

| | Percentage of age group enrolled in primary school[2] | | | | Adult literacy rate, per cent[3] | |
| | Male | | Female | | | |
	1960	1979	1960	1979	1960	1977[1]
Industrial market economies	100+	100+	100+	100+	...	99
Non-market industrial economies	100+	95	100+	96	98	100
High-income oil exporters	44	92	12	70	9	25
Middle-income economies	84	100+	68	93	49	65
Low-income economies:						
China	...	100+	...	100+	...	66
India	80	92	40	63	28	36
Others	50	77	24	47	23	34

Notes:
[1] Or nearest available year.
[2] Pupils of all ages, male and female, as a percentage of the male and female population of primary school age, generally 6–11 years. Gross enrolment rates may exceed 100 per cent because some pupils may be above or below the official primary school age.
[3] The percentage of persons aged 15 and over who can both read and write.
... Not available.
Source: World Bank, *World Development Report, 1982.*

Such rapid development has taken place, no doubt, in response to the perceived inadequacy of traditional education. Perceived, that is, by the modernizing elites, who in Bendix's words (quoted in chapter 6 above) 'put a premium on ideas and techniques which "follower" countries may use to "come up from behind"' in their efforts to rid their societies of the stigma of backwardness. Few questioned that it was highly desirable for the elementary skills of reading, writing, and arithmetic to be widely spread among the people of a modern state, while a need was also experienced for a national elite educated at a higher level in the skills and knowledge of the modern world. The establishment and expansion of formal school systems accordingly became an essential part of the drive to modernity in the cause of nation-building. Schools contributed to that cause by spreading

Table 9.2   *School enrolments, 1960–1979*[a] *Percentage of age group*[b] (*both sexes*) *enrolled*

	Primary school		Secondary school		Higher education	
	1960	1979	1960	1979	1960	1980[a]
Industrial market economies	100+	100+	64	88	17	37
Non-market industrial economies	100+	100	48	93	11	20
High-income oil exporters	28	31	5	44	...	7
Middle-income economies	76	97	15	39	4	11
Low-income economies:						
China	100+	100+	...	79	...	1
India	61	78	20	27	3	8
Others	37	64	6	17	1	2

Notes:

[a] Or nearest available year.

[b] For primary schooling, generally 6–11; secondary, 12–17.

... Not available.

Source: World Bank, *World Development Report, 1982.*

the use of the national language, teaching the nation's history and literature, and fostering national consciousness and pride. Few argued as E. M. K. Mulira did in Uganda for the vernacular in schooling.[24] In general, little but lip-service was paid to transmitting, still less revitalizing, indigenous cultures; the main thrust of nationalist policies was rather to break down tribal, linguistic, and cultural barriers and do away with tribalism.

Those perceptions accorded well enough with the aspirations of many parents in Third World countries to see their children gain a foothold in the modern sector, with its high rewards and glittering prizes. Just how glittering a few statistics will show: in Uganda in 1965, even a junior secondary leaver could expect a salary 7 times the average income per head, a school certificate holder 20 times, and a university graduate 49 times. In India, a secondary school leaver's salary was 7.7 times the national average income, a graduate's 12.4 times; while in Brazil a secondary leaver's income was 2.8 times the national average, and that of a person with higher education nearly 10 times.[25] No wonder people clamour for schools.

Table 9.3   *Illiteracy by sex and urban–rural residence in selected countries*

| | Percentage illiterate[a] | | | |
| | Urban | | Rural | |
Country, date	Male	Female	Male	Female
Peru, 1972	5.9	18.9	33.9	68.0
Nicaragua, 1971	16.0	22.0	63.0	66.4
Philippines, 1970	6.0	8.7	20.4	26.9
Ecuador, 1974	6.9	12.2	32.4	44.6
Honduras, 1974	17.6	24.0	52.1	56.8
Egypt, 1976	28.5	51.8	55.5	86.9
(10 and over)				
Indonesia, 1971	12.4	33.9	34.5	59.9
India, 1971	27.6	54.5	59.4	87.0

Note:
[a] Aged 15 and over unless otherwise stated.
Source: *United Nations Demographic Yearbook* for 1979.

Table 9.4   *School attendance rates by sex and urban–rural residence in selected countries*

| | | Percentage attending school | | | |
| | Ages to which data refer | Urban | | Rural | |
Country, date		Male	Female	Male	Female
Brazil, 1970	11	90.5	90.7	60.6	59.6
Dominican Republic, 1970	11	82.6	83.9	67.3	70.2
Peru, 1972	10–12	95.6	93.3	84.1	69.6
Ecuador, 1974	11	92.8	92.4	75.7	74.3
Guatemala, 1973	10–14	77.5	66.8	43.5	33.0
Liberia, 1970	10–14	53.0	44.2	32.8	29.1

Source: *United Nations Demographic Yearbook* for 1979.

The kinds of skill and knowledge that schooling in the modern sense was intended to transmit and develop involved it, in more cases than not, in a discontinuity with traditional education. In some areas, indeed, the very institution of a school as a place where children assemble, to be formally instructed by specially qualified adults, was an innovation foreign to the indigenous culture. No society lacks the means of socializing the young and transmitting knowledge, skill, and values, but in many pre-industrial

191

societies the ways in which this was done did not correspond to our preconceived notion of the school. A distinction has to be made between education and schooling; while schooling refers to the formal classroom setting, education includes all that people learn in their whole life experience. (Educationists further define formal education as schooling together with other school activities such as sport; non-formal education as organized teaching outside the school, such as adult literacy and agricultural extension; and informal education as the rest, including learning at work.)

Thus in many African traditional cultures, young people learned by doing and by helping their parents and others older than themselves. Some institutions such as tribute labour had educational functions when young men and women called to work at the chief's court saw and heard what went on there. In some African societies there were initiation ceremonies marking the transition from juvenile to adult status, *rites de passage* that included tests of fortitude and some instruction in the duties of men and women; in some cases these were carried out in seclusion over a period and therefore called 'schools'.[26] Although one or two attempts were made to reconcile the new style of schooling with these traditional initiation rites, in general the two were in conflict. For example, in Lesotho the mission schools were reluctant to accept initiated boys or to allow them to resume their studies. That resulted in a sharp division between the schooled and the initiated; the former, who had completed their formal education and attained positions of overt power and responsibility in the modern system, were nevertheless held in contempt as mere boys by those who had undergone the rigours of the initiation lodge and further proved their manhood in the mines of South Africa.[27]

Lesotho was no doubt an extreme case, but it was quite common in Africa for the setting up of schools by the first Christian missionaries to be met with indifference or hostility among the local people, who had to be persuaded to send their children to school. Adult converts were told it was their duty, while both missionaries and government officials put pressure on chiefs to set an example by sending their sons.[28] In some places initial hostility soon gave way to enthusiastic acceptance, when the advantages of employment in the modern sector came to be recognized; and colonial administrations which not long before had been with difficulty pioneering formal education were now criticized for not doing more and doing it faster.

The school was not quite so complete a cultural innovation in areas outside Africa, and in the traditional civilizations of the Arab-Muslim world and India there were institutions resembling schools in the modern sense. It might be thought that the break between old and new would be less sharp, and the possibility of building the new on the old foundations would be greater, in those areas; but on the whole that has not proved to be the case. Thus in Muslim countries the *kuttab* or Koran school generally resisted modernization, except perhaps to a limited extent in Egypt;[29] and the *madrasah* or higher college too was not very adaptable despite attempts in some countries to introduce subjects such as mathematics and the history and geography of the Arab world. In Tunisia, for example, 'it proved impossible to graft a curriculum suited to the modern age on to the traditional framework of Zitouna', the indigenous university, which despite attempts at reform continued to train its students mainly for religious positions or posts in the Islamic courts. The initiative passed to a newly founded secondary school, Sadiqi College, with a western-style pedagogical system nationally adapted to stress Arabic and Islamic studies; and Sadiqi rather than Zitouna set the pattern for the development of Tunisian education.[30]

In India similarly the traditional schools (*pathsala*) and colleges (*tols, vidyalayas, chatuspathis*) were at a low ebb when British education on British lines made a fresh start in the nineteenth century. The result, as mentioned above, was that the intellectual and administrative elite adopted English as their mother-tongue, could hardly read or write any Indian language, and were thus cut off from the great mass of the people. Uneasiness about this led to movements of thought, religion, and education under the influence of such figures as Rabindranath Tagore, Aurobindo, Vivekananda, and Raja Ram Mohan Roy, and the foundation of experimental schools and colleges aiming to balance Indian and western cultures. At the time of independence, then, Kabir wrote of three systems of education in india:

The products of the three systems of education live in the same country, feel the same types of needs, and must meet the same challenge of the modern age. The existence of parallel and at times incompatible beliefs and ideas among the different communities has had an adverse effect... A man lives simultaneously in many ages. We have examples of Indian scientists who are in touch with the latest movements of scientific thought and are at the same time immersed emotionally in customs which defy all reason.[31]

The conventional wisdom justifying the massive expansion of school systems has been expressed in phrases like 'investment in human capital'. Newly independent countries needed secondary-educated people in technical and administrative posts in their expanding economies, and to replace expatriates, while university graduates were likewise needed at higher levels. Universal adult literacy and primary schooling for all children could hardly fail to open doors of opportunity, and especially if accompanied by fair, objective selection for secondary and higher schooling would promote social mobility. Such developments must surely enhance the productivity of labour and contribute to economic development, though that was not

193

necessarily the only reason for pursuing them, and they were fully justified as ends in themselves.

Against this has been set the 'structuralist' view that school systems conserve and perpetuate the existing social structure, especially its disparities of wealth and power. The authority structure of the wider society is mirrored in that of the classroom. So, far from liberating human potential, much of what goes on there stultifies it. Prospective failures are reconciled in advance to their future position as second-class citizens. In fair, objective assessments the children of the well-to-do always tend to achieve high scores because of the advantages they enjoy at home, both of better food and greater mental stimulation. Such tests do nothing to promote social mobility; they only legitimate afresh in each generation the position of a hereditary elite of privileged families.

Up to a point, the conventional wisdom has been vindicated. Certainly, by and large, countries with higher school enrolment rates have higher per capita GNP. Like all correlations, though, that tells us nothing about cause and effect; perhaps schooling has contributed to economic growth, but it may just as well be that countries with greater resources have devoted more of them to schooling, viewing the latter as an end in itself according to the fall-back position of the conventional wisdom. Then there is the impressive evidence of Inkeles and Smith, detailed in chapter 11, that of all the agents of individual modernization schooling is the most effective. Not the most cost-effective; that is work in a factory, or some other modern organization. Schooling costs, but a year at school has more effect in modernizing individuals' attitudes than a year in a factory. More recently, the World Fertility Survey (see chapter 2) found that women with more schooling were more likely to know about birth control and to be using contraceptives; and they had fewer children, in some countries far fewer.[32] The World Bank likewise found that the spread of basic education tended to lower birth-rates as well as to increase economic productivity. Schooling had played an important part in the diffusion of high-yielding crops, which depended greatly on the literacy of farmers. More generally, too, schooling beyond a certain threshold of about six years had been shown to enhance farmers' adaptability to changing circumstances. Indeed, the rate of return on primary schooling – solely in terms of its contribution to farmers' efficiency – was between 7 and 11 per cent in South Korea, between 14 and 25 per cent in Thailand, and between 25 and 40 per cent in Malaysia.[33]

For if schooling really does constitute an investment in human capital, then we can calculate a rate of return on that investment. Rate-of-return studies begin with the well-known fact that people who have had more schooling are generally found as adults to be receiving higher incomes. Relating individuals' net incomes to how much their schooling cost them or their parents gives us a private rate of return. To calculate a social or public rate of return, the individual's gross income is seen as a contribution to the gross national product, and account is taken of the cost to public funds of his or her schooling. A good many such studies have been done, and Simmons has summarized the findings of research carried out mostly in the 1960s in some 32 countries.[34]

First, private returns are consistently higher than social returns because schooling is everywhere subsidized from public funds.

Secondly, the highest returns are those to primary schooling. Returns to secondary and higher education are usually about equal, and much lower than those to primary. Ratios of social benefits to social costs have been estimated to be 9.5 for primary schooling, 2.37 for secondary, and 2.00 for higher education.

Thirdly, 'the social rates of return for secondary and higher education are for most countries surprisingly close to the social rates for investment in other sectors'. However, if allowances are made for extraneous factors, especially family background and work experience, the rates of return are sharply reduced, and those for secondary and higher education are lower than returns to investments of other kinds.

Fourthly, since those studies were done costs have risen, and so has unemployment among school leavers. The returns to schooling may therefore have been lower in the 1970s than they were in the 1960s, and from this point of view there may have been a substantial over-investment in secondary and higher education. Primary schooling, however, still appears to be a worthwhile use of resources even from the point of view of so utilitarian a calculus. And such considerations prompt the further question whether even greater returns might accrue to improving the environment of infants of pre-school age, both nutritionally and in their psycho-motor development, a question to which some research has been addressed.[35]

Unemployment among school leavers was the starting-point for R. P. Dore's critique of educational policy and practice in late-industrializing countries, and his diagnosis of 'the diploma disease'.[36] 'It is far easier to expand the school system than it is to expand the modern sector economy and increase the number of job opportunities.'

For example, in Sri Lanka at the time of Dore's study the population was about 13 million, of whom about 4 million were classed (in the phrase to which I took exception in chapter 4) as 'economically active'. Of those, about 1 million were working in 'jobs' in the modern sector. The wastage of that mostly rather young labour force from death and retirement was taking place at only about 2 per cent annually, creating some 20,000 vacancies a year. Economic growth at an optimistic estimate might attain 7 or 8 per cent, but because of the capital-intensive nature of most new investment it might expand employment by more like 5 per cent or 50,000

195

new jobs a year. At most, then, there were some 70,000 job opportunities a year, perhaps half of them in desirable white-collar professional and administrative posts. For those jobs, there were some 300,000 young men and women reaching working age annually. School enrolment rates are quite high in Sri Lanka, and by 1971 something like one in three went on to secondary and higher education. There were therefore some 100,000 young people each year with 'the ten years of schooling which they thought (because that *was* the case not so very long ago) ought to entitle them to a decent job', to compete for perhaps 35,000 such jobs. At most one in three might be rewarded.

Half a million people openly unemployed (over 15 per cent of the labour force); four-fifths of that unemployment concentrated in the under-25 age group; among the 20–24 year olds with at least three O-level passes, unemployment rates of 55 per cent for men and 74 per cent for women – these in 1971 were the facts of the schools' social context which were overwhelmingly important in determining what went on within them. If there are no jobs for O-level leavers anyway, what is to be lost by taking the examination for a third or even a fourth year running in order to improve the attractiveness of the piece of paper which is all one has to impress possible employers? Why not try desperately hard to press on to the next higher level?...And, at all levels...what could be more reasonable than to concentrate every effort on trying to ensure that one gets into the top quarter of any achievement test ranking that might influence employers' choices?

It is not surprising that examinations *dominate* the curriculum, that all learning is ritualised, that curiosity is devalued, that no one is allowed to stray from the syllabus, that no one inquires about the usefulness, the relevance, or the interestingness of what is learned.

Dore was not the only observer to note a tendency to formalism and ritualism in schools in late-developing countries. Myrdal, quoted above, deplored the emphasis on memory work and rote learning he found in India, while many other critics have characterized what is taught in the classrooms of the Third World countries as not realistically related to life outside ('irrelevant'); and the pursuit of paper qualifications rather than true learning has been much lamented. Nor is the diploma disease confined to the Third World. Dore had some sharp things to say about Japan, while in Britain too he noted a slow shift from qualities to qualifications. Thus whereas in 1900 a young journalist was said to need adaptability, energy, tact, and a good constitution, by 1950 the comparable rubric was 'educational requirements'; and whereas intending librarians in 1900 were expected to have a love of books, by 1930 a school certificate was desirable, by 1950 it was a minimal requirement, by 1970 two A-levels were necessary, and latterly a graduate entry has been the aim. But in Dore's view the later a country started on its modernization drive, the more widely educational certificates were used for occupational selection, the faster the rate of qualification inflation (that is, the tendency for higher and higher qualifications to be required for the same job), and the more examination-oriented schooling became at the expense of genuine education.

Such considerations do much to call in question one major postulate of the conventional wisdom, namely that developing countries need more skilled and educated people for the expansion of their economies and to take over from expatriates. Yet, given that every country has to have a national elite of people who can cope with the modern world – physicians, engineers, bankers, diplomats and other senior civil servants, industrial managers – unemployment among secondary leavers and graduates poses a severe dilemma which Robert McNamara has well called 'one of the most disturbing paradoxes of our time'. If it is the case that many Third World countries have over-invested in secondary and higher education to the detriment of primary schooling, that only poses in an even sharper form the question of how to select from among primary leavers the fortunate few to go on to secondary school, and correspondingly at university entrance and other higher levels, and who will then have a chance of entering the elite. Here the conventional wisdom can surely assert that whatever their other disadvantages examinations are (or can be) at least fair, certainly more so than other modes of selection such as parental influence, tribalism, nepotism, bribery, corruption, or *force majeure*. Dore indeed acknowledged as much, writing of 'the equity requirement' and 'just and acceptable ways of awarding the privileges and amenities that go with different jobs', but he also put forward other suggestions: earlier entry into careers, with more in-service training; and a greater reliance on aptitude tests which, unlike achievement tests, cannot (or cannot much) be crammed for.

Doubt has likewise been cast on another postulate of the conventional wisdom, that schooling opens opportunities and promotes social mobility. As Simmons wrote, 'In most countries the poor quickly learn that schooling is an escape from poverty for only a few.' They are the first to drop out of school because they have to work, or are needed at home; they fall asleep in class because they are underfed, or tired after working at home and walking a long way to school; they do less well in English or French than children whose parents speak it at home. Many studies, including mine, have indicated the selectivity of secondary and higher education and the extent to which the offspring of well-to-do families are over-represented among students, and most of all among women students. Material affluence is not always the point; in East Africa I wrote of education-minded families, in many cases the descendants of the first mission converts, while French sociologists have coined the phrase *familles educogènes*.

And there has been fundamental criticism of rate-of-return studies. On the side of costs, it has been usual in such studies to include the opportunity cost of earnings forgone by staying on at school. But the alternative to school may not be employment but unemployment; and where unemployment is heavy, both the private and the social cost of staying on at school may be much lower than that reckoned in the calculations. On the side of returns, it has been questioned whether the higher incomes of those with more schooling are really attributable to the investment in their skills, knowledge, adaptability, and similar personal qualities. Where the number and nature of modern-sector jobs in a national economy are more or less fixed, the rewards associated with them may have more to do with the nature of the jobs themselves than with the personal qualities of their incumbents. To quote Simmons again, 'A rigid job structure means that the income earned after schooling does not reflect returns to human capital, but to certification.' Thus both the costs and the benefits of schooling have been greatly over-estimated, according to structuralist critics, especially when, following Dore's lead, the school system is seen as being concerned with selection and certification rather than with education and the development of human potential.

Schooling's shortcomings have led some to propose a drastic remedy: abolish it. 'De-schooling society' was advocated by Ivan Illich basically on the ground that compulsory schooling is an affront to individual liberty, and that it is wrong that one person's judgement should determine what another person should learn.[37] The only learning that matters occurs when people want to learn and actively seek out knowledge. Illich envisioned education as a facilitative network in which those who wanted to learn would seek out a teacher or 'skill model', who might be paid either in cash or in vouchers of which each individual would have a life's supply – a scheme for which Illich cited the support of some economists including Milton Friedman. He was also concerned about the extent to which schooling perpetuates inequality, and the ways it indoctrinates people into the pernicious patterns of mass consumption that characterize modern industrial society. Yet his proposed scheme seems itself to be paradoxically elitist, for it would surely be the bright, active, well-nourished children of education-minded families who would do well out of a system of market individualism in teaching and learning, and the poor who would be left behind. Dore concluded that 'Clearly, to deschool is to throw out the baby with the bathwater, for there genuinely *is* an educational baby worth preserving in the institution called school.'[38] As T. H. Marshall observed, the idea of citizenship in the modern world includes the right to participate in the common cultural heritage; and the right of the adult citizen to have been educated necessarily entails the universal compulsory schooling of children.[39]

The mass media of communication

In non-industrial and non-literate societies the predominant form of communication was by word of mouth. In industrial societies, oral communication tends to be regarded as slow, inaccurate, and unreliable, and dismissed as mere rumour. It is well to remember, then, that in poor countries whose systems of mass impersonal communication are as yet less highly developed, 'rumour' may continue to play a more important part in disseminating information – however garbled – and in setting the public mood.

The mass media of communication are among the goods and services that are unequally distributed in the world. Information costs, and the poor countries have less of it in the same way and for the same reason that they lack other goods and services. Most of the news that circulates in the world is news about industrial countries, distributed to the people of those countries, and gathered and disseminated through the five main international news agency networks including Tass, the Soviet news agency. Apart from local news, the media in poor countries are filled with news from rich countries, scarcely at all with news from other poor countries. This emerged very clearly in a study by Schramm, who showed that, for example, in three representative newspapers in Pakistan in 1961 there was as much news about the Soviet Union as there was about India (13 per cent of all foreign news), more about France and the United Kingdom (16 per cent and 17 per cent respectively), and more than twice as much about the United States (33 per cent), while there was little or nothing about countries such as Egypt or Brazil. Similarly, in the Argentine press only 6 per cent of the foreign news was about Brazil, compared with 11 per cent about the United Kingdom, 12 per cent about the Soviet Union, 15 per cent about France, and 43 per cent about the United States.[40]

The mass media of communication generally are institutions of the modern sector, to some extent foreign to Third World countries and cultures in which their implantation has involved a transfer both of technology and of forms of organization. They differ in their history, their characteristics, and their adaptability for the needs of the Third World.

Newspapers are the oldest of the mass media, emerging as they did gradually in western European countries in the seventeenth and eighteenth centuries out of advertisers and occasional broadsheets and pamphlets. Thus in Britain papers such as *The Times* and *The Observer* began regular publication before 1800, and those such as the *Daily Mail* took advantage of the spread of literacy through schooling in the nineteenth century. The essential technology of the printing press is ancient and relatively simple, and a press of modest scale need not involve a high capital cost. Editorial production costs too can be modest, and advertising revenue generally amounts to as much as or more than sales. A newspaper reader incurs no capital cost like that of a radio receiver, only the recurrent cost per copy, which, however, may be high relative to incomes especially in poor countries; thus Schramm calculated that a workman in California with what he earned in an hour could buy fifty copies of a 40-page paper, whereas in Indonesia an hour's labour would buy only seven copies of a 4-page paper.[41] Literacy is of course required, though this limitation can be overcome and costs shared if one person reads the paper aloud to others. Newspapers can be disseminated widely, anywhere there are shops and wholesale deliveries, though like other goods their distribution can be interrupted by bad roads, natural disasters such as floods, and strikes or civil disturbances. They are well suited to local production and distribution, and their linguistic adaptability is in principle high, so that there is no reason why even quite small language groups should not have their own newspaper, weekly perhaps if not daily. Literacy is the limitation, however. In many places, most people who can read and write can also understand a lingua franca or a language of wider communication, and tend to turn to a national newspaper in a language such as Swahili, Spanish, or English rather than to a weekly vernacular newssheet. In poor countries too the national dailies get the lion's share of the advertising of both private firms and government agencies. Though the cost of advertising in a local paper is usually low in terms of actual outlay, it is usually high in relation to the number of people who see each advertisement. It may be worth paying 10 times as much for a column-inch in a national daily if it is seen by 50 times as many people. Large organizations aiming at a national public distribute their advertising accordingly, and advertising in the local press appeals mainly to small firms with limited resources selling only in a local market. Furthermore, the national daily in a poor country is often amply financed and equipped with foreign capital, and may employ some foreign staff on the production and management side, while the locally owned and managed vernacular papers lack these advantages.

The film is generally regarded as a medium of entertainment rather than of information, though it is hard to separate the two. There is a 'demonstration effect' when cinema audiences are shown a way of life other than their own, and exposed to value-assumptions usually implied rather than expressed. Thus according to Lerner it was in American films that the grocer of Balgat saw the well-stocked supermarket he so much admired. With photography as its basic technology, to which sound recording was later added, the film industry rose to prominence after 1900 in a world market long dominated by Hollywood. The capital costs and unit production costs of film-making are widely variable, but tend to be rather high where films are made in permanent studios by professionals, and to recoup these costs requires a large market. Thus notably among low-income countries India has a vigorous film industry that smaller countries lack. As with newspapers, the consumer is involved in no capital cost, and the price of a cinema seat may be quite low especially where the climate – as in India again – makes open-air viewing possible much of the time. Language barriers can be surmounted to a limited extent by sub-titling, but that of course assumes a literate audience. That and the size of the market needed for profitable operation make the film relatively inadaptable to the needs of small language communities. But a mains electricity supply is not indispensable, and portable equipment mounted on vans can bring films to small audiences in widely scattered rural areas, giving this medium a potentially wide coverage.

The technology of both radio and television is electronic, and for technical reasons under international agreements governments have to license transmitting stations and allot them to a limited number of 'channels' or frequencies. As broadcasting media, too, radio and television differ from newspapers and films in lacking a direct revenue from sales, and have to be financed from advertising, licence fees, or general public funds, singly or in combination. For both technical and economic reasons, therefore, governments have to be involved to a greater extent in broadcasting than in other media, though that involvement ranges in different countries from the minimal to the total. In the United States, the traditional role of the federal government has been minimal; although there is public service broadcasting in some states, there is no licence fee, and finance is from advertising. In an endeavour to avoid commercialism, when radio broadcasting started in Britain in the 1920s it was entrusted to an autonomous public corporation, financed by a statutory licence fee collected by the state, but otherwise independent of political control.[42] In the Soviet Union, broadcasting like newspapers and film was from the first completely controlled by the state and party and consistently directed to mass persuasion, mobilizing public opinion behind party policies, and moulding Soviet citizens for the Soviet state.[43] In France, too, despite a widely different political ideology there was central government control, particularly of television, after the second world war. There has accordingly been no lack of models for the broadcasting organizations of Third World countries, though in general they have not found any of them entirely to their liking.

But though alike in some respects, in others the two broadcasting media are very different.

Radio broadcasting began in many Third World countries in the 1920s and 1930s, not long after the pioneering days in industrial countries, though in some not till after the second world war; Tanganyika in 1951, for example. In countries that were not colonies at the time, such as Latin American countries, Thailand, and the Philippines, for the most part a commercial, private-enterprise model like that of the United States prevailed. Colonial governments tended to exercise more control, but their policies were not always very clear, and only minuscule resources were made available. In British colonies many expatriates listened to the BBC Empire (later the World) Service as best they could on short wave transmissions giving poor reception, and some early initiatives on the part of colonial administrations took the form of re-broadcasting that service, by radio or wire, in whole or part, sometimes interspersed with locally produced news and entertainment programmes. Broadcasting for local people in local languages came later with the setting up of corporations modelled on the BBC, and staffed by seconded personnel or local people trained in Britain. However, by the 1950s there was some dawning awareness of radio's potential as a source of trustworthy news, for general development in fields such as health education and agricultural improvement, and for local cultural creativity. Colonial and independent governments alike sought through radio to spread the use of a language of wider communication, Portuguese in Brazil as much as French in North Africa. Mention should be made, too, of the radio stations set up by missionary bodies in Peru, for example, and the Radio Voice of the Gospel in Addis Ababa, which promoted literacy, health, new farming practices, and honest news as well as Christian evangelism.

Radio has many advantages and few disadvantages. The capital cost of a transmitter, roughly proportionate to its power, need not be great if only local coverage is required, while the cost of producing programmes can be very low indeed and there is ample scope for local talent. For the listener, there is the capital cost of a receiver, but that is relatively small. Cheap robust transistor radios, made in some Third World countries, are everywhere among the target goods of young wage workers, while there are radios in village shops, and travellers by taxi are regaled with the output of a car radio at full volume. Radio receivers do not necessarily depend on mains electricity, though without it there is the small recurrent cost of batteries. Radio broadcasting can be nation-wide in scale, but equally it can be local. Of all the media, then, it is the best adapted to the needs of small language groups, and the one that most decisively breaks through the literacy barrier. Its potential coverage is wide; and, as we are often reminded at times of crisis, radio communications are not liable to the hazards that beset surface transport, be they bad roads, floods, or riots.

Television is the newest of the mass media, coming into general use only since about 1950. It is also by far the most costly. Katz and Wedell, in their study of broadcasting in the Third World, noted that in several countries it seemed to have been introduced as a matter of national prestige for curious, haphazard, and even quite frivolous reasons.[44] In Senegal, for example, after an educational experiment sponsored by UNESCO had been

202

closed down, it was revived in 1972 on the French government's initiative for live coverage of the Munich Olympics. In Iran the special occasion that prompted the start of a television service was the coronation of the Shah; in Uganda, the Kampala meeting of the Organization for African Unity. The capital costs of transmitters and studios, and the unit costs of making programmes, are of the order of 30 times as high as those for radio. Virtually all the equipment is made in a few industrial countries, the United States, Britain, Holland, West Germany, and Japan. For most Third World countries, too, the costs of making their own programmes are prohibitive. According to Katz and Wedell, in the mid-1970s the average cost per hour of BBC TV programmes was of the order of £15,000 or $30,000. To make, say, two thousand hours' programmes for a year's broadcasting at a cost of 60 million dollars was clearly beyond the means of most Third World countries, whose television services had funds sufficient only for the most rudimentary chat shows, amateur drama, or variety. They could hope to fill even a minimal five or six hours' broadcasting a day only by hiring imported programmes, mainly from the United States, at much less cost; in 1974 'country prices' varied around $300 to $400 an hour in Iran, $250 to $300 an hour in Thailand and Peru, and in Nigeria as little as $60 an hour. Furthermore, despite heavy reliance on imported programmes, television has tended to impoverish previously established radio services by draining them of resources of money and professional staff.

Television receivers too are expensive, costing around ten times as much as radios, and in poor countries more than an average household's annual income. They are less robust, especially in tropical countries, where repair facilities are not widely available. Battery operation is less satisfactory, and there is a greater reliance on mains electricity. The very high and ultra-high frequencies required for television broadcasts confine them effectively to visual range of the transmitter, so that unless a country is covered by a network of repeater stations – beyond the means of most Third World countries – for technical and economic reasons alike the coverage of television is limited to the immediate vicinity of big cities. There it is mainly a pastime for the well-to-do, who join their counterparts all over the world in relaxing in front of the small screen to watch the same soap-opera series. The adaptability of the medium to different local languages, and its potential for encouraging local cultural creativity, have hitherto proved limited to say the least.

In the 1950s there were high hopes that the mass media of communication could make a big contribution to development. As will be recalled from chapter 6, Daniel Lerner saw them as prime movers in modernization. His ideas were shared by many of his fellow social scientists in the United States, notably Wilbur Schramm; they greatly influenced the policies of UNESCO, and spread to the elites in Third World countries.[45] In their study of 11 low- and middle-income countries in the 1970s, Katz and Wedell found that policy-makers had consistently expected the media to contribute positively to national integration, to social and economic development, and to indigenous cultural creativity. However, those three goals had not proved readily compatible, and pointed in different directions to different policies. National unity involved the media under government control in focussing attention on the national leader, fostering national sentiment, creating a national mythology, and spreading the national language. For broadcasting it implied extending the coverage of a single national channel. Social and economic development, however, were better promoted by a quite different approach. Specialized programmes were needed to reach particular sorts of people, such as farmers and (for health education and family planning) housewives. To be effective, such programmes had to be in vernacular languages, so that the recognition of diverse ethnic groups was necessary; and their style had to be local, familiar, personal, and practical. That pointed rather to a decentralized regional organization of local radio stations. Cultural authenticity too involved encouraging vernacular languages and recognizing ethnic differences, while it also brought into sharp prominence by contrast the world-wide cultural uniformity of television programmes imported from France, Britain, and above all the United States.

Reaction against the modernization school of thought on the part of radical underdevelopment writers took the form in this case of the charge of cultural imperialism. Just as many thoughtful policy-makers in Third World countries complained to Katz and Wedell that their cultures were being overwhelmed by imported television soap-operas, so radical writers regarded the media as part of the US dominated world capitalist system and poured scorn on the doctrine of the free flow of information.

But the issue of freedom is central. The media institutions of western industrial countries are predicated upon freedoms of expression and association that do not prevail elsewhere. Generally speaking, Third World governments have neither permitted the western models of independent newspapers and autonomous broadcasting corporations to be reproduced in the countries under their control, nor wholeheartedly adopted the Soviet model with its relentless dedication and seriousness of purpose.

Thus even in countries where freedom of the press is written into the constitution, and there is no overt censorship, informal constraints may be exerted by diverse means. Where the economy is largely controlled by the state or public corporations, an actual or threatened withdrawal of government advertising can be enough to ruin a newspaper. It has been argued, indeed, that a substantial private sector is a necessary condition for a genuinely free press for that reason alone. Withdrawal of advertising, however, is the mildest of the sanctions; more drastic ones are the destruction of a paper's premises and presses by the youth wing of the government party (a polite name for organized thugs), and the harassment, intimidation, and in the last resort the imprisonment, of its editor. In the face of such overt or covert threats, local papers inclined to criticize the government often succumb altogether; while foreign-owned national dailies, the subsidiaries of big international newspaper chains, are likely to be anxious to retain their foothold in the country, avoid giving offence, and mute their political comments accordingly.

Similarly, even in former British colonies where broadcasting was originally entrusted to an autonomous public corporation modelled on the BBC, it did not long stay that way, and everywhere governments have taken over. Throughout the Third World, indeed, armed guards and security checks around broadcasting studios and transmitter stations are an ever-present reminder of state control. Broadcasters have become civil servants in fact if not in name, and their accountability and loyalty lie to a government minister, in many countries the president him- or herself. They have experienced severe tensions between their professional norms as communicators and the political requirements to which they have been subject, expected as they have been to create new national myths, adjust their news values to what the government wants the people to hear, and project the personalities of national leaders. The management of broadcasting, too, has often been entrusted to people more remarkable for their political loyalty than for their managerial competence. Subordinates have become reluctant to contribute their ideas for fear of offending superiors, and at the very least being passed over for promotion. Muddle and waste have supervened as efficiency has declined.

According to Katz and Wedell, there has been a genuine effort in some countries to counter 'cultural imperialism', make more of their own programmes, and rely less on imports. For example, in Peru a junta representing (unusually) the lower social classes who came to power in 1968 promptly asserted control of the media and insisted that 60 per cent of programmes should be locally produced, 90 per cent of them by Peruvian nationals, and that all advertising should be locally produced. In Tanzania the government took over radio broadcasting in 1965 and established a commercial channel to promote self-reliance by advertising home-produced goods. Though television was introduced in Zanzibar, it was long resisted in mainland Tanganyika as too expensive, to avoid giving city life an attractive advantage, and out of suspicion of the individualism and self-interested values it might represent. In independent Algeria there was a strongly Arabic emphasis, and the proportion of programmes locally produced rose sharply from 25 per cent in 1969 to 49 per cent in 1973. But leading intellectuals, including writers and broadcasting producers, were not entirely happy with the more extreme demands of such a policy

205

and did not want to be cut off from the French language and through it their access to a wider world of culture.

In some countries quietly successful work has been done especially through radio to promote aspects of development such as better farming. Radio has also proved particularly effective for a once-for-all campaign. An example was the brilliant success of the changeover from left-hand to right-hand driving in Sierra Leone in 1971; so aware did the radio campaign make people of the impending change and the need to take care ('drive safle safle') that not only was it accomplished without a single road accident but none was reported in the whole country for a month afterwards.[46]

Such examples are exceptional, however, and in general little thought has been given in Third World countries to the development potential of the media. Nation-building has taken precedence over social and economic development and indigenous cultural creativity, and without coherent policies the activities of the media under state control in independent Third World countries have been no kinder to indigenous cultures than were the earlier colonial regimes. The media are expected to project the image of the national leader, and penalized in various ways if they do not. They are useful channels for the dissemination of such information as the rulers want the people to hear. They can keep people quiet by providing innocuous entertainment. Otherwise they are generally neglected: but not in a time of crisis. Then, suddenly, they come into prominence. The radio station in particular becomes an all-important strategic resource whose seizure is vital to the success of a *coup*; and the announcement over the state radio that a change of government has taken place very largely constitutes that change of regime itself.

SUGGESTIONS FOR FURTHER READING

P. H. Gulliver (ed.), *Tradition and Transition in East Africa*, London: Routledge and Kegan Paul, 1969

W. H. Whiteley (ed.), *Language Use and Social Change*, Oxford: Oxford University Press for International African Institute, 1971

J. Lowe, N. Grant, and T. D. Williams (eds.), *Education and Nation-Building in the Third World*, Edinburgh: Scottish Academic Press, 1971

John Simmons (ed.), *The Education Dilemma: Policy Issues for Developing Countries in the 1980s*, Oxford: Pergamon, 1980

R. P. Dore, *The Diploma Disease*, London: Allen and Unwin, 1976

Elihu Katz and E. George Wedell, *Broadcasting in the Third World: Promise and Performance*, Cambridge, Mass.: Harvard University Press, 1977; London: Macmillan, 1978

10 Religion and economic development: cause and effect

Sociological studies of religion in relation to economic development have hitherto adopted one or other of two approaches. In one, the prime concentration is on a sect or denomination's religious convictions and the characteristic morals and motivations to which they give rise, and the question is then asked: to what extent do they help or hinder their followers' worldly success through economic enterprise? In the other, the initial emphasis is on the social and economic changes, usually for the worse, to which a group have been subjected, and the religious movements that then occur among them are seen as reactions to or against change. In some cases, though, the two approaches may be complementary, and the wheel may come full circle when personal and moral qualities engendered in adversity by religious faith are seen to enable a group not only to survive but also to go on and prosper.

Religion and economic innovation

Max Weber's monumental study linking the Protestant ethic with the spirit of capitalism, to which I alluded in chapter 1, is so well known as to need no recapitulation here.[1] In support of his thesis, Weber assiduously searched the literature then available in European languages about the religions of ancient Judaism and of the East for parallels with the Protestant ethic, only to conclude that European Puritanism was unique. Thus in China, despite the high state of the arts and crafts and the great urban tradition, the currency was frequently mismanaged, the legal and customary institutions favouring business organization were lacking, and there was no adequate system of book-keeping such as would spur Chinese business-men to allow adequately for the depreciation and replacement of their physical capital. Moreover, though there was much rationality in Chinese thought, both orthodox Confucianism and Taoism and the heterodoxies such as Buddhism tolerated magic. 'Like the educated Hellene, the educated Confucian adhered to magical conceptions with a mixture of scepticism while occasionally submitting to demonology ... The preservation of this magic garden was one of the tendencies innate to Confucian ethics.'[2]

Turning to India, Weber analysed both the character of Hindu thought

207

and society, especially the caste system, and the movements of protest against orthodox Brahministical Hinduism, especially Buddhism. The effects of the caste system on economic life he regarded as essentially negative. It was not so much that particular beliefs or ritual prescriptions in themselves placed insuperable obstacles in the way of economic development, for example by making it difficult for men of different castes to work together in the same factory. Obstacles like that could have been circumvented if the will had been there, just as the ban on usury was in the early development of European capitalism. 'The core of the obstruction was rather imbedded in the "spirit" of the whole system',[3] he wrote, which makes it extremely unlikely that an economic and technical revolution such as industrial capitalism could have originated from within Indian society; while if it were introduced from outside, as under British rule, then its development would be correspondingly hampered.

Although he did not altogether neglect the rise of science, Weber may not have made it sufficiently integral to his analysis. The authority of the church over men's minds, supremely symbolized in the treatment of Galileo, was broken by the Protestant reformation, and its collapse left in the end no defence for dogma against rational scientific inquiry. Not that the Protestant sects themselves espoused a scientific view of the universe and human life; on the contrary, they were in many cases as dogmatic and obscurantist as the parent church itself, as was testified in another age by the agonized mental struggles of Edmund Gosse.[4] But when sceptical rebellious scientists were struggling against Protestant dogmatism, they could in the last resort advance the unanswerable argument of freedom of conscience. The Protestant reformation of the sixteenth and seventeenth centuries can thus be seen as clearing away important obstacles to the rise of science in the seventeenth century, and hence the industrial revolution in the eighteenth.

Weber's thesis has inspired continuing controversy from its first publication,[5] and among its many critics has been Hugh Trevor-Roper:

The idea that large-scale industrial capitalism was ideologically impossible before the Reformation is exploded by the simple fact that it existed...Until the invention of the steam engine, its scope may have been limited, but within that scope it probably reached its highest peak in the age of the Fugger. After that there were convulsions which caused the great capitalists to migrate, with their skills and workmen, to new centres.

The convulsions in question were those of the counter-reformation.

The novelty lay not in the entrepreneurs themselves, but the circumstances which drove them to emigrate...not so much Protestantism and the expelled entrepreneurs as Catholicism and the expelling societies.

The alliance of church and state – particularly the Spanish state, which at that time ruled the Netherlands and parts of Italy – suddenly resolved to persecute the ideas of Erasmus and his followers. It was this hardening of the counter-reformation that drove out the merchant aristocracies, some to Protestant countries, others to less intolerant Catholic kingdoms such as France, and put them into an uncomfortable and unsolicited dilemma between the Lutheran and Calvinist versions of Protestantism. They chose the latter, though neither represented the easy-going Erasmianism they would probably have preferred, and Trevor-Roper suggested that many of them were not really very good Calvinists at heart. A far more important thing about them was that they were migrants.

Neither Holland nor Scotland nor Geneva nor the Palatinate – the four obvious Calvinist societies – produced their own entrepreneurs. The compulsory Calvinist teaching with which the natives of those communities were indoctrinated had no such effect. Almost all the great entrepreneurs were immigrants.

Secondly, the majority of these immigrants were Netherlanders: some of them, perhaps, were Calvinists only because they were Netherlanders.

So the counter-reformation resulted in a Flemish diaspora in which the Flemings became the industrial elite of Europe, with the Jews in second place.[6] Trevor-Roper identified migrant status rather than doctrinal attachment as the critical factor in the making of an enterprising minority; the point is of wider application, and I return to it below.

Another criticism of Weber's thesis, this time in its application to India, was that of Trevor Ling. The notably enterprising character of Indians abroad in countries such as Burma and Malaya should alone cast doubt on it, though to be fair to Weber those developments were only just about to manifest themselves at the time when he was recording his negative conclusion. However, at the very time in 1905–11 when Weber was collecting his material and writing his study, which was published in 1912, events were taking place in India which were to falsify it decisively.

From the point of view of Weber's verdict on India the unkindest twist of fate was that in 1911, the first really notable large scale example of all-Indian industrial capitalism, the Tata Iron & Steel Company, began production. J. N. Tata...died in 1904, but the scheme was taken up and pursued by his son, Dorabji Tata. In 1906 rich resources of iron ore were discovered in...Bihar, which the Maharaja was prepared to allow Tata to work, in return for royalties on the ore. The capital needed for the construction of the plant was £1¾ million. A prospectus was issued by Tata in August 1907. Nationalist fervour was at its height and the leaders of the movement were urging all Indians to join in and support the Swadeshi movement – to support Indian-owned production of every kind, and to boycott British goods. The result was that 'from early morning till late at night the Tata offices in Bombay were besieged by an eager crowd of native investors, old and young...at the end of three weeks the entire capital for the construction requirement was secured, every penny contributed by some 8,000 Indians'. The construction of the plant was begun in 1909. In 1911, when Weber was writing his *Hinduismus und Buddhismus*, the first iron ore was being produced by an Indian company.[7]

Many recent studies have been addressed to the search for latter-day functional equivalents of the Protestant ethic, and contrariwise for religious beliefs and practices regarding economic development. As an example we may take a controversy about the disadvantaged position of Malays compared with Chinese and Indians in Malaya in the 1960s. Initiating the controversy, Parkinson pointed to the Malays' general resistance to change, exemplified in their refusal to follow the government's urgings to grow a second rice crop each year, use wet rice fields instead of dry upland for their rice seed-beds, and adopt other recommended improvements. Parkinson showed that these resistances were at least partly rational, but he thought religious and magical beliefs were also relevant, for example in waiting for a propitious day before transplanting; and 'the Islamic belief that all things are emanations from God...tends to make them fatalistic in their approach to life'.[8] Wilder disagreed with Parkinson's diagnosis of 'Islamic fatalism', saying that it presents a caricature of the Malay as 'a blind, irrational slave of history and custom'. Indeed, in one respect Islam could be said to exercise a favourable influence on economic development, namely the *haj*. Saving the money to pay the fare to Mecca gave peasants a goal to which they directed their lives and built up patterns of saving and rational forms of economic organization.[9] Parkinson, however, insisted that this was not a productive use of savings. Money being saved for the *haj* remained largely idle, and was barren and unproductive from the point of view of economic development.[10]

Another case in point is Burma. Mya Maung analysed the blend of new and traditional thought in the Burmese way to socialism, first enunciated in 1947 and embodied in the national plan launched in 1958. The word *Pyidawtha* used for this programme carried overtones of 'a happy and prosperous state with the additional vision of a utopian blend of traditionalism and modernity'. His central theme was that socialist planning had failed to change the cultural patterns of traditional Burmese life, especially including Buddhist cultural values. Efforts to present *Pyidawtha* as a blend of old and new – ranging from the glorification of a golden past and the revival of religion to exhortations to eat unpolished rice – merely concealed their incompatibility, as did the presentation of socialist ideas in words taken from the vocabulary of Burmese Buddhist thought, especially the use of the Buddhist concept of impermanency (*anate-sa*) for the Marxist dialectical materialism. In fact, 'State action has failed to diffuse the socialist concept of the identity of interest between the state and the individual', and indeed deepened the traditional view of government as an enemy to be wooed and feared. 'Similarly, the socialist concept of collective effort and co-operative life within a classless society is contrary to traditional Buddhist cultural values such as Karma (*Kan* in

Burmese)...Distaste for business enterprise (*a-the*) is present in the traditional Burmese culture.'[11]

Ling remarked, however, that Maung's general statement about the resistance to change of Buddhist culture represented an inadmissible simplification. Theravada Buddhism was only one strand in Burmese culture, and the differences between Buddhist and non-Buddhist elements may be important at precisely the points at which economic activity is significant.[12]

Melford Spiro made the further point that even Theravada Buddhism was not a single strand, and there were at least three major systems – nibbanic Buddhism, concerned with release from the unending circle ('The Wheel') of death and rebirth, causation and frustration; kammatic Buddhism, concerned not so much with release from the Wheel as with improving one's position in the next incarnation; and apotropaic Buddhism, concerned with man's worldly welfare, the curing of illness, protection from demons, the prevention of droughts, and so on. In relation to economic activity:

the soteriology of nibbanic Buddhism provides no bridge of any kind to the world. Far from being a means to salvation, worldly activity in nibbanic Buddhism is its irreducible obstacle; rather than a proof, worldly activity constitutes a disproof for one's chances of being saved. But this is not true of the soteriology of kammatic Buddhism, i.e. that of most practising Buddhists. It, on the contrary, provides profound incentives to worldly (economic) behaviour, for economic success is a necessary means for soteriological action, which in turn has important consequences, social and economic alike...It is only through economic action that one can hope to acquire the most soteriologically valuable merit, the merit acquired through giving (*dana*). To be sure, merit is also acquired through morality (*sila*); but giving is the royal road, and (short of inheriting it) the wealth required for giving must be accumulated by economic action.

Spiro reported that many Burmans kept merit account books and the quest for wealth provided a powerful motivation for work. But *dana* was confined to religious giving, and was not a motive for what we should understand as 'charity' like giving money to hospitals. The most spectacular forms of *dana* consisted of building pagodas and endowing monasteries, which earned men great social prestige – expressed in the formal title of 'pagoda builder' or 'monastery builder' prefixed to their names for life, like the Muslim *Haji* – as well as the assurance of bliss in a future existence. Social prestige as well as salvation was also to be gained from lavish expenditure on one's son's ritual initiation, and another meritorious form of *dana* sanctioned by publicity was the collective offering of new robes and other gifts to monks and on monks' funerals. Spiro concluded that in a typical Burmese village something like 25 to 30 per cent of the net disposable cash income was spent on *dana* and related activities. As in the case of saving for the *haj*, such facts may be interpreted from two different points of view. On the one hand, *dana* affords a motive for work, saving, and the systematic management of resources; on the other, the methodically accumulated savings are neither invested, as Weber put it, for 'forever renewed profit by means of continuous, rational, capitalistic enterprise', nor are they well expended for social welfare.

This is all too well recognised by some of the Burmese themselves, although they are too few to change the system. Thus the headman of one village said to me that 'the entire township spends about 10 per cent of its income on provisioning monks, but far less than 1 per cent on education. If we spent, say, 9 per cent on monks and 1 per cent on education, surely that would not harm Buddhism, and how much better off our children would be.[13]

Another study directly inspired by Weber's analysis was that by Bocock of the Ismailis in Tanzania.[14] The Asian population of East Africa as a whole played a notable part in its economic development, pioneering trade and small scale manufacturing industry and dominating the world of finance and the professions, and among this population two communities rivalled each other for leadership – the Shia Ismailia Khoja and the Patidars. The Ismailis were a Muslim group owing spiritual allegiance to the Aga Khan whom they regarded as the extant Imam, while the Patidars were a Hindu community of the general character of a caste. H. S. Morris, who also studied these groups, singled out the Ismailis as the pace-making group.[15]

An important factor in the Ismailis' success was the role and personality of the redoubtable Aga Khan III, Sir Sultan Muhammad Shah, 1877–1960. Believed as he was to be the known, revealed Imam, all his words were regarded as divinely inspired, and he used his power of *ex cathedra* utterance to urge his followers to modernize their attitudes and practices. In the sphere of social welfare, for example, he opposed infant marriage and advocated modern methods of child care; he stimulated the Ismaili communities to efforts of communal self-help in health and education; and he mobilized their lavish gifts to his person to set up trust funds for investment in the enterprises of Ismaili businessmen. To all appearances the Ismailis in East Africa played the same kind of initiatory role in economic development as the Puritans in Europe, and did so in much the same kind of way and by the same kind of means – hard work, frugality, trustworthiness, and consistently shrewd reinvestment of profits. To one who lived in East Africa the comparison with the Protestant ethic has the air of a commonplace.

In a point-by-point comparison of the Ismaili faith with Calvinism, however, Bocock notes the differences as well as the similarities. Where Calvinism was positively individualist, Ismailism relied more on community self-help. On its own Bocock doubts if it could have produced the positive push towards individualism; it was only in contact with British capitalism

212

that the Ismailis were able to adopt some rational capitalist methods, especially when urged to do so by their divinely inspired leader. There was a superficial similarity in the doctrines of predestination of both Calvinism and Islam, but the latter did not put its adherent under the same terrible strain as the former to prove that he was among the elect by his diligence in everyday work. Islam was much more relaxed, and taught that by giving alms, morality, and prayer he could attain heaven. 'Unlike the puritanical Calvinist, the Muslim, including the Ismailis, can enjoy using and consuming his wealth in this life, within reasonable limits.' Both religions were notably congregational in their forms of organization, and the local community of Ismailis who met daily in Jamat Khan, the Ismaili mosque, constituted also a community exercising moral control over its members and providing them – when in good standing – with mutual aid and credit networks. Islam generally, including Ismailism, had more room for mysticism than did Calvinism. Both encouraged education, but Islam was much more tolerant of magic and did not condemn its use by the faithful in allaying anxieties over things like illness, family and personal problems, and travel.

What is the general import of studies of this kind linking religion as a causative factor with economic development? Clearly Weber's thesis is not lightly to be dismissed; as Trevor-Roper has said, it has a 'solid, if elusive, core of truth', though his reliance on so large an abstraction as 'the spirit of capitalism' makes his analysis difficult either to confirm or refute by reference to newly discovered facts. Moreover, Weber's central pre-occupation was with the original emergence of industrial capitalism, a unique historical phenomenon after which nothing could ever be the same again. As Bendix emphasized, once industrialization had occurred anywhere, that alone altered the environment of all other countries. Subsequent industrialization was either derivative, or competitive, or both; and this too makes it difficult to test Weber's ideas by reference to events elsewhere in the world after the industrial revolution in Europe.

In these circumstances there is a decided tendency to weakness in the explanations that are advanced both of economic backwardness and of economic initiative in terms of the religious and general cultural values of the group concerned. This is seen most clearly in the inconsistency between explanations of retardation in terms of the culture of a people who, when they appear outside their own country as a minority in another, abruptly become associated with innovative energy and initiative. Sometimes the contortions of the analysis in these cases can only be described as comic. For example, it was possible to explain the economic backwardness of China before the communist triumph of 1964 in terms of passivity, the Confucian ideal of the cultivated man of the world, lavish expenditure on funerals and weddings, non-rational magical beliefs, and the like; and all this seemed very plausible when applied to China itself. Yet when Chinese emigrated to Indonesia, Malaya, Singapore, Thailand, or even to Hong Kong they suddenly became the energetic innovators whose industry and enterprise stimulated the economy of the region into new life; and it does not seem to have been the case that the religious beliefs and ritual customs of the overseas Chinese were in any important respect different from those of the homeland. In exactly the same way, the economic backwardness of India has been attributed to the other-worldly mysticism of the Hindu faith, the ban on cow-slaughter, the caste system, and similar cultural factors. Yet Indians overseas have been the dynamic source of economic development, initiating industries, pioneering trade, and through kinship and credit networks maintaining financial and trading links with the world outside the countries to which they migrated – East Africa, Burma, Malaya, and elsewhere. And whatever may be said about 'Islamic fatalism' as an obstacle to development among the indigenous Malays, it clearly did not constitute the slightest obstacle to the spectacular success of immigrant Muslim groups like the Ismailis in East Africa.

Clearly we must look elsewhere for explanations of the innovating energy frequently shown by migrant minorities. Here it is possible to do no more than suggest hypotheses.

First, there may be a process of selection of personality types. Migrants may possibly be the more enterprising people – indeed, the ones who show their enterprise by migrating.

Secondly, there may be demographic effects. Migrants tend to be young men, followed by young women. Migrant communities are characteristically short of older people and of teenage children, being made up of young parents and their young children. There are usually more men than women. This means that the ratio of economically active people in the community is higher than would be the case in a 'normal', settled group; or, looking at it the other way, the proportion of dependants is lower.

Thirdly, migrants may be free from some at least of the customary constraints on enterprise and initiative that are effective in the home society and culture. For example, it may be that one factor in the prosperity of the Chinese overseas in the nineteenth century was that they had not got the mandarinate on their backs. Morris reported that among Indians in Uganda it was impossible to observe the minutiae of the caste system, however committed they were to its general principles. Rules of exogamy were strictly observed – were insisted on, indeed, with special emphasis as if to demonstrate a general adherence to the Hindu way of life; but it would have been simply unrealistic to observe prohibitions such as those which would have prevented neighbouring families in a remote trading centre in Africa from accepting goods and water from each other. Morris wrote accordingly of 'the secular outlook of most of the immigrants', and quoted one of his informants as saying: 'The gods are unwilling to cross the sea.

Most of them, I think, stayed in India. The women brought over a few that are important to them; but for me, it will be time to pray to God when I go back to India.'[16]

Fourthly, immigrant groups are in many cases excluded from control of the traditionally legitimate resources that go with high social prestige. These include especially land and political power. The same hypothesis, indeed, may be extended also to non-immigrant minorities like the original Calvinist and Puritan sects in England and Germany. If at the same time such groups are moved to emulation of the rich and powerful (or in the jargon of sociology if they exhibit reference-group behaviour) then success in business may be the only way in which they can rise in the world. This hypothesis would appear to fit cases like the Chinese overseas especially in colonial times, and the East African Asian groups like the Ismailis both under colonial rule, when they were excluded by Europeans from land and power, and after independence when it was Africans who seized both. Clearly a hypothesis of this kind assumes the general framework of a plural society.

Hypotheses such as these turn more on considerations of minority status and the effects of migration than on the specific features of the culture of the group in question; and it may be that the qualities of method, industry, thrift, and asceticism which enable such a group to survive and prosper are developed in response to a situation rather than brought in with their cultural luggage.

Religious movements as effects of profound social disturbance

In many societies and at different periods where there has been a profound disturbance of established forms of social relations, leading to large numbers of people being deprived of access to resources upon which they had been accustomed to rely, such a disturbance has been followed by the rise of religious movements of a characteristic type. These movements have been variously called messianic, millenarian, nativistic, and prophetic. The term *messianic* implies a comparison with ancient Hebrew beliefs in a saviour who should come to deliver his people. *Millenarian* and the equivalent *chiliastic* refer strictly to the doctrine among some Christian sects that Christ will return and reign in bodily presence for a thousand years; in sociological usage the same terms have been given a slightly extended meaning to cover beliefs of the same general nature in an impending overthrow of the present order of society by supernatural means and the coming of a new order in which 'the last shall be first, and the first, last'. *Nativistic* in the colonial context referred to a movement reasserting the values and practices of the native culture as against white administration and Christian missions. *Prophetic* relates to the fact that such movements

215

commonly have leaders who prophesy the new order and urge their followers to adopt the appropriate moral and ritual usages to prepare for it.

Hundreds of such movements are known, and they have occurred from ancient times to the present. In his historical survey Norman Cohn recalled the prophetic movements among the Jews of the ancient world, notably including the 'stream of militant apocalyptic' and the promise of a saviour, the Messiah, which marked the period from 63 BC to AD 72. In medieval Europe, Cohn traced the rise and fall of sects like the Joachimites in the twelfth century who protested against the wealth and worldliness of the church and expected the millennium in 1260, when an 'angelic pope' was to convert the world to voluntary poverty. Although there were generally few links between the fanatical few inspired by millenarian visions and the broad masses of the peasants whose economic interests were threatened, occasionally under the stress of events the two types of movement might come together. Examples are the part played by John Ball in the English peasants' revolt in 1381, and the Taborites during the Hussite revolt in Bohemia in 1419–21.[17]

Among the factors that Cohn identified as favouring millenarian movements, singly or together, were catastrophe or the fear of it – famine, plague, massacre – along with 'the supposed defection of the authority traditionally responsible for regulating the relations between society and the powers governing the cosmos'. Another contributory factor was often 'emotional frustration in women of means and leisure but without social function or prestige'. Such movements occurred where the traditional religion included the promise of future bliss for the faithful (and not where that was absent, as in ancient Greece). That promise could be renewed by a prophet holding out hope of collective salvation, immediate and total, from frustration, anxiety, and humiliation that could not be assuaged either by taking thought or by any institutionalized routine, and were widely enough shared to result in a collective emotional agitation.[18]

Such conditions have clearly been brought about in recent history by European expansion, colonial rule, and the new order of society related to industrial development. There is a considerable literature on the religious movements that have arisen in response to those upheavals, and most of all on anti-European and anti-colonial movements. It is salutary therefore to be reminded by Cohn that movements of this general nature are confined neither to recent history nor to those particular causes.

A pioneer work in this field was the summary and analysis by Peter Worsley of the cargo cults of Melanesia. An early cult of this type was the Tuka movement which arose in Fiji in the 1870s and 1880s, led by a man named Ndugumoi who organized his followers in a quasi-military fashion under 'sergeants' and 'scribes' with high officers called 'destroying angels'. It was mystically revealed to Ndugumoi that the ancestors were shortly to return to Fiji, the shops would be jammed with calico, tinned salmon, and other goods for the faithful, but unbelievers would die or become the slaves and servants of believers. The whites had deliberately deceived them. The bible was really written about the divine Twins of local legend, but the whites had substituted the names Jehovah and Jesus for the names of the Twins. The false Europeans were pretending to be surveying the reef with their instruments, but really they were scanning the horizon for the vessels in which the Twins were returning with the ancestors.

The Tuka cult was followed by a large number of similar movements all over the area of New Guinea and the islands to the east, in which its main themes were taken up repeatedly – the belief in an imminent millennium in which ships would bring ample supplies of the new goods for the benefit of the local people; the further assertion that the missionaries were conniving in the injustice by means of a deceit in which they were deliberately withholding part of the bible; the organization of the faithful to expel the whites and to prepare for the coming of the cargo. In later cargo cults, prophets succeeded in persuading people to stop cultivating and instead build harbours, and after the 1939–45 war in which aircraft and radio became familiar to the islanders these were reflected in cults which prepared by clearing the bush to make airstrips, putting up poles and making wooden radios.

Colonial governments were generally uneasy about such movements and in some cases acted repressively against them. This unease was prompted in some instances by a paternal concern for the welfare of people who under the influence of group hysteria neglected to make ordinary provision for themselves by cultivating. At other times the cult posed a direct challenge to law and order, as for instance when in 1923 a white plantation owner in New Hebrides was killed as a sacrificial victim symbolizing other Europeans, or when the adherents of a cult formed large crowds in a state of high emotion near police or mission stations. Many of the leaders of cargo cults were imprisoned or restrained in mental hospitals.[19]

Worsley's analysis, carried out from documentary sources, was confirmed in a field study by Peter Lawrence who described how he came upon a cargo cult almost by accident. After two months in the field, the people among whom he was working heard that he was expecting his mother and sister, and asked him to inspect a site for an airstrip for the goods they would presumably be bringing with them. Now that they had, as they put it, 'their own European', things were obviously going to change, the secret they had awaited for years would be theirs; he would 'open the road of the cargo' by contacting God, who would send their and his ancestors with goods to Sydney for onward transmission to him and them.[20]

Lawrence detailed the rise and fall of Yali, who became the leader of a cargo cult on the Rai coast in 1946–50. Yali had been a policeman and then during the 1939–45 war a soldier with a heroically distinguished record. Shortly after the war he gained the further approval of the government for his initiative in community development in his home district, but his very popularity with his own people was in the end his undoing. Their dawning belief in his superhuman qualities led to his being cast in the role of the leader of a cargo cult, with which after prolonged misgivings he eventually identified himself. Such a case tragically illustrates the tenacity of these beliefs, which were reported to be still widespread in 1971.[21]

Vittorio Lanternari's summary of the literature on messianic movements traced among others the succession of prophetic cults among the North American Indians.[22] These began in 1799 when a man named Ganioda'yo or Handsome Lake had a vision when near to death and recovered to pass on the message of the three spirits who had visited him with a new doctrine of salvation. This 'Great Message' was a combination of Christian and traditional Indian teachings; conciliatory in tone, it was commended by Thomas Jefferson as 'positive and effective'. During the nineteenth century, however, conflict between the North American Indians and the white Americans who rapidly grew in numbers and occupied more and more of their land was reflected in prophetic movements which were unambiguously anti-white. These culminated in the so-called Ghost Dances between 1870 and 1890, though it is interesting to note that at least two of these movements gained some white supporters from among the followers of the Mormon prophet Joseph Smith – another group at odds with the dominant white American society. They ended in 1890 when a cult under the leadership of the prophet Wovoka spurred a last hopeless armed uprising among the Sioux, which was defeated at the battle of Wounded Knee.

Following the defeat of the Ghost Dance, some Indians then turned to cults of a very different character. Peyote is a small cactus, a part of which when eaten has a mildly hallucinatory effect, and the central rite of the peyote cults consists of the search for peace through its use. The imagery of the movement, though various, has common themes in the revival and restoration of one near to death, which may be held to symbolize the desperation of individuals whose cultural identity seemed threatened by the all-engulfing industrial civilization of white America. The tone is peaceful and conciliatory, with the playing down of intertribal conflicts, an amalgamation of Christian and Indian symbolic elements, and a general tendency towards withdrawal from rather than opposition to the white man and his civilization. Though they came under the suspicion of Protestant missionaries, the peyote cults were long defended by Commissioner John Collier of the US Bureau of Indian Affairs, who after taking scientific advice decided that the peyote was so mild in its effects, and the cults so important to the sense of identity of many Indians, that they should be allowed to continue. With the general apprehension about narcotic and hallucinatory drugs in the USA in later years, however, the attack was renewed, and peyote was ruled illegal by a court decision in California in 1964.

As a postscript to the foregoing, it is of interest that the peyote cult was 'discovered' by the English writer Aldous Huxley who lived for many years in California and knew the plant by the name of mesca or mescal. Huxley's use of mescaline to induce states of mysticism and heightened consciousness, about which he wrote in *The Doors of Perception* (1954), led directly to the use of peyote and other drugs in the movement of 'chemical mysticism' which grew up in literary circles (e.g. the 'Beatnik' poets) and in the cinema industry in California in the 1950s, and hence to the advocacy of far more powerful synthetic hallucinatory drugs in the 1960s.[23] Perhaps these developments can be seen as representing yet another form of rejection of and withdrawal from modern industrial society, this time on the part not of the deprived and dispossessed but the affluent elite.

In Africa, pioneer studies of Bantu independent churches were carried out by the Swedish missionary Bengt Sundkler, who worked among the Zulu people from 1937 to 1942. Sundkler found that there were no fewer than eight hundred such sects in South Africa alone, and he broadly classified them into the Ethiopian and Zionist types, using names which the sects commonly and characteristically gave themselves.*

Ethiopian sects were either direct or indirect offshoots of white mission churches, whose forms of organization and doctrines of biblical interpretation they followed on the whole very closely. Their essential character could be summed up in the slogan 'Africa for the Africans!' Ethiopia was equated with Africa, and biblical references to Ethiopia were cited in support of claims for the antiquity of an African church; it was also identified with the contemporary kingdom of Ethiopia, both interpretations of the name being inextricably intermingled. Some of these churches had

* In sociological usage, a *church* embraces a whole community; *denominations* compete for adherents in a tolerant secular state; a *sect* is a group united by beliefs and practices at odds with accepted norms, especially in its early stages; and the term *cult* refers to beliefs and practices not yet those of an organized group. But sometimes the term a social scientist would apply to a group differs from the name by which its members know it. In particular, the claim to be the authentic church and not a mere sect may be integral to the ideology of the group in question. Accordingly, some scholars including Sundkler adopt the terminology of the groups they study rather than that of social science.

links with Negro sects (as they were then called) in the United States, forged in some cases by Marcus Garvey, a Jamaican who travelled all over the black world during the 1920s and 1930s spreading the idea of independent black churches as a means to liberation. Their essential aims were to be both Christian and African – Christian in the essentials of doctrine and practice with only minor modifications to accommodate the second aim, that of being self-governing and independent of white control.

In contrast, Zionist sects were syncretistic, combining some Christian ideas and practices with elements such as speaking in tongues and Bantu purification rites and taboos. They combated African witchcraft and similar practices, but Sundkler wrote that 'the weapons with which they fight the struggle belong to an arsenal of old Zulu religion'. The name Zionist constituted a kind of mythical charter linking African prophets who performed baptisms with an apostolic succession embracing John the Baptist, the River Jordan, Mount Zion, Jerusalem, and in some cases Nazareth. It followed that their identification tended to be with ancient Israel, the Holy Land, rather than with Ethiopia (the modern state of Israel had not come into being at the time of Sundkler's field work, and no reference was intended to Zionism as a political movement among modern Jews). Some also had links with the Zion church of Zion City, Illinois, USA. Sundkler emphasizes, however, that the boundary between the two types was ill defined. An individual sect might well change its doctrines and practices and move from one category into the other, while there were many borderline cases in which it was hard to tell whether Ethiopian or Zionist doctrines predominated.[24]

Following Sundkler's work, a number of East African religious movements were studied in depth during the 1950s by F. B. Welbourn. Among them was that founded in Uganda in 1929 by two young Anglican teachers, Reuben Spartas Mukasa and Obadaiah Basajjakitalo, as 'the African Orthodox Church – a church established for all right-thinking Africans, men who wish to be free in their own house, not always being thought of as boys'. Welbourn also studied the churches which grew up in association with the independent schools movement among the Kikuyu, which was in turn a part of the reaction to conquest and white settlement in the much harsher atmosphere of Kenya.[25] That reaction had its political aspects in the African nationalist parties and movements which arose during the period from 1920 onwards, most of them to be suppressed by the colonial administration in a conflict which eventually took the form of an armed revolt and guerrilla movement to which Europeans gave the name of 'Mau Mau'. There has been a good deal of dispute about the character of this movement; the colonial administration at first regarded it as yet another 'dini' or religious movement, and it certainly had its ritual side in the form of oathing ceremonies. Later interpretations characterized it as an African nationalist political movement and rejected explanations in religious terms.[26] The truth may well be that it was both, or more exactly that it was hard to disentangle the religious, educational, political, and military aspects of a broad movement of revolt among the Kikuyu against white settlement, Christian missions, and colonial rule. There was in fact a large and numerous growth of sects in Kenya, ranging from groups which, like Sundkler's Ethiopians, aspired to be fully Christian though free from foreign control, through syncretistic movements which admitted a good many more elements from the traditional African cultures of the region, to cults whose predominant character was that of a chauvinistic revival of traditional or quasi-traditional beliefs and practices. I gave an outline account of some of these movements in my general description of East African society,[27] while a notable later study was that by Sangree of the situation in Tiriki, a small area of western Kenya.[28]

In West Africa, Geoffrey Parrinder's comprehensive study of religion in the city of Ibadan included full descriptions of the separatist sects, one of the most picturesque of which was the Sacred Cherubim and Seraphim Society whose practices were drawn from Muslim as well as Christian and pagan customs.[29] Another detailed study of West African religious practices was that by the psychiatrist Dr Margaret Field, for whom they formed a background to the detailed case-studies of mental patients.[30] Field emphasized the continuity between Hebraic, Christian, Muslim, and pagan West African beliefs and practices. Quite apart from the possibility of common origins, 'Christianity has been in West Africa for five centuries', as she put it; it was not a question of a sudden contact with a complete cultural innovation. She rejected the notion that a supposed conflict between Christian and pagan ideas – 'the opposing pulls of tribal gods and the dictates of Christianity' – was responsible for neurosis or other forms of mental trouble. In particular, beliefs in spirit possession were common to all three of the main religious traditions in West Africa, and it was those which were vital to the new shrines at which 'the troubles and desires of ordinary people' found expression and solace.

Movements variously called schisms, secessions, separatist sects, and independent churches have been reported from all parts of black Africa, and four more examples must suffice. In Zaire, then the Belgian Congo, Simon Kimbangu began to see visions and was credited with the power to heal the sick about 1921, and quickly attracted a large following, to the detriment both of the Roman Catholic missions and work on the railway and the plantations. Within months he was arrested, tried, and sentenced to death, which was commuted to life imprisonment; he died in prison in 1951. Missionary hostility notwithstanding, the movement continued to grow throughout Belgian rule. It was legalized in 1959 and took the title *Eglise de Jesus-Christ sur la terre par le prophète Simon Kimbangu* (EJCSK).

Since independence, with its impeccably anti-colonial origins it has grown both in numbers and standing under the leadership of Kimbangu's sons, one of whom was elected a deputy to the parliament of Zaire and served as minister of labour in Patrice Lumumba's government.[31]

Joseph Booth was responsible, directly or indirectly, for starting no less than seven African sects between 1892 and 1910 in the country then named Nyasaland, now Malawi, an area which before the formal declaration of a British protectorate had been ruled in effect for nearly thirty years by Scottish and Anglican missions. As a Baptist and a radical, Booth incurred the suspicion of missions and government alike in his activities as a kind of free-lance missionary, attached successively to parent bodies including Seventh-Day Adventists. He travelled between southern Africa and the United States, in touch with the Watch Tower movement known as Jehovah's Witnesses as well as with 'Ethiopian' sects in South Africa, and supporting African followers in both continents. One such was Elliott Kamwana, to whom Booth taught the Watch Tower doctrine which he returned to Nyasaland to preach, supplied from time to time by Booth with their literature. Watch Tower spread widely throughout colonial Africa, becoming almost wholly independent of the parent American sect, and acquiring a militantly anti-white tone in which the coming millennium was viewed mainly in terms of liberation from colonial rule. The name was rendered into Bantu languages as Ki-Tower or Kitawala, and as lately as the 1950s it was still causing alarm among missions and governments. Another was John Chilembwe, who was influenced by the National Baptist Convention (a black civil rights movement) in the United States, and returned to Nyasaland with a number of black Americans to found the Providence Industrial Mission. After they left in 1906, Chilembwe's mission became the centre for African militancy, and in 1915 he led an armed rising in the Shire Highlands.[32]

In 1953 a Bemba woman named Alice, whose followers called her Lenshina (Regina, Queen) received a call to start a new religious movement which two years later broke away from the Presbyterian church and attracted large numbers of followers from both Protestant and Catholic missions. Known as the Lumpa (Itinerating) church it spread northward into Tanzania and sent a mission southwards to Salisbury in Rhodesia. At its height the movement is said to have had a hundred thousand members. Trouble began when they refused to pay taxes, and in 1964 this led to the movement taking the form of an armed rebellion against the authority of the newly independent state of Zambia. Bloody clashes ensued and several hundred people were killed before the movement was crushed. Alice was put into restriction, but the movement is said still to have some twenty thousand members, half of them in exile across the border in Zaire.

An exhaustive compilation of the data on movements of this kind in

Africa south of the Sahara was carried out by the Reverend David Barrett, who amassed over 1,300 published accounts of movements numbering by 1966 over five thousand. According to his account:

In 1957, a massive secession involving 16,000 members took place from the Anglican Church in western Kenya. The African bishop there had at that time serving under him some thirty African clergy, and a handful of missionary clergy from the Church Missionary Society including myself. We all imagined that the disturbance was a new and unique kind of phenomenon caused by purely local factors and personalities, and the whole affair was handled from the start on that assumption...

What this demonstrates is the alarming fact that decisions of the utmost importance can be made in good faith yet in virtual ignorance of strikingly similar parallels elsewhere, and hence of the underlying realities of the crisis and the dilemma that it poses.[33]

But perhaps the biggest of all these movements was the Taiping rebellion, the most important of a series of religious revolts in China from the eighteenth century onwards, whose suppression, according to Yang, ranked with border defence as one of the two great tasks of the imperial army.[34]

Taiping was led by Hong Xiu Zhuan, son of a peasant of the Hakka tribe, who studied unsuccessfully for the state examinations and became instead a village teacher. In 1837, when he was twenty-three, he came across a Protestant missionary pamphlet from which he learned the elements of Christian belief. In the following year he saw visions which he interpreted to mean that he was the son of God, a younger brother of Jesus, and charged with a mission to establish *Taiping tien kuo*, 'heavenly kingdom of great peace'. Hong later underwent two months' instruction at a mission station, but he had little understanding of Christianity.[35]

From 1847 the followers of Taiping were in open revolt, and with their homes burned and their goods confiscated by government troops they took to a sort of primitive communism. From 1852 to 1856 they extended their hold into Hunan and down the Yangtse, capturing Nanking (Nanjing), the imperial southern capital, where Hong, now styled 'Heavenly King', established his residence. Despite severe internal dissensions and fighting in Nanking, the movement held the city until 1864 when it fell to the 'ever-victorious army' of Zeng Guo-Fan, an army which included Charles George Gordon among its European and American mercenary units.

Taiping's zeal for social reform embraced common property; over and above subsistence needs, families were to hand over crops and money to a central granary and bank. It advocated land reform, with moderate taxes; the equality of women; temperance in the use of alcohol and tobacco, and the suppression of opium; and iconoclasm, which entailed the destruction of works of art embodying outworn beliefs. Foreigners were not regarded as inferior; all men were equal, and some foreign ideas were good, notably

223

those of Christianity; but foreigners ought not to be exempted from Chinese law, and the movement expressed the resentment which many Chinese felt at what they regarded as the imperial government's surrender in this regard. After the capture of Nanking, the movement appears to have lost its moral fervour, and Franke describes its leaders as succumbing to the traditional vices of display, nepotism, and factionalism. This led to cynicism and demoralization in its army; especially when opposed by Zeng, a man of high ideals and upright character. Further, it failed to co-operate with other movements of revolt, although several peasant rebellions and one other religious revolt were going on at the same time. But it certainly shook the empire to its foundations, and both the Kuomintang and the communists may well have learned much from Taiping.

In many monographic accounts the explanatory emphasis has been on the particular circumstances of the religious movement in question. Commonly in recent history they have been the grievances and humiliations of colonial rule, or analogous situations of internalized colonialism. Thus movements among North American Indians arose in the conflict between them and white Americans; cargo cults in Melanesia under white Australian rule; and the Taiping rebellion in large part as a reaction to the incursions of Europeans into China in the 1840s. Similarly in South Africa Sundkler attributed the rise of independent African churches to particular features of life there, including the colour bar, residential segregation, the land question, the Netherlands Reformed Churches' 'golden rule' of '*geen gelijkstelling* – no equality in church or state', and the inscription '*Net vir Blankes* – For Europeans Only' figuratively but no less virtually written on many church doors besides others.[36]

Such explanations seem insufficiently general. Though a colour bar as rigid as that in South Africa could not be paralleled, separatist sects have arisen elsewhere, such as that which according to Barrett's account broke away from the Anglican diocese in Kenya, most of whose clergy were African and over whose doors there was clearly no literal or metaphorical 'For whites only'. In Uganda and Nyasaland (now Malawi) too, both missions and government encouraged African advancement in education, economic life, and (though more hesitantly) public affairs; yet the mere atmosphere of paternalism sufficed to engender separatist movements like the African Greek Orthodox Church in Uganda and those associated with Joseph Booth, Elliott Kamwana, and John Chilembwe in Nyasaland.

Nevertheless, it does seem to be the case that the more pronounced the white domination and the more rigid the colour bar the greater the tendency to form separatist religious movements. Thus among the five thousand or so African independent churches surveyed by Barrett in the 1960s, some two thousand were in the Republic of South Africa, while

224

of a total membership or following of seven million in all Africa, Barrett estimated that three million were in South Africa.[37]

Further, it is too simple to connect religious movements of this type with colonial rule, for they do not come to an end with political independence. As has been seen, the Kimbangu-ist church continued to attract a mass following in the republic of Zaire long after Belgian rule came to an end. Similarly, the Lumpa church of Alice Lenshina clashed violently with the authorities in independent Zambia. Moreover, this simple equation ignores the evidence of numerous movements that have arisen within societies like those of medieval Europe.

Another broad type of explanatory hypothesis is that which regards syncretistic, prophetic religious movements as arising from the contact (or impact, or clash) of Christianity upon an indigenous system of religious beliefs and practices. Such explanations are 'anthropological' in the sense that they consider the religious phenomena in rather strictly local terms. Thus Peter Lawrence related cargo cults to traditional Melanesian beliefs in the need for co-operation between the living and the dead, so that all important work was compounded of secular and ritual techniques, and it was natural to think of the ancestors as being involved in the production of goods for the use of the living.[38] Similarly, Lanternari drew attention to the syncretism that characterized many prophetic movements and wrote of 'the cultural clash between populations in very different stages of development'.

Here again it must be suggested that these explanations, though not false, are incomplete and insufficient. To view religious movements of the type in question purely in terms of a local clash of cultures is to fail to take into account networks of influence, ideology, and social relations which since the early nineteenth century have been world-wide in scale. Thus the African Greek Orthodox Church in Uganda was stimulated by Marcus Garvey's Universal Negro Improvement Association in America, its original connection was with a Garveyite church in South Africa, and its later links were with the Greek Orthodox church. Or consider the networks in which Joseph Booth was involved, moving as he did between England, Australia, the United States, and southern Africa and setting up links between the American Jehovah's Witnesses and the black Kitawala movement of Elliott Kamwana, besides involving himself in 'Ethiopian' movements in South Africa and initiating half a dozen other movements in what is now Malawi. Yet another example is afforded by the links between the white Mormons of Joseph Smith in America and the prophetic movement of Smohalla among the North American Indians.

Among those who have taken a wider view I have already cited Norman Cohn. Another is John Milton Yinger, who has written of sects and cults

225

arising among 'groups caught in conditions of severe disprivilege' following either conquest by a militarily and industrially more advanced society, or domination by a more powerful segment of their own society. The religion of the conqueror, though often strongly promoted by missionary activity, is embedded in the whole social system of the dominant group and thus unacceptable to the subordinate groups. Among the latter, too, despite traditional tribal differences, people find themselves caught up in common situations, so that unifying themes are needed. Yinger cited the cargo cults, the 1890 Ghost Dance, and the Jehovah's Witnesses as examples of 'attack cults':

Such religious attacks on the dominant society are not limited to conquered peoples. If, within a society, a group lacks an independent and successful past which can serve as the focus of the millennial dream, they can affirm that they are the true defenders of a tradition shared with their oppressors, who have fallen into sinful ways; they alone are 'Jehovah's Witnesses'...Thus the Jehovah's Witnesses also attack the rich and powerful, although there is no racial theme involved, as did the members of the Fiji Tuka cult and the Indian Ghost Dance; and they attack the society by downgrading its institutions and refusing to accord it final loyalty.

Such religious movements, as Yinger mildly put it, are seldom regarded with favour by the dominant group:

Through the years, many of the leaders of the Cargo cults in Melanesia have been jailed and the movements suppressed. The Ghost Dance was smashed militarily at the Battle of Wounded Knee. Hundreds of Jehovah's Witnesses have been jailed in the United States because their search for salvation involved a sharp disagreement with dominant institutions.

The 'attack' type of cult, however, is fairly short-lived. If hope for the restoration of the old culture and the independence of the subject group fades, then there is likely to be a transition to a more accommodative type of cult, like the peyote cult which followed the suppression of the Ghost Dance. On the other hand, the 'success' of the sect, and more especially if its members under its influence gain improved status, Protestant-ethic-style, then what began as a militant sect becomes a denomination accepting its place as one of several alternative forms of religion, tolerated by society and accommodating itself to the existing order.[39]

To those considerations must be added another: reaction against the materialism that seems inherent in economic development and the secularism that pervades modernization. In recent times that reaction, as Talcott Parsons foresaw, has taken the form of religious fundamentalism and the re-assertion of a traditional faith not as one denomination among others but as the dominant form of religion in a whole society. Perhaps the most striking case is that of Iran, where the downfall of that modernizing autocrat the Shah was largely the result of an upsurge of Islamic fundamentalism that led to the establishment of a theocratic state under clerical leadership in 1979. There could hardly be a more vivid illustration of the continuing importance of religion.

SUGGESTIONS FOR FURTHER READING

Robert W. Green (ed.), *Protestantism and Capitalism: the Weber Thesis and its Critics*, Lexington, Mass.: D. C. Heath, 1959

Melford E. Spiro, *Buddhism and Society: A Great Tradition and its Burmese Vicissitudes*, London: Allen and Unwin, 1971

Norman Cohn, *The Pursuit of the Millennium*, London: Secker and Warburg, 1957

Peter Worsley, *The Trumpet Shall Sound*, London: Macgibbon and Kee, 1957

Bengt G. M. Sundkler, *Bantu Prophets in South Africa*, London: Lutterworth Press, 1948

Marie-Louise Martin, *Kimbangu*, Oxford: Blackwell, 1975

11 Some psychological aspects of change

Social change occurs when people change their ways. Related to the kinds of change considered in this book are therefore a number of questions or problems for social psychology. A few people initiate change, many adapt themselves to change, yet others resist change. Can we make any general statements about what kinds of people they respectively are? – their characteristic personalities, aptitudes, attitudes, beliefs, and motives? In what social situation, with what degrees of exposure to what kinds of information and persuasion, do people learn effectively or ineffectively to adapt themselves to new circumstances and turn them to their own advantage, or contrariwise fail to learn?

Leonard W. Doob on 'becoming more civilized'[1]

A pioneer study in this field was that of L. W. Doob, whose previous work had included research on public opinion and propaganda. It was a study of 'two principal questions...concerning people in less civilized societies: 1. Why do they become more civilized in certain aspects? 2. What happens to them as they become more civilized?...What changes occur in their way of thinking, in their systems of self-guiding rewards, in their beliefs, and in their personalities?'

Doob's initial orientation was with the modernization school. Among the earlier studies of societies undergoing change on which he drew in framing his hypotheses, many of them the work of anthropologists, were those directed by Daniel Lerner in the Middle East. He adopted Lerner's categories 'traditional', 'transitional', and 'modern', and specified 'the attributes of less civilized people' as small-scale social relations, security and restriction, faith and absolutism, unity of behaviour, and simplicity. Doob's own field studies were carried out in the 1950s in four societies of Africa and the West Indies (Luo, Ganda, Zulu, and Jamaica) by means of systematic interviews comparing the responses of the old with the young and the schooled with the illiterate.

Among Doob's twenty-seven hypotheses, some were quite specific and lent themselves to confirmation or denial from the data. Thus consistent differences were found in his interviews to support the hypothesis that people 'changing centrally from old to new ways' have longer time-horizons. Similarly, people changing in other respects were found to retain traditional attitudes towards family forms and practices – a finding in accord with the analysis in chapter 8. And though the evidence was not quite conclusive, it seemed likely that people changing their ways were apt to join new groups demonstrating the new ways, and to put more value on traits like initiative, independence, and self-confidence.

'People who are confronted with alternative beliefs and values' were found to be 'likely to retain traditional ones which appear to serve a continuing need and to reject those which do not, but always to retain some of the traditional views.' Even among the most educated groups there was scarcely a case in which at least one member of the sample did not assent to a traditional belief or value, even though their general traditionalism was significantly weaker than the less educated. Similar results were obtained in comparing young and old. Elaborating the initial hypothesis, Doob suggested that traditional beliefs and values may be adhered to because they are taught at an early age. The 'continuing need' may include a need to harmonize the views of younger and more-educated with those of older and less-educated members of the same family group, or at least to reduce the dissonance between them. Doob linked this with the well-known phenomena of syncretism in religious and magical beliefs and practices – the tendency for traditional magic to continue to coexist side by side with newly introduced Christianity, for example. Further, he suggested that 'people changing centrally are liable to remain in a state of conflict concerning the advantages and disadvantages of both old and new beliefs and values'. And misunderstandings were likely to arise among the three categories of people – the unchanged, those who are changing, and those who have changed their ways. But there was little evidence either way for the hypothesis that after people 'change centrally' they are less likely to be dogmatic about their own beliefs and values.

In the later chapters of his book, Doob became more concerned to advance and explore hypotheses than to test them. One theory concerned the 'piecemealness' of change. 'Heavily reinforced behaviour that re-mains satisfying...is likely to change only after some of its components have been changed' – in other words it is more likely to change piecemeal than all at once. Similarly, where a new form of behaviour is difficult to learn, it is likely to be learned piecemeal rather than wholly adopted on one occasion. There is something in common here with Rogers' analysis of the characteristics of innovations which make them more or less readily adopted, with which I deal below. Doob suggested that 'the proficiency with which people change from old to new ways is likely to be increased when they seek a central goal that transcends the specific form of behaviour being changed'. The central goal may be simply that of 'becoming more civilized', or it may be more complex. The Ganda were cited as a case in point of an African people whose overriding aim in the twentieth century was that of making a successful adjustment to the modern world without ceasing to be distinctively Ganda or renouncing their cultural inheritance and sense of identity. Western ways were adopted quickly and thoroughly when they appeared to be instrumental to that end – money, education, modern technology, and even Christianity. The distinction between ends which are central and those which are incidental or instrumental, or in Doob's word 'segmental', led him to advance the corollary hypothesis that 'people who retain strong central values are motivated to learn segmental forms of behaviour that do not appear to be at variance with those values'. Presumably the whole history of Japan since the Meiji Restoration affords an even more striking case in point. Another corollary put in general terms the experience of colonial rebellions: 'People who have changed centrally from old to new ways and who then perceive that they are being prevented from achieving some central goal are likely to learn to seek aggressively a different central goal.' Some of the hypotheses near the end of the list, indeed, appeared to be matters for general assent rather than specific verification – what, for example, are we to make of 'All societies eventually become civilized in a distinctive manner or perish'?

So although Doob began with Lerner's opposition of 'traditional' to 'modern', his analysis of central goals and peripheral adaptations among the Ganda cast some doubt on the usefulness of this opposition. In other ways, too, his work transcended its original limitations, and though its breadth and near-comprehensiveness rendered much of it inconclusive, it remains a source of stimulating and suggestive ideas in its field.

Everett M. Rogers on the diffusion of innovation[2]

Rogers' work began with the study of agricultural innovations in the United States and broadened to that of farm practices world-wide and of innovations in general, including medicine, education, family limitation, public health, and industry.

According to his definitions, an innovation is an idea perceived as new by the individual, while diffusion is the process through which a new idea spreads from a source – its original invention by a creative individual – to its adoption by users. Adoption implies a decision to continue full use of the idea as distinct from a decision merely to try it. A typical time-sequence of events is involved in the behaviour of the users or potential users; first they become aware of the idea, next they decide to try it, and then they continue in full use, the three stages being named 'awareness', 'trial', and 'adoption' accordingly. The adoption period is the time which elapses between the user's first hearing of the idea and the decision to continue full use. 'Innovativeness' is the term Rogers uses for an individual's propensity to adopt innovations. People differ in their innovativeness, and can variously be classified as innovators, early adopters, early and late majority, or laggards, according to the length of time it takes them compared with others to adopt a new practice.

Rogers concluded from a number of studies that some cultures are more generally favourable to innovation than others. For example, his own researches in Wisconsin had led him to the conclusion that farmers of Danish descent there were far more innovative than those of Polish descent, even though all were immigrants into the common cultural environment of a single American state. Rogers' discussion of this in terms of a distinction between 'traditional' and 'modern' norms is in general accord with the modernization school.

The adoption process, which involves both learning and decision-making, is elaborated into five stages – (1) awareness, (2) interest, (3) evaluation, (4) trial, and (5) adoption. Rogers carried out a cross-analysis of these five stages with his analysis of individuals' innovativeness, and showed that early adopters not only start on the process ahead of others, but also go through each of the five stages more quickly.

The characteristics of the innovation do matter, however. The innovations which are easily and quickly adopted tend to be those whose relative advantage over previously established methods is immediately obvious and a source of clear gain to the adopter. Readily adopted innovations are also those which are compatible with existing values and past experience, and are simple (from the point of view of the user, that is; a television set is a highly complex product, but all the user has to do is switch it on and off). Readily adopted innovations, other things being equal, are those which are divisible. Users are more likely to try a new method if they can do so on a small scale, as for example when a farmer tries out something on a small portion of his land. Innovations are less likely to be adopted if they involve going over completely to the new method without the possibility of a small-scale trial. Finally, new ideas are more readily adopted if they are communicable. A new breed of farm crop, for example, may advertise itself by its visibly better yields.

From the point of view of development and change in poor countries, some of Rogers' most important findings were in his detailed analysis of adopter categories and individual differences in innovativeness. Early adopters were found to be younger than others, to have higher social status, and to be wealthier – whether as a result of having adopted innovations in the past, or as a factor that enabled them to innovate in the present because their resources were sufficient to fall back on if an experimental

innovation failed. They were found to have distinctive personality characteristics, including less rigidity and greater rationality. Early adopters
made more use than others of impersonal sources of information such as
farming weeklies or medical journals. Late adopters by contrast tended to
rely more on personal sources, the word of mouth of neighbours or
professional colleagues. Further, early adopters relied more on 'cosmopolite'
sources – national or international journals, for example – compared with
the 'localite' sources of late adopters. Early adopters were more commonly
in direct touch with the sources of new ideas themselves; for example,
farmers might be in direct correspondence with agricultural scientists.
They had a wider range of sources of information and wider horizons
generally. They tended to travel more – some American farmers, for
example, had literally travelled the world in search of new ideas of possible
applicability to their own farms. And they were more likely to be opinion
leaders, the first to hear news and pass it on to others.

In relation to such characteristics, innovators sometimes saw themselves
and were seen by others as deviants from the local social system. At home
and in the company of their neighbours they might be regarded as
eccentric; but 'they identify [themselves] with other reference groups
outside their community who consensually validate their behaviour'; they
are 'in step with a different drummer'.

Finally, Rogers drew attention to the important part played in the process
of diffusion by change agents. These are people professionally concerned
with the adoption of innovations, promoting practices considered desirable,
and trying to prevent those regarded as harmful or inappropriate, such as
public health officials, teachers, and agricultural extension workers. Many
of the educated elites of Third World countries are engaged in such
activities and can be called change agents accordingly.

William Ogionwo on Nigerian progressive farmers[3]

Following Rogers' work, Ogionwo studied in detail the circumstances and
characteristics associated with the adoption of innovations among Nigerian
peasant farmers. His sample consisted of a thousand cash-crop farmers
together with a further two hundred who did not grow a cash crop.
Innovativeness was measured by the proportion of government-
recommended practices a farmer had adopted, out of a list generally of
about twelve to fifteen depending on the crop, the climate, and the region.
Some of the data which were then correlated with innovativeness were
comparatively simple, such as age; other qualities, especially the more
psychological attributes such as rationality and change-proneness, were
probed by means of a number of questions.

The most important of Ogionwo's findings are summarized in table 11.1.
The factors most strongly correlated with innovativeness proved to be gross

Table 11.1   *The correlates of innovativeness among Nigerian farmers*

Variable	Partial correlation coefficient	% of total variation explained	Group total	Conclusion
Economic				
1 Gross farm income	0.425	18.06		Strongly related to innovativeness
2 Acres of crop land	0.046	0.21		Not related to innovativeness
3 Size of plant	0.025	0.06		Not related to innovativeness
			18.33	
Social				
4 Age	−0.158	2.50		Inversely related to innovativeness (younger farmers more innovative) but not very strongly so
5 Education	0.171	2.92		Related, but not very strongly so
6 Level of living	0.325	10.56		Quite strongly related to innovativeness
7 Social participation	0.116	1.35		Positively but weakly related
8 Information contact	0.189	3.57		Related to innovativeness
9 Mobility	0.054	0.29		Not related to innovativeness
			21.19	
Personal				
10 Resignation	−0.013	0.02		Not related to innovativeness
11 Traditionalism	−0.029	0.08		Not related to innovativeness
12 Deviancy	0.119	1.42		Positively but weakly related
13 Familism	0.021	0.04		Not related to innovativeness
14 Change-proneness	0.415	17.22		Strongly related to innovativeness
15 Rationality	0.214	4.58		Related to innovativeness
			23.35[a]	

Note:
[a] Failure to agree with items results from rounding.
Source: W. W. Ogionwo, 'The adoption of technological innovations in Nigeria'.

farm income, level of living, change-proneness, and rationality. In Nigeria as elsewhere it is clearly the case that the more innovative farmers are better off, and this may operate both as cause and as effect – farmers with greater resources are more likely to take the risk involved in going over to a new practice. The finding about change-proneness indicates that people who say they are ready to try new ideas prove to be so in action as well as in words. Rationality in Ogionwo's schedule involved 'the use of deliberation, planning, and the best available sources of information and advice as a means of achieving ends', and this quality too was shown to be correlated with innovativeness, albeit less strongly so. Young farmers were somewhat more likely to adopt new ways. Information contact, education and social participation were also positively correlated with innovativeness, but these correlations were somewhat weaker. Innovative farmers were found to be deviant rather than conformist, and somewhat more likely to reply affirmatively to test statements like 'I never worry about being different from others'; but here again the correlation was not very strong. Mobility was found not to be correlated with innovativeness, despite the initial hypothesis that people who had moved around and seen more of the world might be more inclined to adopt new practices.

Neither resignation, traditionalism, nor familism proved to be significantly correlated with innovativeness. These findings run counter to the tenets of the modernization school that tradition and modernity are diametrically opposed and that attachment to the family and resignation to fate or to the will of God are likewise to be regarded as obstacles to modernity and development. Ogionwo considered these questions in some detail. People can adopt new methods because they are seen as more effective means to achieving traditional ends. Thus a farmer may be motivated to adopt government-recommended practices in the belief that they will increase his income in order to enable him better to discharge his family responsibilities. Or he may adopt because people whom he respects as traditional authorities are recommending or urging him to do so – as in Buganda, for instance, where the chiefs joined the government and the Anglican mission in persuading people to grow cotton. So 'tradition and modernity can...be mutually reinforcing rather than in conflict'. Institutions such as kinship and caste should not be seen merely as impediments to economic growth. Against the oft-cited 'plague of family parasitism' should be set the family's contribution to the division of labour, the supply of skill and training, and the accumulation of capital. Pitting tradition and modernity against each other as paired opposites led us to overlook the mixtures and blends that reality displayed. It became 'an ideology of anti-traditionalism, denying the necessary and usable ways in which the past serves as support, especially in the spheres of values and political legitimation, to the present and the future'.

234

Information was collected in some detail about the use and effectiveness of different media of information, and this is of interest in relation to the ideas of Lerner, Schramm, and others. Almost all farmers heard the radio – 88 per cent – and many of those who did not own radios themselves listened to farming programmes in neighbours' houses. The printed word naturally reached a smaller proportion of farmers, about 38 per cent of whom had never been to school at all; less than a half of the sample read newspapers, and about a third received 'printed extension' material directed specifically at farmers. The most effective influences involved personal contact and the spoken word; the peer group of neighbours, kinsmen, and friends was the most important influence, followed by 'oral extension', that is word of mouth of an extension officer. However, this test of effectiveness is not really decisive. 'Learning of a practice from relatives and other farmers is somewhat analogous to lifting oneself by one's own boot-straps, for ego's peers are not likely to be much better informed than ego. The farmer who learns from his peers is learning second- or third-hand information which may have lost its accuracy.' Ogionwo summarized his findings thus:

Personal media tended to be more important than *formal* mass media both in terms of 'total exposure' and 'effective exposure'. But this tendency was not evident when we examined type of information source and the degree of effectiveness. In view of the limited coverage of the printed media, 'unprinted mass media' emerged as the main source of influence apart from 'oral extension'. And it was radio that accounted for the importance of 'unprinted mass media'. It can thus be suggested that the best medium of spreading agricultural information is the radio, provided there is a close personal follow-up by extension officers to assure farmers that 'yes, it is right for you'. The printed word reaches only the literate minority, who are not notably more innovative than the non-literate majority, though hard technical information in print is important for the extension officers.

It was, however, a mistake to think only in terms of the flow of information to an individual who then decided whether or not to act on it. Group interaction was of great importance:

We started with the traditional assumption that individuals have to make up their minds about whether or not to adopt a recommended farm practice, and that once their minds are made up they would go ahead and use it...But the experience of our investigation suggests that in certain societies (and certainly in the society concerned) the individual is not a free agent...He is very often subject to all sorts of pressure to adopt or not to adopt; family, friends, community norms, may all bombard him. It is of interest, therefore, to discover whether the adoption of farm practices in Nigeria requires individual or collective decision.

Ogionwo concluded with a plea for a recognition of the importance of a two-way flow of information. Not only is there a question of the effectiveness or otherwise with which the government's recommendations are communicated 'down' to farmers; there is also the question of the flow of information 'upwards' from the farmers to the government:

In order that this dialogue may take place, there must be an effective and continuous means of taking government information down to the villages and bringing the 'feed-back' of rural opinion up to the government. And to the extent that good communication presupposes both the machinery of communication and the desire to communicate, a degree of mutual confidence between the two sectors is an essential third estate of the communication process.

David C. McClelland on achievement motivation[4]

In his studies of human motivation, McClelland's first concern was to establish that a need for achievement or *n* Ach exists, that it is distinguishable from other needs and drives, and that it occurs to a different extent in individuals and also in cultures. His colleague Winterbottom was then able to show that the development of *n* Ach takes place fairly early in childhood, and depends on parents' expecting of their children a 'self-reliant mastery' at an appropriate age, namely about eight years. 'Self-reliant mastery' includes such things as knowing their way about the neighbourhood, being active and energetic, trying hard to do things for themselves, and doing well in competition with other children. If all this is called for too soon, then children react with discouragement and a reduced self-confidence; if too late, then their *n* Ach remains low. Among contemporary nations, Japanese parents on the average 'hit it right on the nose' by expecting these qualities of their children at the right age, while Brazilians demanded them too young and Germans left it too late.

McClelland pointed out that these findings are consistent with, and give a further depth of understanding to, the classic theory of Max Weber linking the Protestant ethic and the spirit of capitalism, since a 'self-reliant mastery' is what we may confidently suppose Puritan parents expected of their children.

A number of historical studies demonstrated that an upsurge of achievement themes in popular literature, children's stories, and other cultural manifestations was associated, after a time-lag, with an upsurge of economic activity. Such a relation was shown, for example, between *n* Ach derived from English popular literature between 1500 and 1800, and coal shipments to London, with a time-lag of thirty to fifty years. Similarly, *n* Ach in medieval Spain was related to the tonnage of shipping cleared for the New World. In both cases 'the initial high level of *n* Achievement is followed some time later by a period of economic growth which subsides fairly abruptly after the level of *n* Achievement has decisively dropped'.

Turning to contemporary societies, McClelland found a close correlation between *n* Ach on the one hand, and GNP, electric power, or both combined

236

on the other. Comparing the 1925 with the 1950 level of this measure for a large number of countries he showed that *n* Ach is 'positively correlated with subsequent economic growth, and very significantly so for the electrical output measure or for both measures combined'.

The implications for development in the poor countries are obvious. Achievement motivation has been shown without exception to be related to economic development both in the contemporary world and historically, though there is usually a time-lag between the period at which children are being brought up in conditions which arouse high *n* Ach and the country's subsequent actual achievements when they are grown up and reach positions in which they influence its development. In the long term the number of people with high *n* Ach and the *n* Ach level of the people generally could presumably be raised by suitable changes in the generally accepted methods of bringing up children. In at least one sphere this is largely under the direct control of governments, namely in the schools, and there seems no reason why a government which takes McClelland's findings seriously should not act directly on, for example, the content of children's first school reading books.

In the immediate future, the economists' 'short term', however, the poor countries will presumably have to make do with whatever resources of achievement motivation their adult populations already possess. McClelland spelled out the immediate recommendations that follow from his findings.

First, 'the leadership of a country should promote an achievement mystique by every means at its disposal'. A leader who in McClelland's view had notably done so is President Nyerere of Tanzania, whose writings contain frequent references to the ideal of self-reliance: 'Between MONEY and PEOPLE it is obvious that the people and their HARD WORK are the foundation, and money is one of the fruits of that hard work. This is the meaning of self-reliance' (The Arusha Declaration). McClelland commented:

In these and other passages President Nyerere clearly shows an understanding of what the psychologist is saying: it hasn't been money as such that has produced development – ever; rather it has been a particular motive – the need to achieve – that has been critical; he calls it *hard work* which has a common sense relationship to the need to achieve – though it is not precisely the same since many peasants all over the world work very hard without producing rapid economic growth.

Secondly, McClelland advocated motivational training for businessmen, and cites the success of ten-day training seminars which were developed in India for this purpose. More than half the business leaders so trained showed marked increases in business activity. In the two years after attending the seminar they invested twice as much and created twice as many jobs as a comparable group who had not undergone the course. The institutions in which achievement motivation is encouraged among businessmen should be able also to offer material aid in the form of loans and credit. Businessmen attending the seminars would then be planning with reality in mind, while at the same time those conducting the seminars are in a good position to study seminar participants and their plans during training and follow up their progress afterwards. And these institutions should be part of the whole structure of economic planning in the country, so that the seminars could be a means of implementing the general development plans.

Thirdly, higher education for women as well as for men should be insisted on.

The recommendation may seem paradoxical since by and large it is the men who will be responsible for development of the economy. Yet...no modern industrialized nation has so far developed which has not stressed getting women into the higher levels of the working force...Achievement cannot be stressed for one-half the population only – namely, the male half. It appears not to be possible to maintain an achievement ideology in a population which is so to speak 'half slave and half free'. Furthermore, women as wives and mothers play enormously important roles in encouraging achievement in the male half of the population.[5]

At the same time it is necessary to make a number of criticisms of McClelland's work. Achievement motivation is not a simple concept but has several aspects, the relations among which are not clear. The disposition to *set oneself tasks* rather than have tasks set from outside is not self-evidently the same as the search for the satisfaction from *performing a task well* whether it is self-imposed or externally induced. Both should be distinguished from *performing a task better than others*, excelling in competition, or 'winning'. Excelling over others is further to be distinguished from *gaining others' recognition* of work well done, and enjoying the approval of significant others – notably, of course, one's mother in early childhood at least. Recognition is again to be distinguished from *symbolic reward*. As for the desire to *assert oneself over others* in such a way that they *accept one's leadership*, and recalling Winterbottom's question, 'At what age would you expect a son of yours to have learned to be able to lead other children and assert himself in children's groups?' it may be that these qualities are more highly valued, encouraged, and rewarded in the United States than in other cultures. A certain ethnocentricity, too, is evident in McClelland's handling of the concept of other-directed behaviour, which is first diluted from altruism to 'paying attention to the opinion of others as a way of guiding one's own behaviour', and hence degraded into mere market morality.

Alex Inkeles and David H. Smith on individual modernization[6]

Alex Inkeles (most of whose previous studies had been of Soviet society) and David H. Smith conducted research in the mid-1960s into individual modernization in six developing countries: Argentina, Chile, India, East Pakistan (now Bangladesh), Nigeria, and Israel, where almost all their sample were 'Oriental Jews' of non-European origins. Each national sample consisted of about a thousand men aged 20–30 and included industrial workers both experienced and inexperienced, urban non-industrial workers, and countrymen. Interviews lasting about four hours were carried out by locally recruited field staff, and followed a schedule which, while broadly standard for the whole inquiry to ensure comparability, was suitably adapted to each country's circumstances and carefully translated into the appropriate languages. It was designed primarily to measure the subject's 'overall modernity' (OM) as indicated by such traits as his aspirations, readiness for change, attitude to women's rights and to family limitation, sense of personal efficacy, active public participation, media exposure and how much he had learned from it, religious attitudes and behaviour, and kinship attitudes and behaviour. The initial hypothesis to be tested was that there is a *syndrome* of modernity, a systematic tendency for these traits to occur together, so that for instance a man with a strong sense of personal efficacy also tends to favour birth control, to join voluntary organizations, and to take an interest in world affairs. Early designs of the questionnaire embodied this initial approach, clearly based as it was on the ideas of the modernization school. On testing them it was found that most of the traits did cohere, and the initial hypothesis was to that extent confirmed; some did not, and were dropped. The questionnaire and measurement scale progressed through a series of validating steps to their final form, code-named OM500, to be used in the full-scale national surveys. In the light of the discussion in chapter 8, and of Ogionwo's findings about familism, it is of interest to note that among the questions dropped were those about family attitudes, since it was found that men of high overall modernity were no less likely than others to accept their kinship obligations. The final schedule OM500 consisted of questions addressed to thirty 'subthemes' that 'had passed a rigorous test proving that they were indeed unmistakably part of the OM syndrome' while also being free of the 'partialling fallacy', that is, they were not the same thing under different names.

A first analysis showed that individual modernity was associated with schooling, and also with father's schooling; factory experience, skill, and income (as evidenced by consumer goods possessed); living in towns; and media exposure. However, some partialling fallacies were suspected at this stage; in particular, working in a factory is almost bound to entail living in town, and the two influences had to be disentangled.

Schooling's pre-eminence was confirmed in a more detailed analysis by means of partial correlation techniques designed to single out each contributory factor in turn. Disregarding all other influences, each year at school put anything from 1.3 to 2.3 on an individual's OM score out of a hundred, so that a full eight years' primary schooling could raise the OM score by 10–18 percentage points. Schooling was therefore a stronger and more consistent influence than any other. Oddly, though, it did not seem to matter whether it was a good or bad school, nor whether it was in town or country.

Exposure to the mass media, measured by a simple index giving equal weights to radio listening and newspaper reading, also proved to be a strong and consistent modernizing influence.

Factory experience too was closely correlated with modernity, especially for men born in the country. For such men, each year in a factory added 0.5 to 0.9 points to the OM score, while for men born in town it added about 0.4. As a modernizing influence it was second only to schooling, and Inkeles and Smith pointed out that the gain (if it be so regarded) is achieved at no cost in organizations primarily engaged in producing goods or providing services, whereas schooling entails public and private costs; factory experience thus emerges as the most cost-effective. Furthermore, it affords as it were a second chance for those who missed schooling to be exposed to modernizing influences. As with schooling, it did not seem to matter much whether the factory was modern or traditional, large or small, competently managed or not. And the term 'factory' needed to be widely understood in this context. To have a modernizing effect, work experience did not have to be in industry narrowly defined; it could equally well or even better be in a reorganized agriculture. Thus in Israel farmers in the co-operative settlements known as moshavim were about equal to industrial workers in their OM scores; while in the rural development scheme at Comilla set up under government auspices in what was then East Pakistan, the OM scores of members of the village co-operative society actually exceeded those for factory workers, and those of non-member villagers were not much lower. The important thing, it seemed, was to work in a modern organization, whether agricultural or in the narrow sense industrial.

Disentangling work experience from that of town life was the particular reason for including in each national sample some urban non-industrial workers in what later became known as the informal sector (see chapter 7). They included self-employed artisans, taxi drivers and rickshaw pullers, street vendors, and casual labourers, and the findings about their modernity were somewhat equivocal. Their OM scores consistently exceeded those of rural cultivators, but despite their longer experience of town life they mostly scored lower than even new, inexperienced factory workers. It seemed clear that factory work's modernizing effect was direct and independent of the factory's urban setting. When other socializing influences were partialled out, especially schooling, factory experience, and media exposure, the modernizing influence of urban residence alone proved to be little or none in five of the six countries (the exception was Nigeria); and the authors concluded that 'It is not urban experience *per se* which makes men more modern but rather the differential contact with the schools, mass media, and factories which the town contains.'

Comparing early with late socializing experiences in the life of an individual, Inkeles and Smith found that men born in town started with higher OM scores than their country cousins, but once in a factory the latter learned faster. An educated home was an advantage, and father's education was significantly correlated with modernity, but boys from less advantaged homes could and did catch up at school, and boys lacking both an educated home and schooling could and did catch up at work in a modern organization; the latter, indeed, could well be regarded as a second chance for remedial education.

Inkeles and Smith acknowledged that their study was confined to men; that was for practical reasons, since in developing countries at that time there were very few women in the industrial jobs in which they were especially interested. They saw no reason, however, why their findings should not prove equally true of women, since presumably the same forces that had made men modern – schooling, work in modern organizations, and mass-media exposure – would also make women more modern. Rebutting in advance any criticisms of ethnocentricity or a capitalist bias, they cited the 25 years Inkeles had spent studying Soviet society, and pointed to the similarity between most, though not all, of the themes included in the OM scale and the personal qualities officially extolled in the Soviet Union. They concluded that individual modernity could be summed up under four major headings. People who could be characterized as modern were informed participant citizens; they had a marked sense of personal efficacy; they were highly independent and autonomous in their relations to traditional sources of influence, especially when making basic decisions about how to conduct their personal affairs; and they were ready for new experiences and ideas, that is, they were relatively open-minded and cognitively flexible.

Some psychological aspects of change

SUGGESTIONS FOR FURTHER READING

Alex Inkeles and David H. Smith, *Becoming Modern*, London: Heinemann, 1974
John H. Kunkel, *Society and Economic Growth: A Behavioural Perspective on Social Change*, Oxford: Oxford University Press, 1970

12 The political characteristics of new states in poor countries

Political life in Third World countries is shaped by influences to some of which attention has been paid in earlier chapters: low levels of income and of industrial development, the colonial heritage, tribalism or communalism and the plural society, language, schooling, the educated elite, and the mass media of communication. Political life as here understood is concerned with making the major decisions about the life of a country, or other group. Politics is not the implementation of the rules that regulate group life: that is administration. Politics is concerned rather with making and changing the rules, including changing the rules for changing the rules. It involves competition, rivalry, and manoeuvre among individuals and groups for the control of resources; above all, power. In most societies the most important power resource is the state, that unique institution which according to Weber's classic definition successfully asserts a monopoly of legitimate force over a defined geographical area. Politics in the narrow sense is generally thought of as being 'about' who controls the state and for what purposes it is used. It is of great importance, however, to consider politics in a wider perspective. In most poor countries the state is unequivocally an institution – indeed the most important and powerful institution – of the modern sector. In other sectors, however, unofficial ways of exercising power and making decisions operate to a large extent, often in direct continuity with pre-existing traditional political systems; and these articulate only to a limited extent and at particular points with the politics of the state. The study of that very process of articulation between the two systems is an important and fruitful field for social science research. In studying the politics of Third World countries it is therefore specially necessary to keep in mind the politics of local communities such as the village, province, or tribal area, even though – or rather, precisely because – such communities are explicitly deprived of, and often at odds with, the formal central power of the state.

Politics, development, and modernization

In all societies somebody makes the large, final decisions. They may be wise or foolish decisions, well- or ill-informed, well- or ill-considered. The

243

discussion that precedes them may be carried on in public or in private, at a high or low intellectual level. As it is hard to discern any clearly marked evolutionary trend in these matters, it may be suspected that phrases such as 'political development' and 'political modernization' have little meaning.

Modernizing the forms of government is not the point. Public accounts are no longer kept by tying knots in pieces of cord, as in ancient Peru, or cutting notches in pieces of wood, as in medieval England, while messages are no longer sent by the hand of a man on a horse. Typewriters, filing cabinets, telephones, and the new technology for storing and processing information are everywhere in use. But that does not make the political decisions any wiser. And if administrative modernization, though genuine, may be a comparatively trivial aspect of the matter, the same can be said of the outward forms of political institutions. A new state may have a National Assembly, meeting in an imposing building, giving an impression of modernity belied by the actual content of the business transacted there, the low level of debate, its ineffectiveness, its liability to be influenced by corruption, and the widespread belief that it is a mere sham, a 'gas chamber', while the big decisions are made elsewhere by people not accountable to it. On the other hand, some states, such as those 'crowned republics', the monarchies of western Europe, have adapted rather than discarded their antique traditional institutions in response to modern needs. As Dodd remarked, many people find a modernized house more comfortable to live in than a modern one.[1] Accordingly, to quote Apter, 'it is no good evaluating governments on the basis of their organization. A single-party state, for example, may be meaningfully democratic. A supreme court may not be decisive in developing the rule of law.' Clearly what matters is the substance, not the form.[2]

The widely different meanings given to 'political modernization' and 'political development' have been summarized by Dodd. Some have seen political development as a movement towards an end-state regarded as desirable and probably inevitable, be it a communist society, multi-party electoral democracy, or an Islamic state. Others have written in such terms as 'the expansion and centralization of government power, and the differentiation and specialization (and subsequent integration) of political functions and structures'. The slightly different phrase 'the politics of development' can be usefully applied to policies conducive to economic development such as land reform. 'The politics of modernization' comes near to the heart of the matter. If to be modern means to be willing and able to choose, clearly governments differ widely in the extent to which they enable their citizens to exercise choice, especially in the political arena itself.

For the modernization school, as noted in chapter 6, participation is all-important, including the spread of the franchise and equality of opportunity to participate in politics and compete for office. However, experience of 'departicipation' in countries such as Uganda (as detailed below) has led to a reassessment of the concept, notably by Huntington and Nelson. They considered that in the long run modernization did indeed entail broadened participation, but the relations between them were complex and involved other factors, and the processes were neither steady, uniform, nor irreversible. The prevailing view in the United States in the 1950s and 1960s had been that socio-economic development would lead to greater equality, political stability, and democratic political participation. That 'benign line' of the liberal model of development, however, had been shown to be 'methodologically weak, empirically questionable, and historically irrelevant except under specialized circumstances'; and there were other possibilities. For example, in a 'bourgeois model' political participation might be extended to the urban middle class, the leaders of rapid economic development, resulting in increased inequality and demands for participation from the unenfranchised poor, and political instability. Or a modernizing autocrat might deny political participation to the rising middle class while promoting equality in order to mobilize political support from the masses. Land reform would be a key issue in such a case; could the government muster enough support to overcome opposition from the landed aristocracy despite middle-class indifference and an as yet not very participant peasantry? A 'technocratic model' might achieve faster development with greater inequality, less stability, and less participation, unless there were a 'participation explosion' or revolt and an abrupt switch to another path of development. Or a 'populist model' might result in greater equality and more participation, at the cost of slower economic growth and less stability, unless there were a 'participation implosion' with power taken out of the people's hands and politics superseded by central administration. So Huntington and Nelson concluded that 'At least in the short run, the values of the political elite and the policies of government are more decisive than anything else in shaping the participation patterns of a society.'[3]

The colonial heritage

As pointed out in chapter 3, in most Third World countries by far the biggest single legacy of colonial rule was the organized power of the state; and it was for control of that unique resource that the most acute struggle was waged at the time of independence. Moreover, as other sources of wealth and prestige such as large business corporations tend to be either under foreign control or overshadowed by the state, there are few other ways for an ambitious individual to attain control of large resources, so that the pre-eminence of the state and the sharpness of the struggle to control it have continued.

Sometimes the forms of government adopted, initially at least, were closely modelled on those of the former colonial power. One example was the 'Westminster model' adopted by many former British colonies, and sometimes ridiculed for slavish adherence to small details like the design of the mace or the wigs of the clerks at the table. One important reason for this was that, though its insistence did not extend to inessential detail, it was a general condition for the grant of self-government by Britain that parliamentary democracy should be a working reality. In part, however, the adoption of this model reflected an admiration for parliamentary democracy on the part of some members of the political elite of those countries; and indeed, the anti-colonial ideology might in some cases take the form of a simple demand that the political rights and freedoms enjoyed by the British people should be shared by those of their colonies. For example, the Nigerian leader Dr Nnamdi Azikiwe quoted from Locke and Burke in declarations in favour of parliamentary democracy for his country.[4]

In some other cases, however, the experience of colonial rule led to the rejection rather than the acceptance of the practices of the colonial power. In particular, the precedents of Spain and Portugal had little appeal for the successor states of South and Central America. The practices of the United States had some prestige there, as they have in other parts of the world, but there has always been a good deal of ambivalence in Latin American attitudes towards 'the colossus of the north', and a disposition to reject 'Yanqui' models accordingly. ('Poor Mexico!' as General Diaz is reported to have exclaimed, 'so far from God, so near to the United States!') A tendency to look instead for distinctively Latin models led many of these states to adopt features of the French constitution, out of a regard for France as the cultural centre of the Latin world and 'the notion that civilization radiates from Paris'.[5]

A particular legacy of colonial rule in Latin America has been the position of the Roman Catholic church. As successors to the crowns of Spain and Portugal, many of these republics (Mexico being an exception) asserted a state patronage of the church despite the Vatican's objections. It is clear from Willems' account, however, that the formal establishment of the church in these officially Catholic countries is belied by its actual weakness. The clergy are few in number, many rural parishes being without incumbents, while at the same time priests are employed by wealthy families as tutors for their children. Rural life is little touched by clergy who pay hasty and occasional visits, and superstitions flourish. Anti-clerical sentiments are widespread, and there is a common view that 'the Church is something for the rich and women'.[6] Such a discrepancy between formal authority on the one hand and actual power, influence, or control on the other is a common characteristic of poor countries, and constitutes a theme to which I return below.

In more general ways, the style and content of politics after independence as well as its formal institutions have been shaped by the particular experiences of colonial rule. Thus Pye has drawn out the contrasts in south-east Asia, where the British in Burma bequeathed an image of authority committed to the 'proper way of doing things' which was closer to administrative rule than that of popular politicians. The Dutch in Indonesia pursued a policy of cultural relativism, much admired in its time, but one in which the acceptance that there were two essentially respectable worlds left no room for those who sought to become westernized without severing their roots. The result has been 'a highly ambiguous image of the desirable qualities of political authority'. In French Indo-China a different ambiguity prevailed between association and assimilation. French policy permitted the emergence of a remarkably westernized elite, but it was an elite 'who had lost their claim to leadership of the traditional elements of their society [and] could only re-establish such a claim by conspicuously rejecting their affiliations with the French'. Finally, American rule in the Philippines left two distinctive legacies – a highly developed system of public education, and a tradition of rule by elected politicians looking after their supporters' particular interests rather than by competent, impartial administrators.[7] In the same way, Rustow has pointed out the effects of the short and unhappy episode of French and British colonial rule in Arab countries between the two world wars.[8] At the very time when the principle of the self-determination of peoples was being put into practice in Europe with the creation of new states like Czechoslovakia, Poland, and the Baltic republics, it was being denied to the Arabs, giving rise to intense and lasting bitterness.

In many African and Asian countries (the Philippines, as noted, being an exception) an important part of the colonial legacy has been an administration accustomed to think of itself as independent of and superior to the wiles and intrigues of politics. This has led since independence to what Riggs calls the 'interference complex' – mutual accusations of interference by politicians and bureaucrats. The natural claims of the new political leaders to make the important decisions involve the former power-holding elite, the administration, in stepping down gracefully in favour of men whom they may despise and fear. Small wonder, says Riggs, that they protest that such matters as the making of appointments, contracts, and allocations fall within the administrative sphere and ought not to be subject to political interference.[9] The conflict may be particularly acute over military matters, and army officers may be particularly jealous of political interference in matters which affect the national security and prestige; I return to this point below.

Three kinds of nationalism

To pick up another theme from chapter 3, a further effect of colonial rule in many of the new states has been in the nature of the ideology of the groups, individuals, and 'parties' which took over the government.

It is usual to class these ideologies as nationalist, but the term is more often than not misleading. As Worsley has pointed out, the word nationalism has at least three different meanings. In the classical sense in which it was used in nineteenth-century Europe, a movement like that of Polish nationalism was based on a common language, Polish; on a distinctive religious affiliation, Roman Catholic as against Russian Orthodoxy to the east and German Protestantism to the west; and on distinctive historical traditions, including the memories of a period when Poland had been an independent kingdom; and its aim was the establishment of an independent Polish state and the ending of the partition of the country among the empires of Germany, Austria, and Russia. Similarly, nationalist movements in Italy and Germany were aimed at the unification of fragmented small states in an area with a common language and historical traditions; while movements like Czech, Greek, and Irish nationalism aimed at the liberation of those peoples from the foreign rule of the Austrian, Ottoman, and British empires respectively. In the latter cases religion as well as language and a cultural heritage played a part in delineating the community which felt itself to be different, oppressed, and under rule that could be thought of as foreign.

While nationalism in the new states of Africa and Asia originated in the desire to end foreign rule, and has that much in common with many of the nineteenth-century European nationalisms, it differs in other respects. Their nation-building consists essentially of an effort to create sentiments of loyalty to the successor state of a colonial administration. As has been emphasized in chapter 9, most of these are highly arbitrary and in a sense artificial creations, whose borders part like from like as often as they embrace unlike peoples under a single state system. There is not a single symbol capable of being attached to 'Uganda', for instance, which can compare with those that could be attached to 'Poland' – no equivalents for the Polish language, for the common attachment to the Roman Catholic church, for the traditions of the court of King Wladislaw. If there is loyalty and attachment to 'Uganda' it must be of the head and not of the heart.

248

Indeed, it has been convincingly argued that the true twentieth-century counterpart of the nineteenth-century European nationalism is African tribalism.[10] The groups with a common language, a common culture, and a sense of common identity are tribes, not the new states. The emotional sentiments involved in attachments to the new states are shallow indeed compared with the depth and vitality of those toward fellow-tribesmen, traditional forms of social and political organization, and (where applicable) traditional rulers like the Kabaka of Buganda. Yet tribalism is rightly regarded as dangerously destructive of 'national' unity in the new states of modern Africa. As Nyerere said:

There are obvious weaknesses on the African continent. We have artificial 'nations' carved out at the Berlin Conference: we are struggling to build these nations into stable units of human society...Whenever we try to talk in terms of larger units on the African continent, we are told that it can't be done; we are told that the units we would so create would be 'artificial'. As if they could be any more artificial than the 'national' units on which we are now building...

African nationalism is meaningless, is dangerous, is anachronistic, if it is not at the same time Pan-Africanism.[11]

The difficulties inherent in the first two kinds of nationalism in the twentieth century may thus be resolved by an appeal to a third type of attachment, a 'Pan-' movement. As Worsley has succinctly put it, such movements transcend state boundaries and are built on much wider affiliations. These may be religious, as in the case of Pan-Islamism; linguistic and cultural, as with Slavophilism and Pan-Arabism; those of physical appearance, as *négritude* and Garveyism; or geographical, as Pan-Africanism.[12]

Inheritance elites and 'parties' in the successor states

The overriding aim of the political 'parties' which were the immediate successors of the colonial regimes was self-government, or the end of colonial rule by white foreigners. Slogans rather than detailed policies – Free-Dom! Uhuru! – sufficed to embody the universal aim of ending foreign rule. Tiresome questions like 'Who is the self who is to govern?' were brushed aside, in the same spirit as Fanon brushed aside the inquiries of intellectuals and democrats about the objectives of the Algerian resistance to French rule. Vagueness about what was to happen after independence could be countered by attachment to a charismatic leader as a symbol of the popular aspirations. For example, Apter related how the 'more delicate nationalism' of the elite who founded the United Gold Coast Convention in 1946 and called for self-government 'in the shortest possible time' gave way to the more robust slogan of the Convention People's Party, 'self-government now', while Kwame Nkrumah became an almost mythical figure shepherding his faithful flock into the paths of nationalism and independence.[13]

A second major theme in the ideologies of many of the successor states linked imperialism with capitalism. If one was condemned, the other was at least suspect, and there was a preference for economic policies that could in the widest sense be called socialist. Much-needed economic development was to be furthered by central planning and organized by public corporations rather than by private enterprise, and even the small-scale indigenous private enterprise of the informal sector was not always favoured. Thus several of the new states of Africa professed attachment to 'African socialism', though they interpreted the term in their own ways. The materialist premises of the Marxist-Leninist tradition were widely rejected; Senghor wrote eloquently of the spiritual values he thought were lost to Soviet communism under Stalin, Nkrumah found no contradiction between socialism and Christianity, and Nyerere linked African socialism with an image of traditional kinship solidarity in the evocative word *ujamaa*. And when it came to actual policies when in power, there were wide divergences; for example, the government of Tanzania nationalized large private businesses while that of Kenya refused to do so. In Kenya, indeed, Africanization rather than nationalization soon became the aim; foreign firms were pressed to train and employ Africans at managerial levels, and Africans were encouraged to develop commercial banks, even though such policies could hardly fail to result in the rise of an indigenous business class committed to private enterprise.[14]

Yet while ideologies such as African socialism clearly include the aspiration that the emergence of antagonistic classes, like those of nineteenth-century Europe, can be avoided in the newly developing countries, there is nevertheless a clear strand of elitism in them. If there is socialism, it is socialism planned by an elite. As Sigmund pointed out, many nationalist leaders have seen strong government as the only way to achieve development, and coined phrases like Sukarno's 'guided democracy', Ayub Khan's 'basic democracy', and Sékou Touré's 'democratic dictatorship' to express and legitimate the leadership which the modernizing elite must give the people through the government and the ruling party.[15]

Similarly in Ghana, Apter wrote of a tendency to assert that 'the CPP formed the nucleus of a new society. This required the party to "generalise" itself into society'. Thus Nkrumah declared in a speech about academic freedom versus ideological education that:

The Convention People's Party is a powerful force, more powerful indeed than anything that has yet appeared in the history of Ghana. It is a uniting force that guides and pilots the nation, and is the nerve centre of the positive operations in the struggle for African irridentism. Its supremacy cannot be challenged. The Convention People's Party is Ghana, and Ghana is the Convention People's Party.[16]

Such a tendency to declare that the 'party' that had led the country into independence represented in some almost mythical way the 'true will of the people' was a deeply underlying factor in the adoption of one-party systems in many new states. Other groups had to throw in their lot wholly with the 'party' and divest themselves of other links. In Ghana again, for example, first the TUC had to break its links with the International Confederation of Free Trade Unions, then the independent farmer's co-operative movement was eliminated in favour of a new movement, and thirdly the Scout movement was eclipsed by the Young Pioneers; and when the Anglican bishop of Accra objected to the kind of indoctrination carried on in the latter, he was forced to leave the country.[17] Another aspect of the same syndrome has been the nervous suspicion shown in many new states towards the national university. That intelligent and unprejudiced scepticism that has been called the hallmark of a university-trained mind finds little favour from regimes for whom the independent assessment of policies seems indistinguishable from hostility to the party and disloyalty to the government.

Despite their pretensions to be the authentic national movements, however, it is clear from a number of accounts that many of the 'parties' that came to power in new states were in fact weak. For example, the Senegalese national 'party' drew in a wide variety of special interest groups, some picturesquely named, like the Union pour la Défense des Intérêts du Quartier de Guet-n-Dar et des Pêcheurs, founded because 'they had no market for their salted fish, no stable prices; because they felt forgotten, their streets were ugly and unlit, their water supply was short'.[18] Similarly, the Parti Démocratique de Côte d'Ivoire according to Staniland began as an alliance of voluntary associations – a planters' co-operative in which Houphouet himself became prominent, ethnic associations, the teachers' union, and intellectuals' societies. Clearly neither organizational coherence nor ideological precision could be expected of such diverse groups. Further, the actual working of the party diverged substantially from its official structure, with committees at the district level as often nominated as elected; and only four annual congresses were held in 20 years, giving little opportunity to unseat party officials. Staniland concluded that 'However much P.D.C.I. leaders emphasise the grass-roots context of the militant period, historically the evidence would support an opposed hypothesis, one of deliberate involvement of people at the district level by leaders of a party at the territorial level in a conflict which originated at a still higher level.'[19]

Another instance of the weakness of the national 'party' is afforded by

Gertzel's account of the Kenya African National Union. During the last few years of colonial rule, rival leaders whose power was based on strong local support at the district level preferred not to have a strong national party organization which might enable one leader to gain control. This remained the position for some years after independence in 1963, when it is clear that KANU existed in little more than name:

No meeting of the National Executive or the Governing Council was called between 1963 and 1966…KANU headquarters in Nairobi remained empty except for the occasional minor official. The telephone was disconnected because the account was not paid. Party finances were said to be in disarray. At district level branches were equally lacking in formal organization, and membership dues were not collected.[20]

As Staniland pointed out in relation to Africa, politics in the late colonial and immediately post-colonial period could be interpreted in two ways. One was that independence was granted reluctantly as a result of the pressure of mass movements, whose leaders were concerned with integrating sectional interests into 'the nation', and after independence with raising everybody's living standards. Those leaders were democratic and egalitarian, and they stood for modernization (represented by the national movement, and associated with young people and town life) against an opposed traditionalism (associated with the countryside and represented by the chiefs). The second and perhaps truer interpretation was that colonial development created an indigenous elite who had to some extent assimilated the values of the colonial power. After the second world war some of them were admitted, or co-opted, into political participation at the level of the colony or *territoire*. In attempting to enlarge that participation, they resorted to a 'tactical politicization' at local and sectional levels, in which 'only the vaguest formulation of general goals was possible or desirable (rigid definition would have made it harder to get so much support)'. Decolonization then consisted of a bargain between the retiring colonial power and the indigenous 'inheritance elite', whose version of events constituted the first interpretation.[21]

The national 'parties' which represented, in Staniland's terms, the tactical politicization of petty interest groups by the inheritance elite were quite different from the more substantial organizations we know as parties in industrial countries. As with 'church' and 'sect', we should not be misled by the name 'party' in their official titles into thinking of them in the same terms. Further, the discrepancy between proclaimed authority and actual power is here seen in an extreme form. Sweeping assertions of the power of the 'party' and its identity with the 'nation' well illustrate a tendency to state as if it were fact what is no more than a hope, an aspiration, or even a desperate wish – a tendency Riggs has well called 'double-talk'.[22]

Communal breakaway movements

Strong and persistent threats to the integrity of many new states in Asia and Africa have come from separatist movements among tribes, regions, or communities otherwise delineated, sometimes resulting in major conflicts and bloody wars.

Economic and ethnic factors have combined in many such cases to engender a sense that some region or people was not getting a fair share of resources. It was pointed out in chapter 4 that economic development tends to be uneven, and some regions go ahead faster than others. In some cases it has been the leading region that has become impatient with a situation in which it has been contributing to the central revenues of a larger state from which other and more backward regions have been getting most of the benefit, and has come to feel that it would be better off going it alone (e.g. Buganda, Katanga). In other cases it has been the poorer regions that have experienced 'backwash' and attributed it to exploitation by the leading region (e.g. Bangladesh), or have resisted the secession of that region when it appeared to be trying to make off with the loot (as the Nigerian federation resisted the secession of 'Biafra').

Such instances serve to highlight a general tendency in poor countries to what is described, somewhat temperately and formally, as the weakness of local government. Fears that local, regional or tribal patriotisms are liable to result in the break-up of the state altogether are often well-grounded. The governments of new states are inclined to maintain as much central control as they possibly can, and leave as little initiative as possible to local bodies, precisely because they know they cannot trust the latter to act as loyal representatives in the exercise of devolved powers. As Riggs pointed out, this is one of the reasons for the many criticisms from World Bank missions and similar bodies of what they see as overcentralization. The trouble, however, lay deeper:

From this perspective, extreme centralization of authority can be seen as a desperate attempt to bring the bureaucracy and society under control. Indeed, when effective control weapons are so notably lacking, the cheapest and most obvious remaining weapon is the power of formal authority. Unfortunately, this nominal power turns out to be without potency, resulting, often enough, in a final resort to violence and coercion. Thus 'overcentralization' is a vain hope, a groundless aspiration and pretence, masking the actual dispersion and localization of control which is the hidden reality. The mark of prismatic power distribution is 'equivocality', not 'centralization'.[23]

Accordingly, what in formal terms is called 'overcentralization' and 'the weakness of local government' in new states can be regarded from another point of view as just the opposite – the *strength* of local political processes, beyond the power of the centre to control, and the corresponding *weakness*

253

of the centre. Once more we find a discrepancy between formal authority and actual power or control.

Getting people out of politics, particularly in Uganda

Tribalism, or ethnicity, has been seen by Kasfir as one of the principal reasons why political participation in many African countries reached its peak at the time of independence, only to decline thereafter. The advent of independence led the colonial powers, particularly Britain and France, to make hasty efforts to implant the institutions of representative government – national assemblies, political parties, government and opposition, local councils, trade unions, and elections – as preconditions for handing over power. As Staniland too noted, their efforts were reinforced by the demands of nationalist leaders. In Kasfir's words, 'Decolonization meant national control, which in turn meant widespread popular participation.' Thus, 'all over tropical Africa political structures which markedly increased participation were hastily installed in the last hectic years of colonial rule. Since independence they have been unceremoniously dismantled with the same alacrity', as 'departicipation, the elimination of people from political life, has become increasingly common in independent African countries'.[24]

No doubt there are other reasons for it besides tribalism. Politicians generally cling to office, and in many countries are glad enough of excuses to avoid submitting themselves for re-election. A determination to stay in power may arise not only from a desire to hold on to the prestige and material rewards of office, but also from fear of the consequences of relinquishing it. Everyone who exercises power makes enemies, and it is in only a few countries of great political maturity that political leaders can count on magnanimous treatment and an honourable retirement if they step down. More commonly those in power have reason to fear humiliation and indignities, show trials, the confiscation of their possessions, imprisonment, physical maltreatment, and even death at the hands of those who would supplant them. The more strongly they hold on to power, the harder it is to bring about a change of government without force. Thus Hoogvelt has pointed out that not instability, as often alleged, but rather a suspect stability characterizes many Third World regimes.[25] The point has a clear bearing on military *coups*, to which I turn below.

Another reason has been the dedication to economic planning noted above, and the elitism that entails. By its very nature planning tends to be 'from the top down'. Even where, as in Tanzania, there was a sincerely meant gesture in the direction of planning 'from the bottom up', it is clear from Leys' account that the government's main aim in setting up local planning committees was to secure local commitment to the plan and co-operation in its implementation. The initiative still came from the centre; and when the local committees' contributions were adjudged to be of little value, they were dropped.[26] In Uganda, when in 1964 the minister of planning and community development encouraged district councils to prepare three-year plans, what he received were long lists of projects for extending social services with scant regard to costs, revenue, or general economic development. One district's 'plan' would have cost over one and a half times its annual revenue without making any provision for consequential recurrent costs.[27] On the basis of such experiences, central planning ministries came to view local interests as at best ill-informed and parochial, at worst irresponsibly obstructive.

Many local authorities used deficit budgeting as a weapon in their political struggles with the central government, placing upon the latter the political onus of curtailing their proposed extensions of popular social services. Central governments responded by reducing the councils' financial powers. Thus in Kenya in 1969 responsibility for primary schooling, health, secondary road maintenance, and collecting the personal or 'poll' tax was removed from local authorities. As they had no powers over these matters, they could no longer debate them, nor voice complaints and make representations about central government's policies for these services. In Uganda, too, finding local authorities prone to 'financial irresponsibility, factional disputes, administrative inefficiency, and tribal self-interest', the central government took powers to dissolve them and appoint councillors, and even decided what they could discuss, while the very term 'local government' was replaced by 'local administration'. Faced with a challenge to their authority, in Kasfir's words, 'it is little wonder that national leaders moved quickly to dismantle the participatory aspects of local government'.[28]

At the heart of the matter, of course, was tribalism. In a country such as Uganda, elected local authorities were the natural embodiments of tribal loyalties and interests. Under colonial rule administrative districts had corresponded as closely as possible to tribal areas, and a district administration's use of the tribal language for the conduct of official business was not only a matter of practical convenience but also a symbol of tribal identity. However, local government and its friction with the centre were not the only expressions of tribalism. Central government ministers and senior civil servants too were widely regarded, in Milton Obote's words, 'as representatives of their respective tribes, whose function in government was to safeguard and plead tribal interests in matters of appointments, distribution of development projects, and social services'. It was often over issues of centrally planned economic development, such as the siting of large new public enterprises, that rivalry became acute. To quote Obote again, 'A leader who is a fanatic of tribal hegemony will see any project outside his tribal area as having been sited purely on tribal grounds'. Under the influence of 'the pull of tribalism', the institutions of central government were seen as mere arbiters of tribal rivalries; the National Assembly not 'as a national institution but as an assembly of peace conference delegates', and 'the Government of Uganda as a body of umpires or referees in some curious game of "Tribal Development Monopoly"'.[29]

But policies intended to diminish tribalism entailed intractable paradoxes and inconsistencies. The central government appeared to preach against tribalism while actually practising it; Obote's cabinet appointments carefully maintained a tribal balance, and there were proposals to site important projects in his home district of Lango. Dropping a question on tribe from the 1969 census, as in Tanzania, presented no problem. However, a typical paradox arose over the choice of languages for radio broadcasting. Emphasizing the country's central institutions and weakening those at the local tribal level necessitated effective communication from the centre to the people as a whole. But that in turn meant increasing the number of languages used over the state radio, which rose from five at the time of independence in 1962 to fourteen in 1967, eighteen in 1969, and twenty-one in 1972 – so emphasizing cultural diversity and recognizing the existence of tribes.[30]

Even more difficult dilemmas arose over employment. To quote Kasfir again,

To take the best-qualified individual for a job aroused resentment from those denied opportunities for preparation. But to push ahead those from relatively underprivileged areas further embittered those who had acquired higher levels of skill...Whichever decision was made, distrust would be fuelled by increased ethnic suspicion and rivalry.[31]

In Uganda the tribe particularly affected was the Ganda, to whose privileged position I have referred in chapter 9. Equalizing opportunities for the people of Uganda as a whole necessitated some measure of positive discrimination in favour of other tribes; but that could itself with some justification be represented as tribalism. It was certainly resented by the Ganda, and contributed to Obote's unpopularity among them.

Conflict between the central government and the kingdom of Buganda came to a head in 1966 over another tribal issue, that of the 'lost counties'. They were an area inhabited mainly by Nyoro-speaking people seized by Buganda and incorporated within its boundaries by the 1900 agreement with Britain. The kingdom of Bunyoro had never ceased to claim their restoration, but the issue was unresolved at the time of independence. Immediately before that, tactical alliance had been struck between Obote's Uganda People's Congress on the one hand, and on the other the kingdom of Buganda, organized for this purpose under the name – more a slogan than a party – of Kabaka Yekka, literally 'the king alone!' According to that agreement, and following the alliance's victory over the Democratic

Party in the pre-independence election in 1962, Obote became prime minister while Kabaka Mutesa II assumed office as titular head of state of Uganda as a whole. The uneasy alliance broke down when the Kabaka refused to give his formal presidential assent to legislation, implementing a referendum in 1964, that would have diminished his kingdom by transferring the lost counties to Bunyoro. In the ensuing crisis Buganda threatened to secede, as they had before under British rule, and Obote authorized the army under Idi Amin to sack the palace. The Kabaka escaped, was smuggled out of the country by his loyal subjects,[32] and died in England three years later.

But though the central government was now supreme, and able to dismantle tribal institutions such as the traditional kingdoms, it had in the process alienated the most numerous, prosperous, and educated people in the country, while demonstrating that its rule was based on coercion not consent and that it depended on the army for support. That left it wide open to a military *coup*; and when in January 1971 Amin seized power while Obote was in Singapore at a Commonwealth conference, the news was greeted with extraordinary enthusiasm in Buganda, far greater than elsewhere.

Ganda support for Amin continued for a time as he allowed the Kabaka's remains to be brought home for a state burial and his son to return as a private citizen and landowner. He also immediately released from detention a number of Obote's opponents, many of them Ganda; and later, in a move initially popular throughout the country, he expelled Asians. But rejoicing at Obote's downfall soon turned to dismay as the Amin regime degenerated into a reign of terror. Indiscriminate as it later became, there was a tribal element about even that at first, for it began with massacres of Acholi and Langi soldiers at a number of barracks in different parts of the country. Langi were automatically suspect as fellow-tribesmen of Obote; why Acholi were picked on is less clear. Though news of the army massacres appeared abroad, little was heard about them in Uganda itself. Soon, however, there were other victims. They included Benedicto Kiwanuka, prime minister of the pre-independence Democratic Party government of 1961–62, and chief justice at the time of his abduction and disappearance; Frank Kalimuzo, vice chancellor of Makerere University; the Anglican archbishop Janan Luwuum; hundreds of other people prominent in the professions, business, and public life; and many thousands of ordinary people.[33]

And even the victory of the Tanzanian army and the fall of Amin in April 1979 was not quickly followed by the rehabilitation of the country. Irregular forces recruited during the war of liberation soon disintegrated into armed bandits along with remnants of Amin's army, and life continued to be dominated by men carrying arms and wearing some kind of uniform, though whether one should call them soldiers is not clear. The killing became less systematic but the fear was still ever-present, while the armed bands' depredations wrought havoc with economic life and seriously impeded international famine relief efforts in 1980.

In retrospect, Uganda's post-independence history was marked by a severe reduction in political participation at both local and national levels. Military rule of course represents departicipation at its most drastic; but even before Amin's *coup* any national elections would undoubtedly have been contested more on the basis of tribal allegiances than of debate about policy issues. As Kasfir put it, 'Elections mean participation, and participation is likely to lead to ethnic mobilization.' So none were held. The general election due in 1967 was not held precisely because of the Buganda crisis. Serious preparations were made for one to be held in 1971, for which an ingenious electoral system was devised to neutralize tribalism by making each candidate approved by the ruling UPC stand simultaneously in four constituencies, each in a different region; but it was forestalled by Amin's seizure of power in January.[34] Although general elections were held under British rule during the run-up to independence in 1961 and 1962, there was none in independent Uganda until the one in December 1980 that was intended to legitimate Obote's return to power with Tanzanian support.

And though Uganda is an extreme case in that few parallels could be found for the Amin regime, it is not untypical of many African countries in the decline or breakdown of representative government and the strengthening of central administration in the face of tribalism. Kasfir traces similar trends in Kenya (where Gertzel too chronicled the brief heyday of parliamentary rule), in Ghana, and in Zaire, while even in Tanzania socialist measures have been introduced from the top on the initiative of a central government that has grown stronger since independence.

Coercion

Riggs' 'final resort to violence and coercion' is often exemplified in the ferocious brutality with which the army and police of a poor state behave when they go into action against a communal breakaway movement. The actions of such states often display in a dramatic form this aspect of 'equivocality' in the sharp contrast between the laxity with which the law is normally enforced and the bloody ferocity which the agencies of the state are capable of showing on some particular occasions. Besides the suppression of breakaway movements, those occasions include urban riots, strikes, student protests, and peasants' revolts. At the level of violence to individuals, too, it is consistent with this general analysis that many of the new states have retained or revived the death penalty and the use of judicial corporal punishment. Thus Milner and his co-authors showed that in many African countries the treatment of offenders by these methods was falling into disuse in the late colonial period, in line with the movements of penal reform that were taking place in the metropolitan countries of Europe. Since 1960, however, while a country like Britain has abolished both the death penalty and judicial corporal punishment altogether, a country like Tanzania has moved in quite the opposite direction, introducing mandatory corporal punishment for certain offences despite the publicly expressed misgivings of the Commissioner of Prisons. In the same way many of the new states of black Africa have resorted to public executions. Such developments appear to be motivated at least in part by a desire to do something drastic in a situation that is felt to be getting out of hand and to respond to popular clamour for such action to show that the state's authority cannot be lightly flouted. In the case of the state which makes the greatest use of the death penalty, South Africa, there is a further factor; the generally authoritarian cast of mind which is associated with beliefs in racial supremacy also tends to favour the drastically punitive treatment of offenders.[35]

Political middlemen and the articulation between local and national politics

One consequence of the uncertain control of the state over local political processes is the importance of 'middlemen', to whom some social anthropologists have given attention in the societies they have studied. A pioneer in this field was Max Gluckman, who in his studies of Zulu society in the 1930s gave prominence to the occupants of what he called 'inter-hierarchical positions or roles' of this kind, the hierarchies in question being respectively those of Zulu society and those of the white South African government. One class of such roles was that of the government-recognized chiefs and village head-men, and Gluckman quotes the saying that the chief was the only member of the administration who never went to Britain on leave. Another class of inter-hierarchical roles were those occupied by white men like the District Officer, the Native Commissioner, and the agricultural and other technical officers. Just as the black chiefs became to some extent imbued with the ideas of the administration, so the white administrative officers in many cases came to have much sympathy with those of the Zulu, and Gluckman hinted at a tendency for the official policies of Pretoria to be somewhat modified when it came to their actual execution in Zululand.[36]

Summing up a number of such studies (including F. G. Bailey's of 'para-political systems' in an Orissa village, and Friedrich's unforgettable portrait of a *cacique* or local boss in a Mexican rural community), Swartz pointed out that the middleman's authority or influence is exerted in a situation in which there is a gap or incongruity between political cultures. Political middlemen themselves may not fully understand the situations in which they act, but they manage somehow to be sensitive to the cues afforded by other people's actions in the different systems, and to work out *ad hoc* practical techniques for resolving conflicts and getting what they want.[37] More research is needed in this important area, calling for a combination of the approaches of social anthropology and political science.

Corruption

After the scandals associated with such names as Watergate in the United States and Operation Countryman in Britain it ill befits a citizen of a western industrial country to adopt a high moral tone about corruption in the Third World. Nevertheless there may well be a difference of degree; and it is hard to resist the impression that corruption is far more widespread and pervasive in many Third World countries than it is in industrial states, whether western or communist. I have touched on its economic consequences in chapter 4, while as noted in chapter 6 Myrdal linked it with 'the soft state' and the elitist conspiracy.

It is also related to equivocality, 'double talk', and the discrepancy between formal authority and actual power or control. Laws may be put on the statute book because they will look well there, possibly from the point of view of world opinion, rather than with a serious intention to implement them; Myrdal cites the proscription of caste in the constitution of India. The same may apply to tax laws, whose impact on the rich may be much reduced if they bribe the inspectors to accept a low return of income or assets, paying of course less than the tax saved. Besides money, another inducement is kinship sentiment and family influence; a third is the favour of superiors. Thus a superior may ask a subordinate to do something illegal. To refuse is to forfeit the superior's favour; to comply is to be for ever afterwards under the threat of blackmail. It is in these ways, too, that allegiances are formed which enable leaders to mobilize support for their factions in the political arena.

Both Riggs and Scott have noted the ways in which corruption affects minority groups of the kind whom Riggs calls 'pariah entrepreneurs'. Like private capitalists in a developed industrial society, pariah entrepreneurs have to consider the ordinary economic costs and risks; unlike the former, they incur costs and risks for security and access. Even the capital they nominally own cannot effectively be used without the consent of the elite, for which they have to pay a tribute 'defined as shameful, involving resort to "corrupt" practices as a requisite to survival'.[38] Such minorities seldom act openly as lobbies or interest groups when measures affecting them are being mooted. When business people, for example, know perfectly well that the tax they will actually have to pay will bear little or no relation to their liability under the tax law, it makes more sense for each firm quietly to 'buy' what it needs in the way of enforcement or non-enforcement than to campaign for a different law that would be just as formalistic – and risk attracting unfavourable attention to boot.

Equivocality and corruption are linked, too, when politicians pass laws restricting the private sector 'so as to maintain the proper ideological stance' (as Scott put it), while at the same time conniving, for a consideration, at the evasion of the law by private firms.[39]

Not that corruption affects only the rich and the pariah entrepreneurs. On the contrary, peasants and the urban poor are its victims as they pay for services that should be free, and find it easier and cheaper to bribe the government inspector than to comply with the law's formal demands, often expressed in intricate regulations which many of them cannot read, and which may even be written in a foreign language. However, they possess in their sheer numbers a power which the others lack to overawe government inspectors and even sometimes the police, and when really roused to assert themselves through urban riots and peasant revolts. And then, as stated above, the police and army generally retaliate with extreme brutality. Coercion and corruption can be seen as complementary alternatives in a 'soft state' in which the administration of the law lacks predictability and impartiality.

Where law and order are administered in a lax and capricious manner, the patronage of a powerful person becomes all important. Where such protection is the formal, explicit basis of social and political relations, as in medieval Europe, we have a feudal system.[40] At the other extreme, illegal protection rackets constitute a sort of clandestine feudalism in which rival gangs, like feudal lords, have an interest in protecting their client-victims against the competitive extortions of other gangs. In between, relations of a quasi-feudal kind may prevail, tacitly accepted though not formally legitimated. Thus in disordered Uganda after 1979, some armed bands hired themselves out as guards to such institutions as Roman Catholic missions; once on the payroll, they had an interest in repelling other intruding gangs. In such circumstances, prominent people find it imperative to retain personal bodyguards. These can grow into private armies, with obviously important political implications including the possibility of praetorianism, to which I turn below.

Liability to military rule

Third World countries have proved to be particularly vulnerable to the take-over of state power by the armed forces. Hardly a week goes by without our hearing of yet another *coup* in some state of Asia, Africa, or Latin America. The movement of army vehicles into the capital or its outskirts; the seizure of the radio station; the arrest, flight, or murder of the former prime minister, president or other leading politicians; the dawn broadcast commanding the populace to remain calm – all this has become a matter of dreary routine. Then the amplified statement of the reasons for the *coup*. The selfish intrigues of small-minded politicians, intolerable against the background of the country's needs, its economic crisis, its humiliation in the eyes of the world. Political interference in the administration of the country and particularly of the armed forces. Corruption (always corruption). The appointment of a military cabinet together with a few civilian leaders worthy of the public's trust. The announcement of a regime of sensible administration at the hands of experienced administrators capable of putting country before party and before self. The pledge to restore normal democratic political processes as soon as conditions allow – a constituent assembly dangled as a future possibility – but meanwhile the disbandment of the now totally discredited former ruling party, control of the press, control of political meetings, a curfew, the temporary suspension of the legislature. We have heard it many times.[41]

Military intervention in politics is a matter of degree. It is rare indeed for a government to be wholly military, with every ministerial post held by a long-serving regular officer. Almost always some civilians are included for their expertise in fields such as health and foreign relations. As the original *coup* recedes into the past, they may come to be in a majority, and the cabinet may end up almost wholly civilian, yet still owe their tenure of office to their willingness to carry out policies acceptable to the armed forces. Such a government may then seek to legitimate its position by holding elections, usually carefully arranged to secure the desired result; important opposition parties may be suppressed, their leaders jailed or exiled. And there are other possibilities. Military leaders may gain popularity and even become national heroes, like Nasser in Egypt and de Gaulle in France, capable of winning genuinely contested elections. The line between civilians and soldiers may be blurred when civilians appointed to a military government are commissioned as officers and so find themselves under military discipline, including ferocious penalties for disobeying the order of a superior officer, especially the commander-in-chief. And in almost all countries the military have some political influence, if only from making representations about the needs of national defence and the allocation of resources for that purpose.

With all allowance for difficulties of definition, however, it is almost exclusively low- and middle-income countries that are liable to military rule. Since the second world war, multi-party electoral systems have prevailed in all nineteen of the industrial market economies (see chapter

4); there have been attempted *coups* only in France in 1958 and Spain in 1981, both unsuccessful. Among communist regimes, most have come into being through revolution, civil war, or a war of liberation, and been initially sustained by armed force. However, the party has generally maintained its ascendancy over the army even when the two have merged as partisan forces in an armed struggle, and that ascendancy has been consolidated afterwards. It is rare indeed for the army to displace the party as the ruling organization in an established communist state, and to date there is only one instance of that, namely Poland in 1981. By contrast, many Third World countries have experienced some form of military rule. The two great exceptions are India and China. Those apart, in 1980 some 52 per cent of the combined population of other low-income countries lived under military rule, including Pakistan since 1958, Bangladesh since 1977, and Ethiopia since 1974; and 42 per cent of the population of middle-income countries, including Brazil since 1964, Indonesia since 1966, Chile since 1973, and Argentina since 1974. If we add countries where military regimes had only very recently come to an end, including Uganda 1971–79, Ghana and Nigeria 1966–79, and Peru 1968–80, a clear majority of the people of the Third World outside China and India had recent experience of living under military rule.[42] (See table 12.1.)

Praetorianism in the strict sense refers to a state of affairs like that in ancient Rome, where the imperial guard were detached from the main body of the army and loyal to, and paid by, the emperor personally rather than the senate representing the public.[43] In such circumstances, the guards soon recognize that the converse is also true: the ruler is the one to whom they choose to give their allegiance. A need then arises for an inner and even more personal guard to protect the ruler against a change of allegiance by the Praetorians. Foreign mercenaries are often preferred for this purpose, lacking as they do local affections and loyalties. And as an alternative or supplement to paying them in money, a ruler may reward the trusted troops with licence to plunder the civilian populace. There are examples of some or all of these tendencies in recent African history. In Ghana, according to Gutteridge, after an attempt on his life in 1962 Nkrumah turned increasingly to non-Africans for protection. With help from communist countries he formed a President's Own Guard Regiment independently of the regular army at a time when the latter's equipment was becoming run down and its interests neglected. Resentment at this deterioration of the army's national position, and apprehension that before long the only institution capable of resisting Nkrumah would lose its effectiveness, contributed to a 'now or never' feeling that precipitated the *coup* of 1966.[44] In Ethiopia, according to Levine, the imperial bodyguard established as an elite force separately from the army 'specifically to protect the Emperor against *coup* attempts' themselves attempted to overthrow him

263

Table 12.1   *Political regimes, 1980*

Type of economy	Type of political regime						
	Multi-party elect-oral	Comm-unist	Other one-party	Military	Monarchy	Other	Total
(a) numbers of countries							
Industrial market economies	19	—	—	—	—	—	19
Non-market industrial economies	—	6	—	—	—	—	6
High-income oil exporters	—	—	1	—	3	—	4
Middle-income economies	24	8	11	16	2	2	63
Low-income economies:							
China	—	1	—	—	—	—	1
India	1	—	—	—	—	—	1
Others	1	5	8	11	2	4	31
(b) population in millions							
Industrial market economies	714	—	—	—	—	—	714
Non-market industrial economies	—	353	—	—	—	—	353
High-income oil exporters	—	—	3	—	11		14
Middle-income economies	294	86	228	473	23	34	1,139
Low-income economies:							
China	—	977	—	—	—	—	977
India	673	—	—	—	—	—	673
Others	15	80	99	263	16	38	511

Sources: Political data from *Political Handbook of the World 1979* (New York, 1979), updated where possible to 1980 from *Statesman's Yearbook 1981–82* (London, 1981), press reports, etc., for countries listed in World Bank, *World Development Report 1982*. Slight discrepancies in totals arise from rounding.

in December 1960. Antagonism between the two forces contributed to the promptitude with which the army deployed their greatly superior numbers and weapons to thwart the attempted *coup*.[45] But the defeat of the bodyguard left the army in a commanding position in Ethiopian politics, of which they took advantage in their turn in 1974. And, as indicated above, there were many praetorian features about the Amin regime in Uganda.

However, the term praetorianism is also used in a wider sense to mean military intervention in politics generally, including cases where an apparently civilian government hold office at the will of armed forces who can oust them at any time.

Much has been written about this important subject. A pioneer study was that of S. E. Finer, who pointed out in 1962 that armed forces generally have three great advantages over civilian institutions: superior organization, a highly emotionalized symbolic status, and a monopoly of arms. Forming as they do so powerful and prestigious an order, 'the wonder, therefore, is not why this rebels against its civilian masters, but why it ever obeys them'. Finer's explanation was in terms of what he called 'levels of political culture'. The difficulty of establishing army rule over a complex modern society and economy was well illustrated by the experiences of Allied military government in Italy and Germany after 1945, where the occupying forces were able to carry out their task only by heavily reinforcing their military personnel with civilian administrators, and had to relinquish it altogether when policy decisions had to be made. Even more important, though, was the question of legitimacy. 'Where public attachment to civilian institutions is strong, military intervention in politics will be weak.' In societies at a lower level of political culture, however, the society and economy were not so complex as to be beyond the capacity of the army to administer effectively, while at the same time people's loyalties were not strongly attached to civilian institutions at the level of the national state. Where associations such as industrial enterprises, trade unions, churches, the press, and political parties were weak, the procedure for the transfer of power irregular or non-existent, and the location of supreme authority a matter of acute disagreement or else of unconcern and indifference, there the scope for military intervention would be very wide.[46] The army might not have much of a claim to legitimacy, but if the legitimacy of civilian political institutions were at an even lower ebb then there might be little or no popular resistance. Indeed, an army take-over might be welcomed by many as a liberation from the corrupt rule of crooked politicians.

Finer's analysis in terms of levels of political culture, however, has not found general acceptance; as van Doorn has put it, 'It is not a low political culture as such that permits military intervention, but the impotence of the regime to safeguard the political order.'[47]

Janowitz pointed out that in many new nations the armed forces consist mainly of infantry battalions, with little or no artillery, armour, or logistical support, navy or air force. Such forces have 'the maximum potential for involvement in domestic politics. They are in essence a form of super-police.' Even more striking was the rise in the 1960s and 1970s of paramilitary forces, including national police living in barracks and armed with light military weapons and vehicles, and local defence forces or workers' militia supervised by the army living at home and armed against internal insurrection. While such units might have other duties, for instance as frontier guards, their main purpose clearly was internal repression.[48] As Luckham put it, 'Because of their client status in the international system, there are relatively few nations where the military has a particularly important role to play in relation to external security; whereas in most of them, the army cannot avoid being drafted into performing internal security duties.'[49] For example, as Andreski has pointed out, 'The armies of Latin America cannot fight each other, because in virtue of a multilateral treaty the USA would come to the defence of the invaded country,' while the security of the western hemisphere as a whole is also guaranteed by the United States.[50] Accordingly, military officers' self-image as defenders of the nation against external attack is unrealistic in many Third World countries, and in some their actual role in internal politics has been rationalized in doctrines such as that of 'the enemy within'. Thus according to Drury the Escuola Superior de Guerra in Brazil imbued its students with the necessity for the moral and economic redemption of their country to enable it to take its rightful role in the struggle of the Christian West against the communist East, a struggle in which indirect communist aggression was said to capitalize on misery, hunger, and just nationalist anxieties.[51] Such considerations no doubt render more explicable the bold decision of the liberal centrist government of Costa Rica to disband its armed forces entirely in 1948.[52] To adapt a remark of McKown, among the best advice that one could offer to Third World politicians who would like to serve out their allotted term of office peacefully is: do not have an army.[53]

Janowitz and other writers have put forward analyses of military attitudes that have a bearing on their political role in Third World countries. These include a puritanism, based on the ideals of service before self and country before all, that condemns corruption with especial vehemence and extends also to intolerance of such things as homosexuality and drug abuse. Secondly, politics is anathema. On the battlefield as in a ship at sea or an aircraft in flight, he who hesitates is lost, delay is fatal, and what is needed is clear orders promptly obeyed. Politics entails discussion, debate, negotiation, and bargaining, involving delay in which issues are blurred and ambiguities deliberately left unresolved. Politics and corruption are often associated, and the military's task is seen as that of cleansing the nation of both alike. 'After all we have now got experts to do the job rather than profiteers', as the Nigerian Major Nzeogwu said after the *coup* of January 1966. According to Luckham, 'the military view of the proper conduct of government can be summarised in the form of five antinomies: discipline versus disorder; honour versus decadence and corruption; achievement versus ascription; administered consensus versus politics; and the nation versus regionalism and tribalism'.[54] But the pursuit of these aims encounters intractable difficulties. Despite the personal incorruptibility of many military rulers, corruption at lower levels often becomes as rife as under civilian government.[55] As for national unity, in Nigeria the army that prided itself on being the uniquely national institution in a country riven by tribal strife ended up itself tribally divided in an appalling civil war. And the armed forces' impartial public image is shattered as soon as they intervene in internal affairs, so that administered consensus rather than politics may well be unattainable. The dilemma was perfectly expressed in a press interview with the same Major Nzeogwu in Nigeria:

Maj. N. Neither myself nor any of the other lads was in the least interested in governing the country. We were soldiers and not politicians...We were going to make civilians of proven honesty and efficiency who would be thoroughly handpicked do all the governing.
Q. What would you be doing?
Maj. N. We would stand behind them with our fingers on the trigger.[56]

Outside influences

It remains briefly to make the obvious point that the government a country gets is not always wholly decided within its borders. Not that all *coups* have been engineered from outside; for example, even so radical a writer as First searched in vain for reliable evidence of foreign involvement in the *coups* in Nigeria and Ghana in 1966.[57] Some Third World states have intervened in others, as Tanzania did in Uganda. But there have been many interventions by the major powers, and most of all by the United States and the Soviet Union, concerned as each has been not to allow its position to be weakened by a hostile regime anywhere in the world that might threaten its vital interests and serve as a strategic base for the other's forces. Thus although United States policy-makers no doubt favour elected civilian governments in principle, they have judged it even more important in practice to prevent the rise to power of left-wing movements, and above all not to permit another Cuba in the western hemisphere. Thus according to Nordlinger they took economic measures to weaken the Goulart government of Brazil as it became more radical; it is now known that the Central Intelligence Agency gave encouragement and material support to the *coup* that overthrew the elected socialist government of Chile in 1973;[58] and in the early 1980s the US were visibly intervening in Nicaragua and El Salvador. For their part, the Soviet Union supported communist regimes in Vietnam and Cuba; in Africa they intervened, directly in Ethiopia, indirectly with Cuba as proxy in Angola; and, perhaps mistakenly anticipating a US move into Iran, they invaded Afghanistan in December 1979.

SUGGESTIONS FOR FURTHER READING

C. H. Dodd, *Political Development*, London: Macmillan, 1972

Fred W. Riggs, *Administration in Developing Countries: the Theory of Prismatic Society*, Boston, Mass.: Houghton Mifflin, 1964

Samuel P. Huntington and Joan M. Nelson, *No Easy Choice: Political Participation in Developing Countries*, Cambridge, Mass.: Harvard University Press, 1976

Colin Leys (ed.), *Politics and Change in Developing Countries*, Cambridge: Cambridge University Press, 1969

Marc J. Swartz (ed.), *Local-Level Politics*, London: University of London Press, 1969

Nelson Kasfir, *The Shrinking Political Arena*, Berkeley, Calif.: University of California Press, 1976

James C. Scott, *Comparative Political Corruption*, Englewood Cliffs, N.J.: Prentice-Hall, 1972

Eric A. Nordlinger, *Soldiers in Politics*, Englewood Cliffs, N.J.: Prentice-Hall, 1977

13   The world of aid

International economic organizations and the idea of aid

The international institutions of the post-war world took shape in 1944 when, with victory assured, representatives of the allied nations 'determined to save succeeding generations from the scourge of war' held two important conferences at small places in the United States.

At Dumbarton Oaks they agreed to set up the political and diplomatic organizations of the United Nations, its general assembly and security council, which were formally constituted in 1945 and to which were added specialist organizations, some new like the Food and Agriculture Organization (FAO), World Health Organization (WHO), and Educational Scientific and Cultural Organization (UNESCO), others carried over from the old League of Nations particularly the International Labour Office (ILO).

At Bretton Woods the prime aim was to stabilize the world economy and remedy the economic causes of war, which were widely associated with currency crises, slumps, and unemployment, leading to mass unrest and extremist political movements especially the rise of the fascist dictators in Europe in the 1930s. With that aim it was decided to set up an International Monetary Fund (IMF) to which each member state made an agreed contribution, nine-tenths in its national currency, one-tenth in gold, and from which each could borrow in case of need. Each member government declared the value of its currency in US dollars, which were pegged to gold by means of a fixed price. With the Fund's agreement, member states could adjust the value of their currency up or down in an orderly manner, quite unlike the hectic speculative trading of the pre-war world; while to help countries stabilize their currencies the Fund could issue loans to member states to tide them over balance-of-payments difficulties, subject to the appropriate adjustment of their financial policies as agreed with the Fund's officials and set out in a letter of intent when applying for the loan. Also at Bretton Woods it was agreed to set up an International Bank for Reconstruction and Development (IBRD, later more generally known as the World Bank), whose first task was to be to finance the rebuilding of Europe's war-shattered economies.

In all these organizations of the United Nations family, member states' contributions were proportionate to their resources (as agreed after appropriate consultations). But voting rights differed. In the Dumbarton Oaks organizations, subject to a great powers' veto in the Security Council, the general rule was and is one member state one vote. In the Bretton Woods organizations, however, voting rights were proportionate to contributions, so that initially the United States and Britain together had half the total votes.

The Soviet Union was represented at both conferences. They decided not to join the Bretton Woods organizations; they objected to the weighting of votes according to contributions, they were not willing to report their gold and foreign currency reserves, still less transfer any of them, to an international organization located in the United States, and they could not accept some of the IMF's rules. They joined the Dumbarton Oaks organizations, but it often seemed to the West that they did so only to prevent them working as intended by the frequent use of the veto.

In 1947 the United States took a fresh initiative when their Secretary of State, General George C. Marshall, held out the prospect of aid for post-war reconstruction if there were 'some agreement among the countries of Europe as to the requirements of the situation', and substantial funds were in fact forthcoming for the US's own European Recovery Program, rather than through the IBRD, when Congress passed the Economic Co-Operation Act in 1948.[1] If this was another attempt to draw the Soviet Union into peaceful constructive co-operation, this time in a European setting, then it too failed as the USSR rejected Marshall's plan and would not let Poland and Czechoslovakia accept US aid either.[2] However, it succeeded in promoting the remarkably rapid recovery of western Europe; and it gave a strong impetus to the movement towards co-operation there that led eventually to the Treaty of Rome and the formation of the European Economic Community (EEC), above all ending the deadly quarrels between France and Germany that had caused three wars in 70 years and twice engulfed the world in conflict. So while the recipients of Marshall aid set up the Organization for European Economic Co-Operation (OEEC), the Soviet Union and eastern European states formed their counterpart, the Council for Mutual Economic Assistance (officially CMEA in English, also popularly known as Comecon), and only Yugoslavia with its limited participation in both later formed a slender bridge between them.

Encouraged by the success of Marshall aid, and in the face of relations with the Soviet Union that deteriorated into a 'cold war', in the early 1950s the United States sought to extend the idea of aid beyond Europe and make use of their ample resources to build bulwarks against communism in Asia and the Far East. Here, though, their activities were seen by their critics as propping up corrupt and repressive regimes for no other reason than that they were anti-communist – a recurrent dilemma for United States

270

foreign policy, as has been seen. After 1956, the Soviet Union began to enter the field of foreign aid, and though they never committed anything like the same resources to it as those of the West they did so in the form of large spectacular projects such as, notably, the Aswan high dam in Egypt, and a steel mill at Bhilai in India. The United States' response was to link aid more closely to economic development. In John White's words:

The reason why the initial response of the United States to the Soviet challenge had taken the form of a greater emphasis on development uses of aid was that in a competitive situation the attachment of explicit political conditions exposed the US aid programme to contumely, and was as likely to drive the recipients into the arms of the Russians as to win new allies for the United States.

So 'the rhetoric of aid [became] the rhetoric of development'.[3]

In the 1950s, too, there was a great increase in aid from other sources. As Britain and France recovered from the war they extended aid on an unprecedented scale to their colonies and former colonies. For Britain the 1950s were the heyday of the Colonial Development and Welfare scheme which, as noted in chapter 3, was initiated in 1929 and extended in remarkable acts of faith in 1940 and 1945; while France too made much aid available to French African countries, especially for the reconstruction of Algeria after the disastrous civil war there.

In December 1960 the UN General Assembly in Resolution no. 1522 designated the 1960s as a Development Decade, and called upon industrialized countries to contribute 1 per cent of their national incomes as aid for the development of underdeveloped countries. An expert committee subsequently ruled that the term 'national income' should not be interpreted in its strict technical economists' sense, but should be taken to mean Gross National Product – the interpretation more favourable to the developing countries.[4]

In 1961, when the accession of Canada and the United States made it no longer a purely European organization, the OEEC was reconstituted as the Organization for Economic Co-Operation and Development (OECD), and it was in keeping with the spirit of the times that it added development aid to its other aims and set up a Development Assistance Committee (DAC) for that purpose. At that time, too, the United States persuaded West Germany and Japan, former enemy countries now prospering (largely as a result of having been defeated, disarmed, and so relieved of military expenditure), to join the OECD and DAC and take part in development aid. Other countries, including the neutral Switzerland and Sweden, also entered the field of aid. After 1960, countries such as Britain, France, Holland, and Belgium began to run out of colonies. In particular, the British Colonial Development and Welfare Acts made funds available only for dependencies, yet the needs for development assistance certainly did not lessen as former colonies became independent. Accordingly, as CD & W was

271

wound down, more aid was made available under the Overseas Aid Act of 1966. In Britain as in other donor countries, new government departments were set up for this purpose, adding yet more organizations with their initials and acronyms: the British Department of Technical Co-Operation, later re-named the Overseas Development Minitry (ODM); in the United States the Agency for International Development (AID); in West Germany the Bundesministerium für Wirtschaftliche Zusammenarbeit (BMZ).

Meanwhile, among UN organizations, the IMF and World Bank were established in adjacent buildings in Washington, though with separate staffs and different objectives. The IMF continued to operate the Bretton Woods system for stabilizing currencies; while the World Bank, its prime task of reconstructing Europe taken over by US Marshall aid, became the leading organization for multilateral aid to developing countries.

The Bretton Woods system worked as intended for some 25 years, mainly because the United States' balance-of-payments deficit made ample dollars available as a world currency. It broke down in the early 1970s when, among other reasons, the rest of the world began to lose confidence in the United States' ability to maintain the dollar's value. The dollar was in fact devalued (that is, the price of gold was raised) in December 1971; in partial replacement, the IMF responded by creating and issuing Special Drawing Rights (SDRs) as a kind of international fiduciary currency.

The World Bank has operated in many ways like a bank, borrowing money on the open market in industrial countries to augment its fund of member states' subscriptions, on which it pays no interest, and which ultimately secure its credit. It lends to both governments and the private sector, and according to its charter must lend only for productive purposes to stimulate economic growth in developing countries. It must pay due regard to the prospects of repayment, its decisions to lend must be based on economic considerations, and its loans must be guaranteed by the government concerned. In 1956 the International Finance Corporation (IFC) was set up to handle loans to the private sector in developing countries. In 1960 a second affiliate, the International Development Association (IDA), was established to extend credits, derived from surpluses from the Bank's other operations, on the 'softest' or most concessional of terms to the poorest countries. IDA credits are made to governments only; they are interest-free, apart from a small service charge, there is a ten-year grace period, and 50 years are allowed for repayment. Notable among the Bank's activities is that of research and the collection of data about the world economy and that of individual countries. Besides being of the utmost value to social science (as these pages bear ample witness), its fund of information and informed analysis has done much to maintain the Bank as the leading international organization in the world of aid.

The Soviet Union never joined, so that although Yugoslavia has always been a member, and Poland and Czechoslovakia joined for short periods, until China's accession in 1980 there was little participation by communist states. The United States and Britain lost their initially commanding position over the Bank's policies, but in 1980–81 the United States held over 20 per cent of the voting rights, and with Japan (8 per cent), Britain (6 per cent), West Germany and France (just over 4 per cent each), the 'big five' held just short of 43 per cent of the votes and appointed five of the twenty executive directors. The other fifteen were elected to represent groups of countries, though the system of election virtually guaranteed seats to India and China.[5]

Neither the IMF nor the World Bank entirely endeared themselves to all sections of world opinion. It was not only that, for the reasons just indicated, radical critics could readily stigmatize them as 'capitalist'. Political leaders and senior civil servants in member countries, even such a major contributory country as Britain, found it ignominious if not humiliating to have to submit their whole economic policy to criticism by the IMF's officials when applying for a loan. Their location in Washington, their use of English as their sole working language, the extent to which their officials were imbued with the principles of orthodox liberal economic analysis, and above all their voting system, contributed to a widespread belief that their policies represented mainly the views of the western industrial nations and, in matters of aid, those of the donor rather than the recipient countries. Strong criticisms of the IMF in particular were made by the Brandt commission. It had used its unique position in a paternalist way, tending 'to assume that any country needing to borrow conditional liquidity must have been incompetent or careless at running its affairs', formulating policies on the basis of a monetary approach to balance-of-payments problems, and presuming the latter to be due to too much domestic demand. Its insistence on corrective measures – 'balancing the budget, curbing the money supply, cutting subsidies and setting a realistic exchange rate' – in unrealistically short periods had 'tended to impose unnecessary and unacceptable political burdens on the poorest [countries], on occasion leading to "IMF riots" and even the downfall of governments'.[6]

As Third World countries emerged from colonial rule and joined the UN in growing numbers, they tended to make their presence felt in the Dumbarton Oaks institutions of the General Assembly and the specialized agencies rather than the Bretton Woods organizations. In no field was this more important than that of world trade. At Bretton Woods, a proposed International Trade Organization was discussed whose aims were to have been the stabilization of world commodity trade and prices. Following further talks a charter was drawn up at Havana in 1948; but the US Senate refused to ratify it, and without US participation it was clearly pointless. Some of its provisions were incorporated in the 1948 General Agreement on Tariffs and Trade (GATT), under which developing countries have taken an increasing part in successive 'rounds' of conferences and consultations to negotiate mutual reductions of import duties; but the organization of world commodity markets by the proposed ITO did not occur. Following the 'development decade' resolution, the United Nations took to organizing Conferences on Trade and Development (UNCTAD). Since the first at Geneva in 1964 these have been held at roughly three- to four-year intervals, and with a continuing secretariat and board have assumed the character of an organization rather than a succession of *ad hoc* meetings. Like the General Assembly, UNCTAD's membership was 'universal', including the Soviet bloc, and the principle of one member state, one vote was weighted against the western industrial nations in favour of the many small states of the Third World. They found it a congenial forum accordingly; however, as the Brandt report put it, 'The South had majority votes in the General Assembly which gave assurance of passing resolutions; but the North's position in the World Bank and IMF gave it control over key areas of money and finance.'[7]

The Pearson commission, 1968–69

When in 1968 Robert McNamara became President of the World Bank, he at once appointed a commission under the veteran Canadian statesman Lester B. Pearson to 'study the consequences of twenty years of development assistance, assess the results, clarify the errors and propose the policies which will work better in the future'. The commission's report, presented in 1969, set out the case for aid as it was understood at the time with arguments directed at that archetypal donor the United States senator.

That case at its simplest rested on a moral imperative: it was only right that those who have should share with those who have not. There was also the appeal of enlightened self-interest:

Who can now ask where his country will be in a few decades without asking where the world will be? If we wish that world to be secure and prosperous, we must show a common concern for the common problems of all peoples...This means a refusal to tolerate the extreme and shameful disparity in standards of life that now exists within and between nations.

The commission linked aid to development by adopting the DAC definition: 'funds made available by governments on concessional terms primarily to promote economic development and the welfare of developing countries'. Aid so defined excluded official funds made available for purposes other than development, for example military assistance; and it also excluded private investment. Not that they saw anything wrong with the latter; on the contrary, they emphasized its positive contribution to economic development. But aid worthy of the name was something that was given, not a transaction that profited both parties. There were needs for which private capital flows were inappropriate and inadequate, such as schools, roads, hospitals, and irrigation. Private capital flows were 'concentrated in countries with rich mineral resources and fairly high incomes'. Echoing Rostow they added that it was 'fundamental to our strategy that the need for aid should eventually subside. Direct investment and access to capital markets would then increasingly meet the need for development finance... A keynote of aid policy should be the achievement of long-term and self-sustaining development...In most instances...we believe that developing countries can achieve self-sustaining growth at reasonable levels by the end of the century.'

The Pearson commissioners were at pains to dispel any suggestion that poor countries were not doing enough to help themselves. Perhaps their most important single finding was that 'Despite a common impression that poor countries are too poor to save anything, they have in fact mobilized the bulk of their investment capital. In the 1960s, domestic savings financed 85 per cent of total investment.' They were similarly concerned to defend previous aid programmes against allegations of waste, mis-management, and corruption, which they said were no greater than in other public programmes. More effective use of aid resources, however, could be attained if donor governments would give up 'tying' their aid to their own products and allow recipient countries to shop around for the best bargains.

Tying was a persistent feature of bilateral aid, that is aid from one donor to one recipient country. Most aid was of this kind, and the commission recognized why, for example, Britain had primarily assisted newly in-dependent Commonwealth countries, France had concentrated on French-speaking African countries, Japan had concentrated its aid activities in Asia, and the larger part of the United States' assistance had been to Latin America and countries on the periphery of the communist world. Multi-lateral aid channelled through international agencies represented little more than one-tenth of all aid in 1967, but it filled the gaps in countries such as Ethiopia with no obvious bilateral links, and it was free from tying; for these reasons the commission recommended that there should be more of it, particularly through the IDA. Endorsing the General Assembly's 1 per cent target, they further recommended that 0.7 of that 1 per cent should be official development assistance (ODA) according to the DAC definition cited above.[8]

Aid performance[9]

As Pearson pointed out, it was ironic that total resource flows did actually exceed 1 per cent of combined national income in the five years before the DAC adopted that target in 1964, but not after. Likewise, the industrial countries of the OECD were nearer to devoting Pearson's 0.7 per cent of their combined GNP to official development assistance in 1960 than they were at any time during the two succeeding 'development decades'. According to the World Bank's estimates, in 1960 the proportion was 0.51 per cent; it fell steadily until 1977, when it was 0.33 per cent, less than half of what Pearson had urged; it then rose slightly to 0.38 per cent in 1980. (As seen in table 13.1, the OECD themselves reported a very slightly lower figure.) The United States throughout gave far more aid than any other country, but as a proportion of their GNP it was small, ranging between 0.20 and 0.27 per cent during the 1970s. West Germany and Japan ended the 1970s as major donors, while France's ODA was second only to that of the United States in 1980 and came near the Pearson target at 0.64 per cent of GNP. Britain's contributions were at slightly above the average DAC rate in the 1970s and reached 0.51 per cent in 1979 before dropping to 0.35 per cent in 1980. At that date, the only OECD countries to attain and exceed the Pearson target were Denmark (0.73), Sweden (0.79), Norway (0.85), and the Netherlands (1.03).

Meanwhile, private capital flows from DAC countries to developing countries took place at around 0.66 per cent of their combined GNP in 1975–77, rising to 0.75 per cent in 1978–79, and falling to 0.56 per cent in 1980. Thus although their official development assistance fell far short of the 0.7 per cent target, by the late 1970s the total resource flows from OECD countries were enough to fulfil the UN's original target of 1 per cent of their GNP. Moreover, while their ODA as a proportion of their GNPs was less than recommended, those GNPs were growing; consequently, in real terms their aid increased by 73 per cent between 1960 and 1980 as, valued in 1978 dollars, it rose from 13.1 billions to 22.7 billions. Furthermore, they greatly increased the proportion of their ODA channelled through multilateral agencies. In 1967 that proportion was not much more than a tenth, and Pearson had recommended it should rise to a fifth by 1975. In fact, by 1980 more than a third of all OECD aid was multilateral, and a third of that third (one-ninth of all their aid) was through the World Bank and IDA.

On the other hand, tying continued; in 1979 more than half (55 per cent) of OECD countries' bilateral aid was tied, and some of their multilateral aid too was tied to procurement in the EEC or its associated states, so that nearly half of all their aid was to some extent tied. The share of official development assistance in all capital flows fell from 43 per cent

Table 13.1   *Official Development Assistance, 1980*

Donor groups	Value in billions of current US dollars	Per cent of GNP
DAC	26.8	0.37
OPEC	7.0	1.35
CMEA	1.8	0.12

Source: OECD, *Development Co-Operation, 1981.*

in 1970 to 35 per cent in 1979. With certain exceptions, of which technical assistance was the chief, more and more aid tended to be in the form of loans rather than grants. Thus for example, as already noted, whereas almost all Britain's CD & W assistance took the form of grants, the World Bank's charter and its character as a bank confine its aid to loans. There were arguments for this; loans that had eventually to be repaid, even on 'soft' concessional terms, involved recipients as well as donors in hard-headed calculations of aid schemes' likely benefits; while loan repayments to donor countries offset the foreign exchange costs, and contributed to a rotating fund from which more aid could be made available. As a result of these trends, however, poor countries' debts reached astronomic proportions and constituted a major world problem by the early 1980s.

Furthermore, while private capital flows naturally tended to go to the more rapidly developing countries offering the better prospects, concessional official flows too tended to favour middle-income countries. Thus in 1979, according to the World Bank, of all bilateral aid from DAC countries, Egypt received 12 per cent and Israel 14 per cent, mostly from the United States, while 16 per cent went to France's dependencies, mostly in the form of technical assistance. 'Altogether, out of total bilateral aid of $17 billion in 1979, $11 billion went to middle-income countries. 'Though multilateral aid redressed the balance to some extent, low-income countries (excluding China) received only half as much aid per person as middle-income countries.

Accordingly, the net bilateral flow to low-income countries was meagre indeed; in 1980 it amounted to no more than 0.09 per cent of the combined GNP of OECD countries, just a half of what it had been twenty years before.

Meanwhile, during the 1970s the oil-exporting countries devoted a considerable proportion of their rapidly increasing incomes to aid. In 1975–79, official development assistance from OPEC countries averaged nearly 2 per cent of their combined GNP, while from Arab oil-exporting countries (OAPEC) the average was over 3.5 per cent. In 1980, OPEC aid amounting to nearly seven billion dollars made up one-fifth of all official aid. It was, however, heavily concentrated on two countries; in 1979, Syria received 42 per cent of all OPEC's bilateral aid, and Jordan 29 per cent.

Aid from the Soviet Union and other CMEA countries has been on a very much smaller scale as, in the World Bank's words, 'these countries do not consider that the United Nations 0.70 per cent aid target applies to them'. According to the OECD's estimates, in 1980 the Soviet Union's aid disbursements amounted to 0.14 per cent of their GNP while that of the other CMEA countries was 0.06 per cent of theirs. Soviet aid in recent years has been concentrated very largely on Cuba and Vietnam; according to the World Bank, indeed, those two countries received 96 per cent of all financial assistance from the non-market countries, though the OECD's figures suggested that that might be an over-estimate, and they noted also Soviet project and programme assistance to North Korea, Afghanistan, Kampuchea, and Laos.

It remains to mention, however briefly, the voluntary aid agencies in western countries. Official aid in billions of dollars makes OXFAM's £15.7 millions in 1980–81 look small by comparison; and it was estimated that 'in 1967, for example, the reductions in British aid more than offset all the funds collected by the private organizations in that year at great cost in time and effort'.[10] The voluntary agencies, however, are important in two other ways. Their educational and publicity activities keep the issues of disparity and development continually to the fore; while in the field their representatives, unhampered by official protocol, can take aid straight to where it is most needed.

Criticisms of aid

Pearson epitomized what may without disparagement be called the conventional wisdom: aid, viewed as a transfer of resources, was manifestly right and desirable for the purpose of promoting the economic development and general welfare of the people of poor countries. If it did not always succeed in doing so, any gap between promise and performance was seen as failure or ineffectiveness; and, to be sure, there was much to be learned about how to make aid more effective. Aid practitioners – men and women who staffed the innumerable national, international, and voluntary agencies that made up a veritable world of aid – saw their task as learning from experience how to do better next time with the resources available. Often it was represented, though, that aid could not be made more effective unless there were much more of it, and that the central problem was to persuade the governments and people of the rich industrial countries to give more.

Clearly it was hard for the world of aid to accommodate radical critics who disputed its fundamental assumption and maintained that aid could be actually harmful to poor countries, not as a matter of failure or ineffectiveness, but systematically so.

For P. T. Bauer the basic argument was unconvincing because there was nothing wrong with inequality; 'a differentiated social structure may be both a reflection and an instrument of economic development'. Aid benefited those in poor countries who were already better off – town-dwellers, politicians, civil servants, academics, and some businessmen – and was paid for out of taxes levied among others on the poor; it was 'a process by which poor people in rich countries help rich people in poor countries'. Aid was not indispensable for development; the rich countries were all (as he put it) underdeveloped two centuries ago, and 'many underdeveloped countries have advanced very rapidly over the last half century or so without foreign aid'. Some aid projects had absorbed domestic inputs greater than the net output, so that the recipient country would have been better off without them. Reliance on food aid had reinforced governments' tendency to invest in prestige industrial projects and neglect agriculture. And aid in general was a 'dole', tending to erode or sap attitudes and beliefs conducive to self-reliance, thrift, effort, and enterprise.[11]

Teresa Hayter worked for some years in the world of aid, but her studies in Latin America led her to conclude that the conventional wisdom constituted 'a complicated edifice of deception' and that aid itself could be explained only as 'an attempt to preserve the capitalist system in the Third World'. Since capitalism was to be identified with exploitation and dependence, it was clearly not in the interest of the people of the Third World that it should succeed. But though she wrote from an ideological position diametrically opposed to that of Bauer, there were distinct similarities in her criticisms of the effects of aid. It could help to sustain a privileged class; it could be used 'directly as a bribe' to secure the adoption of measures favourable to donors and unfavourable to recipients; deliberately or otherwise, it could be used for projects which made people worse off, not better; and 'it usually adds to the burden of debt carried by the countries receiving it, and hence to their dependence'.[12]

Without rejecting the idea of aid outright, other criticisms indicated reservations and qualifications to the conventional wisdom. Thus Judith Tendler pointed to the paradox that aid practitioners on the one hand maintained that aid funds were pitifully small and much more were needed, yet on the other hand tended to act in practice as if aid funds were abundant and what were really scarce were worthy, viable projects. To safeguard themselves against criticism, aid practitioners could conscientiously recommend only projects that satisfied a number of exacting criteria. They should be practicable and economic, and offer good prospects of contributing to general economic development, preferably with greatest benefits to the poorest people. They should be manageable, and enable the donor organization to monitor their progress and audit their books, with some assurance that donors' money would not be wasted in mismanagement or corruption. Aid organizations often had to move quickly to dispose of their allotted funds before losing them at the end of the financial year. The bigger the project, the more funds could be disposed of with less effort. Capital-intensiveness and import finance made supervision and control possible, whereas many small projects with much local expenditure would be impossible to monitor and audit. Such considerations were important reasons for a bias towards big, capital-intensive projects.[13]

Similarly, John White, a defender of aid, analysed the conditions in which aid might be said to make its recipients worse off. Tying was one, and there had been a number of cases in which the extra cost of an aid project due to tying had exceeded the amount saved by the concessional terms of the associated loan. In such cases it would have been more advantageous to decline aid and carry through the project with money borrowed at commercial terms on the open market. It was simply not true that 'any aid is better than no aid', and there was no excuse for recipients who did not bother to do their sums.

Further, while the conventional wisdom assumed that aid supplemented local resources, left- and right-wing critics alike alleged that it displaced them. Thus Keith Griffin had shown that Latin American countries that received more aid had lower savings rates than those that received less aid. But it could equally well be argued that countries with low domestic savings would naturally seek external aid for their investment programmes, so that such a finding did not invalidate the supplemental view of aid. Conversely, the displacement theory would be vindicated by a case in which a reduction of aid had been followed by an increase in development resources. 'The most frequently cited example is Tanzania, but the example is a bad one, because the introduction of a declared policy of self-reliance in Tanzania was in fact followed by an increase in the amount of aid received.' While it was theoretically possible that aid might displace local resources to such an extent as to make the recipients worse off than they were before, it was hard to find unequivocal evidence of a case in which that had really happened.

White emphasized that while aid could be viewed in economists' terms as a transfer of resources, it was also always a political transaction. Simply by seeking aid, a government – acting for a country as a whole – put itself into a position of dependence which it would see as a set of constraints limiting its freedom of action in domestic policy. Its relations with donor agencies were therefore likely to be fraught. For their part, those agencies would inevitably form judgements about recipients' policies, and find themselves supporting those they judged beneficial and opposing others. Promises of aid on the one hand, and threats to withdraw it on the other, could therefore be used as 'leverage', imposing demands on recipients often with a high political cost. The supplemental view of aid increased the likelihood that the donor would come into conflict with, and try to bring pressure to bear upon, domestic political forces in the recipient country. That would be seen as interference, causing aid to fall into disrepute.[14]

For example, according to Cheryl Payer, Yugoslavia's acceptance of IMF credits and World Bank loans entailed adopting policies that permitted the growth of inter-regional and inter-occupational disparities which the government would rather have prevented had it been able to do so.[15]

The Brandt commission, 1977–80

'By the early 1970s', though, in the words of the Brandt report, 'the focus of debate had shifted away from aid to the structure of the world economic system.'

In 1977 the time seemed ripe for a fresh review of the issues of world development. Perhaps it was thought that the Pearson commission had not had the impact it should have had. It had been appointed by, and reported to, the World Bank, which as already noted did not command universal admiration; and its terms of reference, or the way they were interpreted, had placed prime emphasis on aid as a moral duty owed by the rich to the poor, an appeal to which the rich proved somewhat deaf and which the poor regarded as patronizing.

Accordingly, though the initiative was again that of Robert McNamara, great pains were taken to make the new commission independent not only of the World Bank but also of every other official and non-governmental institution. It was named the Independent Commission on International Development Issues, and its chairman Willy Brandt in effect appointed himself. Ten of its eighteen members were from non-industrial countries. Its financial and administrative support was drawn from a wide spread of countries, international organizations, and research foundations. It met in a number of places, including India, Mali, and Malaysia. Its secretariat was based in Geneva, with help from the Commonwealth office in London where its report was seen through the press by Edward Heath and Shridath Ramphal; and the first copy was presented to the Secretary-General of the United Nations.

The commission considered aid and development in the widest possible setting of a comprehensive analysis of world issues and problems. Many features of the world situation they faced have already been touched on here. While aid from industrial countries had fallen short of the UN target, studies had indicated that their trade with poor countries was on unequal terms that hindered the development of the latter, whose governments pressed for fairer terms particularly through UNCTAD. The dramatic oil price rises of 1973–74 had almost overnight resulted in the rise of a group of non-western, non-industrial countries to a position of great power and wealth. Though suddenly possessed of huge funds, however, these were in the rapidly depreciating currencies of western industrial countries; and since oil in the ground does not depreciate like dollars or pounds in the bank, those countries had an interest in conserving their natural resources and urging industrial countries to save energy. That further strengthened an already growing awareness that industrial countries' prosperity had been based for the last two centuries on using up ever-diminishing natural resources at an ever-increasing rate, and gave new urgency to the debate about ecology and the environment. It also called in question the role of the multi-national corporations, such as the big oil companies, whose command over resources exceeded that of many states. With those developments went the disintegration of the Third World. The days when non-industrial, non-aligned countries could be thought of as a single group were clearly over when OPEC countries became major aid donors and when newly industrializing countries such as Brazil and Korea were achieving economic miracles while others including India stayed poor. China had emerged on the world scene after thirty years' isolation, a communist country but certainly not aligned with the Soviet Union, and one whose accession to the World Bank was a development of great moment at the time of the commission's deliberations. The Bretton Woods system had collapsed, the dollar had ceased to be the leading world currency, and with no new arrangements in sight world trade was being financed by a series of improvisations including the so-called 'Euro-dollars' and 'petro-dollars' as well as the IMF's Special Drawing Rights. Moreover, western industrial economies were affected by both rising unemployment and inflation in puzzling conditions in which the former 'trade-off' between the two through government deficit spending seemed not to work any more. Those conditions heightened the problems of aid and world development in two ways. They strengthened workers' demands in industrial countries for protection through tariffs or controls against manufactured imports from low- and middle-income countries; and western governments' resolve to combat inflation by reducing public expenditure created a difficult atmosphere in which to press for more aid. Finally, though western governments' military expenditure was falling, that of most others was rising, and fears of major military conflicts overshadowed all else.

The commission's analysis of so complex a world situation prompted an equally complex set of inter-related recommendations, not all of which can even be mentioned here.

Central to them, and several times reiterated, was the need for a 'massive' or 'large-scale transfer of resources to developing countries'. The industrial countries should commit themselves to a timetable for reaching the 0.7 per cent target, beginning in 1980 and attaining it by 1985. Eastern European countries and the better-off developing countries should also contribute official development assistance on a sliding scale related to national income.

Equally vital was disarmament, not only for its own sake, but also to free resources for this purpose. 'More arms do not make mankind safer, only poorer. The world's military spending dwarfs any spending on development.' There should be restraints on the sale of arms from industrial countries of 'the North', both west and east, to the developing countries of 'the South'. 'Every effort must be made to secure international agreements preventing the proliferation of nuclear weapons.' And among other recommendations was one for an internationally levied tax on the arms trade, at a higher rate than on other trade, the proceeds of which should be devoted to development purposes.

A special effort should be made to assist 'the poverty belts of Africa and Asia and particularly the least developed countries'. Largely humanitarian, this effort should include water and soil management, health care, and the eradication of diseases such as river-blindness, malaria, sleeping sickness, and bilharzia, as well as afforestation, solar energy development, and support for mining and industrial development. Agrarian reform was important in many countries. Food aid was needed especially in emergencies, and increased provision should be made for it, but without weakening incentives to local food production.

Though the strain on the global environment was due mainly to the growth of the industrial economies, it resulted also from that of the world's population. To achieve a satisfactory balance between population and resources, family planning should be freely available. In this as in other matters, the whole onus did not fall on the North; governments of countries in the South were responsible too, and there were many other measures they needed to take. Prominent among them were the expansion of social services to the poor, agrarian reform, and the encouragement of small-scale enterprises in rural areas and the informal sector in towns.

A world energy policy was required aiming at an orderly transition from non-renewable energy resources. 'The industrial countries will have to alter lifestyles which they have based on abundant energy.' A greatly expanded role for coal seemed inevitable in the next few decades, pending longer-term research on the economical utilization of solar energy which would most benefit the poorer countries of the South.

Urgent action was needed to stabilize commodity prices at remunerative levels; failing a revival of the abandoned ITO, individual commodity agreements should be pressed ahead. Meanwhile, 'Protectionism threatens

283

the future of the world economy and is inimical to the long-term interests of developing and developed countries alike. Protectionism by industrialized countries against the exports of developing countries should be rolled back.'

International agreements were needed to regulate and clarify the position of multi-national corporations. The proposed new regime would include reciprocal obligations by host and home countries covering investment, the transfer of technology, and the repatriation of profits. Uniform legislation should regulate the disclosure of information, restrictive business practices, and labour standards. Governments should co-operate to remove tax anomalies, of which multi-national corporations might take advantage, and monitor the prices at which the corporations transfer their goods to and from their subsidiaries in different countries.

Finally, a thoroughgoing reform of the international monetary system should be urgently undertaken, beginning with the IMF. 'The participation of developing countries in the staffing, management and decision-making of the IMF should be enlarged.' It 'should avoid inappropriate or excessive regulation' of developing countries' economies, 'and should not impose highly deflationary measures as standard adjustment policy'.

The IMF's Special Drawing Rights, however, had already proved their usefulness following the dethronement of the dollar. They were indeed the only form of international currency yet devised whose creation was a deliberate, conscious decision and not the inadvertent outcome of circumstances such as gold discoveries in the nineteenth century and US balance-of-payments deficits in the twentieth. New SDRs should be created to the extent needed to finance world trade without inflation, as a first step towards a stable and permanent international currency, and one greatly preferable to an arrangement based on any dominant national currency.

Most important, the new SDRs should be issued mostly to developing countries, rather than as before to industrial countries on account of their bigger subscriptions to the Fund. Many developing countries, with their dependence on primary exports in uncertain world markets, often experienced balance-of-payments deficits and needed greater access to short-term resources without being forced into measures harmful to themselves and others in the longer term. Besides, putting more purchasing power in the hands of such countries would increase their effective demand for goods produced by the industrial countries and so help to reduce unemployment there, while effectively transferring resources to poorer countries.

Similarly, though the World Bank came in for less stringent criticism, it was urged to modify the conservative regulations that allowed it to lend no more money than it possessed, and to lend out up to twice its capital. To be sure, there were risks; but the commission pointed out that the record of the Bank's borrowers had been excellent, and there had been no case of default in its whole history.[16]

However, the Brandt report itself was not immune from criticism. Most notably the veteran development economists Gunnar Myrdal and Dudley Seers expressed their profound disillusionment, not only with the report, but also with the whole idea of official development assistance, even though none had done more in their time to promote that idea in the western world; and above all with the political regimes of many Third World countries.

'A distinction must be made between aid to the economy and aid to the poor. We have come to be critical of the former, not the latter.' The Brandt commission's failure to make that distinction had been compounded by their confusing countries with governments. Taken together, those confusions had enabled them to argue that because a country's people were poor, financial transfers were justified to its government. But the assumption that a government represents a country and acts on behalf of its people needed to be questioned, and was in many cases false. 'In many countries the problem precisely is the government.' Many governments in the South were no longer short of resources; their revenues had grown faster than their populations, and would have grown faster still if taxes had been properly collected; and they had borrowed heavily. But much of the money had been spent on luxury goods and weapons rather than development, and much aid had trickled away in bribes and administrative salaries.

Much aid, too, went to 'governments that co-operate in the economic and political strategies of the US State Department', some of which did little about social problems and were among the most repressive. (They did not add that, as noted above, OPEC and CMEA governments concentrated their aid much more narrowly than the West on a few congenial regimes).

As for the report's argument that western countries could relieve unemployment by a massive outpouring of aid, to treat that as a policy that rich governments might consider serious was 'naive, if not dishonest', and it would in any case be a very roundabout and uncertain way for them to solve their problems.

It did not follow, however, that all aid commitments should be abandoned. Great damage would be done, especially in some oil-importing countries in Africa and south Asia, by a sudden and complete elimination of aid to their governments. The key to the quandary was to distinguish different types of aid and different recipients. 'The only type that may, in some cases, deserve a word meaning help is aid which the donor is absolutely sure will be used for elementary needs, such as pure water or primary health care, in a really poor country.' Aid in emergencies such as floods, famines, and earthquakes was one such type, and should be administered by new international institutions specializing in this task. And 'the moral motive is now most evident in the voluntary agencies such as Oxfam and the missionary societies...We would once have looked on these as non-professional "do-gooders". They now appear to have certain advantages.' Their officials, not being civil servants, were less vulnerable to diplomatic pressures, could turn down capital-intensive projects like modern factories, and could by-pass recipient countries' governments to deal directly with local groups.[17]

It was in such terms, then, that the debate was being carried on in the early 1980s about the problems of our world, the great issues of disparity and development, and the challenge of our common humanity.

SUGGESTIONS FOR FURTHER READING

Partners in Development (the Pearson report), London: Pall Mall, 1969
North-South: A Programme for Survival (the Brandt report), London: Pan, 1980
John White, *The Politics of Foreign Aid*, London: Bodley Head, 1974

APPENDIX

OECD: the Organization for Economic Co-Operation and Development; reconstituted 1961 from OEEC, the Organization for European Economic Co-Operation, founded 1947–8. Members in 1981: Australia*, Austria*, Belgium*, Canada*, Denmark*, Finland*, France*, West Germany*, Greece, Iceland, Irish Republic, Italy*, Japan*, Luxembourg, Netherlands*, New Zealand*, Norway*, Portugal, Spain, Sweden*, Switzerland*, Turkey, United Kingdom*, United States*, with the participation of the EEC Commission*, and with special status for Yugoslavia.
* denotes member of Development Assistance Committee, DAC.

CMEA: the Council for Mutual Economic Assistance; founder members, 1949: Soviet Union, Bulgaria, Czechoslovakia, Hungary, Poland, Romania; Albania joined 1949, left 1961. Later accessions: East Germany 1950, Mongolia 1962, Cuba 1972, Vietnam 1978. Since 1964 Yugoslavia has participated in some CMEA agencies.

EEC: the European Economic Community: founder members, 1957: Belgium, France, West Germany, Italy, Luxembourg, Netherlands. Later accessions: Denmark, Irish Republic, and United Kingdom 1973; Greece 1981.

OPEC: the Organization of the Petroleum Exporting Countries; founded 1960. Members in 1981: Algeria (A), Ecuador, Gabon, Indonesia, Iran, Iraq (A), Kuwait (A), Libya (A), Nigeria, Qatar (A), Saudi Arabia (A), United Arab Emirates (A), Venezuela.
(A) denotes member of OAPEC, the Organization of Arab Petroleum Exporting Countries.

Sources: World Bank, *World Development Report, 1982*; *Political Handbook of the World, 1979*; *Statesman's Yearbook, 1982–83*.

Notes

Chapter 1. Introduction and argument

1 United Nations, *Measures for the Economic Development of Under-Developed Countries*, E/1986 ST/ETA/10 (3 May 1951).
2 Gunnar Myrdal, *Asian Drama: An Inquiry into the Poverty of Nations* (Harmondsworth, 1968), appendix 1.
3 Ernest Gellner, *Thought and Change* (London, 1964), p. 33n.
4 A. O. Hirschman, *The Strategy of Economic Development* (New Haven, Conn., 1958), p. 11.
5 Myrdal, *Asian Drama*, appendix 2.
6 Paul Streeten, 'How poor are the poor countries?' in Dudley Seers and Leonard Joy (eds.), *Development in a Divided World* (Harmondsworth, 1971), p. 77; *The Frontiers of Development Studies* (London, 1972), p. 31.
7 Auguste Comte, *Positive Politics*, vol. IV, appendix, pp. 149–50, quoted by N. S. Timasheff, *Sociological Theory, its Nature and Growth* (New York, 1955), p. 19; *Positive Philosophy*, transl. Harriet Martineau (London, 1853), esp. vol. II, ch. VI.
8 Herbert Spencer, *Principles of Sociology* (London, 1904), vol. I, part II, chs. X, XI; vol. II, part V, chs. XVII, XVIII.
9 Sir Henry Sumner Maine, *Ancient Law*, 11th edition (London, 1887), p. 170.
10 Emile Durkheim, *The Division of Labour in Society*, transl. G. Simpson (Glencoe, Ill., 1974); *Elementary Forms of the Religious Life*, transl. J. W. Swain (London, 1915).
11 Ludwig S. Feuer (ed.), *Marx and Engels: Basic Writings on Politics and Philosophy* (New York, 1959); George Lichtheim, *Marxism* (London, 1961).
12 Max Weber, *The Protestant Ethic and the Spirit of Capitalism*, transl. Talcott Parsons (London, 1930).
13 Ferdinand Tönnies, *Gemeinschaft und Gesellschaft*, 1887, revised 1922, transl. Charles P. Loomis, *Community and Association* (London, 1955), *Community and Society* (East Lansing, Mich., 1957).
14 L. T. Hobhouse, *Social Development* (London, 1924); J. A. Hobson and Morris Ginsberg, *L. T. Hobhouse, His Life and Work* (London, 1931).
15 Talcott Parsons, *The Structure of Social Action* (New York, 1937).
16 Talcott Parsons and Edward A. Shils, *Toward a General Theory of Action* (Cambridge, Mass., 1951), pp. 49, 76–7.
17 Talcott Parsons, *Societies: Evolutionary and Comparative Perspectives* (Englewood Cliffs, N.J., 1966), pp. 1, 21–3.
18 Louis Dumont, *Homo Hierarchicus* (London, 1970).
19 Aidan Foster-Carter, 'From Rostow to Gunder Frank: changing paradigms in the analysis of development', *World Development*, vol. 4, no. 3 (1976).

20 Larousse, 1978: 'Tiers état...nom donné en France, sous l'Ancien Régime, à la partie de la population qui n'appartenait ni à la noblesse ni au clergé. Tiers monde, ensemble des pays peu developpés économiquement qui n'appartiennent ni au groupe des États industriels d'économie libérale, ni au groupe des États de type socialiste.' Dupré, *Encyclopédie du bon français*, 1972; 'Tiers ...Aujourd'hui, cet adjectif archaïque a connu une fortune nouvelle dans les expressions le tiers monde', etc.

21 Peter Worsley, *The Third World* (London, 1964).

22 Irving Louis Horowitz, *Three Worlds of Development* (New York, 1966).

23 Leslie Wolf-Phillips, 'Why Third World?' *Third World Quarterly*, vol. 1, no. 1 (Jan. 1979), pp. 105–14; Peter Worsley, 'How many worlds?' *ibid.*, vol. 1, no. 2 (April 1979), pp. 100–8; S. D. Muni, 'The Third World: concept and controversy', *ibid.*, vol. 1, no. 3 (July 1979), pp. 119–28.

24 Ruth First, *Libya* (Harmondsworth, 1974); A. S. Al-Ahmar, *The Changing Social Organization of the Libyan Village*, Ph.D. thesis, University of Leeds (1976).

Chapter 2. Technology, society, and population

1 The classic treatment of the neolithic revolution, and probably the source of the phrase itself, is V. Gordon Childe, *Man Makes Himself* (London, 1936), ch. 2. See also Don R. Arthur, *Survival* (London, 1969); S. Lilley, *Men, Machines, and History* (London, 1948; revised edition, 1965); Carlo M. Cipolla, *The Economic History of World Population*, 7th edition (Harmondsworth, 1978); Colin McEvedy and Richard Jones, *Atlas of World Population History* (Harmondsworth, 1978).

2 United Nations, *The Determinants and Consequences of Population Trends* (1953), ch. 2; Marshall Sahlins, *Stone Age Economics* (London, 1974).

3 J. V. Grauman, 'Population growth', *International Encyclopaedia of the Social Sciences* (1968).

4 The authoritative source for estimates of world population from 1650 to 1930 is still A. M. Carr-Saunders, *World Population* (Oxford, 1936). Later figures from UN *Demographic Yearbooks*.

5 C. P. Blacker, *Eugenics, Galton and After* (London, 1952), ch. 8.

6 Michael Drake, *Population and Society in Norway, 1735–1865* (Cambridge, 1969); D. V. Glass (ed.), *Introduction to Malthus* (London, 1953), pp. 30–8.

7 David Montague de Silva, 'Public health and sanitation measures as factors affecting mortality trends in Ceylon', *Proceedings of the World Population Conference, 1954* (UN, 1955), vol. 1, pp. 411–38; UN *Demographic Yearbooks* 1966 and historical supplement 1979.

8 Francis X. Murphy, 'Catholic perspectives on population issues II', *Population Bulletin*, vol. 35, no. 6 (Population Reference Bureau, Washington, D.C., February 1981).

9 *Partners in Development: Report of the Commission on International Development* (London, 1969), pp. 55–8, 194–9.

10 'China's "one-child" population future', *Intercom*, vol. 9, no. 8 (Population Reference Bureau, August 1981); Jonathan Mirsky, 'China and the one-child family', *New Society*, 18 February 1982, pp. 264–5.

11 Lord Blackett, *The Gap Widens* (the Rede Lecture, 1969; Cambridge, 1970).

12 Michael Lipton, 'The international diffusion of technology', in Dudley Seers and Leonard Joy (eds.), *Development in a Divided World* (Harmondsworth, 1971), pp. 45–50.

13 Georges Tapinos and Phyllis T. Piotrow, *Six Billion People* (New York, 1978), pp. 97–124; T. Scarlett Epstein and Darell Jackson (eds.), *The Feasibility of Family Planning* (Oxford, 1977), pp. 9–10.
14 Depending on definition, middle-class infant mortality as late as 1911 was estimated at 55 to 96 per 1,000 live births; R. M. Titmuss, *Birth, Poverty and Wealth* (London, 1943), pp. 23–31.
15 Etienne van de Walle and John Knodel, 'Europe's fertility transition: new evidence and lessons for today's developing world', *Population Bulletin*, vol. 34, no. 6 (February 1980).
16 Amy Ong Tsui and Donald J. Bogue, 'Declining world fertility: trends, causes, implications', *Population Bulletin*, vol. 33, no. 4 (October 1978).
17 International Statistical Institute, World Fertility Survey, *Country Reports* and *Summaries* (Voorburg, 1977–); Robert Lightbourne Jr. and Susheela Singh, with Cynthia P. Green, 'The World Fertility Survey: charting global child-bearing', *Population Bulletin*, vol. 37, no. 1 (March 1982).
18 Frank L. Mott and Susan H. Mott, 'Kenya's record population growth: a dilemma of development', *Population Bulletin*, vol. 35, no. 3 (October 1980).

Case-study 1: India

1 Kingsley Davis, *The Population of India and Pakistan* (Princeton, N.J., 1951).
2 Myrdal, *Asian Drama*, pp. 1489–91, 1518–20, and appendix 12.
3 Quoted in Tapinos and Piotrow, *Six Billion People*, pp. 98–9, 115–16.
4 Pravin Visaria and Leela Visaria, 'India's population: second and growing', *Population Bulletin*, vol. 36, no. 4 (October 1981).

Case-study 2: England and Wales

1 Carr-Saunders, *World Population*, ch. 1.
2 E. A. Wrigley, 'Family limitation in pre-industrial England', *Economic History Review*, XIX (1966), pp. 82–109.
3 G. M. Trevelyan, *English Social History* (London, 1944), pp. 339–46; T. S. Ashton, *The Industrial Revolution, 1760–1830* (London, 1948), pp. 3–6; H. J. Habakkuk, 'The economic history of modern Britain', *Journal of Economic History*, XVIII (1958), pp. 486–501.
4 R. A. Lewis, *Edwin Chadwick and the Public Health Movement, 1832–1854* (London, 1952).
5 J. A. Banks, *Prosperity and Parenthood* (London, 1954).
6 Graham Wallas, *The Life of Francis Place* (London, 1898), ch. 6; St John G. Ervine, *Francis Place* (Fabian biographical tract) (London, 1912).
7 J. H. Clapham, *An Economic History of Modern Britain, 1850–1886* (Cambridge, 1932), ch. IX; W. W. Rostow, *British Economy of the Nineteenth Century* (Oxford, 1948), chs. III, IV, VII.
8 *Royal Commission on Population Report*, Cmd 7695; E. Lewis-Faning, *Family Limitation* (Papers of the Royal Commission on Population) (London, 1949), p. 7.

Case-study 3: Japan

1 Irene B. Taeuber, *The Population of Japan* (Princeton, N.J., 1958).

Chapter 3. The colonial episode and the race question

1 Carlo M. Cipolla, 'Guns and sails', *European Culture and Overseas Expansion* (Harmondsworth, 1970), pp. 104–5.

2 De Kiewiet, quoted in Pierre van den Berghe, *South Africa: a Study in Conflict* (Middletown, Conn., 1965), pp. 13–14.

3 Burton Benedict, *Indians in a Plural Society: a Report on Mauritius* (Colonial Research Studies no. 34) (London, 1961), esp. chs. II and III.

4 References on this and the previous paragraph include: Gunnar Myrdal, *An American Dilemma* (New York, 1944), abridged edition by Arnold M. Rose, *The Negro in America* (New York, 1958); C. W. Wagley, 'The situation of the Negro in the United States', *International Social Science Bulletin* (later *Journal*), IX, no. 4 (1957), pp. 427–38; Roger Bastide, 'Race relations in Brazil', *ibid.*, pp. 495–512; Donald Pierson, *Negroes in Brazil* (Chicago, 1942), esp. pp. 30–7.

5 Trevelyan, *English Social History*, pp. 347, 388–9, 495–6; R. Coupland, *The British Anti-Slavery Movement* (London, 1933); Eric Williams, *Capitalism and Slavery* (Chapel Hill, N.C., 1943).

6 W. E. R. Ward, *The Royal Navy and the Slavers* (London, 1969).

7 Roland Oliver, *The Missionary Factor in East Africa* (London, 1952), ch. I.

8 Myrdal, *Asian Drama*, ch. 5, section 1, 'The advance of colonial rule'.

9 A. Boyd and P. van Rensberg, *An Atlas of African Affairs* (New York, 1962), pp. 24–7; Roland Oliver and J. D. Fage, *A Short History of Africa* (Harmondsworth, 1962), ch. 16.

10 Harry Thuku, *Autobiography* (with assistance from Kenneth King) (Nairobi, 1970).

11 Oliver, *The Missionary Factor in East Africa*, pp. 149–62; D. A. Low, 'British public opinion and the Uganda question, October–December 1892', *Uganda Journal*, 18 (1954), pp. 81–100.

12 Such attitudes are documented in Elspeth Huxley, *White Man's Country* (London, 1956); Elspeth Huxley and Margery Perham, *Race and Politics in Kenya: A Correspondence* (London, 1944); L. H. Gann and P. Duignan, *White Settlers in Tropical Africa* (Harmondsworth, 1962).

13 A. P. Elkin, *The Australian Aborigines*, 4th edition (Garden City, N.Y., 1964), ch. XIV; 'Aborigines and Europeans in Australia', *American Anthropologist*, 53 (1951), pp. 164–86.

14 Myrdal, *Asian Drama*, pp. 449–52, 832–3, 839.

15 A. I. Richards, *Land, Labour, and Diet in Northern Rhodesia* (London, 1939), pp. 256–62; R. L. Buell, 'Forced Labour', *Encyclopaedia of the Social Sciences* (1932).

16 Oliver, *The Missionary Factor in East Africa*, pp. 247–57.

17 Myrdal, *Asian Drama*, pp. 969–71.

18 Boyd and van Rensberg, *An Atlas of African Affairs*, p. 45.

19 Each £100 invested in the company when it began in 1903 earned a first dividend of £2. 10. 0 in 1907. In 1913 it was written down to £50, and no more dividends were declared until 1918. From then till 1925 the company paid dividends at $5\frac{1}{2}$ to 15%, but that was only $2\frac{3}{4}$ to $7\frac{1}{2}$% on the original capital. No more dividends were forthcoming till 1937, by which time the original £100 investment had been further written down to £37. 10. 0. Later the company paid bigger and more regular dividends, but even so the average yield over the first fifty years was little more than 3%. – C. Ehrlich, *The Uganda Company Limited: The First Fifty Years* (Kampala, 1953).

20 C. Wagley and M. Harris, *Minorities in the New World* (New York, 1958), p. 27.
21 F. B. Welbourn, *East African Rebels* (London, 1961), ch. 7; Carl G. Rosberg Jr and John Nottingham, *The Myth of 'Mau Mau': Nationalism in Kenya* (New York, 1966), pp. 112–25.
22 J. E. Goldthorpe, *Outlines of East African Society* (Kampala, 1958), ch. VIII.
23 William Malcolm Hailey (Lord Hailey), *An African Survey* (London, 1938), pp. 413ff; Max Gluckman, 'Analysis of a social situation in modern Zululand', *Bantu Studies*, 14 (1940), pp. 1–30, 147–74, reprinted as Rhodes-Livingstone paper no. 28 (1958); also his 'Inter-hierarchical roles', in Marc J. Swartz (ed.), *Local-Level Politics* (London, 1968); L. A. Fallers, *Bantu Bureaucracy* (Cambridge, 1956), esp. pp. 196–203; D. A. Low and R. C. Pratt, *Buganda and British Overrule* (London, 1960); David E. Apter, *The Political Kingdom in Uganda* (Princeton, N.J., 1961), ch. 13; The Kabaka of Buganda, *Desecration of My Kingdom* (London, 1967).
24 Goldthorpe, *Outlines of East African Society*, ch. X.
25 Arthur Phillips (ed.), *Survey of African Marriage and Family Life* (London, 1953), pp. 179–89.
26 J. E. Goldthorpe, *An African Elite* (Nairobi, 1965).
27 Cyril Sofer and Rhona Ross, 'Some characteristics of an East African European population', *British Journal of Sociology*, II (1951), pp. 315–27.
28 Roger Bastide, 'Dusky Venus, black Apollo', *Race*, III (1961), pp. 10–18; Carl N. Degler, *Neither Black Nor White* (London, 1971), pp. 185–95.
29 Wagley and Harris, *Minorities in the New World*, p. 24; Pierson, *Negroes in Brazil*, pp. 321–50.
30 C. Wagley, *Race and Class in Rural Brazil* (Paris, 1952), pp. 23–4.
31 Bastide, 'Race relations in Brazil'.
32 van den Berghe, *South Africa*, pp. 14–21, 39–42, 55–9; John Dugard, 'Racial legislation and civil rights', ch. 4 of Ellen Hellman and Henry Lever (eds.), *Race Relations in South Africa, 1929–1979* (London, 1980); Sheila van der Horst (ed.), *Race Discrimination in South Africa: A Review* (Cape Town, 1981).
33 The term is generally credited to J. S. Furnivall in 'The political economy of the tropical Far East', *Journal of the Royal Central Asian Society*, XXIX (1942), pp. 195–210, and in his *Colonial Policy and Practice* (Cambridge, 1948), pp. 303–12. See also John Rex, 'The plural society in sociological theory', *British Journal of Sociology*, X (1959), pp. 114–24.
34 Myrdal, *Asian Drama*, p. 425.
35 F. D. Lugard, *The Dual Mandate in British Tropical Africa* (Edinburgh, 1923), esp. ch. III.
36 *East Africa Royal Commission 1953–1955 Report*, Cmd 9475 (1955), esp. map 2.
37 Myrdal, *Asian Drama*, p. 465.
38 *ibid.*, pp. 453–7.
39 Sir Charles Dundas, *African Crossroads* (London, 1955), pp. 123–30; Huxley and Perham, *Race and Politics in Kenya*, pp. 98, 100, 107; Rosberg and Nottingham, *The Myth of 'Mau Mau'*, pp. 74, 207, 304.
40 Myrdal, *Asian Drama*, pp. 144–7.
41 Margery Perham, 'African facts and American criticisms', *Foreign Affairs*, 22, no. 3 (1944), reprinted in her *Colonial Sequence 1930 to 1949* (London, 1967), pp. 250–62.
42 World Bank, *World Development Report 1982*, table 24; Morris Janowitz, *Military Institutions and Coercion in Developing Nations* (Chicago, 1977), table 1 on pp. 38–9.

43 *Colonial Development and Welfare Acts 1929–70: A Brief Review*, Cmnd 4677 (1971).
44 Sofer and Ross, 'Some characteristics of an East African European population', pp. 319–21.
45 George de Vos, 'Conflict, dominance and exploitation in human systems of social segregation: some theoretical perspectives from the study of personality in culture', in A. de Reuck and Julie Knight (eds.), *Conflict in Society* (a CIBA symposium) (London, 1966), pp. 60–81.
46 Jean-Paul Sartre, preface to Frantz Fanon, *The Wretched of the Earth* (London, 1965).
47 G. Andrew Maguire, *Toward 'Uhuru' in Tanzania* (Cambridge, 1969).
48 Kwame Nkrumah, *Ghana: An Autobiography* (Edinburgh, 1957); Tom Mboya, *Freedom and After* (London, 1963); Kenneth Kaunda, *Africa's Freedom* (London, 1964); Oginga Odinga, *Not Yet Uhuru* (London, 1967).
49 Jawaharlal Nehru, *Letters from a Father to his Daughter* (Allahabad, 1930); *Glimpses of World History* (Allahabad, 1934); *An Autobiography* (London, 1936); *The Discovery of India* (Calcutta, 1946).
50 Frantz Fanon, *The Wretched of the Earth*; *A Dying Colonialism* (Harmondsworth, 1970); *Toward the African Revolution* (Harmondsworth, 1970).
51 Jomo Kenyatta, *Facing Mount Kenya* (London, 1938).
52 Aimé Césaire, 'Cahier d'un retour au pays natal', transl. Peter Worsley and quoted in his *The Third World*, p. 124.
53 Quoted in Philip Mason, *Patterns of Dominance* (London, 1970), p. 290.

Chapter 4. Economic conditions

1 C. F. Carter, *The Science of Wealth* (London, 1966), p. 177.
2 World Bank, *World Development Report 1982*, pp. 23, 162–3.
3 Quoted by Myrdal, *Asian Drama*, p. 549.
4 K. H. Connell, *The Population of Ireland, 1750–1845* (Oxford, 1950), pp. 151–6.
5 H. C. Trowell, J. N. P. Davies, and R. F. A. Dean, *Kwashiorkor* (London, 1954).
6 D. P. Burkitt and H. C. Trowell (eds.), *Refined Carbohydrate Foods and Disease* (London, 1975).
7 Lightbourne, Singh, and Green, 'The World Fertility Survey', p. 29.
8 Myrdal, *Asian Drama*, appendix 2, section 21, pp. 1912ff.
9 World Bank, *World Development Report 1981*, pp. 101–7, and *1982*, pp. 86–9.
10 UN *Statistical Yearbook for 1979/80*.
11 Nick Eberstadt, 'The health crisis in the USSR', *New York Review of Books*, 19 February 1981, pp. 23–31, reviewing Christopher Davis, *Rising Infant Mortality in the USSR in the 1970s*, US Bureau of the Census, series P-95 no. 74 (September 1980), and many other sources; Murray Feshbach, 'The Soviet Union: population trends and dilemmas', *Population Bulletin*, vol. 37, no. 3 (August 1982).
12 Hollis Chenery, Moises Syrquin, and Hazel Elkington, *Patterns of Development, 1950–1970* (New York, 1975).
13 Independent Commission on International Development Issues, *North-South: A Programme for Survival* (London, 1980), p. 145.
14 Data from standard sources including UN, World Bank, and *Statesman's Yearbook for 1982/83*.
15 *North-South*, p. 145.
16 *The Economist*, 15 January 1972, p. 40, and 12 February 1972, p. 39.

17 G. L. Beckford, 'The economics of resource use and development in plantation economies', *Social and Economic Studies*, 18 (Jamaica, 1969), pp. 321–47; reprinted in Henry Bernstein (ed.), *Underdevelopment and Development* (Harmondsworth, 1973), pp. 115–51.

18 P. T. Bauer, *Dissent on Development* (London, 1971), p. 263; World Bank, *World Development Report 1981*, p. 23.

19 Roger Ballard, oral communication.

20 *World Development Report 1981*, p. 33.

21 Quoted in Paul Harrison, *Inside the Third World* (Harmondsworth, 1979), p. 407; see also Keith Griffin and Azizur Rahman Khan, 'Poverty in the Third World: ugly facts and fancy models', *World Development*, vol. 6, no. 3 (1978), pp. 295–304.

22 W. A. Lewis, 'Economic development with unlimited supplies of labour', *Manchester School*, XXII (1954), pp. 139–91.

23 Gerald M. Meier, 'Development without employment', in his *Leading Issues in Economic Development*, 2nd edition (New York, 1970), pp. 430–9; see also his comments on Lewis in *ibid.*, pp. 158–62.

24 Quoted in *Unemployment, the Unnatural Disaster* (OXFAM, n.d., 1971?).

25 W. Arthur Lewis, *Development Planning* (London, 1966), pp. 80–1.

26 G. Arrighi and J. S. Saul, 'Class formation and economic development in tropical Africa', *Journal of Modern African Studies*, 6 (1968), pp. 141–69; reprinted in Bernstein, *Underdevelopment and Development*, pp. 284–97.

27 See for instance Godfrey Wilson, *The Economics of Detribalization in Central Africa* (Manchester, 1942); Godfrey and Monica Wilson, *The Analysis of Social Change* (Cambridge, 1945); Audrey I. Richards (ed.), *Economic Development and Tribal Change: A Study of Immigrant Labour in Buganda* (Cambridge, 1954); P. H. Gulliver, *Labour Migration in a Rural Economy* (Kampala, 1955); Walter Elkan, *An African Labour Force* (Kampala, 1956); P. G. Powesland, *Economic Policy and Labour* (Kampala, 1957).

28 World Bank, *World Development Report 1981*, p. 21.

29 M. J. Sharpston, 'The economics of corruption', *New Society*, 26 November 1970, pp. 944–6.

30 Goldthorpe, *An African Elite*, p. 76.

31 Chinua Achebe, *No Longer At Ease* (London, 1960), pp. 5–6.

32 Peter L. Berger, *Pyramids of Sacrifice* (Harmondsworth, 1977), p. 172; Jagdish C. Kapur, *India in the Year 2000* (New Delhi, 1975); Mihir Bose, 'Middle India', *New Society*, 22/29 December 1977, pp. 617–9.

33 J. P. Nettl, *The Soviet Achievement* (London, 1967), p. 254; David Lane, *Politics and Society in the USSR* (London, 1970), ch. 2; *The End of Inequality?* (Harmondsworth, 1971); *The Socialist Industrial State* (London, 1976), ch. 12.

34 World Bank, *World Development Report 1982*, table 25.

35 Richard Jolly, 'Manpower and education', in Seers and Joy (eds.), *Development in a Divided World*, pp. 211, 219–21.

36 Chenery, Syrquin, and Elkington, *Patterns of Development*, fig. 12 on p. 62.

37 Hollis Chenery et al. (eds.), *Redistribution with Growth* (New York, 1974).

38 Peter T. Knight, 'Brazilian socioeconomic development: issues for the eighties', *World Development*, vol. 9, no. 11/12 (1981), pp. 1063–82; World Bank, *World Development Report 1981*, p. 70.

39 David Stephen, 'South America's new dictators', *New Society*, 16 October 1980, pp. 109–11.

293

40 Robert M. Levine, *Race and Ethnic Relations in Latin America and the Caribbean* (Metuchen, N.J., 1980); see esp. art. on the TV series 'Roots'.
41 Dudley Seers in Chenery, *Redistribution with Growth*.
42 Claes Brundenius, 'Growth with equity: the Cuban experience (1959–1980)', *World Development*, vol. 9, no. 11/12 (1981), pp. 1083–96.
43 Pranab K. Bardhan in Chenery, *Redistribution with Growth*.
44 Lal Jayawardena in *ibid.*
45 World Bank, *World Development Report 1982*, p. 87.
46 Irma Adelman in Chenery, *Redistribution with Growth*.
47 Chenery, *Redistribution with Growth*, p. 14.
48 Gustav Ranis in *ibid.*
49 *Ibid.*, p. 14

Chapter 5. Environmental constraints

1 Paul and Anne Ehrlich, *Population, Resources, Environment* (San Francisco, 1970); Paul R. Ehrlich and Richard L. Harriman, *How to be a Survivor* (New York, 1971).
2 John Maddox, *The Doomsday Syndrome* (London, 1972).
3 Donella and Dennis Meadows et al., *The Limits to Growth* (New York and London, 1972).
4 Thomas L. Boyle, 'Hope for the technological solution', *Nature*, 245, pp. 127–8 (21 September 1973).
5 H. S. D. Cole et al., *Thinking about the Future* (Brighton and London, 1973).
6 Mihajlo Mesarovic and Eduard Pestel, *Mankind at the Turning-Point* (London, 1975).
7 Dennis Gabor et al., *Beyond the Age of Waste* (Oxford, 1978).
8 Everett E. Hagen, *The Economics of Development* (Homewood, Ill., 1968), pp. 39–40; 2nd edition (1975), pp. 29–70.
9 S. Fred Singer, 'Human energy production as a process in the biosphere', *Scientific American*, September 1970, pp. 184–6.
10 L. C. Cole, 'Man and the Air', *Population Bulletin*, vol. XXIV, no. 5 (December 1968), pp. 109–10.
11 Paul and Anne Ehrlich, *Population, Resources, Environment*, pp. 146–7.
12 Uvedale Tristram, 'Fertilisers in Africa: self-sufficiency in five years', *World Hunger*, vol. II, no. 9 (May 1971), p. 13.
13 Michael Lipton, 'The international diffusion of technology', in Seers and Joy, *Development in a Divided World*, pp. 53–4.
14 Paul and Anne Ehrlich, *Population, Resources, Environment*, p. 187; Gabor, *Beyond the Age of Waste*, p. 175.
15 John R. Postgate, *Nitrogen Fixation* (London, 1978); R. H. Burris, 'Non-leguminous N_2-fixing systems', in W. Newton, J. R. Postgate, and C. Rodriguez-Barrueco (eds.), *Recent Developments in Nitrogen Fixation* (New York, 1977), p. 489.
16 *The Guardian*, 21 May 1971.
17 *The Guardian*, 4 August 1971.
18 'Dr Borlaug condemns DDT "hysteria"', *World Hunger*, vol. III, no. 1 (January 1972), p. 11.
19 A. H. Bunting, 'Pests, population, and poverty', a lecture at the University of Nottingham, December 1971, reported in *World Hunger*, vol. III. no. 1 (January 1972), pp. 6–10.

20 Georgeanne Champin and Robert Wasserstrom, 'Agricultural production and malaria resurgence in Central America and India', *Nature*, vol. 293, pp. 181–5; correspondence, *Nature*, vol. 294, pp. 302, 388 (1981).
21 World Bank, *World Development Report 1981*, pp. 101–7.
22 Lester R. Brown, 'World food resources and population: the narrowing margin', *Population Bulletin*, vol. 36, no. 3 (September 1981).
23 World Bank, *World Development Report, 1981*, pp. 80, 104; Pravin Visaria and Leela Visaria, 'India's population: second and growing', *Population Bulletin*, vol. 36, no. 4 (October 1981).
24 Gabor, *Beyond the Age of Waste*, p. 166.
25 World Bank, *World Development Report 1981*, p. 102.
26 World Bank, *World Development Report 1982*, p. 68.
27 Erich H. Jacoby, 'Effects of the "green revolution" in South and South-east Asia', *Modern Asian Studies*, vol. 6, no. 1 (1972), pp. 63–9; see also Griffin and Khan, 'Poverty in the Third World'.
28 Gabor, *Beyond the Age of Waste*, pp. 115–37; World Bank, *World Development Report 1981*, p. 44.
29 Cole, *Thinking About the Future*, p. 33.
30 Frank Fraser Darling and J. Morton Boyd, *The Highlands and Islands* (London, 1964), ch. 4.
31 Cipolla, *The Economic History of World Population*, p. 62.
32 World Bank, *World Development Report, 1981*, p. 42.
33 Walter C. Patterson, *Nuclear Power* (Harmondsworth, 1976).
34 M. King Hubbert, 'The energy resources of the earth', *Scientific American*, September 1971, p. 67; Harrison Brown, 'Human materials production', *Scientific American*, September 1970, p. 208.
35 Gabor, *Beyond the Age of Waste*, pp. 53–6.
36 World Bank, *World Development Report, 1981*, pp. 44 5.
37 Thierry de Montbrial, *Energy: the Countdown* (Oxford, 1979), p. 93; Patterson, *Nuclear Power*, pp. 246, 253–5.
38 World Bank, *World Development Report, 1982*, p. 61.
39 World Bank, *World Development Report, 1981*, pp. 40–2.
40 Knight, 'Brazilian socioeconomic development'; Population Reference Bureau, *Intercom*, vol. 8, no. 3 (March 1980), p. 7.
41 Consumers' Association, *Which?* (May 1981).

Chapter 6. The social sciences and the Third World

1 Bronislaw K. Malinowski, *A Scientific Theory of Culture* (Chapel Hill, N.J., 1944).
2 Margaret Mead, *Growing Up in New Guinea*, ch. I.
3 J. E. Meade, 'On becoming an economist', *Christ's College Magazine* (Cambridge), May 1970, p. 123.
4 UN, *Measures for the Economic Development of Under-Developed Countries*.
5 W. W. Rostow, *British Economy of the Nineteenth Century*; 'The take-off into sustained growth', *Economic Journal*, LXVI (1956), pp. 25–48; *The Stages of Economic Growth: A Non-Communist Manifesto* (Cambridge, 1960; 2nd edition, 1971).
6 Paul A. Baran and E. J. Hobsbawm, 'The stages of economic growth', *Kyklos*, XIV (1961), pp. 234–42.
7 Hagen, *The Economics of Development* (2nd edition, 1975), p. 214.
8 Myrdal, *Asian Drama*, appendix 2, pp. 1852–5.

9 P. N. Rosenstein-Rodan, 'Problems of industrialization of eastern and south-eastern Europe', *Economic Journal*, 53 (1943), pp. 205–11.

10 Ragnar Nurkse, 'The conflict between "balanced growth" and international specialization', *Lectures on Economic Development* (Istanbul, 1958); reprinted in Meier, *Leading Issues in Economic Development*, pp. 362–6.

11 Jacob Viner in a paper to the International Economic Association congress, 1956, quoted in Meier, *Leading Issues*, p. 399.

12 A. J. Youngson, 'Development myths', *Bulletin of the Institute of Development Studies* (University of Sussex), May 1969, pp. 22–3.

13 Albert O. Hirschman, *The Strategy of Economic Development* (New Haven, Conn., 1958).

14 David Apter, *The Politics of Modernization* (Chicago, 1965), pp. 9–10.

15 Hagen, *The Economics of Development* (2nd edition, 1975), p. 73.

16 Daniel Lerner, *The Passing of Traditional Society* (Glencoe, Ill., 1958).

17 Fred W. Riggs, *Administration in Developing Countries: the Theory of Prismatic Society* (Boston, Mass., 1964), p. 36.

18 See for example Baidya Nath Varma, *The Sociology and Politics of Development* (London, 1980).

19 Reinhard Bendix, 'Tradition and modernity reconsidered', *Comparative Studies in Society and History*, IX (April 1967), pp. 292–346; reprinted in his *Embattled Reason* (London, 1970), pp. 250–314.

20 J. P. Nettl and Roland Robertson, 'Industrialization, development, or modernization?', *British Journal of Sociology*, XVII (1966), pp. 274–91; reprinted in their *International Systems and the Modernization of Societies* (London, 1968), part I.

21 Teodor Shanin, lecture at the University of Leeds, 6 March 1980.

22 It is never easy to date an intellectual movement; some regard this as having been initiated by Paul Baran, *The Political Economy of Growth* (New York, 1957).

23 Philip J. O'Brien, 'A critique of Latin American theories of dependency', in Ivar Oxaal, Tony Barnett, and David Booth (eds.), *Beyond the Sociology of Development* (London, 1975), pp. 7–27.

24 Celso Furtado, *Development and Underdevelopment*, transl. R. W. de Aguiar and E. C. Drysdale (Berkeley and Los Angeles, 1964); *Diagnosis of the Brazilian Crisis*, transl. Suzette Macedo (Berkeley and Los Angeles, 1965).

25 Teresa Hayter, *Aid as Imperialism* (Harmondsworth, 1971).

26 A. G. Frank, *Capitalism and Underdevelopment in Latin America* (New York, 1967), pp. 9–11, 242; 'The sociology of development and the underdevelopment of sociology', *Catalyst*, 1967, pp. 20–73' *Latin America: Underdevelopment or Revolution* (New York, 1969), pp. 21–94.

27 Frank, *Capitalism and Underdevelopment*, pp. 221–5, 239.

28 Immanuel Wallerstein, *The Modern World System* (New York, 1974–80), vol. 1, pp. 1, 67, 87–8; vol. 2, pp. 5–6n.

29 John Taylor, 'Neo-Marxism and underdevelopment', *Journal of Contemporary Asia*, vol. 1, no. 4 (1974), pp. 9–10.

30 Barry Hindess and Paul Q. Hirst, *Pre-Capitalist Modes of Production* (London, 1975).

31 Samir Amin, *Unequal Development: An Essay on the Social Formations of Peripheral Capitalism* (Hassocks, 1976).

32 See for instance Robin Jenkins, *Exploitation* (London, 1970); Hayter, *Aid as Imperialism*; Colin Leys, *Underdevelopment in Kenya* (London, 1975).

33 P. W. Preston, *Theories of Development* (London, 1982), ch. 5.

34 Karl Gunnar Myrdal, *An American Dilemma* (1944); *Economic Theory and the Underdeveloped Regions* (London, 1957); *Value in Social Theory* (London, 1958); *Asian Drama* (1968); *Objectivity in Social Research* (London, 1970); 'Underdevelopment and the evolutionary imperative', *Third World Quarterly*, vol. 1, no. 2 (April 1979), pp. 24–42.

35 Dudley Seers, 'The limitations of the special case', *Bulletin of the Oxford Institute of Economics and Statistics*, 25 (May 1963), pp. 77–98.

36 Streeten, *The Frontiers of Development Studies*.

37 Polly Hill [Humphreys], *Studies in Rural Capitalism in West Africa* (Cambridge, 1970).

Chapter 7. The rise of towns

1 Nathan Keyfitz, 'Political-economic aspects of urbanization in South and South-east Asia', in P. M. Hauser and L. F. Schnore (eds.), *The Study of Urbanization* (New York, 1965), pp. 265–309.

2 Homer Hoyt, *World Urbanization* (1962), quoted in G. Breese, *Urbanization in Newly Developing Countries* (Englewood Cliffs, N.J., 1966), p. 16.

3 E. A. Kracke, 'Sung society: change within tradition', *Far Eastern Quarterly*, XIV (1955), pp. 479–88.

4 R. E. Pahl, *Patterns of Urban Life* (London, 1970), p. 19; Phyllis Deane and W. A. Cole, *British Economic Growth, 1688–1959* (Cambridge, 1962), pp. 7–8.

5 Davis, *The Population of India and Pakistan*, p. 127.

6 Kingsley Davis, 'The urbanization of the human population', *Scientific American*, September 1965, pp. 40–53; reprinted in Gerald M. Breese (ed.), *The City in Newly Developing Countries* (Englewood Cliffs, N.J., 1969), pp. 5–20.

7 Breese, *Urbanization in Newly Developing Countries*, p. 19.

8 Population Reference Bureau, *World Data Sheets*, 1980–82.

9 World Bank, *World Development Report 1982*, table 20.

10 Davis, 'The urbanization of the human population'.

11 Peter Lloyd, *A Third World Proletariat?* (London, 1982), pp. 53–65.

12 Robert McNamara, Presidential address to the World Bank, 1975.

13 S. N. Sen, *The City of Calcutta: A Socio-economic Survey, 1954–55 to 1957–58* (Calcutta, 1960).

14 Paul Bairoch, *Urban Unemployment in Developing Countries* (Geneva, 1973), quoted in Harrison, *Inside the Third World*, p. 146.

15 Glenn T. Trewartha, 'Chinese cities: origins and functions', *Annals of the Association of American Geographers*, XLII (1952), pp. 91–3.

16 Morton White and Lucia White, *The Intellectual versus the City* (Cambridge, Mass., 1962).

17 Lerner, *The Passing of Traditional Society*, pp. 58ff.

18 Sir Joseph Hutchinson, 'Reflections on African development', Presidential address to the African Studies Association of the United Kingdom, 1968.

19 Julius K. Nyerere, *Socialism and Rural Development* (Dar es Salaam, 1967), pp. 5–6, 10–11.

20 *The Arusha Declaration* (Dar es Salaam, 1967), pp. 11–13, 17; Julius K. Nyerere, *Education for Self-Reliance* (Dar es Salaam, 1967).

21 François Ponchaud, *Cambodia: Year Zero* (Harmondsworth, 1978); William Shawcross, *Sideshow: Kissinger, Nixon, and the Destruction of Cambodia* (London, 1979), pp. 240–4, 365–78; Ben Kiernan, 'Conflict in the Kampuchean communist movement', *Journal of Contemporary Asia*, vol. 10 (1980), pp. 7–74;

Gavan McCormack, 'The Kampuchean revolution, 1975–1978: the problem of knowing the truth', *ibid.*, pp. 75–118.

Chapter 8. The family and kinship in a changing world

1 E. E. Evans-Pritchard, 'The Nuer of the southern Sudan', in M. Fortes and E. E. Evans-Pritchard (eds.), *African Political Systems* (London, 1940), pp. 272–96.
2 For a warning against this particular error, which may in its turn go too far to the other extreme, see Ruth Finnegan, 'The kinship ascription of primitive societies: actuality or myth?', *International Journal of Comparative Sociology*, XI (1970), pp. 171–94.
3 J. van Velsen, 'Labour migration as a positive factor in the continuity of Tonga tribal society', in Aidan Southall (ed.), *Social Change in Modern Africa* (London, 1961), pp. 230–41.
4 A. I. Richards, *Bemba Marriage and Present Economic Conditions* (Rhodes-Livingstone paper no. 4) (Manchester, 1940).
5 Michael Young and Peter Willmott, *Family and Kinship in East London* (London, 1957); *Family and Class in a London Suburb* (London, 1960).
6 Colin Bell, *Middle Class Families* (London, 1968), pp. 90–5.
7 Peter Townsend, *The Family Life of Old People* (London, 1957).
8 R. W. Firth (ed.), *Two Studies of Kinship in London* (London, 1956), p. 42.
9 Peter Laslett, 'Size and structure of the household in England over three centuries', *Population Studies*, XXIII (1969), pp. 199–223; *Household and Family in Past Time* (Cambridge, 1972), ch. 4.
10 Peter Laslett, *Family Life and Illicit Love in Earlier Generations* (Cambridge, 1977), p. 34.
11 Michael Anderson, *Family Structure in Nineteenth Century Lancashire* (Cambridge, 1971), pp. 85, 124.
12 Chie Nakane, *Kinship and Economic Organization in Rural Japan* (London, 1967).
13 Fujiko Isono, 'The family and women in Japan', *Sociological Review*, 12 (1964), pp. 39–54.
14 Ezra F. Vogel, *Japan's New Middle Class* (Berkeley and Los Angeles, 1963), ch. VIII.
15 W. J. Goode, *World Revolution and Family Patterns* (New York, 1963; revised edition, 1970).
16 Clark Kerr et al., *Industrialism and Industrial Man* (Cambridge, Mass., 1960; Harmondsworth, 1973).
17 Yonina Talmon-Garbier, 'Social change and kinship ties', in Reuben Hill and René König (eds.), *Families in East and West* (Paris and The Hague, 1970), pp. 511–17.

Chapter 9. Cultural diversity, language, education, and the mass media

1 H. Kloss and G. D. McConnell, *Linguistic Composition of the Nations of the World*, vol. 3 (Quebec, 1979); Dankwart A. Rustow, *A World of Nations* (Washington, D.C., 1967), p. 286.
2 On the peoples and cultures of Uganda see the appropriate volumes in the International African Institute's Ethnographic Survey of Africa series; also Goldthorpe, *Outlines of East African Society*; J. E. Goldthorpe and F. B. Wilson, *Tribal Maps of East Africa and Zanzibar* (Kampala, 1960); A. I. Richards, *The*

Multicultural States of East Africa (Montreal, 1969); L. P. Mair, *Primitive Government* (Harmondsworth, 1962); P. H. Gulliver (ed.), *Tradition and Transition in East Africa* (London, 1969); W. H. Whiteley (ed.), *Language Use and Social Change* (London, 1971), esp. ch. VII; P. Ladefoged, R. Glick, and C. Criper, *Language in Uganda* (London, 1972).

3 Low and Pratt, *Buganda and British Overrule*; Apter, *The Political Kingdom in Uganda*; L. A. Fallers (ed.), *The King's Men: Leadership and Status in Buganda on the Eve of Independence* (London, 1964).

4 J. S. La Fontaine, 'Tribalism among the Gisu', in Gulliver (ed.), *Tradition and Transition*, p. 178.

5 Evans-Pritchard, 'The Nuer of the southern Sudan'.

6 Gulliver, *Tradition and Transition*, p. 24.

7 See for instance S. H. Ominde, *Land and Population Movements in Kenya* (London, 1968).

8 Goldthorpe, *An African Elite*.

9 David Parkin, *Neighbours and Nationals in an African City Ward* (London, 1969).

10 R. D. Grillo, *African Railwaymen* (Cambridge, 1973).

11 Richards, *The Multicultural States of East Africa*, pp. 102, 107–8.

12 Joan Vincent, 'Anthropology and political development', in Colin Leys (ed.), *Politics and Change in Developing Countries* (Cambridge, 1969), p. 59.

13 Raymond Apthorpe, 'Does tribalism really matter?' *Transition*, no. 37 (1968), p. 18.

14 Diana Crampton, research in progress.

15 Ladefoged et al., *Language in Uganda*, p. 25.

16 W. H. Whiteley, *Swahili: the Rise of a National Language* (London, 1969); B. Heine, *Status and Use of African Lingua Francas* (Munich, 1970), pp. 80–105.

17 Ali A. Mazrui, 'The king, the king's English, and I', *Transition*, no. 38 (1971), p. 66; reprinted in his *The Political Sociology of the English Language* (The Hague, 1975), p. 37.

18 I. M. Lewis, *The Modern History of Somaliland* (London, 1965); 'Integration in the Somali Republic' in A. Hazlewood (ed.), *African Integration and Disintegration* (London, 1967), pp. 251–84; 'Nationalism and particularism in Somalia', in Gulliver (ed.), *Tradition and Transition in East Africa*, pp. 339–61.

19 Nigel Grant, 'Education and language', in J. Lowe, N. Grant, and T. D. Williams (eds.), *Education and Nation-Building* (Edinburgh, 1971), pp. 189–99.

20 Myrdal, *Asian Drama*, pp. 81–9, 1639–50, 1742–3.

21 Eugene A. Nida and William A. Wonderly, 'Communication roles of language in national societies', in Whiteley (ed.), *Language Use and Social Change*, pp. 62–3.

22 Christopher Freeman, 'The international science race', in D. O. Edge and J. N. Wolfe (eds.), *Meaning and Control: Essays in Social Aspects of Science and Technology* (London, 1973), p. 233.

23 Jonathan R. Cole and Stephen Cole, *Social Stratification in Science* (Chicago, 1973).

24 E. M. K. Mulira, *The Vernacular in African Education* (London, 1951).

25 John Simmons (ed.), *The Education Dilemma: Policy Issues for Developing Countries in the 1980s* (Oxford, 1980), ch. 2.

26 Edwin Smith, 'Indigenous education in Africa', in E. E. Evans-Pritchard et al. (eds.), *Essays Presented to C. G. Seligman* (London, 1934), pp. 319–34.

27 Hugh Ashton, *The Basuto*, 2nd edition (London, 1967), pp. 46–61; Austin Coates, *Basutoland* (London, 1966), pp. 75–80, 109–11.

28 P. T. W. Baxter in A. I. Richards (ed.), *East African Chiefs* (London, 1960), p. 294.

29 R. D. Matthews and M. Akrawi, *Education in Arab Countries of the Near East* (Washington, D.C., 1949), pp. 24, 40, 540.

30 Ruth Sloan and Helen Kitchen (eds.), *The Educated African* (London, 1962), ch. 3, pp. 45–6.

31 Humayun Kabir, *Indian Philosophy of Education* (Bombay, 1961), p. 209.

32 Lightbourne, Singh, and Green, 'The World Fertility Survey'.

33 World Bank, *World Development Report 1982*, pp. 29, 81.

34 Simmons, *The Education Dilemma*, pp. 58–9.

35 Marcelo Selowsky, 'Preschool age investment in human capital', in *ibid.*, ch. 6.

36 R. P. Dore, *The Diploma Disease: Education, Qualification, and Development* (London, 1976).

37 Ivan Illich, *De-Schooling Society* (London, 1971); *Celebration of Awareness* (London, 1971), chs. 8 and 9.

38 Dore, *The Diploma Disease*, ch. 12.

39 T. H. Marshall, *Citizenship and Social Class* (Cambridge, 1950), pp. 25–6.

40 Wilbur Schramm, *Mass Media and National Development: the Role of Information in the Developing Countries* (Stanford, Calif., and Paris, 1964), p. 60.

41 *Ibid.*, p. 101.

42 C. A. Siepmann, *Radio, Television, and Society* (New York, 1950).

43 Alex Inkeles, *Public Opinion in Soviet Russia* (Cambridge, Mass., 1950); 'Mobilizing public opinion', in A. Inkeles and K. Geiger (eds.), *Soviet Society* (London, 1961), pp. 219–28.

44 Elihu Katz and E. George Wedell, *Broadcasting in the Third World: Promise and Performance* (Cambridge, Mass., 1977; London, 1978).

45 Jeremy Tunstall, *The Media are American: Anglo-American Media in the World* (London, 1977), pp. 204ff.

46 Donald S. E. Taylor, *The Mass Media and National Development with special reference to Broadcasting in Sierra Leone*, M.Phil. thesis, University of Leeds, 1980.

Chapter 10. Religion and economic development: cause and effect

1 Parts of Weber's posthumous *Gesammelte Aufsätze zur Religions-soziologie* (1920–1) have appeared in English translations as follows: *The Protestant Ethic and the Spirit of Capitalism*, transl. Talcott Parsons (London, 1930); *The Religion of China*, transl. Hans H. Gerth (New York, 1951); *The Religion of India*, transl. Gerth and Don Martindale (New York, 1958); *Ancient Judaism*, transl. Gerth and Martindale (New York, 1952). The following references are to the English translations cited by title only.

2 *The Religion of China*, chs. I and IV, pp. 173–95, 227–9, 243.

3 *The Religion of India*, pp. 111–12.

4 Edmund Gosse, *Father and Son: A Study of Two Temperaments* (London, 1907).

5 Robert W. Green (ed.), *Protestantism and Capitalism: the Weber Thesis and its Critics* (Lexington, Mass., 1959).

6 Hugh Trevor-Roper, *Religion, the Reformation, and Social Change* (London, 1967).

7 T. O. Ling, 'Max Weber in India', inaugural lecture at the University of Leeds, 11 December 1972.

8 Brien K. Parkinson, 'Non-economic factors in the economic retardation of the rural Malays', *Modern Asian Studies*, vol. I, no. 1 (1967), pp. 31–46.

9 William Wilder, 'Islam, other factors and Malay backwardness: comments on an argument', *Modern Asian Studies*, vol. II, no. 2 (1968), pp. 155–64.

10 Brien K. Parkinson, 'The economic retardation of the Malays – a rejoinder', *Modern Asian Studies*, vol. II, no. 3 (1968), pp. 267–72.

11 Mya Maung, 'Socialism and economic development of Burma', *Asian Survey*, vol. IV, no. 12 (1964), pp. 1182–90.

12 T. O. Ling, 'Religion and economic development in Burma and Malaya', paper presented to the Development Seminar, University of Leeds, 8 December 1971.

13 Melford E. Spiro, *Buddhism and Society: A Great Tradition and its Burmese Vicissitudes* (London, 1971), pp. 12, 453–4, 463–7.

14 Robert J. Bocock, 'The Ismailis in Tanzania', *British Journal of Sociology*, XXII (1971), pp. 365–80.

15 H. S. Morris, *The Indians in Uganda* (London, 1968); Goldthorpe, *Outlines of East African Society*, pp. 125–6.

16 Morris, *The Indians in Uganda*, pp. 51–4.

17 Norman Cohn, *The Pursuit of the Millennium* (London, 1957).

18 Norman Cohn, 'Medieval millenarism: its bearing on the comparative study of millenarian movements', in Louis Schneider (ed.), *Religion, Culture and Society* (New York, 1964), pp. 168–78.

19 Peter Worsley, *The Trumpet Shall Sound* (London, 1957), pp. 20–2, 144.

20 Peter Lawrence, *Road Belong Cargo* (Manchester, 1964), pp. 2–3, 116–221.

21 Robert Forster, 'The cargo cults today', *New Society*, 7 January 1971, pp. 10–12.

22 Vittorio Lanternari, *The Religions of the Oppressed*, transl. Lisa Sergio (London, 1963).

23 Weston La Barre, *The Peyote Cult*, enlarged edition (Hamden, Conn., 1964), pp. 205–6, 227–37.

24 B. G. M. Sundkler, *Bantu Prophets in South Africa* (London, 1948).

25 F. B. Welbourn, *East African Rebels: A Study of some Independent Churches* (London, 1961).

26 Carl G. Rosberg, Jr, and John Nottingham, *The Myth of "Mau Mau": Nationalism in Kenya* (New York, 1966).

27 Goldthorpe, *Outlines of East African Society*, ch. VIII.

28 Walter H. Sangree, *Age, Prayer and Politics in Tiriki, Kenya* (London, 1966), esp. chs. VI and VII.

29 Geoffrey Parrinder, *Religion in an African City* (London, 1953), ch. 6.

30 M. J. Field, *Search for Security: An Ethno-Psychiatric study of Rural Ghana* (London, 1960), part I.

31 Georges Balandier, *Sociologie Actuelle de l'Afrique Noire* (Paris, 1955), transl. Douglas Garman, *The Sociology of Black Africa* (London, 1970); Dominique Desanti, 'The golden anniversary of Kimbanguism, an African religion', *Continent 2000*, April 1971, pp. 7–19; Marie-Louise Martin, *Kimbangu* (Oxford, 1975).

32 George Shepperson, 'The politics of African church separatist movements in British Central Africa, 1892–1916', *Africa*, XXIV (1954), pp. 233–45; George Shepperson and T. Price, *Independent African: John Chilembwe and the Nyasaland Rising of 1915* (London, 1958); R. L. Wishlade, *Sectarianism in Southern Nyasaland* (London, 1965).

33 David B. Barrett, *Schism and Renewal in Africa* (Nairobi, 1968), pp. xvii, 25, 114, 139, 285.

34 C. K. Yang, *Religion in Chinese Society* (1961), pp. 218–29, reprinted in Franz Schurmann and Orville Schell, *Imperial China* (Harmondsworth, 1967), pp. 157–68.
35 Wolfgang Franke, 'The Taiping rebellion', transl. from the German and reprinted in Schurmann and Schell, *Imperial China*, pp. 170–82.
36 Sundkler, *Bantu Prophets*, p. 37.
37 Barrett, *Schism and Renewal*, p. 71.
38 Lawrence, *Road Belong Cargo*, pp. 225–6.
39 J. M. Yinger, 'Religion and social change: functions and dysfunctions of sects and cults among the disprivileged', *Review of Religious Research*, vol. 4, no. 2 (1963); reprinted (abridged) in Richard D. Knudten (ed.), *The Sociology of Religion: An Anthology* (New York, 1967), pp. 482–95.

Chapter 11. Some psychological aspects of change

1 Leonard W. Doob, *Becoming More Civilized: A Psychological Exploration* (New Haven, Conn., 1960).
2 Everett M. Rogers, *Diffusion of Innovations* (New York, 1962).
3 W. W. Ogionwo, *The Adoption of Technological Innovations in Nigeria: A Study of Factors Associated with Adoption of Farm Practices*, Ph.D. thesis, University of Leeds, 1969.
4 David C. McClelland, *The Achieving Society* (Princeton, N.J., 1961).
5 David C. McClelland, 'A psychological path to rapid economic development', *Mawazo*, vol. 1, no. 4 (December, 1968), pp. 9–15.
6 Alex Inkeles and David H. Smith, *Becoming Modern: Individual Change in Six Developing Countries* (London, 1974).

Chapter 12. The political characteristics of new states in poor countries

1 C. H. Dodd, *Political Development* (London, 1972), pp. 9–15.
2 Apter, *The Politics of Modernization*, p. 14.
3 Samuel P. Huntington and Joan M. Nelson, *No Easy Choice: Political Participation in Developing Countries* (Cambridge, Mass., 1976).
4 *Zik: A Selection from the Speeches of Nnamdi Azikiwe* (1961), quoted in Paul E. Sigmund, *The Ideologies of the Developing Nations* (New York, 1963), pp. 212, 215.
5 George I. Blanksten, 'The politics of Latin America', in Gabriel A. Almond and James S. Coleman (eds.), *The Politics of the Developing Areas* (Princeton, N.J., 1960), p. 521.
6 Emilio Willems, *Followers of the New Faith: Culture Change and the Rise of Protestantism in Brazil and Chile* (Nashville, Tenn., 1967), pp. 34–44.
7 Lucian W. Pye, 'The politics of South East Asia', in Almond and Coleman (eds.), *The Politics of the Developing Areas*, pp. 87–97.
8 Dankwart A. Rustow, 'The politics of the Near East', in *ibid.*, pp. 382ff.
9 Riggs, *Administration in Developing Countries*, p. 236.
10 W. J. Argyle, 'European nationalism and African tribalism', in Gulliver (ed.), *Tradition and Transition in East Africa*, pp. 41–57; George Bennett, 'Tribalism in politics', in *ibid.*, pp. 59–87.
11 Speech to the second Pan-African seminar, World Assembly of Youth, 1961; quoted in Sigmund, *The Ideologies of the Developing Nations*, pp. 209–11.

12 Worsley, *The Third World*, p. 69.
13 David E. Apter, *Ghana in Transition*, revised edition (New York, 1963), pp. 167, 173–4.
14 William H. Friedland and Carl G. Rosberg, Jr, *African Socialism* (Stanford, Calif., 1964).
15 Sigmund, *The Ideologies of the Developing Nations*, pp. 18–24.
16 Apter, *Ghana in Transition*, p. 326.
17 *Ibid.*, pp. 345–6.
18 Thomas Hodgkin, *African Political Parties* (Harmondsworth, 1961), p. 48.
19 Martin Staniland, 'Single-party regimes and political change', in Leys (ed.), *Politics and Change in Developing Countries*, pp. 147, 152.
20 Cherry Gertzel, *The Politics of Independent Kenya, 1963–68* (Nairobi, 1970), p. 58.
21 Staniland, 'Single-party regimes and political change', p. 139.
22 Riggs, *Administration in Developing Countries*, p. 201.
23 *Ibid.*, pp. 254, 282, 340.
24 Nelson Kasfir, *The Shrinking Political Arena: Participation and Ethnicity in African Politics, with a Case Study of Uganda* (Berkeley and Los Angeles, 1976), pp. 3, 227.
25 Ankie M. M. Hoogvelt, *The Sociology of Developing Societies* (London, 1976), pp. 144–6.
26 Leys, *Politics and Change in Developing Countries*, pp. 272–3.
27 Colin Leys, quoted in Kasfir, *The Shrinking Political Arena*, p. 272n.
28 Kasfir, *The Shrinking Political Arena*, pp. 147–50, 272.
29 *Ibid.*, pp. 117, 207, 211.
30 *Ibid.*, pp. 180, 204, 208–10.
31 *Ibid.*, p. 211.
32 For his version of these events see the Kabaka of Buganda, *Desecration of My Kingdom*.
33 Henry Kyemba, *State of Blood* (London, 1977).
34 Kasfir, *The Shrinking Political Arena*, pp. 206–8.
35 Alan Milner (ed.), *African Penal Systems* (New York, 1969).
36 Max Gluckman, 'Analysis of a social situation in modern Zululand', *Bantu Studies*, 14 (1940).
37 Swartz, *Local-Level Politics*, pp. 199–204.
38 Riggs, *Administration in Developing Countries*, pp. 189–90.
39 James C. Scott, *Comparative Political Corruption* (Englewood Cliffs, N.J., 1972), pp. 15, 24–5.
40 Marc Bloch, *Feudal Society* (London, 1961).
41 Edward Luttwak, *Coup d'Etat: A Practical Handbook* (London, 1968).
42 Data compiled from Arthur S. Banks (ed.), *Political Handbook of the World 1979* (New York, 1979), up-dated where possible to 1980 from *Statesman's Yearbook 1981–82* (London, 1981), press reports, etc., for countries listed in World Bank *World Development Report 1982*.
43 Edward Gibbon, *The History of the Decline and Fall of the Roman Empire* (London, 1781–88, and many subsequent editions), chs. III–V.
44 William F. Gutteridge, *The Military in African Politics* (London, 1969), pp. 104–7.
45 Donald N. Levine, 'The military in Ethiopian politics', in Henry Bienen (ed.), *The Military Intervenes: Case Studies in Political Development* (New York, 1968), pp. 28–33.

303

46 S. E. Finer, *The Man on Horseback: the Role of the Military in Politics* (London, 1962), pp. 6, 16, 21.

47 Jacques van Doorn, *The Soldier and Social Change* (Beverly Hills, Calif., 1975), p. 83.

48 Morris Janowitz, *Military Institutions and Coercion in the Developing Nations* (Chicago, 1977, incorporating *The Military in the Political Development of New Nations*, 1964), pp. 28, 36–40, 108–9.

49 Robin Luckham, *The Nigerian Military: A Sociological Analysis of Authority and Revolt 1960–67* (Cambridge, 1971), p. 202.

50 Stanislav Andreski (formerly Andrzejewski), *Military Organization and Society*, 2nd edition (London, 1968), p. 214.

51 Bruce R. Drury, 'Civil–military relations and military rule: Brazil since 1964', in George A. Kourvetaris and Betty A. Dobratz (eds.), *World Perspectives in the Sociology of the Military* (New Brunswick, N.J., 1977), p. 240.

52 G. Pope Atkins, 'The armed forces in Latin American politics', in Charles L. Cochran (ed.), *Civil–Military Relations: Changing Concepts in the Seventies* (New York, 1974), pp. 229, 237.

53 Roberta E. McKown, 'Domestic correlates of military intervention in African politics', in Kourvetaris and Dobratz, *World Perspectives in the Sociology of the Military*, p. 196.

54 Luckham, *The Nigerian Military*, pp. 254, 281.

55 Scott, *Comparative Political Corruption*, p. 10.

56 Luckham, *The Nigerian Military*, pp. 284–5.

57 Ruth First, *The Barrel of a Gun: Political Power in Africa and the Coup d'Etat* (London, 1970), pp. 363–83.

58 Eric A. Nordlinger, *Soldiers in Politics: Military Coups and Governments* (Englewood Cliffs, N.J., 1977), pp. 9–10.

Chapter 13. The world of aid

1 W. G. Zeylstra, *Aid or Development* (Leyden, 1975), p. 33.

2 George C. Herring, *Aid to Russia, 1941–1946* (New York, 1973), pp. 271–2; Thomas G. Paterson, *Soviet-American Confrontation: Postwar Reconstruction and the Origins of the Cold War* (Baltimore, Md., 1973), pp. 208–21.

3 John White, *The Politics of Foreign Aid* (London, 1974), pp. 130, 215.

4 UN, *Measurement of the Flow of Resources to Developing Countries*, E/4327 ST/ECA/98 (1967); *Partners in Development*, p. 144.

5 *The World Bank Annual Report 1982*, appendices F and 7.

6 *North-South: A Programme for Survival* (Pan, 1980), p. 216.

7 *Ibid.*, p. 38.

8 *Partners in Development*, pp. vii, 9–10, 30, 122–6, 134–40, 148–9, 168–9, 215, 229–30.

9 Sources: World Bank, *World Development Reports 1981* and *1982*; OECD, *Development Co-Operation, 1981*.

10 Andrzej Krassowski (ed.), *ODI Review*, no. 4 (1970), pp. 48–50.

11 P. T. Bauer, *Dissent on Development* (London, 1971).

12 Hayter, *Aid as Imperialism*.

13 Judith Tendler, *Inside Foreign Aid* (Baltimore, Md., 1975).

14 White, *The Politics of Foreign Aid*, pp. 78–81, 121–5, 161–3.

15 Cheryl Payer, *The Debt Trap: the IMF and the Third World* (Harmondsworth, 1974), ch. 6.
16 *North-South*, pp. 14, 67–8, 78, 117, 119, 209, 219, 225, 241–2, 249, 278, 282–90, 293–304.
17 *The Guardian*, 2 July 1982.

Index

Index

Baptist Church, 222
Baran, Paul A., 295n.6, 296n.22
Bardhan, P.K., 101
Barrett, David, 223–5
Basajjakitalo, Obadaiah, 220
Bastide, Roger, 60, 290n.4, 291n.28
Bauer, P.T., 279
Baxter, P.T.W., 300n.28
Beckford, G.L., 85–6, 89
Beijing (Peking), 104, 159
Belgium, 136, 152, 182; Belgian colonies, 56–7, 92, 221, 225; loss of, 271
Bell, Colin, 166
Bemba, 127, 165
Bendix, Reinhard, 135–7, 149, 189, 213
Benedict, Burton, 209n.3
Bennett, George, 302n.10
Berger, Peter L., 293n.32
Berghe, Pierre van den, 290n.2, 291n.32
Besant, Annie, 24, 33, 39
Bhutan, 16
Biafra, 253
'big firm, small country', 49, 85–7, 93
birth control, see family planning
birth-rate, 2, 23–41, 80, 169, 173, 194
'black triangle', 46
Blacker, C.P., 23, 40
Blackett, Lord, 30
Blanksten, George I., 302n.5
Bloch, Marc, 303n.40
Bocock, Robert J., 212–13
Bogue, Donald J., 34
Bolivia, 74, 83, 177
Booth, Joseph, 222, 224, 225
Borlaug, Norman, 111, 116–17
Borup, K.E., 51
Bose, Mihir, 293n.32
Boyd, A., 290n.9, 18
Boyd, J. Morton, 295n.30
Boyle, Thomas L., 107
Bradlaugh, Charles, 24, 33, 39
'brain drain', 96, 188
Brandt, Willy, 83, 273–4, **281–6**, see also North–South
Brazil, economy, 15, 16, 71, 83, 86, 94, **97–9**, 120, 124–5, 137–8, 282; population trends, 30, 34, 98; slavery and race, 45–6, 52, 59–61; politics, 43–4, 98–9, 263, 268; language, 56, 202; psychology, 236
breast-feeding, 76
Breese, Gerald M., 152, 162
Bretton Woods, 269–70, 272–3, 282
Britain: economy, 3–4, 88, 120, 125, 129, 203; education, 146, 196; mass media, 199, 201–2, 205; politics, 46, 112, 175, 259; urban growth, 151–2; rôle in

internat. organisations, 270, 273; aid, 65, 271, 272, 275, 276–8; see also Scotland
British empire, 17, 44–7, 54, 56, 63–6, 68, 248
  rule in India, 36–7, 158, 193, 208; in Uganda, 178–9; in Tanganyika, 183; in Burma, 247; in Arab countries, 247; in Africa, 254
  slave trade, 45; abolition, 46
broadcasting, 201–6
Brown, Harrison, 295n.34
Brown, Lester R., 115
Brundenius, Claes, 100
Buddhism, 29, 177, 207, 208, 210–12
Buell, R.L., 290n.15
Buganda, 50, 178–81, 183–4, 234, 253, 256–7; see also Ganda
Bulgaria, 33
Bunting, A.H., 112
Bunyoro, 178, 256–7
bureaucracy, see administration
Burkitt, D.P., 292n.6
Burma, 50, 177, 187, 210–12, 214, 247
Burris, R.H., 294n.15
Burundi, 92

Cabora Bassa, 125
Calcutta, 156–8
Calvin, Calvinism, 129, 209, 212–13, 215
Cambodia (Kampuchea), 17, 70, 157, 160–2, 278
Campbell, Lord, 90
Canada, 74, 88, 113–15, 122–3, 125, 182, 271
capital, 3, 14, 87–8, 104, 107, 116, 128, 141, 143, 146, 152, 199–203; c. flows (aid), 274–7
capital-intensive methods, 3, 72, 88, 90–1, 96, 98, 103, 107, 110, 131, 150, 154–5, 188, 195, 280, 286
capitalism, capitalist, 6, 13–14, 16, 18, 139–42, 181, 204, 207–8, 212–13, 250, 273, 279
carbon dioxide, 108–9
cargo cults, 215–18, 224, 225–6
Carr-Saunders, A.M., 32, 36, 39
cars, see motor vehicles
Carson, Rachel, 111
Carter, C.F., 292.n.1
cash sector, 80–4; see also modern sector
caste, 11–12, 66, 208, 214
Castro, Fidel, 17, 140
Catholic, see Roman Catholic
censorship, 204–6
census, 36, 38, 40, 151, 180, 181, 256

McEvedy, Colin, 288n.1
McKown, Roberta E., 266
McNamara, Robert S., 156, 197, 274, 281
Madagascar, 179
Maddox, John, 106–7, 126
magic, 207, 210, 213, 229
Maguire, G. Andrew, 66–7
Maine, Sir Henry, 5, 10
Mair, L.P., 299n.2
maize, 75, 116, 124
malaria, 25, 111–12, 283
Malawi, 92, 164, 222, 224, 225
Malaya, 47, 50, 62, 210, 214
Malays in S. Africa, 61
Malaysia, 95
Mali, 92
Malinowski, Bronislaw, 8, 10, 12, 295n.1
Malthus, Thomas; Malthusian, 27, 30, 39, 113–15
manager, management, 117, 131, 155, 182, 200
Manchuria, 43
Mansfield, Lord Justice, 46
Maoris, 48
marriage, 2, 24, 33, 34, 38, 55, 59–61, 163–76
Marshall, George C.; Marshall aid, 270, 272
Marshall, T.H., 198
Martin, Marie-Louise, 227
Marx, Marxist, 6, 14, 27, 129–30, 140–2, 146, 210
Mason, Philip, 68
mass media, 2, 134, **199–206**, 235, 239–41
Matthews, R.D., 300n.29
Mau Mau, 63, 220
Maung, Mya, 210
Mauritius, 45, 62, 83, 89
Mazrui, Ali A., 184
Mboya, Tom, 292n.48
Mead, Margaret, 127
Meade, J.E., 295n.3
Meadows, Donella and Dennis, 107–8, 126
meat, 74–5, 115
medicine, medical service, *see* health
Meier, Gerald M., 90
Mesarovic, Mihajlo, 294n.6
metals, metallurgy, 21, 82–4, 117–18, 120; *see also* mining *and under individual metals*
metropolis and satellite, 13, 139
Mexico, 30, 34, 36, 95, 116, 157, 246, 259
middlemen, political, **259–60**
Midgley, James, 105
migration: in colonial history, 45–6, 50;

and plural societies, 62; of workers, 92; to towns, 89, 90, 150–7, 164, 168–9, 182; and mines, 164; study of, 180; and religious persecution, 209; and enterprise, 213–15
military: *coups*, rule, 84, 98–9, 206, 254, 257–8, **261–7**; elites, 11, 95; expenditure, 65, 77, 271, 274, 282–3
milk, 75
millenarian movements, 215–27
millet, 75
Milner, Alan, 259
mining, 1, 50–1, 63, 86–7, 92, 192, 283
Mirsky, Jonathan, 288n.10
misplaced aggregation, 107, 147
missions, 45, 50, **51–3**, 66, 178–9, 184, 192, 197, 219–26, 286
mixed descent, 59–61
modern, modernity, 132–7, 181, 189, 228–31, 234, 239–41
modern sector of dual economy, 13, 80–84, 91–2, 96, 140, 176, 195, 199
modernization, 10–12, **132–7**, 164, 173, 181, 189, 196, 203, 226, 228–31, 243–5, 252; individual m., **239–41**; modernizing autocrats, 136, 226; elites, 135–7, 181, 189
money, 21, 54, 72, 80–2, 100, 157, 230, 237, 263
Mongolia, 43
monogamy, 128, 133, 139–41
Montbrial, Thierry de, 295n.37
Mormons, 218, 225
Morris, H.S., 212, 214–5
mortality, **23–42**, 80, 87; *see also* death-rate, infant mortality
mother-tongue, 181–3, 186
motor vehicles, 86, 98–9, 124, 125, 129, 131, 161
Mott, Frank L. and Susan H., 289n.18
movements, religious, **215–27**
Mozambique, 16, 45, 56, 92, 125, 183
Mukasa, Reuben Spartas, 220
Mulira, E.M.K., 190
multi-national corporations, 14, 49, 85–7, 96–7, 138, 158, 282–4
Muni, S.D., 288n.23
Murphy, Francis X., 288n.8
Muslim, 61, 173, 177, 192–3, 210, 212–13, 221; *see also* Islam
Myrdal, Karl Gunnar, 4, 12, 37, 49, 50, 63, 64, 76, 130, 142–5, 149, 181, 186, 196, 260, 285–6

Nakane, Chie, 169–70
Nasser, Gamal Abdul, 262

315

Taiwan, 15, 17, 43, 56, 71, 87, 95,
104–5
take-off into sustained growth, 129, 143,
275
Talmon-Garbier, Yonina, 175
Tanganyika, 63–4, 66–7, 201, 205
Tanzania: socialism and self-reliance, 155,
160, 205, 250, 254–5, 280; cultural
diversity, 179, 181, 183, 256; sects,
212, 222; penal policy, 259;
intervention in Uganda, 257–8, 267
Taoism, 207
Tapinos, Georges, 42
tariffs, 2, 63, 86–8, 131, 274, 282
Tasmania, 45
Tata, 209
taxes, 2, 21, 50, 54, 63, 69, 145, 150,
151, 157, 255, 260–1, 279, 283, 284
Taylor, Donald S.E., 300n.46
Taylor, John, 296n.29
tea, 83–4
teachers, 94, 96, 232; *see also* education,
schools
technology, **20–23**, 47, 86–90, 107–25,
129, 137, 187–8, 199–201
television, 21, 99, 201–5
Tendler, Judith, 279–80
text-books, 51, 146, 180, 237
Thailand, 30, 34, 64, 75, 187, 201, 203
Third World, origins and usage of term,
15–18
Thuku, Harry, 47
tin, 50, 83, 106
Tiriki, 221
Titmuss, R.M., 289n.14
Tokugawa, 40
Tonga, kingdom of, 55
Tonga of Malawi, 164–5
Tönnies, Ferdinand, 7, 10
Toro, 178
tourists, 82, 182
towns: origins, 21, 52, 58, 150–2; health
in, 38–9, 76, 77; population, 34, 70–1,
151–2; leading sectors, modernizing
influence, 82, 134, 139, 239–41;
migration to, 89, 90, 150–7, 164,
168–9, 182; workers' remittances, 92,
157; urban–rural disparities, 96, 157;
informal sector, 156, 283; urban poor,
261; foreignness, anti-urban bias,
158–61; language, 182; television, 203,
205; aid, 279
Townsend, Peter, 166
trade: origins, 21, 48; in slaves, 45–6; in
contraceptives, 32; world, 72, 273–4;
terms of, 128, 281–2; and towns, 150,
156–7; language, 182–3

trade unions, 3, 86, 90–1, 96–7, 98–9,
103, 104, 251, 265
tradition, 11, 13, 89, 130, 132–3, 164,
181, 189, 228–31, 233–4, 243, 249,
252; traditional sector of dual economy,
80–2, 140, 176
transition, 11, 133, 135, 228–30
Trevelyan, G.M., 289n.3, 290n.5
Trevor-Roper, Hugh, 208–9, 213
Trewartha, Glenn T., 159
tribes, tribalism, 2, 6, 153–4, 164, 166,
178, **179–81**, 190, 249, **253–8**, 267
trickle-down effects, 132, 143
Tristram, Uvedale, 294n.12
Trowell, H.C., 292n.5,6
Tsui, Amy Ong, 34
Tuka, 216–17, 226
Tunisia, 77, 193
Tunstall, Jeremy, 300n.45
Turkey, 30, 95, 120, 134–5
tying, 275–6, 280

Uganda: cultural diversity, 2, 178–80,
248; British rule, missions, 48, 51–2,
54, 55, 57, 59, 63, 66; health, 73; diet,
75; languages, 81, 182, 183; migration,
92; disparities, 96, 190; towns, 160;
African Orthodox Church, 220, 224,
225; recent history and politics, 84,
181, 203, 210, 248, **254–8**, 263, 267
Uganda Company, 290n.19
underdevelopment, 4, 12–14, 127, 130,
137–42, 204, 279
unemployment, 86, 89, 90–1, 127, 143,
147, 155, 195–8, 269, 282, 284, 285;
underemployment, 90, 127, 147
United Fruit Company, 85–6
United Kingdom, 95, 182, 199; *see also*
Britain
United Nations (UN), 30, 34, 37, 191,
269–74, 276
United Nations Conference(s) on Trade and
Development (UNCTAD), 274, 282
United Nations Educational, Scientific and
Cultural Organization (UNESCO), 202,
203, 269
United States of America: economy, 4, 95,
106, 109, 113–15, 125, 129, 136, 146;
slavery and race, 44–6; towns, 152;
language, 182; mass media, 199,
201–4; sects and cults, 218, 220, 225;
social thought, 11, 132–5, 146, 159;
psychology, 230–1; influence abroad,
17, 65, 99, 102, 104, 138, 140, 145,
161, 246, 247, 267–8, 269–76
universities, 13, 57, 65, 96, 100, 139,
180, 193, 250–1, 257

319